Imagining Home

THE HAYMARKET SERIES

Editors: Mike Davis and Michael Sprinker

The Haymarket Series offers original studies in politics, history and culture, with a focus on North America. Representing views from across the American left on a wide range of subjects, the series will be of interest to socialists both in the USA and throughout the world. A century after the first May Day, the American left remains in the shadow of those martyrs whom this Haymarket Series honours and commemorates. These studies testify to the living legacy of political activism and commitment for which they gave their lives.

Imagining Home

Class, Culture and Nationalism in the African Diaspora

Edited by
SIDNEY J. LEMELLE
and
ROBIN D.G. KELLEY

VERSO

London • New York

For Salima and Diedra

First published by Verso 1994
© Verso 1994
All rights reserved

Verso
UK: 6 Meard Street, London W1V 3HR
USA: 29 West 35th Street, New York, NY 10001-2291

Verso is the imprint of New Left Books

ISBN 0-86091-386-4
ISBN 0-86091-585-9 (pbk)

British Library Cataloguing in Publication Data
A catalogue record for this book is available from the British Library.

Library of Congress Cataloging-in-Publication Data
A catalog record for this book is available from the Library of Congress.

Typeset in Baskerville by NorthStar, San Francisco, California
Printed and bound in Great Britain by Biddles Ltd, Guildford and King's Lynn

Contents

Contents

Acknowledgements

In all stages of this work, from the 1988 conference that produced many of these papers to the final editing of the manuscript, we have had the help and support of colleagues, friends and loved ones. A tremendous source of encouragement came from members of the Intercollegiate Department of Black Studies of the Claremont Colleges, sponsors of 'Pan-Africanism Revisited: Liberation Movements in Africa and the Diaspora'. Of particular note were the contributions of Ruth Wilson Gilmore, who co-convened the conference with Sidney J. Lemelle. When things seemed to fall apart, Ruth was always there to pick up the pieces and set things straight. Likewise, Sue and Frankie Houchins and Agnes Moreland Jackson were unwavering in their support for the conference. We are also indebted to Neva and Zeph Magetla, Kathy Ogren, Craig Gilmore, Consuella Lewis, Cynthia Linton, Alden and Mary Kimbrough, Ione Graves, Helen Young, Marjorie Richardson, Shauna Mulvihill, Cathy Pet, Juliette Allasbrook, and a host of students and faculty whose energy and hard work made the conference a success.

Special thanks to Mike Davis and Colin Robinson at Verso Books for their support for our project, and to Steven Hiatt and Megan Hiatt for their expert editorial assistance. We are also grateful to Sam Floyd, editor of *Black Music Research Journal,* for allowing us to reprint Paul Gilroy's essay; and to A. Sivanandan, editor of *Race and Class,* for granting permission to reprint the essays by Sidney J. Lemelle and Cedric Robinson.

Several institutions and foundations provided valuable funding for the conference, including the Pomona College Centennial Fund, the Claremont Links, Alpha Kappa Alpha Sorority, and the Office of Black Student

Affairs of the Claremont Colleges. Writing and preparation of the manuscript were made possible by generous grants from the Ford Foundation, the History Department of Pomona College, and Emory University's faculty research fund. To all of these institutions we express our gratitude.

We extend our thanks to all the conference participants and supporters, most notably members of the African National Congress and the South West African People's Organization, who supported our efforts, and to Robert A. Hill, Vincent Harding, and Cedric Robinson for their stimulating discussions and for their useful suggestions for this book.

Finally, we want to express our deepest gratitude to our families, who endured and supported the completion of this collection – in particular, Salima M. Lemelle (who put up with Sid's late hours and weekends in the office) and Diedra Harris-Kelley (who put up with Robin's late hours and weekends at home). Diedra, once again, deserves special props for her artistic output. If you haven't figured it out yet, the beautiful pastel on the dust jacket is hers; a fitting representation of the dilemma Africans of the diaspora face when they 'imagine home' in the modern West.

Introduction

Imagining Home:

Pan-Africanism Revisited

Sidney J. Lemelle and Robin D.G. Kelley

I

Most of the essays in this volume grew out of the 1988 conference held at Pomona College titled Pan-Africanism Revisited: Liberation Movements in Africa and the Diaspora. Motivated in part by the past decade of upheaval in Southern Africa and the worldwide divestment movement, the conference organizers, Sidney J. Lemelle and Ruth Wilson Gilmore, and many of the participants viewed the gathering as an opportunity to critically assess the 'rebirth' of radical Black/Pan-Africanist movements. It was this renewed interest during the 1980s that also exposed the shortcomings of the literature on Pan-Africanism – both liberal/nationalist and (its more modern manifestation) afrocentric/cultural nationalist interpretations.

Although Pan-Africanism Revisited was conceived as an opportunity to reassess the achievements and failures of various Pan-African movements and ideologies, examine their political, historical and cultural salience, and ruminate on the role Pan-Africanism has played in the struggle for liberation on the continent and in the diaspora, many of the participants presented work that shifted the conference's focus in significant ways. By the final day of the meeting, it had become clear that the central project of the conference was not to recuperate and assess the Pan-African ideal as it emerged in the Manchester conference of 1945 or in the heady days of the founding of the Organization of African Unity, but to interrogate the very meaning of the term and search for the often ambivalent place Africa holds in the imaginations of its 'New World' descendants – the daughters and sons of Africa who are either not associated with what we traditionally

1

label Pan-Africanism or whose relationship to Africa has been oversimplified by previous scholarship. Indeed, most conference participants tended to shy away from a single working definition of Pan-Africanism and concluded that it has taken different forms at different historical moments. Sometimes it has taken the form of a tangible political movement; at other times it has been an expression of consciousness animated by various cultural forms. And more often than not, it has been a combination of the two. One thing is certain: no matter how conservative or atavistic the rhetoric, Pan-Africanism was intended to be an oppositional ideology. As Bernard Magubane put it recently, 'The Pan-African consciousness has always been a determined effort on the part of Black peoples to rediscover their shrines from the wreckage of history. It was a revolt against the white man's ideological suzerainty in culture, politics, and historiography.'[1]

We situate this collection of essays within a broader radical literature that regards Pan-African politics as the construction and reconstruction of a diasporic identity and as the product of racial capitalism, cultural hegemony and self-activity. Following the pioneering tradition of C.L.R. James, W.E.B. Du Bois, Eric Williams and Walter Rodney,[2] most of these contributions might be seen as a continuation of projects outlined by several radical Black scholars in books published in the mid to late 1980s. Their works grappled with the historical and philosophical contradictions within the Pan-African movement, challenged the liberal historiography of Pan-Africanism, invoked a class analysis, employed a much more complicated interpretation of culture and cultural politics, and criticized what they viewed as dogmatic or overly economistic, reductionist interpretations.[3]

At the center of their 'revisionist' histories lies the problem of Black liberation – the problem of the relations between modern capitalist countries, their racial policies and economic exploitation. For these radicals a critical assessment of Black liberation involved a materialist analysis of Pan-African history over the past three hundred years. It also necessitates a broad analysis of the contemporary economic, political and cultural life of Africans and diasporan Africans. To this end, they attacked (either directly or indirectly) the older established liberal historiography of Pan-Africanism – most of which had its roots in nineteenth-century European liberal thought. In particular they focused on the liberal assumptions and beliefs in the basic unity and goodness of humankind, the benefits of liberal education, the power of reason and the possibility of uplift and progress within the capitalist system.

Ironically, liberal historiography has been particularly influential among Black nationalist writers and historians – despite its racist/ethnocentric origins in Western Enlightenment thought and, in part, Social Darwinism. Paul Gilroy's essay makes explicit the philosophical links between the nationalists and the liberal school when he writes, 'European romanticism and cultural nationalism contributed directly to the development of modern Black nationalism. It can be traced back to the impact of European theories of nationhood, culture and civilization on elite Afro-American intellectuals in the early and mid nineteenth century.'[4]

The liberal/nationalist school of Pan-African historiography began to take form in the nineteenth century and flourished after the founding of the Pan-African Congress Movement. The main characteristic of early Black nationalism was a concern with intellectually establishing the existence of a racial-cultural bond between continental Africans and diasporan Africans, and demonstrating the importance of Pan-African unity in building an emancipatory movement. People like William Wells Brown, Robert Benjamin Lewis, Martin Delany, Edward W. Blyden, Alexander Crummell, J.E. Caseley-Hayford and many others wrote extensively on African history and its connection to 'New World Negroes', though their critiques were generally constrained by a highly moralistic and nationalistic Western epistemology grounded in a hybrid discourse that combined Christian rationalism and its attendant notions of 'civilization' or 'progress' with a Black prophetic tradition of Ethiopianism.[5]

The Negritude movement of the 1920s and 1930s, the subsequent decolonization of Africa in the post–World War II era, and the expansion of historical training in English-speaking and French-speaking universities produced a spate of liberal professional historians and activist/politicians who challenged 'colonial' interpretations of African history and placed greater emphasis on cultural unity, resistance, and the recuperation of a glorious precolonial past. Although these critiques tended to be far more secular than the writings of nineteenth-century Pan-Africanists, many authors were still constrained by Western notions of civilization and progress and few adopted a critical stance toward capitalism and class struggle within African and diasporan communities.[6] Here, in the works of authors such as J.A. Rogers, William Ferris, William Leo Hansberry, Willis N. Huggins, John Jackson, and later in the works of George E.M. James, Chancellor Williams, Ivan Van Sertima, John Henrik Clarke and Yosef ben-Jochannon, we see the roots of Molefi Asante's interpretation of Afrocentrism. These writers not only employ the dominant notions of 'civilization', 'progress', even 'technology', to prove the antiquity and superiority of Africa – mainly Egypt – but they are also locked into the discourse of race and nation, foregrounding the argument that Egypt was a 'Black' civilization. As Horace Campbell writes in his contribution, 'Afrocentric intellectual culture was a part of the opposition to the ideation system of European chauvinism. Yet in its opposition to Europe it internalized some of the principal aspects of that ideation system.'[7]

Unlike much of the previous liberal/nationalist literature on the topic, the essays included here are only briefly concerned with the *origins* of Pan-Africanism. Rather, our contributors are more interested in rethinking Pan-Africanism and re-evaluating its various expressions and manifestations. For this reason most of the authors tend not to invoke a single working definition of Pan-Africanism, choosing instead to situate a wide variety of diasporic social, political and cultural movements within specific historical contexts. Besides, while many earlier efforts to define Pan-Africanism have been useful, they have not been entirely adequate for the sort of work included in our collection. For example, George Shepperson and St. Clair Drake had insisted that a distinction be made between *Pan-Africanism* and *pan-Africanism*.[8]

According to these scholars *Pan-Africanism* 'consciously and deliberately attempts to create bonds of solidarity based upon a commonality of fate imposed by the trans-Atlantic slave trade and its aftermath.'[9] This is typified by organized political activity like the Du Boisian conferences or the Garvey movement. On the other side, *pan-Africanism* refers to the activities of individuals and groups 'that kept alive the memory of African origins . . . and to informal activities of various sorts.'[10] Similarly, Immanuel Geiss, in his book *The Pan-African Movement,* views Pan-Africanism in dualistic terms; he defines it in both a 'narrower and a broader sense'. He limits the narrower definition to the political movement for the unification of the African continent and relates it to the so-called 'Pan-Negro movement' or Pan-Africanism defined primarily in racial terms. His broader definition, on the other hand, incorporates a wide range of diasporic cultural and intellectual movements.[11]

The essays in this volume suggest that the ideological and practical, or discursive and nondiscursive, aspects of Pan-Africanism are so inseparable as to render such distinctions meaningless. Indeed, this kind of dualism tends to obfuscate the contradictory nature of Pan-Africanist movements and ideologies, or the myriad ways in which grassroots religious and cultural movements either inform Pan-Africanist political organizations or constitute a political force in their own right. More significantly, most of the early liberal/nationalist authors fail to come to terms with the reality of class and gender divisions amongst diasporan Blacks and the meanings of 'difference' for the development of political movements, ideologies, and cultural forms. Most of our contributors are concerned with questions such as, Which class or classes led these movements and formulated their ideologies? How did various cultural forms reflect contending class and gender ideologies? To what degree was the ideology of Pan-Africanism and the iconography of Africa employed to mobilize masses of Black people around local and domestic issues? How important has a consciousness of Africa been to the construction of cultural identities in the diaspora, and how have class, gender, and race shaped or constrained those identities?

The essays' emphasis on class relations and class consciousness is one of the critical features of this volume distinguishing it from earlier works. For most of our contributors, a person's class is established by his or her position in the network of ownership relations and the objective place occupied in a historically definite system of social production. Yet, although class is an objective relationship, class consciousness is not a mechanical product of one's position in social production or one's relations to the means of production – even though the latter conditions consciousness. While these essays recognize that people understand their experiences in cultural terms (manifested in tradition, value systems, ideas and institutional forms), they also realize that class consciousness cannot be reduced to a single culture or cultural form. Kelley's and Ogren's chapters show that there was no single class culture in the Pan-African (or Black Nationalist) movement. Instead they demonstrate that culture is never 'pure', nor void of contradiction; it is basically interactive, multi-leveled, and intertwined with (and interpenetrated by) other cultures.

By paying particular attention to class, class consciousness and class struggle in the formation of Pan-Africanist movements and Black New World identities, these authors are not denying or diminishing the importance of race and racism. As several of our contributors (Seidman, Tongun and Watkins) show, far from being a hindrance, racism has been crucial to capital accumulation, making possible the division of the working class and its control, and determining the distribution of surplus. Instead, these essays point to a decidedly more complex relationship between class and race than that suggested by either the liberal/nationalist school or its modernized Afrocentric version.

When gender is also employed as a category of analysis, as some of our contributors demonstrate, the relationship between class, culture and consciousness in the diaspora becomes even more complicated. In fact, the failure to adopt a serious gendered analysis has been perhaps the biggest weakness in diaspora studies, in general, and the historiography of Pan-Africanism, in particular. Despite the proliferation of feminist scholarship during the last decade or more, gender has only slowly been integrated into the field of diaspora studies, mainly by African-American and African feminist scholars whose work is all too often ignored.[12] Although some of these initial contributions have tended to conflate gender as a category of analysis with the study of women, more recent scholarship has extended the discussion to how gender shapes dominant discourses and how Black male constructions of masculinity shape culture, ideology, and politics in the diaspora. Given the close association between nationalism and masculinity, and the gendered iconography of Pan-Africanism – Black men coming to redeem the soil of a 'Mother Country' 'raped' by Europe – gender offers perhaps the freshest and most exciting possibilities for the study of diasporic political and cultural movements.[13] Indeed, in a recent essay on nationalism and gender, critical theorist R. Radhakrishnan asks several provocative questions which have yet to be interrogated: 'Why is it that the advent of the politics of nationalism signals the subordination if not the demise of women's politics? . . . Why is it that nationalism achieves the ideological effect of an inclusive and putatively macropolitical discourse, whereas the women's question – unable to achieve its own autonomous macropolitical identity – remains ghettoized within its specific and regional space?'[14]

A few of our contributors illustrate what a difference gender can make. Barbara Bair's intepretation of the life of Adelaide Casely Hayford, which draws on a wide range of feminist theorists, illustrates that the class and cultural identities of Pan-Africanist intellectuals cannot be understood without reference to gender, and vice versa. Her essay shows that gender is not static but a constellation of fluid lived experiences. As a product of both Africa and the West, communally based dual-sex institutions and the bourgeois family, Casely Hayford practiced a hybrid form of feminism combining bourgeois Victorian values with what she believed was African communalism, though her class prejudice and distrust of militant nationalism limited her sphere of political struggle and closed off the possibility of a more inclusive 'sisterhood' that would include peasant and working-class women. Gender, along with class and race, also made a difference for understanding Black and white (mostly male) writers and critics in the cultural politics of US communism. As Kelley shows in his essay, the common theme of masculinity served to bridge the gap between racial and class politics in a political climate in which they appeared to be mutually exclusive. Nevertheless, while a few of our own contributors make a sustained effort to incorporate gender in their essays, the volume as a whole still falls short of the kind of work that needs to be done.

Despite the collection's shortcomings, however, what follows constitutes a significant break with the liberal/nationalist paradigm. These essays not only move well beyond the glory story narratives of resistance and race *over* class dichotomies, but they break with much prevailing literature by collapsing the boundaries between cultural movements and formal politics. Indeed, by including discussions of class (and to a lesser extent gender) distinctions, the construction of cultural identities and the formation of diasporan/Black nationalist political organizations, we essentially bring together a number of different approaches to diaspora studies.

II

One of the central themes that runs through most of the essays is the *construction* of a diasporic identity. Although Benedict Anderson's notion of an 'imagined community' was not explicitly invoked by most of our contributors, we feel that his ideas are implicit in most of the essays. The authors move beyond the diaspora studies' focus on cultural survivals from Africa and explore how diasporic identities are constituted, reconstituted and reproduced; how even the most inchoate sense of solidarity among Black peoples in the New World, Europe and Africa is contingent, constantly shifting, and socially constructed. Of course, the contributors to this volume realize that Anderson's notion of 'an imagined community' – employed originally to analyze nationalisms situated in nation-states – could not be directly applied to the African diaspora without some substantive revision or qualification. First, the diaspora is not a sovereign territory with established boundaries, though it is seen as 'inherently limited' to people of African descent. Second, while there is no official language, there seems to be a consistent effort to locate, no matter how mythical, a single culture with singular historical roots. Third, many members of this diaspora see themselves as an oppressed 'nation' without a homeland, or they imagine Africa as their (future?) home. Finally, linked to the search for a homeland is the fourth barrier to the wholesale adoption of Anderson's concept to the African diaspora. As Paul Gilroy points out in his seminal book, *There Ain't No Black in the Union Jack,* most Black folk outside of Africa and the Caribbean live in countries where they are 'external to and estranged from the imagined community' of the dominant culture.[15]

Nevertheless, most of the authors understand and, implicitly at least, adopt Anderson's dictum that imagined communities 'are to be distinguished, not by their falsity/genuineness, but by the style in which they are imagined.'[16] But, more than style itself, it is important to bear in mind that hegemonic institutions construct and maintain systems of knowledge/information that reproduce (or attempt to reproduce) the imagined community, a sense of national obligation, patriotism, and familiarity necessary for the success of nationalism. Anderson himself examined some of these systems in his analysis of maps, museums and the census. Because these systems operate both within the nation-state and globally, they have a tremendous effect on the construction of a diasporic identity – both in terms of subverting or contesting this transnational and racialized 'imagined community' and reproducing it. Valentin Mudimbe's recent treatise, *The Invention of Africa,* makes an even stronger case for the role of dominant systems of power and thought in the construction of a hybrid diasporic identity. He asserts that Africa as a coherent ideological and political entity was, indeed,

invented with the advent of European expansion and continuously reinvented by traditional African and diasporan intellectuals, not to mention
metropolitan intellectuals and ideological apparatuses – educational institutions and their attendant disciplines, traveler accounts, popular media, and
so forth.[17]

In other words, the making of a Black Atlantic culture and identity, in
general, and Pan-Africanism, in particular, was as much the product of 'the
West' as it was indigenous to Africa. But racial capitalism, imperialism, and
colonialism – the process that created the current African diaspora in the
first place – could not shape African culture(s) without Western culture
itself being transformed. Realizing this, several of our contributors have
turned or extended their analytical gaze to the 'master', so to speak, and
begun to interrogate the ways in which ideological and institutional arrangements replicate and/or subvert hegemonic forms of class and gender
domination within diasporic movements and communities. Cedric Robinson, Lako Tongun, Barbara Bair, and William Watkins, for example,
ground their projects at the site where power – through various systems of
knowledge, institutions, physical and social spaces – is constituted, reconstituted and struggled over.

The other tendency in Pan-African scholarship has been to identify African survivals in the New World in order to make a stronger case for
cultural continuities between Africa and the diaspora. This historiographi-
cal tradition actually has its roots in the work of Melville Herskovitz. His
book *The Myth of the Negro Past* (1941) pioneered the field of diaspora studies while a number of Black social scientists, though still glorifying the
ancient past, were rejecting the idea of African survivals.[18] Nevertheless, at
the present moment the intellectual trend toward diaspora studies has as its
main proponent Black historian Joseph Harris. Harris's *Global Dimensions of
the African Diaspora* contains a series of papers produced for the First African
Diaspora Studies Institute in August 1979. Methodologically, diaspora studies focuses on three broad topics: African survivals in the 'New World';[19]
the movement of population throughout the diaspora;[20] and the movement
of 'ideas' or the intellectual 'roots' of Pan-Africanism. The latter body of
scholarship, which flourished in professional academic circles during the
1960s and early 1970s, was an attempt to historicize the very movement
that gave rise to the new historiography celebrating Africa's past and pre-
sumed cultural unity – a movement that included Pan-Africanist political
and cultural struggles in the diaspora.[21]

Although this large body of scholarship cannot be easily grouped together, some generalizations can be made about the more common approaches to diaspora studies. Methodologically, much (though by no
means all) of these works do not take into account the similar *historical*

conditions in which African people produced and transformed culture. As several of our contributors make clear, forced labor, European hegemony, and racial capitalism constituted a critical matrix through which most Black Atlantic as well as African cultures were produced. Thus the cultural practices that might have survived the middle passage could never be the same, either in the New World or in Africa. Unfortunately, several diaspora studies scholars ignore or deemphasize this matrix and adopt an ahistorical and often romantic view of African culture. Implicit in this analysis is the notion of a 'traditional' or 'authentic' African culture that is timeless, unchanging. 'Folk', often regarded as the descendant of 'traditional', has been invoked as well as a way to talk about New World diasporan cultural practices, though folk culture is almost always limited to that which has not been mass marketed or 'contaminated' by other cultures. The problem, of course, is that such an interpretation obscures the degree to which 'traditional' culture in any given historical moment is the product of bricolage, cutting, pasting and incorporating various cultural forms which, in modern times at least, become categorized in a racially/ethnically coded aesthetic heirarchy. Indeed, most nationalist interpreters of African and African-American culture have ignored or played down its cultural hybridity in order to demonstrate the presence of some pure African essence untouched by commercial or Western influence.[22]

On the other hand, as Paul Gilroy argues in this collection, the hybridity of Black Atlantic culture does not negate its commonalities, the links that enable critics to locate a diasporic identity within difference. More important, critics and cultural workers construct a discourse of racial/ethnic authenticity that is, in some ways, more central to sustaining Pan-African links than some elusive common structural or discursive component of African and diasporic culture.

III

The essays in our collection try to address the theoretical categories we have just discussed. At the same time our contributors realize that there is no way they can provide an overall or comprehensive view of the topic; nor do they necessarily aim to do so. The first section of the volume looks at the issues raised above through an examination of the cultural politics of Pan-Africanism. Ogren's, Kelley's, and Gilroy's essays examine the highly charged literary and artistic movements of working-class and middle-class Blacks. The chapters by Nelson, Bellegarde-Smith and Conde begin to unravel the phenomena of culture and consciousness as embodied in the 'practices and institutions' of religion (associated with Rastafarianism,

Ethiopianism and Vodun) and political organizations. Collectively, the essays reveal not only the degree to which a consciousness of Africa has been central to political discourse among the *masses* of Africans in the so-called New World during the nineteenth and twentieth centuries, but they illumine the ways in which a Pan-African sensibility manifested itself in multiple and contradictory ways.

Kathy Ogren's essay, 'What Is Africa to Me?: African Strategies in the Harlem Renaissance', reconsiders the significance of Africa on cultural movements like the Harlem Renaissance. Focusing on the debates about the 'New Negro' as represented in art, literature and music, she analyzes the influence of Pan-Africanism on African-Americans in Harlem and, in turn, their influence on the movement itself. In Chapter 2, Kelley investigates the Black cultural tradition of radicalism in the United States and its relationship to the Communist Party USA. He attempts to explain why Party cultural critics would tolerate Black nationalist and racial themes in the cultural production of African-American Communists while simultaneously resisting any form of 'petty-bourgeois nationalism' in explicit political movements. He argues that African-Americans found surprisingly open spaces within Communist circles for cultural expression because of the CP's essentialist view of Black culture, the logic of the Party's demand for self-determination in the 'Black belt' counties of the South, and the fact that most radical Black poets of the 1930s shared with the mainstream white left a common, gender-based imagery that equated proletarian/African-American struggle with manhood.

Paul Gilroy's essay examines contemporary Black music, ethnicity and Black popular culture in the Pan-African diaspora. He gives a critical account of the dynamics of Black subordination and resistance, and the fundamental dislocation of Black popular music. He rejects the criticism, posited by some critics, that dismisses all attempts to locate the cultural practices, motifs and political agendas that connect the Pan-African diaspora as exercises in essentialism or idealism or both. Gilroy maintains that any attempt at theorizing the construction of a Black Atlantic identity must understand it as, among other things, a product of lived experiences under racial capitalism and an 'imagined community' that is discursively constituted and reconstituted through localized and diasporic popular cultures.

The next three essays – by Maryse Conde, Gersham Nelson and Patrick Bellegarde-Smith – turn our attention to grass-roots cultural and political movements in the Caribbean. Conde's essay examines culture and Pan-Africanism in the context of Antillean/Diasporan liberation and the development of feminist awareness. Using her own experiences as a novelist and activist, she explores the role of the West Indian writer and contextualizes the utility of Pan-Africanism as a tool for achieving cultural, economic and political freedom.

Gersham Nelson also explores the links between political and economic liberation of diasporan Africans and the cultural vehicles used to achieve that goal. He challenges scholars who have insisted on reducing Ethiopianism and Rastafarianism in Jamaica to merely a messianic movement. These movements, Nelson argues, were more than simply attempts at 'deliverance' (that is, to return to some idealized 'Africa'). Indeed, the Ethiopianists' and Rastafarians' use of culture was the key to destroying 'the chain of oppression' in Jamaican society.

Bellegarde-Smith's article, 'Renewed Traditions: Contrapuntal Voices in Haitian Culture and Politics', also concentrates on cultural forms of resistance. He analyzes how 'Voodoo' as a cultural manifestation of Pan-African liberation has had a profound effect in Haitian politics. Both Nelson and Bellegarde-Smith explore the antagonistic relationship between popular cultural movements and ruling elites. They clearly demonstrate that these movements derive their energy from working-class and peasant culture, representing the primary force behind popular resistance. In Jamaica, Haiti and elsewhere in the Caribbean, these movements were forces of counter-legitimization against the cultural hegemony of the state.

The second section of the book reconsiders some of the intellectuals who were influential in the development of Pan-Africanism. The essay by Barbara Bair examines the life and works of a female Pan-Africanist thinker whom scholars had ignored in the past. Bair's biographical portrait of Adelaide Casely Hayford illustrates the degree to which a female leader within the Garvey movement crossed boundaries usually circumscribed by gender. In the process she assumed positions and secured rights usually designated for men, transcended international boundaries by identifying with Africa and the Americas and crossed political boundaries by exhibiting both left-wing and right-wing tendencies. By exploring the relationship between her ideology and her politics through the prism of feminist standpoint theory and the construction of 'woman as nature and culture', Bair reveals how Adelaide Casely Hayford helped reformulate the UNIA's basic platform.

Cedric Robinson's paper, 'W.E.B. Du Bois and Black Sovereignty', offers many interesting and controversial insights into the man whom many consider the father of Pan-Africanism. Robinson contends that Du Bois, 'blinded by the elitism characteristic of his class's prerogative', fell prey to American colonialism by supporting US reduction of Liberia to an American colony. In the essay Robinson 'assails the current ambiguous conjuncture of the discourses of race and class', thereby underscoring the contradictory nature of Pan-Africanism. Similarly, Paul Buhle's essay, 'C.L.R. James: Paradoxical Pan-Africanist', provides brief but penetrating insights into the contradictory evolution of another intellectual giant of Pan-Africanist philosophy. His primary focus is on James's literary evolution and his contributions to the genesis of the modern Pan-African movement.

The next essay in this section is Barbara Harlow's examination of Pan-Africanism in a broader oppositional context; she investigates the assassinations of several prominent Pan-Africanist writers/politicians and other political artists/artist politicians. Through critical analysis she examines the lives of these figures, notes how each eschewed the structures of power as sanction for their work and chose instead to draw from the arena of popular struggle to transform the existing distorted relations of power. Her approach allows her to problematize the deeper reasons for their murders.

Finally, in an essay entitled 'Max Yergan and South Africa: A Transatlantic Interaction', David Anthony explores some of the dimensions of Yergan's particular brand of leadership. Yergan, a leading Pan-African radical who eventually turned rabidly anti-Communist during the Cold War, was perhaps the most highly visible Black intellectual in the US left. Anthony highlights the profoundly perplexing ideological transformations that Yergan underwent and the historical elements that made them possible. He also sheds light on Yergan's public and personal fate and his possible influence on a number of South African revolutionaries.

Part III consists of three chapters that deal primarily with Southern Africa, contemporary US politics and economics and the resurgence of Pan-Africanist ideologies among African-Americans. Ann Seidman's essay 'Apartheid and the US South' identifies and examines the role apartheid has played in shaping the political economy of the southern US. Given the material linkages between the South African and southern US political economies, Pan-Africanism has been a powerful force for mobilizing African-Americans and Black South Africans to oppose the racist power structure in their respective regions. Knowledge of the common contradictions Black people face, she argues, could play a key role in the final destruction of all forms of racist and class domination.

The last two essays in this section examine independence struggles in Southern Africa and America. William Watkins's essay examines the relationship between power and ideology in the education of African and African-American peoples. He points out that recent forms of control, though subtle, are as insidious as the neocolonial social policies that they supposedly replaced. He exposes the vested economic and power relationships of educational policies in Africa and its corporate-industrial-philanthropic origins in American imperialism. Lako Tongun closes with a broad discussion of the political and ideological ramifications of the Congressional Black Caucus's struggle for South African sanctions.

Part IV, 'Theory of Liberation or Liberation from Theory?', consists of three broad theoretical essays critically assessing the scope and vision of Pan-Africanism. Horace Campbell summarizes the major contradictions evident when the modern Pan-African movement came into existence – many of which continue today. Following a brief overview of the movement, Campbell proceeds to link it to historical developments in the Caribbean, particularly to Garveyism, and to recent struggles to liberate Southern Africa. His essay asks crucial questions about the movement's class basis and the impact of Eurocentrism/racism on the development Pan-African thought and the politics of African liberation.

Like Campbell, Ntongela Masilela and Sidney J. Lemelle call in their essays for a radical critique of Pan-Africanism and its various manifestations, and insist that Marxism still has something to offer Africans and people of African heritage in the late twentieth century. In an essay titled 'Pan-Africanism or Classical African Marxism?', Masilela offers a fascinating intellectual history and critique of the fusion between classical European Marxist thought and Pan-Africanism. Masilela illustrates how the reconstruction of African, European and 'New World' history, and the African revolutions of the 1950s and 1960s, have been the terrain on which classical Marxists and Pan-Africanists struggled to create a sharper radical vision. Paying special attention to the contributions of Amilcar Cabral and Frantz Fanon, Masilela not only argues that classical African Marxism grew out of the efforts of African and Afro-diasporic intellectuals to unite theory and praxis, but he suggests that their contributions constitute a serious challenge to the entire Western Marxist tradition.

Sid Lemelle turns his attention to the US equivalent to Masilela's 'classical Pan-Africanism'. In 'The Politics of Cultural Existence: Pan-Africanism, Historical Materialism and Afrocentricity', Lemelle offers a stinging rebuke of Molefi Asante's Afrocentrism, particularly the claim that there is a single, unified culture in Africa. As an alternative to Asante's essentialism, Lemelle suggests that we return to a modified historical materialism that takes seriously the cultural and psychological dimensions of identity struggles.

Imagining Home, then, is an effort to rethink the history of Pan-Africanism and to historically document the multifaceted ways in which people of the African diaspora have continually reinvented and imagined the home of their ancestors. At the very least, these essays widen the debate over the material force of identity politics. No matter how invented the 'imagined diaspora' might be, the memory of Africa and imaginary links have inspired some of the most dynamic political, intellectual and cultural movements of our century.

Notes

1. Bernard M. Magubane, *The Ties That Bind: African-American Consciousness of Africa,* Trenton, N.J. 1987, p. 230.

2. In particular, I'm thinking of C.L.R. James, *The Black Jacobins,* New York 1963 [1938], and *A History of Pan-African Revolt,* Washington, D.C. 1969 [1938]; Eric Williams, *Capitalism and Slavery,* New York 1966; W.E.B. Du Bois, *Black Reconstruction in America: An Essay Toward a History of the Part Which Black Folk Played in the Attempt to Reconstruct Democracy in America, 1860–1880,* New York 1935; Walter Rodney, *How Europe Underdeveloped Africa,* Washington, D.C. 1980, and 'Towards the Sixth Pan African Congress: Aspects of the International Class Struggle in Africa, the Caribbean and America', in Horace Campbell, ed., *Pan Africanism: Struggle Against Neo-Colonialism and Imperialism,* Toronto 1976, pp. 18–41.

3. Vincent Thompson, *Africa and Unity: The Evolution of Pan-Africanism,* New York 1969, and *The Making of the African Diaspora in the Americas, 1441–1900,* New York 1987; Horace Campbell, *Rasta and Resistance: From Marcus Garvey to Walter Rodney,* London 1987; Wilson J. Moses, *The Golden Age of Black Nationalism: 1850–1925,* New York 1978; Cedric Robinson, *Black Marxism: The Making of the Black Radical Tradition,* London 1983; Magubane, *The Ties That Bind;* Paul Gilroy, *There Ain't No Black in the Union Jack: The Cultural Politics of Race and Nation,* Chicago 1991; A. Sivanandan, *Communities of Resistance: Writings on Black Struggles for Socialism,* London 1990, and *A Different Hunger: Writings on Black Resistance,* London, 1982.

4. See Gilroy's essay in this volume.

5. William Wells Brown, *The Black Man: His Antecedents, His Genius, and His Achievements,* Boston 1863; Robert Benjamin Lewis, *Light and Truth: Collected from the Bible and Ancient and Modern History, Containing the Universal History of the Colored and Indian Race, From the Creation of the World to the Present Time,* Boston 1844; J.E. Casely Hayford, *Ethiopia Unbound: Studies in Race Emancipation,* London 1969, 2nd edn; Alexander Crummell, *Africa and America: Addresses and Discourses,* Springfield, Mass. 1891; Wilson J. Moses, *Alexander Crummell: A Study of Civilization and Discontent,* New York 1989; Martin R. Delany, *The Condition, Elevation, Emigration, and Destiny of the Colored People of the United States,* New York 1968 (reprint).

6. See Kwame Nkrumah, *Africa Must Unite,* New York 1970, and *Consciencism: Philosophy and Ideology for Decolonization and Development with Particular Reference to the African Revolution,* London 1964. For a critique of the nationalist historiography of Africa, see especially Arnold Temu and Bonaventure Swai, *Historians and Africanist History: A Critique,* London 1983; Henry Slater, 'The Dar es Salaam Contribution to the Post-Nationalist Historiography of Africa: Towards Methodology and Practice of Proletarian Socialist Historiography', paper presented to the 13th Annual Conference of the Canadian Association of African Studies, Laval University, 1983.

7. Willis Huggins and John Jackson, *A Guide to Studies in African History,* New York 1934, and *Introduction to African Civilization,* New York 1970 [1937]; J.A. Rogers, *World's Greatest Men of African Descent,* New York 1931, *World's Greatest Men and Women of African Descent,* New York 1935, *The Real Facts about Ethiopia,* Baltimore 1982 [1936], and *World's Great Men of Color,* New York 1947; Valerie Sandoval, 'The Brand of History: A Historiographic Account of the Work of J.A. Rogers', *Schomburg Center for Research in Black Culture Journal,* (Spring 1978), pp. 11–17; Ivan Van Sertima, *They Came Before Columbus,* New York 1976; George E. M. James, *Stolen Legacy,* New York 1976 [1954]; William Leo Hansberry, *Pillars of Ethiopian History,* Joseph Harris, ed., Washington, D.C. 1974; *Africa and Africans as Seen by Classical Writers,* Joseph Harris, ed., Washington, D.C. 1977; Yosef ben-Jochannon, *Africa: Mother of Civilization,* New York 1971; John Henrik Clarke, 'African-American Historians and the Reclaiming of African History', in Molefi Kete Asante and Kariamu Welsh Asante, eds, *African Culture: The Rhythms of Unity,* Westport, Conn. 1985; Cheikh Anta Diop, *Nations negres et culture,* Paris 1955, and *African Origins of Civilization,* New York 1974; Chancellor Williams, *The Destruction of African Civilization: Great Issues of Race from 4500 B.C. to 2000 A.D.,* Chicago 1974; Molefi Asante, *The Afrocentric Idea,* Philadelphia 1987.

8. For a discussion of this distinction, see Shepperson and St. Clair Drake, 'Diaspora Studies and Pan-Africanism', in Joseph E. Harris, ed., *Global Dimensions of the African Diaspora,* Washington, D.C. 1982, pp. 13, 353.

9. See Harris, *Global Dimensions*, p. 9, or Shepperson's original essays, 'Notes on Negro-American Influences on the Emergence of African Nationalism', *Journal of African History*, vol. 1 (1960), p. 309–10; '"Pan-Africanism" and "pan-Africanism": Some Historical Notes', *Phylon*, vol. 23 (1962), pp. 353–4; and 'The African Diaspora – or the African Abroad', *African Forum*, vol. 2 (Summer 1966), pp. 76–93.

10. Harris, *Global Dimensions*, p. 13.

11. Immanuel Geiss, *The Pan-African Movement*, London 1974, p. 7.

12. Pioneering contributions include Beverly Lindsay, ed., *Comparative Perspectives of Third World Women: The Impact of Race, Sex, and Class*, New York 1980; Filomina Chioma Steady, ed., *The Black Woman Cross-Culturally*, Cambridge, Mass. 1981; Rosalyn Terborg-Penn, Andrea Rushing, and Sharon Harley, eds, *Women in Africa and the African Diaspora*, Washington, D.C. 1987; E. Frances White, 'Africa on My Mind: Gender, Counter Discourse and African-American Nationalism', *Journal of Women's History*, vol. 2, no. 1 (Spring 1990), pp. 73–97.

13. Examples include bell hooks, *Ain't I A Woman: black women and feminism*, Boston 1981, pp. 87–117; Paula Giddings, *When and Where I Enter: The Impact of Black Women on Race and Sex in America*, New York 1984, pp. 299–335; Joyce Hope Scott, 'From Foreground to Margin: Female Configurations and Masculine Self-Representation in Black Nationalist Fiction', in Andrew Parker, Mary Russo, Doris Sommer, and Patricia Yeager, eds, *Nationalisms and Sexualities*, New York 1992, pp. 296–312; Barbara Bair, 'True Women, Real Men: Gender, Ideology, and Social Roles in the Garvey Movement', in *Gendered Domains: Rethinking Public and Private in Women's History: Essays from the 7th Berkshire Conference on the History of Women*, Susan Reverby and Dorothy O. Helly, eds, Ithaca, N.Y. 1992. E. Frances White, on the other hand, looks at the masculinist impulses of contemporary Afrocentricism by writers like Molefi Asante in addition to earlier manifestations ('Africa on My Mind', pp. 73–97), while cultural critics Paulla Ebron and Tricia Rose explore Black masculinity in rap music (Paulla Ebron, 'Rapping Between Men: Performing Gender', *Radical America*, vol. 23, no. 4 (June 1991), pp. 23–7; Tricia Rose, 'Never Trust a Big Butt and a Smile', *Camera Obscura*, vol. 23 (1991), pp. 109–31).

14. R. Radhakrishnan, 'Nationalism, Gender, and the Narrative of Identity', in Parker et al., *Nationalisms and Sexualities*, p. 80.

15. Benedict Anderson, *Imagined Communities: Reflections on the Origins and Spread of Nationalism*, revised edn, London 1991; Gilroy, *There Ain't No Black*, p. 153.

16. Anderson, *Imagined Communities*, p. 6.

17. 18. V.Y. Mudimbe, *The Invention of Africa: Gnosis, Philosophy, and the Order of Knowledge*, Bloomington, Ind. 1988.

18. Melville Herskovitz, *The Myth of the Negro Past*, London 1941; see also Herskovitz, *The New World Negro: Selected Papers in Afro-American Studies*, Bloomington, Ind. 1966. The pioneering works by Black sociologists who rejected the idea of African survivals included E. Franklin Frazier, *The Negro Family in the United States*, Chicago 1939, pp. 21ff, and Charles S. Johnson, *Shadow of the Plantation*, Chicago 1934, p. 3.

19. Harris, *Global Dimensions*, and *The African Presence in Asia*, Washington D.C. 1971; Leonard Barret, *Soul-Force: African Heritage in Afro-American Religion*, New York 1974; Graham W. Irwin, ed., *Africans Abroad: A Documentary History of the Black Diaspora in Asia, Latin America, and the Caribbean During the Age of Slavery*, New York 1977; Robert Farris Thompson, *Flash of the Spirit*, New York 1983; Winifred Vass, *The Bantu-Speaking Heritage of the United States*, Los Angeles 1979. The most sophisticated volumes on the subject of African survivals not only avoid many of the pitfalls of assuming an undifferentiated African culture but attempt to historicize the subject by examining the dialectical process by which culture is continuously made and re-made. And yet they also make a strong case for privileging the African roots of African-American culture. See, for example, Joseph Holloway, ed., *Africanisms in American Culture*, Bloomington, Ind. 1990; Sterling Stuckey, *Slave Culture: Nationalist Theory and the Foundations of Black America*, New York 1987; Margaret Washington Creel, *'A Peculiar People': Slave Religion and Community-Culture among the Gullahs*, New York 1988.

20. Floyd Miller, *The Search for a Black Nationality: Black Emigration and Colonization, 1787–1863*, Urbana, Ill. 1975.

21. Colin Legum, *Pan-Africanism: A Short Political Guide*, London 1962; Kenneth King, *Pan-Africanism and Education: A Study of Race, Philanthropy and Education in the Southern States of America*

and East Africa, Oxford 1971; J. Ayodele, *Pan-Africanism and Nationalism in West Africa, 1900–1945: A Study in Ideology and Social Classes*, Oxford 1973; Ajala Adakunle, *Pan-Africanism: Evolution, Progress and Prospects*, London 1973; Robert Weisbord, *Ebony Kinship: Africa, Africans, and the Afro-American*, Westport, Conn. 1973; Imanuel Geiss, *The Pan-African Movement*, New York 1974; Robert Chrisman and Nathan Hare, eds, *Pan Africanism*, Indianapolis, Ind. 1974; Jacob Drachler, *Black Homeland/ Black Diaspora: Cross-Currents of the African Relationship*, New York 1975; Shaukat Ali, *Pan-movements in the Third World: Pan-Arabism, Pan-Africanism, Pan-Islamism*, Lahore 1976; S.K.B. Asante, *Pan-African Protest: West Africa and the Italo-Ethiopian Crisis, 1934–1941*, London 1977; P. Olisanwuch Esedebe, *Pan-Africanism: The Idea and Movement, 1776–1963*, Washington, D.C. 1982; Kinfe Abraham, *From Race to Class: Links and Parallels in African and Black American Protest Expression*, London 1982; Kwesi Krafona, *The Pan-African Movement: Ghana's Contribution*, London 1986; W. Ofuatey-Kodjoe, ed., *Pan-Africanism:, New Directions in Strategy*, Lanham, Md. 1986; and Magubane, *The Ties That Bind.*

22. See, especially, Andrew Ross, *No Respect: Intellectuals and Popular Culture*, London 1989, p. 68; Simon Frith, 'The Cultural Study of Popular Music', in Grossberg et al., *Cultural Studies*, pp. 180–81; Wahneema Lubiano, 'But Compared to What?: Reading Realism, Representation, and Essentialism in *School Daze, Do the Right Thing*, and the Spike Lee Discourse', *Black American Literature Forum*, vol. 25 (Summer 1991), pp. 253–82, for an excellent discussion of the problems of 'authenticity' in Black film. Some of these ideas are further developed in Robin D.G. Kelley, 'Notes on Deconstructing "the Folk"', *American Historical Review*, vol. 97, no. 5 (December 1992), pp. 1400–1408.

PART I

The Cultural Politics

of Pan-Africanism

1

'What Is Africa to Me?':

African Strategies in the

Harlem Renaissance

Kathy J. Ogren

> What is Africa to me:
> Copper sun, a scarlet sea,
> Jungle star and jungle track,
> Strong bronzed men and regal Black
> Women from whose loins I sprang
> When the birds of Eden sang?
> One three centuries removed
> From the scenes his fathers loved,
> Spicy grove and banyan tree,
> What is Africa to me?
>
> *Countee Cullen, 'Heritage'*

When Henry Sylvester Williams, W.E.B. Du Bois and others organized the first four Pan-Africanist conferences between 1900 and 1927, their efforts paralleled the emergence of significant new developments in Afro-American art, literature and music. A 're-visitation' of Pan-Africanism in America includes, therefore, not only a re-evaluation of political and economic relationships between Africa and the Diaspora, but also a reconsideration of the significance of Africa in cultural movements like the Harlem Renaissance. American social and intellectual historians have debated the role of Africa as a political and aesthetic inspiration on participants in the Harlem Renaissance from a variety of standpoints – each of them offering a firm response to poet Countee Cullen's plaintive question 'What Is Africa to Me?' Most commentators share a common perception that Africa was a significant part of a discourse asserting political rights and aesthetic goals during the Harlem Renaissance.[1]

Analyzing the uses of Africa in Harlem Renaissance debates about the representation of the New Negro in art, literature, music, history and politics provides one way to understand the influence of Pan-Africanism on American Blacks and their occasional influence, in turn, on the Pan-Africanist movement itself. Using a literal as well as a figurative Africa to evoke artistic and aesthetic antecedents, Harlem Renaissance writers and artists echoed Marcus Garvey's call for a 'return to Africa' – although they did not always distinguish clearly between individual African nations or ethnic groups. Recent historians and literary critics have also reconsidered the meaning of Africa in their evaluations of the Harlem Renaissance.

Editor Alain Locke's collection *The New Negro* (1925) is the most representative text to begin this exploration because it contains a variety of views on Africa, concluding with W.E.B. Du Bois's Pan-Africanist essay 'The Negro Mind Reaches Out'. A professor of philosophy at Howard University, Locke was asked to edit a special Harlem edition of the *Survey Graphic* magazine in 1924, which formed the basis for *The New Negro* several months later. The volume contains political, sociological and historical essays, poetry, art and music criticism and illustrations by Aaron Douglas and Winhold Reiss.[2] Three main strategies emerge from this important collection suggesting connection to, mediation between and detachment from Africa. Similarly, these same approaches characterize influential histories and reconsiderations of the Harlem Renaissance. Thus, one can revisit Pan-Africanism by comparing the artistic strategies of selected participants in the Harlem Renaissance with the interpretive schemes of contemporary critics David Levering Lewis, Nathan Huggins and Houston A. Baker, Jr.[3]

Essays in *The New Negro* exemplifying a connective strategy towards Africa typically concerned historical, anthropological and folkloric data. For example, bibliophile Arthur A. Schomburg's 'The Negro Digs Up His Past', recommended that Black Americans reject the dominant American delusion that the United States was 'the one country where it is unnecessary to have a past'. According to Schomburg, the legacy of slavery and negative racist stereotypes necessitated 'a group tradition' that 'must supply compensation for persecution' so that 'history' could 'restore what slavery took away'.[4] Reconstructing an accurate history of Africa was the starting point for this project, Schomburg explained, and he outlined the strengths of major collections of Africana and Afro-American materials. Schomburg stressed the importance of seeing the African past as dynamic and 'civilized' in order to counteract static and pejorative Social Darwinist portrayals of a monolithic 'backward' continent. Reclamation of the African past, according to Schomburg, was the most important way to 'open up the closed Negro past'.[5]

Schomburg pointed out that the establishment of accurate historical data on Africa would help correct racist distortions in the official American historical record. He welcomed the development of professional societies devoted to Black history, especially The Negro Society for Historical Research, that brought together African, West Indian and Afro-American scholars. Schomburg wanted scientific historical methods to replace the amateur history that he believed evolved from the 'race issue' that had been 'a plague on both our historical houses'.[6] In addition, Schomburg cited the importance of Gustavus Vassa's autobiography to British abolitionists as an example of those situations in which he believed accurate historical knowledge had aided larger political struggles.[7]

Anthropologist Arthur Huff Fauset also emphasized the connections between Africa and Afro-Americans by documenting African characteristics of selected folktales. Fauset first detailed the distortions he found in Joel Chandler Harris's Uncle Remus stories. Decrying the tendency of Harris's readers to misinterpret Harris's version as authentic portrayals of Black folk life, Fauset recommended that 'scientific collecting' of Afro-American folklore be expanded as an antidote. He lauded the 'competence' of ethnologists Franz Boas and Elsie Clews Parsons.

Fauset identified as African several features of Black American folktales, especially the use of anthropomorphic figures as a source of proverbial advice. Two of the tales Fauset had collected, 'T'appin' and 'B'rer Rabbit Fools Buzzard', followed his essay. According to Fauset, 'T'appin' had been 'brought to America from West Coast, Africa, 1859'. Like Schomburg, Fauset believed that professional standards would preserve accurate and authentic tales and prevent the distortions that accompanied literary mediations.[8]

W.E.B. Du Bois's 'The Negro Mind Reaches Out' represented the fullest expression of the connective strategy. In it, Du Bois reflected on the statement he had made twenty-two years earlier in *The Souls of Black Folk*: 'The problem of the twentieth century is the problem of the color line, – the relation of the darker to the lighter races of men in Asia and Africa, in America and the islands of the sea'.[9] Reporting on the Third Pan-African Congress, Du Bois extended his color line analogy by examining the effects of World War I and imperialism on Africa.

Using the 'dark colonial shadow' over Africa as his unifying metaphor in each section, Du Bois then illuminated in turn the consequences of Portuguese, Belgian, French, Spanish, Italian and English colonial domination. The 'shadow' metaphor provided an interesting contrast to one of Du Bois's famous passages in *The Souls of Black Folk*. In that 1901 text, Du Bois described the identity of American Blacks as being like those 'born with a veil', leading to 'a peculiar sensation' of 'double-consciousness'. Du Bois elaborated:

> It is a peculiar sensation, this double-consciousness, this sense of always looking at one's self through the eyes of others, of measuring one's soul by the tape of a world that looks on in amused contempt and pity. One ever feels his twoness – an American, a Negro; two souls, two thoughts, two unreconciled strivings; two warring ideals in one dark body, whose dogged strength alone keeps it from being torn asunder.[10]

Interestingly, living beneath a 'shadow' does not suggest a deterministic dynamic that keeps one enmeshed in a veil. And in fact, Du Bois's evaluation of each area of colonial domination in Africa emphasizes the efforts of Africans, Pan-Africanists and others to remove these shadows. For example, Du Bois described 'insurgent Morocco, independent Abyssinia and Liberia' as 'shadows of Europe on Africa unattached and as such they curiously threaten the whole imperial program'. Du Bois mused:

> On the one hand they arouse democratic sympathy in homeland which makes it difficult to submerge them; and again, they are temptations to agitation for freedom and autonomy on the part of other Black and subject populations. What prophet can tell what world-tempest lurks in these cloud-like shadows?[11]

Unlike the 'warring ideals in one dark body' he describes in the articulation of the veiled double-consciousness, Du Bois's survey of Africa recorded examples of external political struggles aimed at diluting the intensity of the colonial shadow.

In his analysis, Du Bois emphasized the relationship between racism and working-class consciousness. 'Modern imperialism and modern industrialism are one and the same system; root and branch of the same tree', wrote Du Bois. Then, with an ironic inversion of the well-known Rudyard Kipling poem 'The White Man's Burden', Du Bois continued, 'The race problem is the other side of the labor problem; and the Black man's burden is the white man's burden'.[12] Du Bois pointed out that the potential political power of labor was undermined by a white racism that divided the working class. White laborers, he complained, 'still lean rather toward the attitude of South Africa than that of Russia'. As Black laborers became 'more organized and more intelligent', Du Bois's analysis used the origins and consequences of World War I as a way of connecting economic developments with the struggle for national liberation against the 'shadows' of colonialism.[13]

Du Bois also discussed differences between a 'happy Africa' and a West defined by the 'command of technique or mastery of physical force'. One of the political aims for Pan-Africanism that he promoted was to eliminate colonial and capitalist domination and extend the benefits of modern life to Africans. In Du Bois's view, Black Americans should lead this effort. Thus in content, metaphor and program, Du Bois's essay stressed connections between America, Africa and the rest of the world.[14]

Many writers discussed the ways in which Africa had been mediated by European or American cultural forms, rather than trying to reveal connecting links. Alain Locke's essays on African art and the spirituals and J.A. Rogers's essay on jazz both began with the premise that slavery cut off all direct experience of Africa and thereby prevented Africans and Afro-Americans in the diaspora from preserving most African traditions. Locke's essay 'The Legacy of the Ancestral Arts' opens with his interpretation of the difference between African and American cultures:

> Music and poetry and to an extent dance, have been the predominant arts of the American Negro. This is an emphasis quite different from that of the African cultures, where the plastic and craft arts predominate; Africa being one of the great fountain sources of the arts of decoration and design. Except then in his remarkable carry-over of the rhythmic gift, there is little evidence of any direct connection of the American Negro with his ancestral arts.[15]

Locke argued, nevertheless, that Africa was a valuable source of artistic ideas and disciplines. Visual artists could benefit from experimenting with the mediums and ideas typical of African art and in the process learn what Locke called the 'lesson of a classic background, the lesson of discipline, of style, of technical control pushed to the limits of technical mastery'.[16]

Locke used photographs of masks and statues from Bushongo, Sudan-Niger, the Ivory Coast, Dahomey and the Congo as illustrations for his essay. But Locke also envisioned that the illustrations in *The New Negro* itself could serve as a 'path-breaking guide and encouragement to this new foray of the younger Negro artists', and emphasized that the experiments in a new idiom would 'point the lesson that contemporary European art has already learned – that any vital artistic expression of the Negro theme and subject in art must break through the stereotypes to a new style, a distinctive fresh technique and some sort of characteristic idiom'.[17]

Significantly, Locke expected European modernists to provide an important path to finding this African inspiration. American art had neglected African and Afro-American themes, according to Locke, and he was skeptical it could provide much positive guidance. Locke suggested that painters and sculptors might learn from 'African influences' in the works of artists like Henri Matisse, Pablo Picasso, André Derain, Amedeo Modigliani, Maurice Utrillo, Max Pechstein and Elaine Stern. In making his recommendation in *The New Negro,* Locke did not comment in detail on the political or economic contexts in which the African art had been 'collected' by Europeans. In later articles, Locke would address this subject in more detail.[18]

As Jeffrey Stewart has pointed out in *The Critical Temper of Alain Locke: A Selection of His Essays on Art and Culture,* Locke was often ambivalent about his respect for European art, while at the same time asserting a unique cultural or emotional bond to Africa; he would become one of the most important critics and collectors of African art in America.[19] In *The New Negro,* Locke enthusiastically celebrated the attempts already made by American artists Meta Warrick Fuller, Archibald Motley, Otto Farrill, Albert Smith, John Urquhart, Samuel Blount and Charles Keene.

Fuller's work is especially important to a consideration of Pan-Africanism. She had been working with African and Black American subjects prior to Locke's call for a new, African-inspired art in 1925 and has been credited with being one of the 'earliest examples of American art to reflect the formal exigencies of an aesthetic based on African sculpture'.[20] Fuller embraced W.E.B. Du Bois's Pan-Africanism and one contemporary art critic attributes her choice of African subjects to a 'desire to awaken Black people to the consciousness of nationhood and anti-colonialism'. Locke considered Fuller's 1914 sculpture 'Ethiopia Awakening' an outstanding example of the kind of art young artists should aspire to create.[21]

The two essays on music in *The New Negro* also highlight the mediating influence of European and American music forms, although the argument is somewhat different from the one for the visual arts. Locke's 'The Negro Spirituals' mentions the importance of African rhythms to Black folk music and consequently to the spirituals. J.A. Rogers's 'Jazz at Home' claimed that the origins for both jazz and ragtime were 'atavistically African'. Rogers argued that the influence of modern civilization had transformed these African beginnings, however, 'because . . . jazz time is faster and more complex than African music'. Rogers's dubious assumption about 'African' music was followed by an equally curious list of novelty effects that he credits with 'civilizing' jazz:

> With its cowbells, auto horns, calliopes, rattles, dinner gongs, kitchen utensils, cymbals, screams, crashes, clankings and monotonous rhythm it bears all the marks of a nerve-strung, strident, mechanized civilization. It is a thing of the jungles – modern man-made jungles.[22]

Generally, Rogers's comments were typical of those critics who wanted to assert a positive folk origin and world-wide appeal for jazz against its detractors' labels of the music as merely a bunch of tricks or noise. Like most analyses of jazz in the 1920s, Rogers's acknowledged African origins for jazz but emphasized the transforming effects of America's musical influences. Rogers also quoted Leopold Stowkowski's favorable judgement of jazz and reminded his readers that 'serious modernist music and musicians ... have become the confessed debtors of American Negro jazz'. Rogers, like many others, celebrated the possibilities of jazz to become an international music.

These strategies of mediation, in which African influences are either preserved, appreciated or improved by the intervention of European and American culture or 'civilization', are quite interesting when compared to the primitivism vogue of the 1920s. Some Harlem Renaissance writers, inspired in part by the fascination of white European and American writers with Native American, Asian and African cultures, also labelled themselves 'primitives': Claude McKay was probably the best known 'primitive' Black writer. Primitivist strategies celebrated purportedly noncivilized societies that had avoided the alienation of industrialized life. African and Afro-American folk cultures were often cited as repositories of 'primitive' virtues.[24]

Bruce Nugent's 'Sahdji', for instance, typifies some of the primitivist conventions. A stream-of-consciousness vignette, 'Sahdji' contains a tale about an East African chieftain Konombju and his 'favorite wife' Sahdji. Inspired by Konombju's son Mrabo's longing for Sahdji, a young 'buck' named Numbo stages a hunting accident in which Konombju is killed. Numbo's plans are thwarted when Sahdji joins her husband on the funeral bier. The story's atmosphere depends on descriptions of a generic Africa and a sensuous Sahdji, consequently projecting a mythological Africa with little accurate ethnographic information. But Nugent's purpose, of course, was merely to evoke certain conventional images of Africa and transform them into a primitivist sketch.[25]

Primitivist experiments can be seen as part of a mediating strategy, since the conventions of dominant white critical definitions come between the Black artist or writer and their attempts to use African or Afro-American vernacular culture. Writers like Langston Hughes and Claude McKay tried to create an alternative to the primitivist conventions established by white writers by developing their own visions of Black folk and working-class culture. *The New Negro* contains a few of their attempts to do so, such as Countee Cullen's 'Heritage', Claude McKay's 'The Tropics in New York', and Langston Hughes's well-known 'The Negro Speaks of Rivers'. Hughes took his first trip to [West] Africa in 1923, but *The New Negro* contains only one of the poems it inspired – 'Dream Variations'.[26]

One final strategy that emerges from the pages of *The New Negro* reverses the impetus of connective and mediating uses of Africa. Many contributors did not discuss Africa at all, and a few rejected the notion that Africa had any long lasting influence on American Blacks and therefore on the Renaissance. Anthropologist Melville Herskovitz, for example, contributed 'The Negro's Americanism', in which he stressed the acculturation of Black Americans. Herskovitz used Reconstruction as his starting point and argued that freed Blacks borrowed social and institutional structures from the dominant white American culture. For example, Herskovitz wrote that '[s]chools sprang up in which they might learn, not the language and technique of their African ancestors, but that of this country, where they lived'.[27] Although Herskovitz would later be credited with cataloguing 'Africanisms' throughout the diaspora, each example in this piece reinforced his relativist view that Black American and African cultures be judged primarily on their own terms and not through their relationships to one another.

Herskovitz attributed the differences between cultures to their historical and political development and argued against racially determinist views. Herskovitz's example of the gulf that might exist between Africans and Americans suggests that Black Americans had accepted industrial regimen in their lives, while Africans had not:

> To the Negro in Africa, it would be incomprehensible for a man to work at a machine all day for a few bits of paper to be given to him at the end of his work-day and in the same way, the white traveller stigmatizes the African as lazy because he will not see the necessity for entering on a gruelling forced march so as to reach a certain point in time.[28]

The 'African' under discussion in Herskovitz's essay is not specifically identified, but his imagery poses an interesting comparison to Du Bois's Africans, who are much more clearly integrated into modern capitalist societies. Herskovitz concluded that despite its origins, Black American culture was 'the same pattern as white', only a 'different shade'.

The dissociative strategy can also be mapped by noting that the numerous essays in *The New Negro* discussing social, political and educational advances in America had little to say about comparable African developments. This is not surprising, since *The New Negro* was conceived, of course, to reach a broad and sympathetic audience primarily concerned with American intellectual and social life. Having acknowledged this orientation, however, it is important to realize that *The New Negro* still did not capture the full spectrum of Harlem politics. The most deafening silence in *The New Negro* concerns Marcus Garvey and the Universal Negro Improvement Association.

Perhaps contributors were overly concerned with what historian David Levering Lewis calls 'civil rights by copyright', that is, a determination not to offend potential Black and white supporters and patrons of younger artists by publicizing subjects that portrayed the Black community in a negative light.[29] Since *The New Negro* was published in 1925, many of the contributors had not yet asserted their artistic and political independence from what they perceived as a constricting older generation. Writers like Langston Hughes, Claude McKay, Eric Walrond and Zora Neale Hurston had not yet published the iconoclastic journal *Fire,* for instance, and Hughes and McKay had just begun their travels to Europe, Africa and the Soviet Union.

In fact, McKay's only trip to Africa, where he visited Casablanca, Rabat, Fez, Marrakesh and other parts of North Africa, took place in 1928. His novel *Banjo* (1929) is often interpreted as reflecting McKay's attitudes towards his travels in the Mediterranean and North Africa. The novel concerns a protagonist named Ray who rediscovers his African roots and thus an alternative to the repression of civilization by his association with Africans, West Indians and others in Marseilles. Garveyism is one of the subjects discussed by the men on the docks. Hurston would discuss possible African influences on Afro-American folklore later on in her career, but she did not take her first collection excursions in the American South and the West Indies until late in the 1920s.[30]

Garveyism was discussed only tangentially in *The New Negro*, usually as part of a broader topic. Charles S. Johnson, director of research and publicity for the National Urban League and editor of *Opportunity* in 1925, briefly discusses Garvey as a symbol of the Black 'peasantry's' race pride and desire for a better life in 'The New Frontage on American Life'. Journalist W.A. Domingo, who wrote the sole essay in Locke's volume devoted to the relationship between the West Indies and America and, to a lesser extent, Africa, also gave Garvey brief mention. In 'The Gift of the Black Tropics', Domingo rejected the accusation that the Garvey movement represented 'the attempt of West Indian peasants to solve the American race problem'. Domingo saw West Indian support for Garvey as an expression of solidarity against 'attacks made upon him because of his nationality'. Domingo pointed out that West Indians, specifically Cyril Briggs, had provided the 'earliest and most persistent exposures' of what Domingo called Garvey's 'multitudinous schemes'.[31] Aside from Du Bois's essay on Pan-Africanism, then, there are few discussions of Africa or Garveyism in the pages of *The New Negro*.

A thorough examination of all the literature of the Harlem Renaissance years would reveal many more examples of the political and cultural relevance of Africa. Clearly, one needs to give full attention to the African strategy represented by Garveyism, which can be gleaned from the growing scholarship on Garvey. One writer who specifically addresses the relationship between Garvey and participants in the Harlem Renaissance is

Tony Martin, whose book *Literary Garveyism: Garvey, Black Arts and the Harlem Renaissance* provides an interesting contrast to the Renaissance as represented by *The New Negro*.[32]

In addition to the example set by Garvey, one would also need to look at the analysis of Africa that emerged from the socialist press, particularly if, as historian Mark Naison claims, Black American socialists developed many of their arguments in the 1920s as a response to Garvey. In *The Messenger,* for example, A. Philip Randolph regularly denounced Garvey for what Randolph saw as Black capitalist delusions of empire in Africa. Cyril Briggs, writing in the African Blood Brotherhood's newspaper, *The Crusader,* denounced imperialism in Africa and called upon all 'blood brothers' to unite in a symbolic rendering of ancient rituals in which blood is shared between fathers and sons.[33]

The connective, mediative and dissociative strategies towards Africa that emerged from the pages of *The New Negro* also characterize most evaluations of the Harlem Renaissance. Historians and critics of the Renaissance differ in their evaluation of the significance of African themes and ideas – developing their own strategies of return and renewal. Several participants, notably James Weldon Johnson, Langston Hughes and Claude McKay, were quite harsh in their ultimate judgements of the Renaissance. Johnson spoke about the Renaissance as a time of 'disillusionment and disappointment', and Langston Hughes ridiculed the idea that the 'vogue' for Black culture would bring about significant social change, commenting, 'The ordinary Negroes hadn't heard of the Negro Renaissance. And if they had, it hadn't raised their wages any.'[34] McKay complained about the genteel pretensions of Renaissance spokespersons.

Contemporary reassessments sometimes echo this dim view. For example, in his comprehensive survey *When Harlem Was in Vogue* (1982), historian David Levering Lewis found the optimism of *The New Negro* contributors ridiculous:

> To suppose that a few superior people, who would not have filled a Liberty Hall quorum or Ernestine Rose's 135th Street library, were to lead ten million Afro-Americans into an era of opportunity and justice seemed irresponsibly delusional.[35]

Since Africa does not emerge as a prominent theme in the cataloguing of Renaissance inadequacies or failures, one could conclude that the dissociative strategy dominates most scholarship about the perception of Africa in the Harlem Renaissance.

But two of the most influential studies of the Harlem Renaissance do give African themes serious consideration. Furthermore, they should be analyzed as part of the revisitation of Pan-Africanism. Historian Nathan Huggins's *Harlem Renaissance* (1971) and literary and cultural critic Houston A. Baker, Jr's *Modernism and the Harlem Renaissance* (1987) both provide important critiques of the role of Africa in the Renaissance, although the authors reach a different conclusion.[36]

The earliest study to systematically explore African influences in the Renaissance was Nathan Huggins's text. Huggins judged most experiments with African themes within the context of the cult of primitivism. Huggins provided an extended discussion of 'pagan/primitive' motifs in the works of writers Nella Larsen, Countee Cullen, Jean Toomer and Claude McKay and in the art of Richmond Barthe, Aaron Douglas and Palmer Hayden.[37] Huggins suggested that since Black American writers had a 'superficial' understanding of Africa, they wrote 'romantic' and naïve primitivist fantasies. 'The final and perhaps supreme irony of the primitives', wrote Huggins, 'was that they were in their quest for Africa, in their fancy Timbuctoo and Alexandria, forsaking their actual past'.[38] Huggins judged the Renaissance primarily to be a case of 'ethnic provincialism', characterized by art that was 'problematic, feckless, not fresh and not real' and therefore a 'failure'. Huggins objected to these 'primitivist' experiments, which I have judged mediative strategies, and in fact suggested that searching for a mythical Africa may have impeded a clear understanding of the Afro-American folk cultural roots available in America.

Likewise, Huggins characterized as 'thwarted' W.E.B. Du Bois's 'efforts to lead Afro-Americans toward a world-view of race – away from their provincialism. . . .' In his analysis of Du Bois's Pan-Africanism, Huggins paints the civil rights leader as stranded between the 'complexities of international politics' and the 'restraints imposed by his American progressivism'.[39] By contrast, Huggins credited Marcus Garvey with giving Africa a 'tangible and visible reality' to large numbers of Black Americans under the aegis of the Universal Negro Improvement Association.

Huggins also found the popular theatrical acts of Bert Williams and George Walker to be redeeming portrayals of Africa. The shows, *In Dahomey* (1902) and *Abyssinia* (1906), were based on white-determined minstrel stereotypes, but Williams and Walker transformed the format, according to Huggins and 'they served to shift the focus from the arid and artificial minstrel stereotypes and to give the Negro a context in which to work that was more culturally and historically rich'.[40] Williams and Walker were inspired to develop the African themes because they had been employed as 'sham Africans' at an 1893 San Francisco fair exhibit, temporarily replacing a delayed delegation from Dahomey. The two vaudeville performers watched the Dahomians carefully when they finally did appear and, according to Huggins, 'Walker saw that the addition of African themes to be a real freedom for the Black performer'.[41] Significantly, then, Huggins judged most favorably those African strategies that appeared through popular political and cultural formats and which subverted the dominant white culture's distortions of Africa.

A fairly recent study of the Harlem Renaissance, Houston Baker's *Modernism and the Harlem Renaissance*, approaches the Renaissance from what Baker considers a new 'problematic'. Baker challenges the premise of Huggins and other scholars who felt that the Renaissance failed to produce change or a significant contribution to modernism. Baker proposes that we see the Renaissance as a product of 'modern Afro-American sound' that is a 'function of a specifically Afro-American discursive practice'.[42] Baker offers two related concepts to use in evaluating several major writers from the Renaissance. The first he calls 'mastery of form', especially as represented by Booker T. Washington's *Up from Slavery* (1901) and Charles W. Chestnutt's collection of short stories *The Conjure Woman* (1899). Baker locates his second concept, the 'deformation of mastery' primarily in the poetry of Paul Laurence Dunbar and W.E.B. Du Bois's *The Souls of Black Folk*. These concepts converge in his analysis of *The New Negro* as a 'singing book' of 'extreme deformation'.

Baker sees these 'forms' not as static objects but as symbolizing fluidity, and he suggests that one can concretely imagine this process by remembering that the mask as 'a center of ritual' can only be defined – like form – from the perspective of action, *motion seen* rather than 'thing' observed'.[43] Because the minstrel mask became a pervasive medium for communicating the purported sounds of Africa and Black America, Baker begins his critique by describing how Booker T. Washington and Charles Chestnutt master the mask or literary 'form' to show that 'there *are* rhetorical possibilities for crafting a voice out of tight places'. Baker sees *Up from Slavery* as Washington's oratorical guide to survival in the South. Consequently, Baker labels Washington the 'quintessential herald of modernism in Black expressive culture' because Washington wrote for the Black American nation – not merely his own individual goals.[44]

Baker's explanation of the mastery of form and, as we shall see, his interpretation of the deformation of mastery both presume that the soundings communicated through or in spite of the masks or forms are African. Baker writes, for example, that 'Chestnutt's effectiveness as a "modern" lay in his ability to give the trick to white expectations, securing publication for creative work that carries a deep-rooted African sound.'[45] Similarly, Baker labels Du Bois '. . . the most articulate adherent of African sound'. Baker sees the Sorrow Songs that Du Bois used to organize *The Souls of Black Folk* as 'masterful repositories of an African cultural spirit'. As a central example of this sensibility, Baker quotes Du Bois's explanation for the songs:

The songs are indeed the siftings of centuries; the music is far more ancient than the words and in it we can trace here and there signs of development. My grandfather's grandmother was seized by an evil Dutch trader two centuries ago; and coming to the valleys of the Hudson and the Housatonic, Black, little and lithe, she shivered and shrank in the north winds, looked longingly at the hills and often crooned a heathen melody to the child between her knees, thus. . . .[46]

This passage was followed by Du Bois's rendition of the old song.

Baker argues that Du Bois, unlike the more accommodating survivalist Washington, asserts a positive and transforming 'folk'. Thus, Baker concludes, 'Washington remains the spokesperson *on behalf* of the folk . . .; Du Bois, by melodious contrast lifts his voice and transmutes his text into the FOLK's singing'. Baker himself echoes the first phrase of the Black National Anthem, 'Lift Every Voice and Sing', in this tribute to Du Bois.[47]

I quote Baker at length because he is providing an innovative look at mediating strategies. Each of the writers, artists and musicians discussed in his argument is performing from behind a veil, mask or form. In the spirit of Du Bois's 'double-consciousness', Baker sees the process of emerging 'African' soundings as a specifically Afro-American modernism. Baker is not concerned with evaluating the authenticity of African objects, ideas or memories in the Harlem Renaissance. By treating the mediative strategies regarding Africa as sufficient and definitive for the establishment of an Afro-American modernism, Baker himself argues for a strong connection to Africa.

Thus, Baker's discussion of Alain Locke's *The New Negro* grants it unparalleled legitimacy as 'our first national book'. Although Locke and the other contributors created a text that conformed to and often advocated Western aesthetic standards, Baker believes they functioned as a maroon community engaged in guerilla warfare: 'The world of *The New Negro* represents a unified community of national interests set in direct opposition to the general economic, political and theological tenets of a racist land'.[48] Furthermore, Baker sees Du Bois's Pan-Africanist goals as a 'sounding' by Du Bois to the younger generation to lead not only at home but in the fight against colonialism.[49] For Baker, the Harlem Renaissance is not chronologically or geographically bounded. 'Renaissancism' is a continuous process within the diaspora that

> . . . not only summons a mass image but converts it into a salvific sound that becomes a spirit house and space of Black habitation. For the very sufferers imagined are a people of will and strength who convert *marronage* into song, story, arts of liberation and guerilla war. There is quite frequently among them a communicating by horns. And their image translates at last into the mask of a resounding and venerable ancestry of the fields. The task of the spokesperson

who would engage the sound of folk conversion is to situate himself or herself in productive relationship to a field marked by awesome strategies of deformation and mastery. It is this discursive field that links us bone of the bone, flesh of the flesh and note by resounding blue note to contours of those transforming African masks that constitute our beginnings.[50]

For Baker, 'Renaissancism' becomes the cultural expression of Pan-Africanism. And, just as one might periodically revisit Pan-Africanist political and economic critiques, so too, according to Baker, will Black Americans continually draw on their Renaissance.

The strategies outlined in this essay reflect a number of re-occurring approaches taken to interpret the influence of Africa on early-twentieth-century Black American writers, artists and cultural critics of the Harlem Renaissance. Writers in the Harlem Renaissance argued for connective, mediative and distancing relationships with Africa. Contemporary historians and critics echo many of the same themes. When W.E.B. Du Bois titled his *New Negro* essay 'The Negro Mind Reaches Out', he was accurately characterizing the vast majority of these figurative reconnections to Africa. Cultural Pan-Africanism celebrates these spiritual, symbolic or in the case of Baker's 'soundings', performative identifications with Africa.

Notes

1. 'Heritage' was included in Alain Locke's edited collection, *The New Negro*, New York 1975, p. 250.

2. I have chosen to limit most of my observations to the materials collected in Alain Locke's *The New Negro* in order to present a brief overview of African themes in Harlem Renaissance literature. I suspect that the strategies described in this paper can be used to explore a much wider sample, although I have not yet tried to do so. There are some limitations presented to using *The New Negro*; in particular, it does not contain any essays devoted to political debate and discussion. Consequently, I have tried to evaluate its weak areas where relevant to my purposes. My own conception of strategies has been strongly influenced by the rhetorical strategies analyzed by Houston Baker, although, as readers will see, I have applied them somewhat differently.

3. The three historical and critical studies of the Harlem Renaissance discussed in this essay are Nathan Irvin Huggins, *Harlem Renaissance*, New York 1971; David Levering Lewis, *When Harlem Was in Vogue*, New York 1982; and Houston A. Baker, Jr, *Modernism and the Harlem Renaissance*, Chicago 1987.

4. Arthur A. Schomburg, 'The Negro Digs Up His Past', Locke, ed., *The New Negro*, New York 1975, p. 231.

5. Schomburg, 'The Negro Digs Up His Past', Locke, ed., *The New Negro*, p. 237.

6. Schomburg wrote: 'The blatant Caucasian racialist with his theories and assumptions of race superiority and dominance has in turn bred his Ethiopian counterpart – the rash and rabid amateur who has glibly tried to prove half of the world's geniuses to have been Negroes and to trace the pedigree of nineteenth-century Americans from the Queen of Sheba' ('The Negro Digs Up His Past', Locke, ed., *The New Negro*, p. 236).

7. Schomburg, 'The Negro Digs Up His Past', Locke, ed., *The New Negro*, pp. 231–7.

8. Arthur Huff Fauset, 'American Negro Folk Literature', 'T'appin', and 'B'rer Rabbit Fools Buzzard', in Locke, ed., *The New Negro*, pp. 238–49. Fauset's discussion compares favorably to the argument presented by Roger D. Abrahams, ed., *Afro-American Folk Tales: Stories from Black Traditions in the New World*, New York 1985.

9. W.E.B. Du Bois, *The Souls of Black Folk*, New York 1969 [1903], p. 54. The most thorough explanation for how Du Bois's historical and literary training contributed to his idea of folk culture appears in Arnold Rampersad, *The Art and Imagination of W.E.B. Du Bois*, Cambridge 1968.

10. Du Bois, *Souls of Black Folk*, p. 45.

11. Du Bois, 'The Negro Mind Reaches Out', in Locke, ed., *The New Negro*, p. 389.

12. Ibid., pp. 406–8.

13. Du Bois's analysis of the relationship between white and Black labor in 'The Negro Mind Reaches Out' prefigures the analytic framework of *Black Reconstruction: An Essay Toward a History of the Part Which Black Folk Played in the Attempt to Reconstruct Democracy in America, 1860–1880*, New York 1935. There are several commentators one can consult concerning Du Bois's views on socialism. Manning Marable, *W.E.B. Du Bois: Black Radical Democrat*, Boston 1986, is a good starting place.

14. Du Bois, 'The Negro Mind Reaches Out', in Locke, ed., *The New Negro*, pp. 385–414.

15. Locke, 'The Legacy of the Ancestral Arts', in *The New Negro*, p. 256.

16. Ibid., p. 256.

17. Ibid., pp. 266–7.

18. For the discussion of Locke's attitudes toward African art and culture, see Johnny Washington, *Alain Locke and Philosophy: A Quest for Cultural Pluralism*, Westport, Conn. 1986, especially Ch. 11, and James M. Barnes and J. Linnemann, eds, *Alain Locke: Reflections on a Modern Renaissance Man*, Baton Rouge, La. 1982. Interestingly, Washington finds no correlation between Locke's axiological philosophy and Africa. Washington wrote: 'It is curious that Locke did not utilize his own values theory to explain the nature of values and value judgments as they pertained to African art culture', p. 208.

The current debate about 'primitivism', stimulated by the Metropolitan Museum of Modern Art's 1984 exhibit 'Primitivism and 20th-Century Art: Affinity of the Tribal and Modern', provides a context in which to read Locke's exhortations. Interested readers should consult the catalog for that show, 'Modernist Primitivism: An Introduction', in *Primitivism in Twentieth Century Art: Affinity of the Tribal and Modern*, New York 1984, pp. 1–78, and reviews such as James Clifford, 'Histories of the Tribal and Modern', and Yve-Alain Bois, 'La Pensee Sauvage', both in *Art in America*, vol. 73 (1984), pp. 164–89. See also Dore Ashton, 'On an Epoch of Paradox: "Primitivism" at the Museum of Modern Art', and Gail Levin, '"Primitivism" in American Art: Some Literary Parallels of the 1910s and 1920s', in *Arts Magazine*, November 1984, pp. 76–80 and 101–5, respectively. Historian Patrick Manning uses the MOMA exhibit as a starting point for his discussion of how African sculpture appealed to 1920s European artists and audiences, providing 'the successful maintenance of non-hierarchical values in a conflict-ridden modern world', because the Europeans drew on 'sculpture representing communitarian and antiauthoritarian values, rather than on court art with its hierarchical tradition', against the 'pressures of capitalist development' (unpublished paper, 1985, pp. 2 and 5).

19. Stewart's study suggests that Locke developed a strong pluralist vision during the 1920s and 1930s. See Jeffrey Stewart, ed., *The Critical Temper of Alain Locke: A Selection of His Essays on Art and Culture*, New York 1983. On African influences in Harlem Renaissance art, see Samella Lewis, *Art: African American*, New York 1969; David Driskell, *Two Centuries of Black American Art*, New York 1976; and The Studio Museum in Harlem, New York, *The Harlem Renaissance: Art of Black America*, New York 1987.

20. Mary Schmidt Campbell, 'Introduction', The Studio Museum in Harlem, *Harlem Renaissance: Art of Black America*, p. 27.

21. David Driskell, 'The Flowering of the Harlem Renaissance: The Art of Aaron Douglas, Meta Warrick Fuller, Palmer Hayden and William H. Johnson', in The Studio Museum of Harlem, *Harlem Renaissance: Art of Black America*, pp. 108–9; Locke, 'Ancestral Arts', in Locke, ed., *The New Negro*, p. 266.

22. Rogers, 'Jazz At Home', in Locke, ed., *The New Negro*, p. 218.

23. Ibid., p. 222.

24. On McKay's primitivism, see Michael B. Stoff, 'Claude McKay and the Cult of Primitivism', Arna Bontemps, ed., *The Harlem Renaissance Remembered*, New York 1972, pp. 126–46.

25. This sketch apparently contributed to Nugent's collaboration with William Grant Still in the choral ballet 'Sahdji', first performed in 1932. Music historian Eileen Southern describes it as ' . . . a ballet with chorus and a narrator who recited African proverbs', in Eileen Southern, *The Music of Black Americans: A History*, New York 1971, p. 457.

26. For a discussion of Hughes's first trip to Africa and the poetry it provoked, see Arnold Rampersad, *The Life of Langston Hughes, vol. 1, 1902–1941: I, Too, Sing America*, New York 1986, pp. 73–81.

27. Melville Herskovitz, 'The Negro's Americanism', in Locke, ed., *The New Negro*, p. 354.

28. Ibid., p. 358.

29. Lewis analyzed the political issues that motivated some of the aesthetic judgements of the Harlem Renaissance in 'Parallels and Divergences: Assimilationist Strategies of Afro-American and Jewish Elites from 1910 to the early 1930s', *Journal of American History*, vol. 71 (1984), pp. 543–64.

30. On McKay's attitude toward Africa, see Wayne F. Cooper, *Claude McKay: Rebel Sojourner in the Harlem Renaissance*, Baton Rouge, La. 1987, pp. 248–54; on Hurston, see Robert E. Hemenway, *Zora Neale Hurston: A Literary Biography*, Urbana, Ill. 1977.

31. Charles S. Johnson, 'The New Frontage on American Life', and W.A. Domingo, 'The Gift of the Tropics', in Locke, ed., *The New Negro*, pp. 296, 348.

32. On Garvey, see Robert A. Hill and Barbara Bair, eds, *Marcus Garvey: Life and Lessons*, Berkeley, Calif. 1987; Judith Stein, *The World of Marcus Garvey: Race and Class in Modern Society*, Baton Rouge, La. 1986; Tony Martin, *Literary Garveyism: Garvey, Black Arts and the Harlem Renaissance*, Dover, Mass. 1983; and E. David Cronin, *Black Moses: The Story of Marcus Garvey*, Madison, Wis. 1955.

33. Mark Naison, *Communists in Harlem During the Depression*, Urbana, Ill. 1983, Ch. 1, especially pp. 5–8. Selections from the political press of Harlem are anthologized in Theodore E. Vincent, ed., *Voices of a Black Nation: Political Journalism in the Harlem Renaissance*, San Francisco and Trenton, N.J. 1991, pp. 117, 126. A complete set of *The Crusader* has recently been compiled by Robert A. Hill, ed., *The Crusader: Official Organ of the African Blood Brotherhood and the Hamitic League of the World, 1918–1922*, New York 1987.

34. Johnson, quoted in Houston A. Baker, Jr., *Modernism and the Harlem Renaissance*, Chicago 1987, p. 9; Langston Hughes, *The Big Sea: An Autobiography*, New York 1940, p. 228.

35. David Levering Lewis, *When Harlem Was in Vogue*, p. 117.

36. Nathan Irvin Huggins, *Harlem Renaissance*, New York 1971; Baker, *Modernism*.

37. Huggins, *Harlem Renaissance*, pp. 157–89.

38. Ibid., pp. 188-9.

39. Ibid., p. 41.

40. Ibid., p. 281.

41. Ibid., p. 282. A 'Dahomian Village' was also a popular attraction at the 1893 Columbian Exhibition in Chicago. For a discussion of the musicians who performed in or who were influenced by the Columbian Exhibition, see Southern, *Music of Black Americans*, p. 272.

42. Baker, *Modernism*, p. xiv.

43. Ibid., p. 17.

44. Ibid., pp. 33–7.

45. Ibid., p. 49.

46. Ibid., p. 60.

47. Ibid., pp. 62–9.

48. Ibid., p. 77.

49. Ibid., pp. 188–9.

50. Ibid., p. 95. This section of Baker's text is accompanied by the observation that Marcus Garvey considered himself a 'modern', which leads Baker to suggest that the present generation follow Garvey's 'confidence' and 'critical invulnerability'.

2

'Afric's Sons with Banner Red':

African-American Communists and

the Politics of Culture, 1919–1934

Robin D. G. Kelley

> Rise, Afric's sons with banner red.
> Freedom's path we too must tread.
> We've fought for it and bled.
> Black men, United!
>
> Long we've borne the nation's shame.
> Long we've bow'd both meek and tame.
> 'Tis right that now our anger flames.
> In its might. . .
>
> Face the lynchers, the Southern Cossacks.
> Face the demons. Strike them back.
> Face them dying but striking back. For our right. . . .
> *J. Thompson, 'Exhortation'*

I

I first discovered Thompson's poem a few years ago buried in a barely readable microfilm edition of the *Liberator*.[1] Though the poem had no direct bearing on my research (I was working on a dissertation about Communists in Alabama), I was fascinated by it because it struck me as so peculiar and out of place. Published in 1933, it appeared during a time when the Communist Party was waging war against 'petty bourgeois Negro nationalism' and 'racial chauvinism'. Yet 'Exhortation' is in many ways a Black nationalist manifesto. Thompson does not paint the portrait one might expect of Black and white workers together fighting the bosses; rather, he introduces us to a different sort of Manichean world in which white lynchers and Black men are poised to battle. The implication that dignity is embodied in the masculine act of resistance places 'Exhortation' in the tradition of Claude McKay's celebrated poem 'If We Must Die', which also inspired many of Thompson's contemporaries who published in the Garveyite *Negro World*. Like McKay, Thompson's appeal for the united resistance of Black men centers not on the fruits of possible victory, but on the very act of fighting. Indeed, except for keywords like 'banner red' and 'Southern Cossacks', there is nothing in 'Exhortation' that would indicate he is a Communist writing for a Communist paper.

As I continued perusing Communist publications for obscure information about the South, these kinds of creative expressions of Black nationalism became less anomalous and more pervasive, particularly in Communist publications geared toward the African-American community. It seemed to fly in the face of everything I had thought to be 'proletarian internationalism', and the very presence of this work – irrespective of its aesthetic worth – seemed to undermine the common assertion that the Communists imposed integrationist values on Black artists.[2] Of course, studies of the politics of culture during the Popular Front and the recent string of biographies of Black radical artists – Langston Hughes, Claude McKay, Richard Wright and Paul Robeson – have already challenged the notion that Party discipline transformed these artists into Moscow automatons.[3] But most of this work still assumes that the Communists had a clear-cut 'line' on cultural production that was naturally in conflict with the work of Black artists. What scholars have yet to explain is how, especially during the more radical 'Third Period' (1928–33), Party theoreticians simultaneously thwarted 'racial chauvinism' and 'petty-bourgeois nationalism' in all manifestations of political action, while race-conscious themes and nationalist sentiment appeared in so much Black expressive and literary culture inside and on the margins of the Communist Party.

The following, then, is a preliminary effort to unravel this paradox by exploring the relationship between Communist political and aesthetic discourses and the cultural production of African-American radicals from the mid 1920s to the mid 1930s. It is my contention that some of the answers can be found partly in the changing make-up of the Party during the Third Period, which enabled African-American working people – many of whom had left Garveyite movements in various stages of decline – to insinuate themselves into the Party's culture. I want also to suggest that the Communists' position on the 'Negro Question' (implicitly, at least) and the Party's interpretation of 'proletarian realism' unintentionally opened up discursive space for an articulation of Black nationalist ideologies in spite of the

Party's formal opposition to 'Negro nationalism'. In other words, by the late 1920s and early 1930s, Black nationalism(s) – especially as it was expressed in culture – had much more in common with American Communism than most scholars have admitted. Thus, for African-American Communists, like American Jewish and Finnish Communists, whose cultural and national identities constituted a central element of their radical politics,[4] ethnic nationalism and internationalism were not mutually exclusive.

II

African-Americans who joined the Party in the 1920s and 1930s were as much the creation of American Communism as of Black nationalism; as much the product of African-American vernacular cultures and radical traditions as of Euro-American radical thought. Many were products of Garveyism and/or the emerging postwar Black left that had been deeply touched by the Bolshevik Revolution as well as by workers' uprisings and racial violence in American cities during and after World War I. While these events did not propel large numbers of African-American radicals into the American Communist Party, it did reinforce their belief that socialist revolution was possible within the context of a complicated matrix of 'race politics' and working-class unity. A. Philip Randolph and Chandler Owen attempted to build African-American support for the Socialist Party of America (SPA) by emphasizing class as well as race-specific goals, but the Socialists' official position regarded racist oppression secondary to the class struggle and held steadfastly to the idea that socialism was the only way to solve the problems of Blacks.[5]

Perhaps the most enigmatic group among the postwar Black left was the African Blood Brotherhood (ABB), a secret, underground organization of radical Black nationalists led largely by West Indian immigrants. Founded in 1918 by Cyril Briggs, the ABB advocated armed defense against lynching, the right to vote in the South, the right to organize, equal rights for Blacks and the abolition of Jim Crow laws. According to Briggs, the ABB was the first organization to demand self-determination for Afro-Americans in the southern United States. Although it is doubtful that the ABB's leadership worked out a theory based on the image of an oppressed nation, Briggs consistently demanded self-determination, in some form or another. As early as 1917, while editor of the *Amsterdam News*, Briggs advocated the creation of a 'colored autonomous state'. In the pages of the *Crusader*, he attacked Woodrow Wilson for not applying the concept of self-determination to Africa, and during the 'Red Summer' of 1919, Briggs demanded 'government of the Negro, by the Negro and for the Negro'. A unique experiment in Black Marxist organization, the ABB was short-lived, killed by its own internal logic; by the early 1920s its Marxist leadership decided that an interracial proletarian party would be a more effective form of organization and therefore opted to join the CPUSA.[6]

Like the Socialists before them, American Communists initially regarded Black radicalism as a subset of the class struggle. The Party's 1921 program asserted that 'the interests of the Negro worker are identical with those of the white.' Two years later, Communist leadership recognized that Black people in the United States constituted an 'oppressed race' but considered Black nationalism 'a weapon of reaction for the defeat and further enslavement of both [Blacks] and their white brother workers.' However, pressure from the Communist International, primarily V.I. Lenin and Indian Communist M.N. Roy, and popular support for Black nationalist movements within African-American working-class communities, compelled the CPUSA to reconsider its approach to the 'Negro Question'.[7]

The Fourth Congress of the Comintern in 1922 adopted a set of theses describing Blacks as a nationality oppressed by worldwide imperialist exploitation.[8] Because Black workers' struggles were now considered inherently anti-imperialist, American Communists were obliged to view Garveyism and other notable nationalist movements anew. During the 1924 UNIA Convention, the *Daily Worker* thoroughly covered the proceedings and praised the organization for its militancy. And at the 4th National Conference of the Communist Party in 1925, it recognized that the Garvey movement was 'an almost universal phenomenon among American Negro workers'. While Party leadership praised the UNIA for its mass base and anti-colonial position, it was critical of its strategy and rhetoric. The Party opposed the UNIA's mass-based nationalism and emphasis on race pride; its 1925 platform equated Garveyism with 'reactionary' Jewish Zionism. On the other hand, the same platform expressed faith in the ability of Communists to work within the UNIA and transform it into 'an organization fighting for the class interests of the Negro workers in the United States.'[9] The CPUSA's new-found respect for Garvey's appeal came a bit too late, however, since the UNIA was already on the verge of collapse. The Party responded by forming the American Negro Labor Congress (ANLC) in 1925, an organization led chiefly by former ABB leaders whose primary purpose was to build interracial unity in the labor movement. Chapters were to be established throughout the United States, particularly in the South, but because of poor leadership and ill-conceived planning, the ANLC never gained popular support.[10] In the end, although the Communists utterly failed to redirect Garveyism, they did attract a handful of ex-Garveyites into their ranks.

The Communists' failure to mobilize significant Black support in the early and mid 1920s can be partially attributed to the Comintern's vision of internationalism, which extended beyond Pan-Africanism and/or racial solidarity. While Comintern officials recognized differences between anti-colonial and European working-class movements, peasants and proletarians, they still insisted that these struggles be united under the same banner. Even their conferences emphasized an international unity that few Americans, Black or white, could ever imagine. In 1927, for example, African-American delegates were invited to attend a conference in Brussels held under the auspices of the League Against Colonial Oppression. Organized in 1926 by the German Communist Party to combat pro-colonial sentiments emerging in Germany, the League was an important step toward coordinating various struggles for national liberation in the colonies and 'semi-colonies', and it served as an intermediary between the Communist International and the anti-colonial movement. It was at this conference that former ABB leader Richard B. Moore witnessed Europeans, Asians and Africans pass a general resolution that proclaimed: 'Africa for the Africans, and their full freedom and equality with other races and the right to govern Africa.' It was indeed a remarkable sight for anyone who believed the struggle for African freedom was *only* an African struggle.[11]

The Communist movement's internationalism not only appropriated the familiar idioms of Pan-Africanism, but in many ways it created space for a vision of Black anti-imperialism that could transcend without negating a completely racialized world view. Moreover, internationalism became a vehicle for African-American radicals to cross cultural boundaries, to escape and challenge essentialist presumptions common among some segments of the CP about what the 'authentic' Negro proletariat looked and talked like. Lovett Fort-Whiteman, an early recruit who rose quickly within the Chicago CP's ranks, was emblematic of this sort of cultural internationalism. Soon after his return from the Soviet Union, the Texas-born Communist became a popular spectacle on the South side of Chicago, strolling the streets draped in a Russian *rubaschka*. Nonetheless, this same internationalist vision sometimes hindered the Party's work in the African-American community. For example, Black delegates from the Workers (Communist) Party and the ABB attending the first All-Race Conference in 1924 were treated with suspicion when they attached to their proposal for armed self-defense and working-class organization a statement endorsing the 'Internationale' as the 'anthem of Negro Freedom'. Similarly, at the ANLC's first mass meeting in Chicago, organized by the infamous Lovett Fort-Whiteman, hundreds of Black workers in attendance became disenchanted with the Congress as soon as the entertainment appeared: a Russian ballet and a one-act play written by Pushkin – performed entirely in

Russian![12]

A major turning point for the Party's racial politics occurred in 1928. That year, the Sixth World Congress of the Comintern passed a resolution asserting that African-Americans in the Black Belt counties of the American South constituted an oppressed nation and therefore possessed an inherent right of self-determination. Not surprisingly, the resolution met fierce opposition from white, and some Black, Party leaders, but for many Black Communists, particularly those in the urban North, the resolution on Black self-determination indirectly confirmed what they had long believed: African-Americans had their own unique revolutionary tradition. As historian Mark Naison observed, 'By defining Blacks as an oppressed nation . . . the Comintern had, within the Leninist lexicon of values, endowed the Black struggle with unprecedented dignity and importance.' Black Communists published dozens of articles in the Party press supporting the idea that African-Americans have their own identifiable, autonomous traditions of radicalism. 'Aside from the purely Marxian analysis', wrote one Black CP organizer, 'the Negro's history is replete with many actual instances of uprising against his exploiters and oppressors.'[13] In short, history and culture – whether to celebrate the traditions of Black resistance or recuperate the 'folk' art of the Black working class – became the vehicles through which Black Communists could both 'express' and justify their collective right to self-determination.

III

The Comintern's new position on the 'Negro Question' compelled Black Communists to call upon African-American writers, artists and historians to focus their work on the age-old tradition of Black rebellion. As early as 1928, William L. Patterson, a prominent Black Harlem lawyer who had joined the Party in the mid 1920s, criticized virtually all contemporary Black poets in an article entitled 'Awake Negro Poets'. Although Patterson was pleased that they 'have persistently called themselves Black men, have proclaimed their songs Negro songs, have triumphantly hailed the emergence of a *Negro* culture', he hoped more young writers would write revolutionary verse that described the conditions of the Black masses and captured the tradition of resistance instead of catering to patrons.[14]

Writers of the genre Patterson supported were drawn to left-wing circles during the 1930s because of the Party's new focus on African-American issues. Even more than the self-determination slogan, the Party's defense of the Scottsboro Nine and Angelo Herndon, its vigorous denunciation of racism and its unrelenting fight for the concrete economic needs of poor

Blacks attracted a significant section of America's submerged Black intelligentsia, many of whom were former Garveyites or Pan-Africanist ideologues. Many were drawn to the League of Struggle for Negro Rights, a CP-sponsored auxiliary created in 1930 intended to replace the defunct American Negro Labor Congress. Its somewhat radical nationalist program supported Black self-determination in the South, advocated militant resistance on the part of African-Americans and called for a resolute campaign against lynchings and white terrorist organizations.[15] The LSNR newspaper, established under the able editorship of former ABB founder Cyril Briggs, was conceived as the 'agitator and organizer of the Negro Liberation Movement.'[16]

Yet, while the Central Committee of the CPUSA agreed to the formation of the LSNR and the publication of the *Liberator*, it did not agree with Briggs's assessment that the movement and its paper should be in the vanguard of the 'Negro Liberation Movement.' Indeed, white Communist leaders exhibited ambivalence toward the LSNR as early as the League's first national convention in St. Louis in 1931. The Central Committee resolved that the LSNR should not become 'a substitute for the Party, which at all times must retain its leading role in the struggle for full equality, and in the South, for the right of self-determination.' Most revealing, however, was the Central Committee's insistence that the League not become a 'Negro organization' and that the *Liberator* not be characterized as a 'Negro' paper.[17] These kinds of political pressures from national CP leadership ultimately led to the demise of the *Liberator*. After first suspending publication in January 1932, it resumed again a year later but was limited primarily to Harlem. By 1934, the League had been reduced to little more than a paper organization.[18]

During the five years the *Liberator* remained in existence, however, its readership understood it to be a 'Negro paper' irrespective of Central Committee concerns. As veteran Alabama Communist Hosea Hudson remembered, the *Liberator* 'carried news items on the whole question of the oppressed people, like Africa. . . . It always was carrying something about the liberation of Black people, something about Africa, something about the South. . . . We would read this paper and this would give us great courage.'[19] The *Liberator* incubated a renascent Black nationalist literary movement, publishing not only the verse of writers such as Langston Hughes but also more obscure works like Thompson's 'Exhortation'. And like Thompson's poem, much of the verse which appeared in the *Liberator* combined class consciousness, prevailing Pan-Africanist ideas and an emphasis on struggle as a form of masculine redemption. A provocative example is Ruby Weems's 'The Murder of Ralph Gray', a narrative poem about the Communist-led Share Croppers' Union's first martyr. One of the founders of the all-Black union, Gray was murdered in a shoot-out with law enforcement officials near Camp Hill, Alabama. Like Thompson, Weems transcends the simple class basis of anti-labor repression and goes directly for the racial jugular vein. Her opening stanza reads:

> O white masters of the mulatto South,
> Thin lips emitting froth,
> Pale eyes shining like the upturned belly
> Of a decaying snake carcass,
> You killed Ralph Gray. . . .

It is hard not to notice her reference to Caucasian physical features and the white ruling class's profligate character. Not only does Gray's willingness to die for the cause of freedom epitomize a kind of symbolic manhood, but his individual death cannot stop the millions of Black people who allegorically stood behind Gray and the SCU. As if a massive ghost were rising from Gray's grave, Weems warned the 'landowners and slave-drivers' of the consequences of their actions:

> But white masters,
> Why do you hurry through the cornfields late at night?
> Are you running away from Ralph Gray?
> Too late, too late!

> His muscles swelling into a mighty challenge
> Mount into a vision of a million clenched fists.
> He wears his death like a joyous banner of solidarity,
> A specter of militant Negro manhood.
> He lies still and silent – but under his unmoving form
> Rise hosts of dark, strong men,
> The vast army of rebellion![20]

Much of this poetry could have easily appeared in the *Negro World's* column, 'Poetry for the People'. Although the themes were far more varied and eclectic than those which appeared in the *Liberator*, Garveyite poems shared the gendered language which defined the act of resistance as a masculine rite of passage. Garveyites published poems whose titles include 'A Call to Race Manhood'; 'The Message of Freedom'; 'Ku Klux Klan Beware'; and numerous others which imply the redeeming quality of male violence against their oppressors. Witness, for instance, Robert Poston's poem, 'When You Meet Member of the Ku Klux Klan' (1921):

> When you meet a member of the Ku Klux Klan,
> Walk right up and hit him like a natural man;

Take no thought of babies he may have at home,
Sympathy's defamed when used upon his dome. . . .[21]

Thus, whereas racial themes might have been in conflict with the Communists' version of proletarian realism, these Black artists – including most male writers outside of the Party – found common ground on the terrain of gender. Proletarian realism consciously evinced masculine images and defined class struggle as a male preserve. Communist cultural theoretician Mike Gold did not mince words in 1926 when he wrote: 'Send a strong poet, a man of the street . . . send a man.' As Paula Rabinowitz insightfully points out, 'By linking the proletariat, and its culture, with masculinity, the metaphors of gender permeated the aesthetic debates of male literary radicals throughout the 1930s.'[22] In fact, dozens of poems written by white Communists dealing directly with race made their pleas for interracialism in a wholly masculinist discourse. As Sadie Van Veen wrote in her poem 'Scottsboro', published in the *Liberator*, 'Scottsboro long will you be remembered / By men and the children of men. / For all that you stand for.'[23] Kenneth Patchen's 'Southern Organizer' invokes an image of state-sanctioned vigilante violence, in which men are its victims, and 'true' men, Black and white, are those who stand against it:

> . . . Badges gleam; they dump the sack into the water, turn and go.
> It is peaceful in the Southland; tommorrow
> They will hang and shoot some more
> Of ours: but tonight, as all true men with southern blood will tell you,
> The possum is abroad, the bloodhounds sleep,
> And it is beautiful. Comrades.
>
> Let us do this thing together.
> Black man, comrade, we must together.
> And he is dead. There is work for living
> Men to do. We salute him.
> We have no tears for him.[24]

Similarly, V.J. Jerome's poem, 'To a Black Man', written as a companion to Langston Hughes's 'An Open Letter to the White Men of the South', counters what he perceives to be Black racial separatism with a sustained appeal for unity against capital, but his appeal is to men about men. And like all of these authors, retaliatory violence is as much a matter of male redemption as it is class struggle. The final stanza reads:

> Call back your sons,
> brother and tell them

the cause is not in the skin
It's war over wheat-fields and coal pits
over clothing and houses milk and bread.
We against them.
Slaves against masters.
Fuse the fires
you from the black breast
I from the white
It's war for the earth!
Workmen fieldmen
Every hammer a gun
Every scythe a sword
War for the earth![25]

The language of masculinity, in fact, dominated representations of grass-roots organizing and Party propaganda, especially during the 1930s. Elizabeth Faue makes this point in her excellent study of working-class struggles in Minneapolis. Speaking of the labor movement's iconography as a whole, Faue writes: 'They forged a web of symbols which romanticized violence, rooted solidarity in metaphors of struggle, and constructed work and the worker as male.'[26] It stands to reason, then, that African-American radical writers' and artists' persistent theme of manhood and violent resistance struck an enticing chord that probably reverberated louder than allusions to racial pride. This tendency was even evident among Communist music critics: in the pages of the *New Masses*, writer Richard Frank proclaimed that Black music deserved high status within proletarian culture because it 'possesses such virility'.[27] Besides, the Party's position on Black liberation after 1928 – namely, its insistence on self-determination for African-Americans – not only took precedence over women's struggles, but essentially precluded a serious theoretical framework that might combine the 'Negro' and 'Woman' questions. Furthermore, the Party's advocacy of Black self-determination conjured up masculine historical figures such as Toussaint L'Ouverture, Denmark Vesey and Nat Turner, and writers such as Eugene Gordon and V.J. Jerome portrayed the movement as a struggle for 'manhood'. Armed resistance, in particular, was deemed a masculine activity. When the central Black character in Grace Lumpkin's novel *A Sign for Cain*, a young southern-born Communist, observed 'shotguns stacked in the corner of the cabin', he assured his comrades, 'we ain't dealing with cowards, but men.'[28]

But this is only part of the story. Those who entered radical circles toting the baggage of cultural nationalism found reinforcement in Communist theory. Ironically, Stalin's mechanical definition of a nation, which embraced a 'community of culture' as a central concept, persuaded Black Communists to search everywhere for the roots of a national culture. As William L. Patterson wrote in 1933, the African-American nation was bound by a common culture: 'The "spirituals," the jazz, their religious practices, a growing literature, descriptive of their environment, all of these are forms of cultural expression. . . . Are these not the prerequisites for nationhood?'[29] Black Party leader Harry Haywood traced the roots of a 'national Negro culture' in 'ancient African civilization [and] Negro art and literature reflecting the environment of oppression of the Negroes in the United States.'[30]

The self-determination slogan might have inspired a few Black intellectuals already in the CP, but it was not the key to building Black working-class support. The horrendous conditions brought on by the Great Depression, the Party's defense of the Scottsboro Nine and Angelo Herndon, its vigorous denunciation of racism and its unrelenting fight for the concrete economic needs of the poor attracted a considerable section of America's submerged Black working class and intelligentsia. The presence of Black working-class activists, especially from the South, infused Communist Party circles with what might best be described as radical 'folk' traditions. Like other visible ethnic groups before them, working-class African-Americans brought their grass-roots, race-conscious cultural traditions to the Party.

Although the songs, rituals, religious practices and styles of ordinary Black working people were in conflict with Communist ideology (many African-Americans not only showed irreverence for the Party's interracialism but refused to even consider questioning their religion), this level of Black cultural production rarely faced the critical scrutiny of CP cultural critics. In his critique of the Harlem Renaissance poets, Black Communist William L. Patterson, for example, vacillated between demanding a culture that would focus on and celebrate the Black masses, and rejecting the very idea that working-class African-Americans in the South – those whom he designated as 'pure-Black' – ever made any cultural contributions. He not only attacked the Harlem writers for voicing 'the aspirations of a rising petty bourgeoisie', but he challenged them for refusing to 'echo the lamentations of the downtrodden masses.' While he rejected racialist claims that the emergence of a Negro literati can be explained by intermixture, his attack on that argument implicitly accepted that 'racially pure' Blacks do not or cannot make the same sort of cultural contribution: 'Obviously, it is easy to say that the fact that the new Negro culture is the creation of a white-black group proves that the white blood is dominant. Not at all. The scientific explanation is simply that the pure-blacks, living in the South, are so oppressed, so debased by white exploiters, that any cultural expression is impossible for them.'[31] Patterson's elitism notwithstanding, what is important about his critique is the degree to which it is entangled in the dominant discourse of race – a discourse set firmly in the idioms of science.

Patterson's views were in the minority, however, and even he developed a greater appreciation for the culture of the Southern Black masses. Nevertheless, Communist cultural critics generally accepted the same essentialist, race-bound definition of culture – a tendency by no means limited to the Left. Furthermore, like most American interpreters of culture, they tended to place virtually everything Black people did under the rubric of 'folk', which ultimately had the affect of insulating even the most nationalist expressions from censure. As Paul Buhle explains, 'folk' expressions within Communist cultural criticism were sheltered from the current debates which raged over the meaning of 'proletarian realism': 'Few guidelines already existed on the left or elsewhere for popular art. That very absence provided breathing space for the cultural innovator. . . . No one could say what the significance might be, for instance, between Marxism and Black field hollers. . . .'[32] In other words, folk artists were not subject to the same criticism and scrutiny that 'legitimate' intellectuals faced. With the possible exception of Langston Hughes, most of the contributors whose work appeared in the *Liberator,* and in other Party-related publications were usually treated as folk or popular culture.[33]

Most Communist theoreticians assumed (even during the Third Period) that 'genuine' Black folk culture was at least implicitly, if not explicitly, revolutionary. This is precisely why a Communist critic as anti-religious as Mike Gold could describe the spiritual expressiveness of Black vernacular culture in such celebratory terms. Writing about the Black cadre in the South Side of Chicago, Gold writes: 'At mass meetings their religious past becomes transmuted into a Communist present. They follow every word of the speaker with real emotion; they encourage him, as at a prayer meeting with cries of "Yes, yes, comrade" and often there is an involuntary and heartfelt "Amen!"'[34] Likewise, for white Communists such as Harold Preece, 'the throbbing note of protest . . . is even in the spirituals. The Negroes were denied the most elementary civil rights. But they could sing and those songs were living prophesies of deliverance.'[35]

Of course, not all CP cultural critics agreed. A handful of left-wing musicologists of the Third Period found revolutionary content in Black secular song, but displayed greater ambivalence with respect to spirituals. Critical of Hollywood's attempted cooptation of African-American religious music, one writer remarked that 'music which was once so soothing a balm for their oppression has misled most of America's cultural world into a belief that these songs are the only genuine artistic expressions of the the Negro.' Instead, 'workaday songs' constituted the only 'pure' musical expression of the Black working class. Lawrence Gellert, probably the Party's most enthusiastic champion of Black music, thought the content of Black religious music from the institutional church was essentially reactionary, but the *form* of the spiritual provided a foundation for revolutionary music. He explained secular songs with anti-clerical undertones as a reaction to the Black preacher, 'a pompous, fat-headed, blow-hard parasite, prating meaningless platitudes about "de Lawd an' his By an' By Kingdom."'[36] Nevertheless, all of these writers agreed that there was a common, identifiable, 'pure Negro culture', and that culture was the most genuine expression of the most submerged segment of the American proletariat.

Ironically, while the Party's essentializing of Black culture created more space for cultural expressions which otherwise would be in conflict with Communist ideology, it also obscured the degree to which 'folk' culture was actually bricolage, a cutting, pasting and incorporating of various cultural forms which then became categorized in a racially/ethnically coded aesthetic hierarchy. Consider, for instance, the way in which Black Party members transformed old spirituals into Communist anthems or secular protest songs. African-American Communists gave classics like 'We Shall Not Be Moved' and 'Give Me That Old Time Religion' new lyrics and completely new messages. In the latter, the verse was changed to 'Give Me That Old Communist Spirit', and Party members closed out each stanza with 'It was good enough for Lenin, and it's good enough for me.'[37] The lyrics were also rewritten as 'The Scottsboro Song' after nine young defendants were spuriously found guilty of raping two white women:

> The Scottsboro verdict,
> The Scottsboro verdict,
> The Scottsboro verdict,
> Is not good enuf for me.
>
> It's good for big fat bosses,
> For workers double-crossers,
> For low down slaves and hosses.
> But it ain't good enuf for me. . .[38]

In some respects, these kinds of alterations were very much in the tradition of improvisation, and the insertion of secular lyrics into spiritual song forms was certainly not unique to Black Communist culture. But by employing a Marxist-Leninist discourse with its attendant language, idioms and metaphors, the way in which African-American Communists transformed 'traditional' music subverted both the Party's own racialized cultural categories as well as the Black musical forms upon which they inscribed new lyrics. What they produced was hardly 'folk' music; it was a bricolage drawn from the Party's ideology, Black cultural traditions and collective memories and a constellation of lived experiences. Black radical artists, in particular, self-conscious of this sort of pastiche of proletarian internationalism and 'pure Negro' folk culture, were frequently prone to more parodic or satirical expressions. Black Chicago Communists, for instance, came up with a hilarious, tongue-in-cheek rendition of 'Lift Every Voice and Sing' (which is acknowledged as the Black national anthem) by James Weldon Johnson and J. Rosemond Johnson. It provides an implicit critique of mainstream Black leadership for failing to adopt a radical internationalist vision, and yet acknowledges what is possible when Black and Red traditions of resistance come together:

> Sing a song full of the strife that the dark past
> has taught us.
> Sing a song full of the hope Communism has
> brought us.
> Facing a Red! Red! Sun of a new day begun
> Let us fight on till victory is won.[39]

Similarly, a contributor to the *Liberator* borrowed a nineteenth-century slave song to create a humorous parody entitled, 'No Mo', No Mo''. While the song embodies practically all of the elements found in the Communist literary tradition, including anti-clericalism and a prophetic vision of an indomitable revolutionary movement, it contains a whole host of 'cotton patch' stereotypes. And like the poetry of Weems and Thompson, the creator of this song makes no reference to Black and white marching together:

> No mo' pickin cotton fo' ten cents a day,
> No mo' raisin' taters without gittn' pay.
> Yo gits no bread in church fo' pray:
> No mo' God, no mo' bosses, we folkses say. . . .
> No mo' KU-KLUX KLAN with
> their burnin' crosses.
> No mo' chain-gangs, we's no
> dogs no' ho'ses.
> The NAACP, God no' Moses
> Can stop us Blackies fightin' the bosses. . . .
> [chorus]
> Negroes ain' Black-but RED!
> Teacher Lenin done said
> Brothers all oppressed an' po.'
> Ain't it so? Sho! . . .[40]

The chorus leaves one with an image of an army of militant, atheist 'Darkies' poised for a battle against racism *and* the Black middle class, yet guided by the teachings of Lenin. Once again, both the popular conception of the 'Negro folk' and the Communists' own image of the proletariat are subverted. Ironically, although the song's explicit anti-religious tone reflected the Party's ideology, given the tendency of critics like Harold Preece and Michael Gold to associate religiosity with an authentic Black 'folk' culture, it is altogether possible that 'No Mo', No Mo" undermined the popular image of the 'ordinary Negro' held by a number of Communist intellectuals.[41]

This last point can only be speculative, for we still do not know how the Party's intelligentsia collectively fashioned a notion of 'folk' culture that differed from, say, high culture, modernism, or Socialist realism. That the Communist interpretation of the 'folk', especially 'Negro folk', was socially constructed and contingent goes without saying. But several questions remain: To what extent does the presence of a singular 'Negro Question' constrain or structure efforts to interpret African-American culture? Does the very idea of a 'Negro Question' assume the existence of a single Black community, and thus a single, 'authentic' culture to be reckoned with? By what criteria do Communist critics categorize Black cultural forms as 'folk'? These and other questions will have to await further research and reflection.

IV

The cultural world of African-American Communists and sympathizers was a mosaic of racial imagery interpenetrated by class and gender. During the 1930s the Party attracted thousands of African-Americans who toted their cultural and ideological baggage to the movement, shaped the cultural landscape of American Communism and occasionally found spaces within Communist circles to create an expressive culture which, in some respects, contradicted the movement's goal of interracial solidarity. Indeed, while some Black Communists were being charged with 'petty-bourgeois nationalism' or reactionary 'Negro chauvinism', the Communist-sponsored *Liberator* published poems celebrating the beauty, militancy and determination of the 'Negro race'.

As I have tried to demonstrate, this dichotomy between representations in Communist literary culture and politics in part reflects a political concession to its new constituency. Advocating an idiosyncratic concept of Black liberation, the Party presented itself as the legitimate heir of Garveyism, particularly in communities like Harlem and Chicago. Moreover, a number of factors converged within Party politics and culture that opened up space for creative expressions of Black nationalism and race pride. For one, despite all the antagonism and invective separating Communists from Garveyites and other Black nationalists during this period, their writers and artists had one thing in common: they agreed that struggle was a man's job. The languages of class struggle and 'race' struggle employed a highly masculinist imagery that relied on metaphors from war and emphasized violence as a form of male redemption. Thus on the terrain of gender Communists and Black nationalists found common ground – a ground which rendered women invisible or constructed them in an auxiliary relationship.

Second, the Comintern's thesis on self-determination in the Black Belt – frequently pointed to as evidence *par excellance* of the CPUSA's dictatorial relationship with Moscow – contributed to Blacks' greater cultural freedom within the Party. It might not have directly *encouraged* the development of an artistic expression of Black self-determination, but what *was* produced exemplified the kind of rebellious, nationalist sentiment implicit in the notion of self-determination. Besides, white Party critics and theoreticians tended to accept without criticism anything they believed was 'folk' culture, for this was presumably the genuine expression of the laboring and farming masses. Since much of Black expressive culture was categorized as 'folk', some surprisingly race-conscious, nationalist-inspired art survived in Party circles without censure.

Although the Party rejected racial politics in favor of interracial action, it did not (and could not) stifle the creative contributions of Black radicals. On the contrary, during the Third Period African-American culture created a home for itself in Communist circles because of the growing presence of Black working people – a presence that persuaded left-wing musicologists, theoreticians and literary critics to accept (or tolerate) their racial world view and search for meaning in their various texts.

Notes

1. *Harlem Liberator,* 24 June 1933.

2. Harold Cruse, *The Crisis of the Negro Intellectual,* New York 1964, pp. 144, 149, 150–51; James O. Young, *Black Writers of the Thirties,* Baton Rouge, La. 1973, pp. 40, 157–60; Ernest Allen, 'The Cultural Methodology of Harold Cruse', *Journal of Ethnic Studies,* vol. 5, no. 2 (1977), pp. 26–50; Arthur Paris, 'Cruse and the Crisis in Black Culture', *Journal of Ethnic Studies,* vol. 5, no. 2 (1977), pp. 63–6; Jabari Simama, 'Black Writers Experience Communism: An Interdisciplinary Study of Imaginative Writers, Their Critics, and the CPUSA', Ph.D. dissertation, Emory University 1978, p. 270.

3. The works of Mark Naison and Paul Buhle, in particular, have explored the politics of Black culture during the Popular Front. It was a critical moment, since Black culture was elevated to the status of a revolutionary component of American culture, as Communists – especially in Harlem – successfully drew African-American artists and performers into their ranks. See Mark Naison, *Communists in Harlem During the Depression,* Urbana, Ill. 1983, pp. 193–219;

Naison, 'Communism and Harlem Intellectuals in the Popular Front: Anti-Fascism and the Politics of Black Culture', *Journal of Ethnic Studies*, vol. 9, no. 1 (1981), pp. 1–25; Paul Buhle, *Marxism in the United States: Remapping the History of the American Left*, London 1987. The more recent important biographies of Black radical artists include Wayne F. Cooper, *Claude McKay: Rebel Sojourner in the Harlem Renaissance, A Biography*, Baton Rouge, La. 1986; Arnold Rampersad, *The Life of Langston Hughes, Volume 1, 1902–1941: I, Too, Sing America*, New York 1986; Margaret Walker, *Richard Wright – Daemonic Genius: Portrait of the Man, A Critical Look at His Work*, New York 1988; Martin Duberman, *Paul Robeson*, New York 1989; see also Sam G. Kim, 'Black Americans' Commitment to Communism: A Case Study Based on Fiction and Autobiographies', Ph.D. dissertation, University of Kansas 1986.

4. David John Ahola, *Finnish-Americans and International Communism*, Washington, D.C. 1981; Auvo Kostiainen, *The Forging of Finnish-American Communism, 1917–1924: A Study in Ethnic Radicalism*, Turku 1978; Michael Gary Karni, 'Yhteishyva – Or for the Common Good: Finnish Radicalism in the Western Great Lakes Region, 1900–1940', Ph.D. dissertation, University of Minnesota 1975; Al Gedicks, 'The Social Origins of Radicalism Among Finnish Immigrants in Midwest Mining Communities', *Review of Radical Political Economics*, vol. 8 (1976), pp. 1–31; Peter Kivisto, *Immigrant Socialists in the United States: The Case of the Finns and the Left*, London and Toronto 1984; George P. Hummasti, 'Finnish Radicals in Astoria, Oregon, 1904–1940: A Study in Immigrant Socialism', Ph.D. dissertation, University of Oregon 1975; Paul Buhle, 'Jews and American Communism: The Cultural Question', *Radical America*, vol. 23, Spring 1980, pp. 9–33; David P. Shuldiner, 'Of Moses and Marx: Folk Ideology Within the Jewish Labor Movement in the United States', Ph.D. dissertation, UCLA 1984.

5. On the Socialist Party and African-Americans, see Philip Foner, *American Socialism and Black Americans: From the Age of Jackson to World War II*, Westport, Conn. 1977; Jervis Anderson, *A. Phillip Randolph: A Biographical Portrait*, New York 1973, pp. 85–137; Theodore Kornweibel, *No Crystal Stair: Black Life and the Messenger, 1917–1928*, Westport, Conn. 1975; Henry Williams, *Black Response to the American Left*, Princeton, N.J. 1971; Robert Allen, *Reluctant Reformers: Racism and Social Reform Movements in the United States*, Washington D.C. 1983, pp. 212–15; Sally Miller, 'The Socialist Party and the Negro, 1901–1920', *Journal of Negro History*, vol. 56 (July 1971), pp. 220–39; Lawrence Moore, 'Flawed Fraternity: American Socialist Response to the Negro, 1901–1912', *The Historian*, vol. 33, no. 1 (1969), pp. 1–14; Mark Naison, 'Marxism and Black Radicalism in America: Notes on a Long, and Continuing Journey', *Radical America*, vol. 5, no. 3 (1971), pp. 4–10; David A. Shannon, *The Socialist Party of America*, Chicago 1967, pp. 49–52; James Weinstein, *The Decline of Socialism in America, 1912–1925*, New York 1969, pp. 69–70.

6. First quote, *Amsterdam News* 5 September 1917; second quote, *Crusader*, vol. 1, no. 8 (April 1919), pp. 8–9; *Crusader*, vol. 1, no. 12 (August 1919), p. 4; Briggs, WPA interview. Anselmo R. Jackson, associate editor of the *Crusader* wrote that the paper was dedicated 'to the doctrine of self-government for the Negro and Africa for the Africans.' *Crusader*, vol. 1, no. 3 (November 1918), p. 1. Despite statements in the *Crusader*, Richard B. Moore and W.A. Domingo, two former leaders of the ABB, deny that Briggs or the ABB ever advocated such a position. 'Richard B. Moore, interview, 15 January 1958', and 'W.A. Domingo, interview, 18 January 1958', Box 21, Folder 3, Theodore Draper Papers, Emory University. For more on the ABB, see 'Cyril Briggs and the African Blood Brotherhood', WPA Writers' Project, No. 1, Reporter: Carl Offord, Schomburg Collection; *Crusader*, vol. 2, no. 2 (October 1919), p. 27; 'Program of the African Blood Brotherhood', *Communist Review*, London (April 1922), pp. 449–54; Mark Solomon, 'Red and Black: Negroes and Communism, 1929–1932', Ph.D. dissertation, Harvard University 1972, pp. 80–83; Harry Haywood, *Black Bolshevik: Autobiography of an Afro-American Communist*, Chicago 1978, pp. 122–30; Naison, *Communists in Harlem*, pp. 3, 5–8, 17–18; Theodore Vincent, *Black Power and the Garvey Movement*, pp. 74–85; Tony Martin, *Race First*, Westport, Conn. 1976, pp. 237–46; Theodore Draper, *American Communism and Soviet Russia*, New York 1960, pp. 322–32; Philip S. Foner, *Organized Labor and the Black Worker, 1619–1981*, New York 1981, pp. 148–9; Cedric J. Robinson, *Black Marxism: The Making of the Black Radical Tradition*, London 1983, pp. 296–301; David Samuels, 'Five Afro-Caribbean Voices in American Culture, 1917–1929: Hubert H. Harrison, Wilfred A. Domingo, Richard B. Moore, Cyril Briggs and Claude McKay', Ph.D. dissertation, University of Iowa 1977; Theman Taylor, 'Cyril Briggs and the African Blood Brotherhood: Effects of Communism on Black Nationalism, 1919–1935',

Ph.D. dissertation, University of California, Santa Barbara 1981.

7. Workers (Communist) Party of America, *Program and Constitution: Workers Party of America*, New York 1921, p. 14; Workers (Communist) Party of America, *The Second Year of the Workers Party of America: Theses, Programs, Resolutions*, Chicago 1924, p. 125; V.I. Lenin, 'The Socialist Revolution and the Right of Nations to Self-Determination, Theses', in *Lenin on the National and Colonial Questions: Three Articles*, Peking 1967, p. 5; 'Theses on the National and Colonial Question Adopted by the Second Congress of the Comintern Congress', in *The Communist International, 1919–1943, Documents*, Jane Degras, ed., London 1956, 1:142. Roy's contribution to the Theses, as well as to the general direction of the Commission, was quite substantial. Among other things, he recognized the existence of class distinctions in the colonies and he placed the peasantry in a pivotal position for waging the anti-colonial struggle. See Manabendra Nath Roy, *M.N. Roy's Memoirs*, Bombay 1964, p. 378; see also John Haithcox, *Communism and Nationalism in India: M.N. Roy and Comintern Policy, 1920–1939*, Princeton, N.J. 1971, pp. 14–15; D.C. Grover, *M.N. Roy: A Study of Revolution and Reason in Indian Politics*, Calcutta 1973, pp. 2–13. A copy of Roy's theses are available in V.B. Karnik, *M.N. Roy: A Political Biography*, Bombay 1978, pp. 107–110. For Lenin's views on Roy's supplementary theses, see 'The Report of the Commission on the National and Colonial Questions, 26 July 1920', in *Lenin on the National and Colonial Questions*, pp. 30–37; Draper, *American Communism*, p. 321. As early as 1913, Lenin wrote a short article entitled 'Russians and Negroes', in which he compared the plight of Blacks to that of emancipated Russian serfs., *Collected Works*, vol. 18, pp. 543–4. In his 'Notebooks on Imperialism', put together in 1916, he was critical of the Socialist Party's position on Afro-Americans, as well as of the Mississippi Socialist Party's policy of segregation: *Collected Works*, vol. 39, pp. 590–91. Lenin's criticism of the American Communists' failure to work among Blacks was based on research he had conducted regarding the plight of Black sharecroppers and tenant farmers in the United States. And it was in these works, completed in 1915 and 1917, that Lenin suggested that Blacks constitute an oppressed nation in the United States: V.I. Lenin, 'New Data on the Laws Governing the Development of Capitalism in Agriculture', in *Collected Works*, vol. 22, pp. 13–102; 'On Statistics and Sociology', in *Collected Works*, vol. 23, p. 276.

8. Draper, *American Communism*, pp. 320–21, 327–8; Robinson, *Black Marxism*, p. 304; Roger E. Kanet, 'The Comintern and the "Negro Question": Communist Policy in the United States and Africa, 1921–1941', *Survey*, vol. 19, no. 4 (Autumn 1973), pp. 89–90; Haywood, *Black Bolshevik*, p. 225; Claude McKay, *A Long Way from Home*, New York 1937, pp. 177–80; Billings [Otto Huiswoud], 'Report on the Negro Question', *International Press Correspondence*, vol. 3, no. 2 (1923), pp. 14–16. The full text of the 'Theses on the Negro Question' is available in *Bulletin of the IV Congress of the Communist International*, no. 27 (December 1922), pp. 8–10.

9. Quotations from Workers (Communist) Party of America, *Fourth National Convention of the Workers (Communist) Party of America*, Chicago 1925, pp. 121 and 122; on the CP and Garveyism, see Vincent, *Black Power and the Garvey Movement*, p. 211; Robert Hill, ed., *The Marcus Garvey and Universal Negro Improvement Association Papers*, vol. 3, Berkeley, Calif. 1984, pp. 675–81;, quotation Workers, Communist Party of America, *Fourth National Convention of the Workers (Communist) Party of America*, Chicago 1925, p. 122; James Jackson [Lovett Fort-Whiteman], 'The Negro in America', *Communist International*, February 1925, p. 52; Robert Minor, 'After Garvey – What?' *Workers Monthly*, vol. 5 (June 1926), pp. 362–5.

10. Haywood, *Black Bolshevik*, pp. 139, 140–46; 'Report of National Negro Committee, CPUSA', (tsc., 1925), box 12, Folder, 'Negro–1924–25', Robert Minor Papers, Butler Memorial Library, Columbia University; James Ford, *The Negro and the Democratic Front*, New York 1938, p. 82; Harvey Klehr, *The Heyday of American Communism: The Depression Decade*, New York 1984, p. 324; Wilson Record, *The Negro and the Communist Party*, Chapel Hill, N.C. 1951, pp. 29–33.

11. Willy Munzenberg, 'Pour une Conference Coloniale', *Correspondance Internationale*, vol. 6, no. 9 (August 1926), p. 1011; Munzenberg, 'La Premiere Conference Mondiale Contre la Politique Coloniale Imperialiste', *Correspondance Internationale*, vol. 7, no. 17 (5 February 1927), p. 232; Robin D. G. Kelley, 'The Third International and the Struggle for National Liberation in South Africa, 1921–1928', *Ufahamu*, vol. 15, nos. 1 and 2 (1986), pp. 110–11; Edward T. Wilson, *Russia and Black Africa before World War II*, New York and London 1974, p. 151; *South African Worker*, 1 April 1927, 24 June 1927; 'Les Decisions du Congres: Resolution Commune sur la Question Negre', *La Voix des Negres*, vol. 1, no. 3 (March 1927), p. 3.

12. 'Resolutions Proposed by Workers Party of America at the Negro Sanhedrin, 12 February 1924', pp. 4, 7, 9, 13, Box 13, and 'Report of National Negro Committee, CPUSA', (tsc., 1925), Box 12, Robert Minor Papers; W.A. Domingo Interview, 18 January 1958 (tsc.), p. 4, Box 21, Folder 3, Theodore Draper Papers, Emory University; Ford, *The Negro and the Democratic Front*, p. 82; Haywood, *Black Bolshevik*, pp. 143–6; Klehr, *The Heyday of American Communism*, p. 324; Naison, *Communists in Harlem*, p. 13.

13. Naison, *Communists in Harlem*, p. 18; (quotation) Gilbert Lewis, 'Revolutionary Negro Tradition', *Negro Worker*, 15 March 1930, p. 8. Cyril Briggs published a whole series of essays on this score, such as 'Negro Revolutionary Hero – Toussaint L'Ouverture', *Communist*, vol. 8, no. 5 (May 1929), pp. 250–254; 'The Negro Press as a Class Weapon', *Communist*, vol. 8, no. 8 (August 1929), pp. 453–60; and 'May First and the Revolutionary Traditions of Negro Masses', *Daily Worker*, 28 April 1930.

14. William L. Patterson, 'Awake Negro Poets', *New Masses*, vol. 4 (October 1928), p.10.

15. 'Draft Program of the League of Struggle for Negro Rights', (tsc., n.d.), pp. 1–3, Box 12, Folder – 'Negroes, 1931', Robert Minor Papers; LSNR, *Equality, Land and Freedom: A Program for Liberation*, New York 1933.

16. *Liberator*, 21 February 1931.

17. Resolution of the Central Committee, CPUSA, on Negro Work, 16 March 1931 (tsc.), pp. 2–4, Box 12, Folder – 'Negro, 1931', Robert Minor Papers, Butler Memorial Library, Columbia University; *Daily Worker*, 23 March 1931; *Liberator*, 28 March 1931.

18. *Daily Worker*, 19 January 1932; Harvey Klehr, *The Heyday of American Communism*, p. 332; [Herman] Mackawain, 'The League of Struggle for Negro Rights in Harlem', *Party Organizer*, vol. 8 (April 1934), p. 60; 'The Reminiscences of Earl Browder', interview conducted by Joseph R. Starobin, 1964 (tsc.), vol. III, p. 285, Columbia Oral History Project, Butler Memorial Library, Columbia University; Harry Haywood, *Black Bolshevik*, pp. 439–40.

19. Nell Irvin Painter, *The Narrative of Hosea Hudson: His Life as a Negro Communist in the South*, Cambridge, Mass. 1979, p. 102.

20. *Liberator*, 21 November 1931.

21. Tony Martin, *Literary Garveyism: Garvey, Black Arts and the Harlem Renaissance*, Dover, Mass. 1983, pp. 43–6, 73.

22. Michael Gold, 'Send Us a Critic', in *Mike Gold: A Literary Anthology*, Michael Folsom, ed., New York 1972, p. 139; Paula Rabinowitz, 'Women and US Literary Radicals', in *Writing Red: An Anthology of American Women Writers, 1930–1940*, Charlotte Nekola and Paula Rabinowitz, eds, New York 1987, p. 3; see also Charlotte Nekola, 'Worlds Moving: Women, Poetry, and the Literary Politics of the 1930s', pp. 129–31; Stanley Burnshaw, 'Notes on Revolutionary Poetry', *New Masses*, vol. 10 (20 February 1934), p. 22; V.F. Calverton, 'Leftward Ho!' *Modern Quarterly*, vol. 6 (Summer 1932), pp. 26–32; Paula Rabinowitz, *Labor and Desire*, Chapel Hill, N.C. 1991.

23. *Liberator*, 22 August 1931.

24. *Daily Worker*, 10 August 1935.

25. *Daily Worker*, 3 December 1932.

26. Elizabeth Faue, *Community of Suffering and Struggle: Women, Men, and the Labor Movement in Minneapolis, 1915–1945*, Chapel Hill, N.C. 1991, p. 71; Sharon Hartman Strom, 'Challenging "Woman's Place": Feminism, the Left, and Industrial Unionism in the 1930s', *Feminist Studies*, vol. 9, no. 2 (Summer 1983), pp. 359–86.

27. Richard Frank, 'Negro Revolutionary Music', *New Masses*, vol. 11, no. 7 (15 May 1934), p. 29.

28. Eugene Gordon, 'Alabama Massacre', *New Masses*, vol. 7, August 1931, p. 16; *Daily Worker*, 3 December 1932; Ruby Weems, 'The Murder of Ralph Gray', *Liberator*, 21 November 1931; Grace Lumpkin, *A Sign for Cain*, New York 1935, p. 223; Robin D. G. Kelley, *Hammer and Hoe: Alabama Communists During the Great Depression*, Chapel Hill, N.C. 1990, p. 146.

29. William L. Patterson, 'The Negro Question', (tsc., unpublished ms., April 1933), 1, microfilm, reel 2, International Labor Defense Papers, Schomburg Collection.

30. Harry Haywood, 'Against Bourgeois-Liberal Distortions of Leninism on the Negro Question in the United States', *Communist*, vol. 8, no. 9 (August 1930), p. 700; also Haywood, 'The Theoretical Defenders of White Chauvinism in the Labor Movement', in *The Communist*

Position on the Negro Question, New York n.d., p. 31.

31. Patterson, 'Awake Negro Poets', p. 10.

32. Buhle, *Marxism in the United States*, p. 157. On the debate over proletarian literature, see Buhle, *Marxism in the United States*, Ch. 5; Lawrence Schwartz, *Marxism and Culture: The CPUSA and Aesthetics in the 1930s*, Port Washington, N.Y. 1980; Alan M. Wald, *The New York Intellectuals: The Rise and Decline of the Anti-Stalinist Left from the 1930s to the 1980s*, Chapel Hill, N.C. 1987, p. 78.

33. See for instance Walter Carmon's review of Hughes's *Not Without Laughter*, *New Masses*, vol. 6, no. 5 (October 1930). The beginning of a serious Black literary critique within Party circles dates to 1935 with the founding of the American Writers' Congress. See especially, Henry Hart, ed., *American Writers' Congress*, New York 1935, pp. 139–53; Eugene Clay, 'The Negro in Recent American Literature', *International Literature*, vol. 6 (1935), pp. 79–80; and of course, Richard Wright, 'Blueprint for Negro Writing', *New Challenge*, vol. 1 (Fall 1937), pp. 53–61.

34. Michael Gold, 'The Negro Reds of Chicago', *Daily Worker*, 30 September 1932.

35. Harold Preece, 'Folk Music of the South', *New South*, vol. 1 (March 1938), p. 13; also see Harold Preece to Anne Johnson, 25 December 1936, Clyde Johnson Papers, microfilm reel 13.

36. Philip Schatz, 'Songs of the Negro Worker', *New Masses*, vol. 5, no. 12 (May 1930), pp. 6–8; Lawrence Gellert, 'Negro Songs of Protest', *New Masses*, vol. 6, no. 11 (April 1931), pp. 6–8.

37. *Daily Worker*, 7 April 1934; *Southern Worker*, July 1936. As early as 1932, the same song was sung by Black Communists in Chicago, but their version was slightly different in that it referred to the 'New Communist Spirit'. *Daily Worker*, 30 September 1932, quoted in Denisoff, *Great Day Coming*, p. 37. For examples of adaptations of 'We Shall Not Be Moved', see *Labor Defender*, vol. 9, no. 11 (December 1933), p. 80; Harold Preece to Anne Johnson, 25 December 1936, Clyde Johnson Papers, microfilm, reel 13.

38. *Southern Worker*, 18 July 1931.

39. *Daily Worker*, 2 October 1932.

40. *Liberator*, 14 November 1931.

41. Poet Langston Hughes was unusual among Black poets who contributed to the Communist press for his often explicit depiction of ordinary Black folk dispensing with or questioning religion altogether. See especially Langston Hughes's works published in *New Masses*, the *Liberator* and the *Negro Worker*. The more profane works include 'Goodbye Christ', 'God to Hungry Child', 'A Christian Country', 'The New Black Blues', and 'A New Song'. Much of this work has been reproduced in Langston Hughes, *Good Morning Revolution: Uncollected Writings of Social Protest*, Faith Berry, ed., Westport, Conn. 1973; see also *Liberator*, 15 and 31 October 1931. The characters in Hughes's poems, however, were not unusual. As I have demonstrated elsewhere, it is likely that some Blacks were drawn to the Party as a result of their personal disillusionment with the church. Robin D. G. Kelley, '"Comrades, Praise Gawd for Lenin and Them!": Ideology and Culture Among Black Communists in Alabama, 1930–1935', *Science and Society*, vol. 52, no. 1, Spring 1988, pp. 64–6.

3

Pan-Africanism,

Feminism and Culture

By Maryse Conde

I am from the Caribbean island of Guadeloupe which, along with its sister island Martinique, is still a French overseas department, a French colony. Many people like myself do not accept this colonial status, and are actively supporting the independence movements. We realize that if this situation is to end we must do it ourselves; we cannot expect any help from the French government, even a so-called socialist one. We know full well, as the French political scientist Yves Bénot, has put it, 'De droite ou de gauche Metropole reste la Metropole', meaning 'left wing or right wing, a colonial power remains a colonial power.' Several years ago we convened a conference to discuss strategies to achieve our independence, but, unfortunately, we accomplished very little. As we continue to search for a unifying force to facilitate our struggle for independence, it might be opportune to review Pan-Africanism and its possibilities in relation to our struggle.

Pan-Africanism and Guadeloupe

When my political colleagues learned that I was going to a conference on Pan-Africanism in the United States, they asked, 'What are you going to tell people over there?' I responded, 'I am going to tell them the truth.' My presentation will look at Pan-Africanism in an attempt to determine the truth – as I see it. It will be an informal talk because I am a novelist; and what is a novelist but someone who tells stories. Therefore, I am going to tell a few stories; together we shall try to make sense of them in the context of Pan-Africanism and culture.

At the end of 1987, French authorities arrested three leaders of the Popular Movement for the Independence of Guadeloupe (MPGI) for acts of 'terrorism'. Several years earlier they had been accused of bombing an administration building on the island and burning automobiles belonging to French citizens. Soon after their arrest, however, they managed to escape. They went into hiding in the rural areas of the island. Remember, Guadeloupe is a very small island; therefore, for them to remain free, they must have had the complicity of the people.

At the beginning of 1987, when a series of bombings rocked Paris and many people died, French authorities decided that they had had enough and would mount a campaign to 'wipe out terrorism'. Thus, they offered a very large reward for the capture of the three Guadeloupean leaders still at large. In a country like Guadeloupe, where the rate of unemployment is as high as 30 percent, it was only a matter of time before someone turned them in to the police. Realizing this, the men decided to leave Guadeloupe and ask for political asylum in another Caribbean country. They hired an airplane and attempted to flee to Surinam, but authorities there denied them entrance. They then tried Trinidad and were again refused. One after another the islands in the Caribbean declined to accept them. Finally Saint Vincent gave permission to land, but in the meantime notified French officials, who arrested the three on arrival. Eventually they were returned to Guadeloupe and then taken to France for trial. They were sentenced to thirty years in prison. The most popular of the three was a thirty-year-old revolutionary named Luc Reinette.

It was not surprising that the weak political regimes of the various Caribbean islands gave in to French pressure. But what was surprising and upsetting for people like myself was the lack of interest from the outside world. Neither French, British nor American newspapers published a single line protesting the fate of the three liberation leaders. In despair, a group of young Guadeloupeans and Martiniqueans demonstrated in the streets of Paris. They carried large banners reading 'Free Nelson Mandela and Luc Reinette'. In the minds of these protesters Mandela and Reinette were the same, political prisoners fighting for the independence of their people. Most people who saw them marching in the streets of Paris laughed, including many so-called leftists. They all knew the Black South African leader Nelson Mandela, but none of them had any idea who Luc Reinette was – or even cared.

After the failure of the demonstration, we began to ask ourselves questions: Was the life of one man not equal to the life of another? Were Luc Reinette and Nelson Mandela not fighting injustice and oppression? Were they to be treated differently just because one came from a large and well-known country, while the other came from a small and desolate island?

Does one have to be from South Africa, or Angola, to receive attention? These were very important questions. Certainly, some of those who ridiculed our demonstration were ignorant; however, we became convinced that there was a conspiracy of silence about our plight. So you understand why my political friends were shocked at the idea of my coming to speak about Pan-Africanism, when our leaders are still in jail. When not even one of those self-proclaimed leftists or Pan-Africanists had raised a finger to help liberate them.

Does this mean that Pan-Africanism is dead? Or does it mean that the concept must be redefined in the context of present realities? Before I attempt to answer these questions, let me tell you a second story.

Unity Among Peoples of the Caribbean?

Due to the political and economic conditions existing in Haiti, there are many Haitians who have migrated to Guadeloupe and, to a lesser extent, Martinique and French Guiana. In Guadeloupe, they are primarily low-paid migrant laborers who work in the sugarcane fields and in private gardens. Therefore, the local population despises them. There is a common saying on the island: 'I'm not your Haitian', meaning, 'I am not your slave.' At various times French authorities expelled all Haitians from Guadeloupe, when their labor was no longer necessary. There are also many people from Dominica who live in slum areas on the island. They too will eventually be expelled and few people on the island will care. The French will put new buildings where the old shacks once stood, and everyone will forget about the Dominicans. My point is that it is difficult to achieve unity within the Caribbean, even among people who share a common history and language, in this case, Creole. So how can we talk of Pan-Africanism in Guadeloupe? I know you will ask, What am I doing as a writer and a Pan-Africanist to improve this situation? I must explain these contradictions in human terms.

As far as Luc Reinette and the other political prisoners are concerned, I did what I could given the limitations imposed by colonialism. I signed petitions, marched in the streets and protested whenever and wherever I could. For the Haitians, I did a bit more, using the main weapon at my disposal – I wrote a book for children. Several years ago, in 1985, a boat full of Haitian migrants fled the turmoil of their country, a turmoil mostly created by American imperialist policies, and tried to find refuge in the United States. Off the coast of Florida the United States Coast Guard approached them and, terrified, they jumped into the sea. They were all drowned, and for weeks afterwards their bodies were scattered along the coast of Florida – a truly tragic story.

A Haitian novelist, Jean-Claude Charles, wrote a very moving book about the incident, which he titled *De si jolies petites Plages/Such Lovely Little Beaches*. The tragedy so distressed me that I decided to also write a story – but mine would be for kids. Why so? Because in the schools of Guadeloupe and Martinique, our kids sit next to the children of Haitian migrants without understanding them. In fact, they are filled with a contempt that they learned from their parents. It seemed to me that writing a book about this event would be a way of fighting prejudice at its root. That is why I wrote *Haiti cherie* in 1988. I also spent a great deal of time going to the schools explaining to the children of Guadeloupe that the Haitians are their brothers and sisters.

I had to fight to have *Haiti cherie* included in the syllabus of the Guadeloupean primary schools. In fact, I managed to have it included only because I received support from two education officers (one Guadeloupean, one French), as well as from parents, teachers and others. And it became a success. Now whenever I go to schools or children come to my home I discuss Haiti with them. Here I must say that there have been changes in the school system since my school days in the 1940s and 1950s, but they remain limited. Now kids learn a little about the geography of their island, its mountains and rivers, much more than I learned as a child, when I could not name one of the island's mountains – although I knew all about the Alps and Pyrenees.

The children of today also learn a bit of history; but what kind of history? Among other things, they learn that slavery was not that bad. Although they are not as explicit as they used to be, hidden in their textbooks are justifications for the slave trade. They are taught that Africans were happier in the West Indies than they were in Africa. They are told that while it was certainly wrong to kidnap and harm the slaves during the Middle Passage, when they arrived on the plantations they were content. This is the type of nonsense still existing in the school syllabus. However, increasing numbers of Guadeloupeans and Martiniqueans are writing books to correct these racist notions. We hope that the texts and the memories will change accordingly. I realize that my contributions may not seem much, given the situation; but it is what I, as a writer, can do to contribute to the unity of the Caribbean and to keep the idea of Pan-Africanism alive. Unity within the Caribbean is something one does not really see. And when it comes to Africa there is even less awareness.

Pan-African Consciousness and the New Generation

How do the people of Guadeloupe feel about Africa and other areas of the diaspora? People of my generation expected too much of Africa. In the 1960s we had too much hope and faith in Africa. I believe that the time has now come for a certain re-evaluation and/or self-criticism. It was naive, simplistic and overly idealistic to assume that African countries, just liberated from the yoke of colonization, and facing so many problems and subject to so many pressures from the imperialist powers, could provide the model we were looking for. We expected to be welcomed by the Africans with open arms and seen as long-lost brothers and sisters. We expected them to help us in our struggles while their's were still raging. But this was not possible. The concept of Pan-Africanism, as espoused by intellectuals, was not understood by the people – at least at the level of an abstract ideology. Now the intellectuals and artists of my generation have come to realize that it was almost inevitable that the majority of Africans treated us with distrust. We were viewed as foreigners and this frustrated many of us. I, however, have gotten rid of this feeling. When I wrote my first novel, *Heremakhonon* (1976), I had just returned from Africa and was terribly hurt by the experience. I have since recovered. Now, I only remember what was good about my years there, and what I learned living there.

What seems frustrating to me is the complete absence of any understanding of Africa in the minds of Guadeloupe's people. I see this particularly among the very young. They often ask me why I went to Africa in the first place. When I try to explain the African independence movements of the 1960s, or speak of the magic of leaders like Sékou Touré or Kwame Nkrumah, they simply do not understand. For them Sékou Touré was just another dictator who unfortunately died in his bed. They do not even think about Africa. Instead, they look to the United States, to Black America, for their inspiration. They idolize people like Jesse Jackson and other popular African-American politicians, artists and sportsmen. They see the United States as a place where a Black man or a Black woman can reach the top. It is very difficult to explain to them that this is not the case without disillusioning and discouraging them.

Even those who belong to the older generation have a similar approach to Africa and its culture. In 1983, a Haitian writer named Anthony Phelps caused a stir when he attended a conference in Padua, Italy. He stated openly, 'Moi Negre des Ameriques je ne suis pas un ecrivain Negro-Africain. Je ne suis pas un ecrivain Negro-Americain. Il n'existe pas de literature Negro-Americaine, nous Negres du Noveau Monde, nous ne sommes pas des Africaines en exil en Amerique.' Paraphrased in English, he said: 'I, a Black man from the Americas, am not an Afro-American writer. There is no Afro-American literature. We Blacks from the New World (Americas) are not Africans in exile in America.' He pointed out that there was no reason to brand a writer with prefixes. He went on to explain the complete originality of his world, the Haitian one, the Caribbean one. As you might guess, his remarks were met with a good deal of hostility, since they challenged notions of the African personality, Pan-Africanism and Négritude.

At one point in our history, we looked to Négritude in particular as champion of cross-cultural communication and Pan-Africanism. But there are elements inherited from that movement which we must discard. Du Bois, Garvey, Padmore and Malcolm X put forth the idea that Africa was the cornerstone of the Black world. According to them, if Africa was powerful the other Black communities throughout the world would have a different image of themselves. Is that true?

I also question the idea perpetuated by Négritude that all Blacks are the same. It is as Sartre put it in *Orphée Noir*, it is a type of racism inherited from the whites who believe that all 'niggers' look alike, thus they are all similar. This is certainly not true. Every Black society is different. By overlooking that fact, the proponents of Négritude made a big mistake and caused a lot of suffering in the minds of West Indians and African-Americans as well. As I mentioned before, we were led to believe that Africa was an ideal home. When we discovered it was not, we suffered. Without Négritude, we would not have experienced the degree of disillusionment that we did. The issue of 'likeness' or 'similarity' is erroneous even in the Antilles. Guadeloupe is very different from Martinique. Each island has an identity of its own, even if we cannot divorce our problems from theirs.

We can see this rejection of Africa in the writings of West Indian author Patrick Chamoiseau – the spiritual son of Edouard Glissant (father of Antillanite). Chamoiseau's work does not even mention Négritude. Instead, he is an advocate of *Creolite*. This, in Guadeloupe and Martinique, is a syncretic culture which meshes French, Blacks from Africa, East Indians from India, and other Asians into a new culture. The new concept of Creolite does not refer to race or color. It refers only to culture. In fact, the exponents of Creolite are simply repeating what Frantz Fanon and Amilcar Cabral said before them.

In *The Wretched of the Earth*, Fanon stated that Blacks were 'disappearing' from the surface of the earth, adding, 'There can be no two cultures which are completely identical.'[1] Likewise, Amilcar Cabral in one of his political speeches said [in paraphrase], 'You will think that people fight for their material needs. When people fight, it is just to preserve their culture. Culture, that is all that matters.'[2] This is precisely the Creolite attitude toward culture. In Guadeloupe and Martinique this is most important, as their culture is constantly under attack. In 1992 the citizens of both islands would have officially become Europeans when their countries joined the EEC. This represented a challenge to West Indian cultural identity, and we wondered how to preserve it in that political context.

You will certainly ask, How can one define West Indian culture? The best answer is that culture is not an entity to be defined; a culture is something to be lived. So the people of the Caribbean do not have to define exactly what they are, who they are, what constitutes their culture. They just have to live as West Indians.

A good illustration of this new Creolite culture is found in music; it has become the crucible in which the ideas of people are emerging in Caribbean.[3] Many Guadeloupeans and Martiniquans have come to know about Jamaica through Bob Marley; not only his music, but the lyrics as well. Even though the words were in English, they understood the meaning. We had a lot of Antillean Rastafarians wearing dreadlocks, living in small colonies up in the hills, trying to imitate Marley, but who never knew exactly what it was to be a Rastafarian. Jamaica came to be regarded as a sister island because of its musicians. Now the chain of influence has been redirected; other islanders, who once despised Martinique and Guadeloupe because they were French dependencies, have been drawn to *Kasav* and *Zouk* music. Guadeloupe and Martinique are now known, even in West Africa. *Kasav* in Zaire, interacting with an established popular music tradition there, has built a firmer base of understanding and appreciation perhaps than we writers ever did. People have to read to understand us, but music, you just have to feel.

Returning Home

When I returned to Guadeloupe after thirty years of living in Europe, Africa and the United States, these were the things I faced. Guadeloupe was in transition; communication in Creole rather than French had become an obvious and intimate sign of belonging. Also one's political position on Guadeloupean independence overshadowed the old social divisions based on differences of color and ethnicity. The role of the writer must necessarily evolve in this new environment. I had to be born again. Initially, I had to re-evaluate my role as a writer, and reassess the negative images of Antillean culture I inherited from my parents' generation.

Aimé Cesairé defined in poetic terms what the role of the Antillean writer had been in the early days when he wrote: 'Je suis venu acclimater un arbre de soufre et de lave parmi un peuple de vaincus.' In other words, 'I come to plant a tree of sulphur and lava among a vanquished people.'[4]

He means that it is the writer who gives people power, strength, unity and faith. Césaire's was an intellectual attitude toward culture that nobody believes in now. You must know how the profession is perceived in Guadeloupe. As our books are published in France and written in French, our reputations are generally developed in France and in the outside world. Yes, we have been to America, but who in Guadeloupe cares about American universities? Our people pay no attention to that kind of scholarly acclaim. As an author, you must try to be adopted for other reasons. To give examples of the humbling process that occurs, let me relate a number of incidents.

How does an author in present-day Guadeloupe inspire the general public to read, adopt and admire his/her work? I am not sure. I have succeeded in some ways, but I am not certain that the recognition I am now enjoying is based on any of my written text. *Segu* was hardly read in the West Indies; those who did read it found the novel bizarre and alien. It seemed almost science fiction. After my return to Guadeloupe, I met a woman who told me, 'I admire you a great deal; whenever you appear on television, my children call me in to see you because they know I like you so very much. Tell me, what is your name and what do you do for a living.' That was one of the first shocks I faced. Another woman stopped me in a supermarket, saying, 'Oh, congratulations for all your wonderful books.' To myself, I thought, 'At last here is someone who has read them.' So I asked, 'You've read my novels?' She replied, 'No, but I like the way you speak about them on TV.' Now I no longer ask the question.

A final example: when I talk about literature and culture on the independent radio station, Radio Tambour, listeners do not pay attention to what I say. Rather they call in to comment on my progress in speaking Creole. Last year, when I invited Paule Marshall and Louise Merriwether to a conference in Guadeloupe, I wanted to prepare the audience, and somehow achieve unity within the diaspora by speaking in advance about their work. Having recently returned to the country, I spoke in French. Callers phoned in to the station complaining, 'But who is Maryse Conde? She speaks French, is she a white woman?' To be a writer is almost meaningless for the majority of our people. While this first problem was simply a matter of overcoming my own pride, the second was far more painful, for it involved a reassessment of West Indian culture.

West Indian culture: what is it after all? As I said before, I learned that culture, unlike Césaire's definition cited above, is something that you live and not a phenomenon you simply discuss in detail. I did not, however, reach that conclusion immediately, as my quest for understanding over the years indicates. When I sought to find out what West Indian culture is, I compared it with the cultures of Africa, which seemed to be stronger. During my childhood, to be a West Indian was a misfortune, a disease of sorts. Coming from that background and returning to a country where people are proud to be West Indian requires the acceptance of the culture on its own terms. I had to reassess indigenous dance and folktales in the context of modernity. It has been an extremely difficult experience which is not yet completed. I am still in the process of re-evaluating West Indian culture.

A Woman in the Movement

There is also a third thing which I was forced to do on my return to Guadeloupe; I had to reassess my role as a woman in the independence movement. In my mother's generation, women believed that education was the key to social mobility. One was educated by going to museum exhibits or to churches to hear music – all the while having a French education and French culture forced upon you. Yet by looking at the older generation, the people of today can also learn some valuable lessons. In fact, the younger generation has lost something which is essential. They have become *consumers* instead of *producers:* consumers of foreign films, of TV programs, etc., whereas their mothers were producers of songs, of folktales, of food in their small villages. These women were independent; but the women of my mother's generation have forgotten all about that. The women that I see in Guadeloupe today, who are mostly uneducated, have a tendency to regard me as totally useless. Why? Because they do not read my books, they do not travel, they do not know anything about being producers. I, therefore, feel it is my duty to make them understand that writing is a way of producing, comparable to the creativity of their mothers. Of course, times have changed; I cannot sing a song, or tell a tale the way their mothers did – but I can write.

I must show them that writing is not something useless, but rather that it is something full of creativity for them. Yet convincing today's women of this point is a long and difficult task, which I have only begun. I must convince them that I am writing for them – because I am part of them, of our people. Unfortunately, they want to dictate what I should write. But if I do that I shall lose the freedom which is necessary to any artist. So after I complete the process of being adopted, I shall have to be let free. This is the battle I must fight. But I cannot fight the two battles simultaneously.

What do I see as 'the role of women' today? The women of my mother's generation had a stereotypical view of their mothers as being too submissive and servile. They also believed that they, through education, would liberate themselves. But they also became dependent on their husbands. Formerly, the majority of Guadelopean women had no husbands;

men went about fathering children outside the institution of marriage. Thus one could say that women were submissive, but in another sense they were not. They put up with this situation without shedding a tear for the wayward husband. (They lived alone – without a man – and made their lives harmonious and whole.) They raised their children alone, and turned them into capable men and women. Therefore, in a manner of speaking, they were freer than the following generation of women – my generation. Again, we should try to understand and value our mother's and grandmother's attitudes more.

Today, there is a great deal of confusion among women about their role in the independence struggle and their role in liberating women. Many of the educated women of my age consider themselves militant, liberated women, fighting for the independence of Guadeloupe. But often when I (and some of my more militant friends) are in the field talking to women active in the struggle, we notice that when their husbands appear they become silent. This is a contradiction. In such circumstances, we try to emphasize that they must fight for the independence of Guadeloupe, but they must not forget about the liberation of women. In Algeria, for example, during the liberation war women were in the streets – without veils – fighting for the end of colonialism. Yet when the war was over and independence won, they were told to go back to their 'place'. We cannot accept this in Guadeloupe. In particular, husbands continue to dominate their peasant wives. Their lives are similar to those of their grandmothers'. There are other women, unfortunately a minority in the population, who continue to raise feminist slogans. At the same time, they also warn peasant women that shouting slogans is not enough, they must be strong and independent in their own minds. So the struggle continues. Most of the women I know are just ordinary people living in villages who face the immediate problem of finding money for food, clothing and schooling for their children. They do not have time to actively participate in the liberation of Guadeloupe, much less attacking men or pondering the relevance of Pan-Africanism to their lives. Rather they go about finding their own power and energy to create a world for themselves and for the children that they bring forth.

Many people might say that we in Guadeloupe (and the Caribbean at large) are very far from the principles of Pan-Africanism: but I do not believe we are. There is a West Indian proverb: 'It is only when you have swept your house that you can go out.' I believe we are in the process of sweeping our houses, achieving our independence. Only after that can we begin to think about something more ambitious. I, personally, still believe in Pan-Africanism; but the idea was born in the minds of diasporan people at a time of great racial and physical oppression. Now it appears that the physical and racial oppression, while still extant, is not as severe today as it was then. For this reason I believe we should shift our interest to culture. We should busy ourselves by protecting our culture, making an inventory of it, and trying to see exactly what we are and what we possess. I think that when we finish that inventory we will better understand Pan-Africanism. Du Bois, Garvey, Nkrumah and the rest had beautiful and grandiose ideas, but they were ahead of their times. We shall come to that at a later stage – when we have finished cleaning our houses. I believe it will be the role of future writers, male and female, to turn the minds of the people towards the other world and to make them understand that there is a need for unity, diversity and Pan-Africanism. If we are not allowed to be diverse and different, we cannot be united. Diversity within unity is the definition of our shared objectives of national autonomy and cooperation within the larger Caribbean. So Pan-Africanism is not that far off; what we are witnessing now are the beginnings, the birth of a new stage of Pan-Africanism.

Notes

Note: This text was edited and revised by Sidney J. Lemelle and Barbara Bair from the transcript of the original talk, entitled 'The Making of a West Indian Feminist', given on 8 April 1988 at the Pan-Africanism Revisited Conference, Claremont, California. Some portions of the text also appeared in 'I Have Made Peace with My Island: An Interview with Maryse Conde', by VeVe Clark, which appeared in *Callaloo*, vol. 12, no. 1 (Winter 1989).

1. Frantz Fanon, *The Wretched of the Earth*, New York 1963, p. 234.
2. See Amilcar Cabral, 'National Liberation and Culture', in *Return to the Source*, New York 1973.
3. The following section was excerpted from Clark, 'Interview', pp. 111–15.
4. See Aimé Césaire, 'The Responsibility of the Artist', in W. Cartey and M. Kilson, eds, *The African Reader: Independent Africa*, New York 1970, pp. 153–62.

4

Rastafarians and

Ethiopianism

Gersham A. Nelson

According to Albert Memmi, colonized peoples have historically employed two approaches in response to colonialism and its legacies. The first is cultural adoption, in which the colonizer is emulated and traditional values that conflict with the new culture are submerged. The second takes the form of a cultural revival. Here the colonized search for and seek to recapture cultural elements torn away by colonization.[1] The Land and Freedom Movement of Kenya, for example, confronted British colonialism by laying claim to traditional rights which had been denied them by the colonizer. In this effort the Kikuyu nationalists sought to authenticate their claim to the Rift Valley by calling on the name of their forefathers who had bequeathed the land to them.

The Lenshina Movement of Northern Rhodesia (now Zambia), though different in many ways from the Land and Freedom Movement, shared the common objective of casting off the yoke of colonialism in the name of ancestral rights. Some Black South Africans who accepted Christianity were faced with the incongruity of the church being a collaborating agent in colonial oppression yet preaching a gospel of love. To address this contradiction these believers organized their own church and replaced European saints and heroes with their own. Since the economic, political and social structures of South Africa alienate the indigenous people and deprive them of human dignity, these churches have become concerned as much with issues of political liberation as they are with those of spiritual liberation.

It is a major challenge for any colonized people to reconstruct the past, even when it is preserved in written form. The difficulty is even more formidable for those like Africans south of the Sahara who, for the most part, preserved their heritage through oral transfer. This cultural reconstruction, however, is clearly most difficult for Africans of the diaspora such as the Rastafarians of Jamaica.

The Rastafarians, like other Blacks of the diaspora, are the descendants of Africans who were torn away from their past and through enslavement denied their cultural heritage. This essentially meant denying them a future as well. Despite the difficulty involved in employing the pre-slavery past to create a positive identity to counteract subservience, as well as the economic, social and cultural deprivation imposed by the slave masters, who later became colonial masters, this is the task upon which the Rastafarians embarked. And probably the most impressive aspect of the movement is that it emerged from among the most deprived sector of Jamaican society. This makes Rastafari an authentic grassroots movement struggling for liberation.

Given the problems surrounding African historiography, the Eurocentric views of colonials and the high rate of illiteracy which existed among the Jamaican masses during and even after the colonial period, it is not surprising that Rastafarians were dismissed as madmen with no knowledge of Africa or African history. They were said to have fallen prey to ignorance and misguided sentiment. This attitude, however, merely reflects blindness and insensitivity to the plight of the victims who had suffered decades of oppression and deprivation without political recourse.

In this essay the objective is not so much to examine the extent to which Rastafarians understood African history and their relationship to it. Instead, this is an attempt to understand Ethiopianism as used by these social outcasts to give hope and meaning to their lives. Among the questions examined here are the following: What motivated the emergence of Rastafarianism? What is the relevance of Ethiopia and that nation's principal religion (before the 1975 revolution) to Rastafarian doctrine? And why has the movement continued to survive even after the dethronement and subsequent demise of its messiah, Haile Selassie I?

An examination of these questions reveals more than a mere protest movement against colonialism; it reveals in a dramatic way the indomitability of the human spirit, epitomises cultural creativity and demonstrates the power of symbolism. The Rastafarians, representing a microcosm of Africans of the diaspora, demonstrate the ability and will of a people to survive amidst adversity. They use as their principal source of motivation Ethiopianism with a messianic component.

Colonized Africans and Ethiopianism

Ethiopianism as a form of cultural and religious rebirth has been the source of inspiration to people of African descent in the Caribbean and the Americas, as it has been to Africans on the continent. Sundkler's work on religion among the indigenous peoples of South Africa throws some light on the history of Ethiopian and Zionist churches in that country, where the struggle for emancipation has met with the most violent form of government repression.

The first 'Ethiopian Church' in South Africa was founded in 1892 as a result of discontent in the Wesleyan church. African leaders grew tired of racial segregation advocated by church leaders who professed to be followers of Biblical teachings, which acknowledge the equality of all human beings before God. Here the colonized do not totally reject the colonizer's religion but seek to address contradictions in its practice. While some African religious leaders accept the European notion that Africa was alienated from God, they see in the Bible evidence that this alienation will end, bringing with it self-government for the church. Thus Psalm 68:32, which states that Ethiopia will reach out to God, is 'interpreted to mean the self-governments of the African church under African leaders'.[2] These leaders also came to understand the correlation between self-government in the church and political emancipation.

Many of these independent church movements were seen by the European rulers of South Africa as a serious threat to the system of white supremacy in that society. The government, therefore, took various steps to make it difficult for churches operated and governed by indigenous Africans to receive any form of official recognition. In fact evidence that the Ethiopian Church was attempting to assert itself against government oppression resulted in the appointment of a government commission in 1921 to study and recommend a strategy for effective monitoring and control. The commission expressed the conviction that 'so long as the movement is not mischievous it should be tolerated and where it springs from a worthy motive and is working in harmony with the government it should be encouraged. . .'[3] Some general requirements were established to determine which of these churches could register and be officially recognized. To these was added a provision which left judgement on each application to the then newly formed Native Affairs Commission, which was to advise the government on the merits of each church.

A notable development from the independent church movement has been the rejection of a white Christ by some of its leaders. They have sought instead to present a Black Christ and a Black God, neither of whom is physically alienated from the people. One leader, Isaiah Shembe, is quoted as having said: 'You, my people, were once told of a God who has neither arms nor legs, who cannot see, who has neither love nor pity. But Isaiah Shembe showed you a God who can be known by man, a God who loves and who has compassion.'[4] When asked about her conception of Jesus, a woman from Zululand responded: 'Jesus! Him we have only seen in photos! But I know Shembe and I believe in him. He is the one who created heaven and earth: he is God for us Black people'.[5] Thus, Ethiopianism is manifested in Africa as a force in the struggle for liberation.

The Emergence of Ethiopianism in Jamaica

The name Ethiopia became identified with salvation in Jamaica, if only indirectly, as early as 1784. In that year an African-American Baptist preacher, a former slave, founded the first Baptist church on the island, calling it the Ethiopian Baptist Church.[6] While there might be no direct relationship between this church and the Rastafarian movement, the Baptist denomination in Jamaica has the historic reputation of having been one of the strongest voices on behalf of the masses. It is, therefore, not surprising that Rastafarians consider themselves disciples continuing the work that certain Baptist leaders left off. Names such as William Knibb, Paul Bogle and George William Gordon, all former Baptist church leaders, are held in high esteem by the Rasses.

The religious significance of the name Ethiopia was not given much emphasis until after Marcus Garvey founded the Universal Negro Improvement Association in 1916. Garvey emphasized the theme 'Africa for Africans at home and abroad' and presented Ethiopia as the source of inspiration for the liberation of Africans in the West. To counteract the massive, and sustained cultural assault mounted against Africans and their descendants by Europeans, Garvey presented God to Africans through a vision of Ethiopia rather than through Abraham, Jacob and Isaac as did the Europeans:

> We Negroes have found a new ideal. Whilst our God has no colour, yet it is human to see everything through one's own spectacle, and since the white people have seen their God through white spectacles, we have only now started out (late though it be) to see our God through our own spectacles. The God of Isaac and the God of Jacob let him exist for the race that believe in . . . him. We Negroes believe in the God of Ethiopia, the everlasting God – God the Son, God the Holy Ghost, the one God of all ages. That is the God whom we believe, but we shall [see him] through the spectacle of Ethiopia.[7]

Followers of Garvey, therefore, came to view Ethiopia as the symbol of freedom from 'Babylonian' oppression. This meant cultural, religious and political liberation.

Garvey's dream, rooted in the concept of Pan-Africanism, was that Africans of the diaspora would some day return to their ancestral home and, reunited with their brothers after a long separation, build an African kingdom which would recapture some of the continent's ancient glories:

> The power and sway we once held passed away, but now in the twentieth century we are about to see the rebuilding of Africa; yes, a new civilization, a new culture shall spring up from among our people and the Nile shall once more flow through the land of science, of art and of literature, wherein will live Black men of the highest learning and the highest accomplishments.[8]

It is through such proclamations and Biblical references to Ethiopia that Rastafarians have come to reconstruct what they consider to be their true identity. They no longer had to be ashamed of the color of their skin, the hovel in which they lived, the absence of adequate nutrition in their diet, the lack of education or the general lack of material possessions. They finally knew who they were, from whence they came and whither they were going.

The choice of Ethiopia and Haile Selassie to replace Europe and the Christian saviour is not without logic. Ethiopia, which alone survived Europe's scramble for Africa, is one of only two African countries which European writers gave credit for having a recorded history going back over 2,000 years. It is also the only African country to which the Old Testament consistently makes positive reference. In addition, the Ethiopian monarchy claimed to have descended directly from the line of David through Solomon and the Queen of Sheba. And there existed in Ethiopia the tradition of an ancient Christian faith.

Due largely to Garvey's vision, Ethiopia would take on a symbolic meaning not unlike Jerusalem to the Jews, Christians and Arabs. But, despite the unmistakable religious theme which he articulated, Garvey was more a politician than a religious zealot. And as noted above, Ethiopia was being used largely because the human being needs 'spectacles' through which to view God.

Garvey was not uncritical of Haile Selassie. He made his view of the emperor quite clear on more than one occasion. Not long after the Italian invasion and occupation of Ethiopia in 1935, Garvey observed that the dilemma faced by the emperor was 'only another example of what unpreparedness means to a people'.[9] Garvey was not only critical of Selassie's failure to modernize Ethiopia, he was also critical of the Emperor's failure to establish closer ties with Africans of the diaspora:

> If Haile Selassie had negotiated the proper relationship with hundreds of millions of Negroes [outside of Abyssinia in Africa], in South America, in the United States of America, in Canada, in the West Indies and Australia, he could have had an organization of men and women ready to do service, not only in the development of Abyssinia, as a great Negro nation, but on the spur of the moment to protect it from any foe.[10]

So while Garvey can be credited with having Africans of the diaspora seek salvation through a vision of Africa, for him Haile Selassie *lacked* this Pan-African vision.

Rastafarianism: A Response to Oppression

It is difficult to determine all the factors which gave rise to the Rastafarian movement, but there are a few events and developments which must be borne in mind as one seeks to understand Rastafarianism. First among them is the history of resistance and revolt against enslavement and colonialization in Jamaica. Second, a pattern of racism on the island granted and denied social and economic privileges largely on the basis of skin pigmentation. Third is the teachings of Marcus Garvey and the impact of his Universal Negro Improvement Association, which attracted a large following among Blacks in the United States, in the Caribbean, in Latin America and in Africa during the 1920s. Fourth, the worldwide economic depression of the 1930s, which was most devastating among the deprived sectors of colonial societies. Fifth is the regency of Ras Tafari and his ascendancy to the Ethiopian throne in 1930. The sixth and final factor is the strong appeal of messianism to many who are oppressed, exploited and deprived. Although the scope of this essay does not allow for a full discussion of all these events and developments, the historical background given here is adequate for the reader to make the relevant connections.

Although slavery had been legally abolished in Jamaica almost one hundred years before the birth of the Rastafari movement, the attitudes of the planter class and those of their mulatto children towards Africans of the diaspora had not changed. Between 1838 and 1930 the masses faced varying degrees of oppression, ranging from legislative action aimed at keeping them dependent on the plantation to outright military repression. This period was one of constant struggles between unmatched forces. The plantocracy had exclusive access to the island's political, economic and legal structures, buttressed by the military power of Britain, the 'mother country'.

The principal sources of conflict between the plantocracy and the masses were wages and land. In their effort to keep wages as low as possible, planters, in close collaboration with the colonial government, embarked on a grand labor importation scheme in the 1840s. But, while this helped depress wages, it did not save the plantation system from economic collapse.[11]

Despite the failure of half the plantations between 1844 and 1854, neither the plantocracy nor the colonial government would seriously consider pleas from the masses for greater access to land. Indeed, the hard line taken against the masses would lead to the Morant Bay protest of 1865, called a rebellion by the local administration. Convinced that the Black masses would eventually become a force too powerful for the plantocracy to control, Governor Eyre used force to crush the protest and then convinced the legislature to give up its autonomy in exchange for more direct control and presumably greater protection from Britain.

While the new administrative arrangement proved to be somewhat more efficient and less hostile to the masses, it never seriously addressed the land tenure system, so structural deprivation remained. By the latter part of the nineteenth century those among the rural Jamaican masses who had the opportunity to migrate did so in search of employment. Some travelled abroad while others went to Kingston, which had emerged as the principal city on the island. In the face of a finely tuned system of color prejudice and an undeveloped capitalist economy, many found the move to Kingston painfully disappointing. The prevailing attitude that Africans and their descendants were inferior and should be treated accordingly imposed profound limitations on their access to opportunities for personal growth and development in an already limited economic climate. The result is that economic and social conditions for them remained almost identical to those of their ancestors. The following observation, made in 1930 by a visitor, betrays not only the observer's condescending attitude, but offers us a glimpse into the nature of the discrimination that the Jamaican masses faced:

> Coloured girls are the office workers and shop clerks and school teachers. In large offices in Kingston, employing scores of workers, practically everyone is coloured; as a rule they are a clean, well-dressed, well-behaved and self-respecting group. Many [are] lawyers, and doctors, usually brown or lighter. Many of these people are as cultured as white people of the same economic status. There is admittedly a colour line or colour lines, but there is as much caste feeling and caste practice between the light coloured Negroes and full Blacks as between whites and coloured groups.[12]

Amid the general practice of discrimination along class and color lines, the 'wretched of the earth' rejected the status imposed on them by an alien culture and looked to their distant roots for cultural identity.

The Emergence of Rastafarianism

It was in New York that Marcus Garvey had his greatest success as a leader, but he also had devout followers in Jamaica, his homeland. As discussed earlier, the major focus of Garvey's message was unmistakably clear. Africa had had its days of imperial glory with significant achievements in science, the arts and state craft, but decay had occurred and with it came the loss of respect for members of the Black race as a whole. Respectability could be recaptured only after Blacks again established and successfully ruled their own great kingdom. Garvey therefore advocated that Africans of the diaspora return to Africa and found a nation. His own dedication to this ideal would cause his name to be placed on the secret security files of the most powerful western nations.

It is alleged that he once said to some of his followers in Jamaica, 'Look to Africa when a Black king shall be crowned, for the day of deliverance is near.'[13] If indeed Garvey made this statement, it is not clear exactly what he meant. However, it was to be taken as a prophecy that had its fulfillment in 1930. While shock waves were going through the capitalist world and economic specialists were scrambling for answers to questions about the disaster that had befallen the New York stock market and subsequently the global economy, a special event was taking place in St George's Cathedral, Addis Ababa. Ras Tafari, the son of Ras Makonnen, who was the cousin of Emperor Menelik II and great-grandson of King Sahela Selassie of Shoa, was being crowned Negus (king) of Ethiopia. He assumed the title Haile Selassie I, Conquering Lion of the Tribe of Judah. This was an extraordinary event, attended by official representatives and journalists from the great nations of the world. When the Jamaican press reported on this auspicious coronation of an African king, there were no doubts in the minds of some Garveyites that the prophet's words had come to pass.

It is quite difficult to accurately establish who the founders of the Rastafarian movement were, but a 1960 study sponsored by the University College of the West Indies at Mona noted that among the first individuals to preach Ras Tafari's divinity were Leonard P. Howell, Joseph Nathaniel Hibbert, H. Archibald Dunkley and Robert Hinds. These men were followers of Marcus Garvey and, with the possible exception of Hinds, had substantial travel and work experience outside of Jamaica.[14] According to this report, Howell had not only lived in North America, but in Africa as well. He had reportedly fought in the Ashante War of 1896 and even learned to speak an African language. Like Howell, Hibbert and Dunkley returned to Jamaica after the Emperor's coronation and began preaching that Haile Selassie was the Messiah who had returned in the flesh to bring redemption to the downtrodden.

It is apparent that the fundamental doctrine of Rastafarianism, namely belief in the divinity of the Ethiopian emperor, was developed independently by a number of individuals who later became aware of each other's beliefs. In the early stages of its development, Rastafarianism assumed different characteristics. For example, Hibbert, who was a master mason and a member of the Ancient Order of Ethiopia for many years, founded what he called the Ethiopian Coptic Church. He used extracts from the Ethiopic Bible of St. Sosimas and created a highly disciplined religious organization. On the other hand, the group led by Paul Erlington was initially more politically oriented. They called for social reform in Jamaica and the right of passage back to Africa.[15]

Because the Bible became widely used to demonstrate that Haile Selassie was the Messiah, the movement became more firmly religious. Among the many Biblical passages used as proof of the Messiahship of the Ethiopian monarch is Revelation 5:2-5:

> And I saw a strong angel proclaiming with a loud voice: who is worthy to open the book and loose the seals thereof? And no man in heaven, nor in earth, neither under the earth, was able to open the book, neither to look thereon. And I wept much, because no man was found worthy to open and to read the book – And one of the elders saith unto me, Weep not: behold, the Lion of the tribe of Judah, the root of David, hath prevailed to open the book, and to loose the seven seals thereof.

Revelation 19:16 is also widely used and is considered particularly important for its simple message: 'And he hath on his venture and on his thigh a name written, "KING OF KINGS AND LORD OF LORDS"'. As the reader will recall this was, in part, the name assumed by Ras Tafari at his coronation.

In 1935, when the Italians invaded and occupied Ethiopia, these prophecy-oriented Rasses turned to the Bible for an explanation and found the answer in Revelation 19:19: 'And their armies, gathered together to make war against him that sat on the horse and against his army'. After the temporarily dethroned King of Ethiopia addressed the League of Nations, world opinion turned in his favor but little real support was forthcoming from other members of the League until it was generally understood that Mussolini, in collaboration with Hitler, had ambitions which posed a threat to the balance of power in Europe. With the necessary support, the Ethiopian monarch regained his throne in 1941. At this point the Rastafarians turned to Revelation 19:20, 'And the beast was taken and with him the false prophet that wrought miracles before him, with which he deceived them that worshipped his image. These both were cast alive into a lake of fire burning with brimstone.' To Rastafarians it was clear that Haile Selassie was King of Kings and Lord of Lords, the conquering Lion of the tribe of Judah who was not vicar of God, but Jah himself, the Annointed One to whom the prophecy referred. He was to be their deliverer from colonial bondage.

Rastafarians, Ethiopianism and Struggles

The emergence of the Rastafarian movement reflects not only the failure of the colonial government to create a climate in which people of African descent could expect just and equal treatment, it also highlights the failure of traditional Christian denominations on the island. These organizations were unwilling or unable to effectively champion the cause of those who were neglected and oppressed. Thus, Rastafarians rejected mainstream Eurocentric denominations and looked to Africa not only for a king, but for a god. It is hardly surprising then that when Howell, Hibbert, Dunkley and others got the revelation and started to proclaim the good news that Haile Selassie I, King of Kings, Lord of Lords and conquering Lion of the tribe of Judah was the Black redeemed, they found receptive ears among elements of the social outcasts.

The author observed Rastafarians and their practices at close quarters for many years, but like many Eurocentric Jamaicans, gave little serious attention to the menacing message which they proclaimed on the streets of Spanish Town, Kingston and Montego Bay, on the buses and later, through reggae music, on local radio stations and jukeboxes throughout the island. The message was eventually carried to Europe, Africa, North and South America, as well as to other parts of the world.

The Rastafarian movement emerged in the 1930s, but it received very limited objective attention before the 1970s. Among the early attempts to examine the movement were two studies: one undertaken by an American scholar in 1953,[16] and the other carried out jointly by three scholars from the University College of the West Indies, Mona Campus, in 1960.[17] Reports on the Rastafarians were to be found in the local newspapers on occasion, but generally referred to raids on their compounds and arrests by the police.

Although the West India Commission made reference to Rastafari in 1938, and in 1943 the census for Trench Town (one of the slum areas of

Kingston) listed several Rasta men, the Rastafarian movement remained obscure for over two decades. Many of the movement's leaders were imprisoned from time to time, yet little was known about the group until 1954 when police raided a camp which had been established by Howell at Pinnacle near Spanish Town. A substantial quantity of marijuana was captured and the brethren dispersed, many of them to Kingston. The study done by University College of the West Indies scholars M.G. Smith, Roy Augier and Rex Nettleford in 1960 revealed that, despite repeated arrests by the police, some Rastafarians under the leadership of Howell had continued to run their own government not unlike that of the Maroons:[18]

> By all accounts, Pinnacle seemed to have been rather more like an old Maroon settlement than a part of Jamaica. Its internal administration was Howell's business, not the Government's. It is therefore understandable that the unit could have persisted as a state within a state for several years without the people or the government of Jamaica being aware of it.[19]

The government had obviously hoped that raiding Pinnacle and the detention of over a hundred Rastafarians would destroy the movement. But from all appearances, the attack on the settlement served to strengthen their faith in the Black messiah and their commitment to destroying Babylon.

> Rastafarians with their dreadlocks roamed the streets like madmen calling down fire and brimstone on Babylon, using the most profane language to shock the conservative establishment. Their wild behavior attracted large audiences and their rhetoric of defiance made their presence felt in Kingston. Although many were shocked by their appearance and behavior, hundreds of the dispossessed began to receive their message and soon several small camps had sprouted in Shanty-Town.[20]

Although Rastafarians successfully presented the message of Ethiopianism, or liberation from bondage, beginning in the 1930s, the closest contact they had with Ethiopia before the 1960s was probably through their relationship with the Ethiopian World Federation, Inc. This relationship, which was a very positive one, began shortly after the Jamaican branch of the E.W.F. was established in 1938.[21]

In 1955 the Rastafarian movement gained impetus as a result of two announcements, both of which received liberal coverage from the island's newspapers. The first was made by a leading official of the Ethiopian World Federation. On 30 September the *Daily Gleaner* carried the following headline, 'Large Audience Hears Message From Ethiopia'. The messenger was Mamie Richardson of New York, who told Jamaicans that Emperor Haile Selassie was in the process of building a merchant navy which would link

Addis Ababa and American ports in trade. She then held out the possibility of the Ethiopian ships one day calling on Jamaica. This news was particularly welcomed by Rastafarians because they believed that deliverance from 'bondage' in Jamaica by the African king was imminent.

Shortly after Mamie Richardson's return to New York, the second announcement, a gesture of appreciation from the Emperor of Ethiopia, was made in the local press. The Emperor had granted five hundred acres of fertile land to Blacks of the West who, through the Ethiopian World Federation, had aided his country in resisting Italian occupation.[22] Not surprisingly Rastafarians dramatically increased their following after these announcements. The brethren adopted the slogan 'repatriation now', and insisted that the government set them free to emigrate to Ethiopia, the promised land.

After the Rastafarians could no longer be ignored, the government and members of the middle class tried to dismiss them as madmen, but this strategy would change by 1960. Not only were the masses becoming increasingly attracted to the Rastafarian message of deliverance, it became increasingly evident that ignoring the problems which were driving the movement could produce unacceptable consequences.

Between 1958 and 1960 a series of incidents forced the local intelligentsia, the middle class and the government to take a closer look at the Rastafarian movement. The first of these events surrounded what the Brethren called a *groundation,* or convention. This event was organized by Prince Edward Emanuel and his followers. *The Star* (Jamaica's evening paper) of 6 March 1958 carried the following front page report:

> For the first time in local history members of the Rastafarian cult are having what they call a 'Universal Convention' at their headquarters known as the Koptic Theocratic Temple in Kingston Pen. Some 300 cultists of both sexes from all over the island have assembled at the Back-O-Wall headquarters since Saturday 1 March ... The convention was said to be 'the first and last' in that they were expected to migrate to Africa their homeland.[23]

Fliers were used to give the upcoming event wide publicity. While the *Star* reported on 6 March that there were some three hundred Rastafarians, two days later the *Jamaica Times* estimated that some 3,000 individuals had attended the event.[24] Many were obviously curious observers, but a large number were people who wanted to leave the island for Africa. Some had even sold or given away their possessions in anticipation of their departure from the land of bondage.

The response to Prince Emanuel's convention clearly indicated that many Jamaicans were desperate in their search for a way out of the system which had created and maintained formidable barriers to their growth and development. But the government and middle-class Jamaicans viewed this Ackee Walk, Kingston Pen affair as backward and embarrassing. To no one's surprise the convention area was kept under constant surveillance by law enforcement agents. While there was no direct challenge to the government, the Rastafari staged a symbolic takeover of Kingston early on the morning on 24 March:

> The city of Kingston was 'captured' near dawn on Saturday by some 300 bearded men of the Rastafarian cult along with their women and children. About 3:30 a.m. early market goers saw members of the Rastafarian movement gathered in the center of Victoria Park with towering poles atop of which fluttered black, green and red banners and loudly proclaiming that they had captured the city. . . . When the police moved towards them, a leader of the group, with his hands raised, issued a warning to the police: 'Touch not the Lord's annointed'. . . The police finally moved them.[25]

There was much disappointment among Rastafarians and other individuals who had hoped to leave for Africa. However, the coming together of so many believers inspired hope. Furthermore, the promise of land in Ethiopia along with the idea that an Ethiopian vessel could some day visit Jamaica continued to reassure many deprived Jamaicans.

Following the convention, Prince Edward Emanuel and his followers were harrassed by the police. Emanuel was then arrested and his settlement leveled with fire. He was later released when the government failed to prove that he was guilty of violating any law. This was only the continuation of an established pattern of persecution. The other events in the series referred to above surround Claudius Henry, one of the participants in Prince Emanuel's convention. Henry founded the African Reform Church, otherwise referred to as the Seventh Emanuel Brethren, at Rosalie Avenue early in 1959 and declared that he had been annointed to be the 'Repairer of the Breach' (R.B.). In the summer of that year the Reverend Claudius Henry, R.B. distributed thousands of cards with the following announcement:

> Pioneering Israel's scattered children of African origin 'Back home to Africa'. This year 1959, deadline date – Oct. 5th. This New government is God's Righteous Kingdom of Everlasting Peace on Earth. 'Creation's Second Birth'. Holder of this certificate is requested to visit the Headquarters at 18 Rosalie Avenue August 1st 1959 for our emancipation Jubilee, commencing 9 a.m. sharp. Please reserve this certificate for removal. No passport will be necessary for those returning to Africa, etc. We sincerely, 'The Seventh Emanuel's Brethren' gathering Israel's scattered [children] – and [the] annointed prophet, Rev. C.V. Henry.

Given this 2nd day of March 1959, in the year of the reign of His Imperial Majesty, 1st Emperor of Ethiopia, 'God's Elect' Haile Selassie, King of Kings and Lord of Lords, Israel's returned Messiah.[26]

Thousands of these cards were sold for a shilling each and on 5 October people from all over the island arrived at the headquarters of the African Reform Church on Rosalie Avenue. Hundreds of Rastafarians and non-Rastafarians alike gathered in anticipation of the departure to Africa. Henry had no plans to support his announcement. He is said to have explained to a representative of the *Daily Gleaner* that 5 October was not meant to be the date for departure to Africa but the date on which he expected the Jamaican government to explain how it would seek to meet the demands of the people.[27] Not unlike the case with Prince Emanuel's convention the previous year, many of those who waited in vain at Rosalie Avenue had sold and given away what few possessions they had. With nowhere to live they would come to constitute a new group of squatters in Kingston. After a brief detention, Henry was fined £100, freed and ordered to keep the peace.

A few months later it was rumored that Reverend Henry was planning to overthrow the government. Although this seemed ludicrous, the government was prepared to take no chances. Police raided the headquarters of Henry's African Reform Church at 18 Rosalie Avenue and found a .32 caliber revolver, a shotgun, over 2,000 electrical detonators, a large number of machetes sharpened on both sides and several sticks of dynamite. Henry was again arrested along with some of his followers. This time he was sentenced to ten years in prison on felony charges.

Not long after Henry was sentenced, his son Ronald, who lived in New York, was reported to have returned to the island and was training a group of Rastafarians in guerilla warfare to release his father from jail. Some of Reverend Henry's followers interviewed by this author years after these events had taken place insisted that there was no connection between the operation of the son and that of his father. This, however, is in conflict with other reports.[28]

The government declared a national state of emergency and launched a massive manhunt which resulted in the capture of Ronald Henry and some of his men, but not without several casualties on both sides. The rebels were tried and sentenced to death.

The foregoing events beginning with the 1958 convention and ending with the Ronald Henry episode gives one a glimpse of the power and potential of Ethiopianism. The climate for revolution has long existed among the masses. The massive support given to obscure but charismatic figures regardless of whether the issues involved were religious or political testifies to that. Alexander Bedward, who spoke defiantly against colonial oppression during the late nineteenth and early twentieth centuries, remains a formidable figure in Jamaica. Marcus Garvey was regarded as a national hero among the masses long before it was made official. Alexander Bustamente was unknown when in 1938 the masses gave him their devotion because he boldly marched in protest against the economic elite and the colonial government. And a number of Rasta men like Emanuel and Henry were able to amass large followings with very limited resources or organizational effort.

General concern among various groups, including some Rastafarians, led to the 1960 study of the Rastafarian movement. The University College of the West Indies scholars who carried out the study made a number of recommendations, including the following:

> The government of Jamaica should send missions to African countries to arrange for immigration of Jamaicans. Representatives of Ras Tafari brethren should be included in the mission. The Ethiopian Orthodox Coptic Church should be invited to establish a branch in the West Indies.[29]

In addition, the scholars gave a clear and timely warning to the leaders of Jamaica: 'It would be a pity if either [political] party failed in its duty to the Jamaican people and the Rastafarian brethren at this time. It would also be disastrous.'[30]

While the UCWI scholars clearly demonstrated that they understood the gravity of the prevailing condition in Jamaica, it is not clear how well they understood Ethiopianism. As demonstrated earlier, Ethiopianism emerged on the continent of Africa as well. Thus, as desirable as greater familiarity with Africa was, the fundamental need was not for the brethren to visit the continent which, for the most part, remained under European colonization. A mission to Africa including Rastafarians could probably serve to demythologize Africa, but could do little to address matters of employment and educational opportunities. And although Rastafarians would have liked nothing better than the opportunity to emigrate to an African country, this was no solution to the problems which gave birth to the movement. African countries, for the most part, were searching for solutions to problems similar to those which the Rastafarians were struggling against in Jamaica. And whereas cultural exchange with Africa, not specifically recommended, could prove invaluable, introducing a branch of the Ethiopian Orthodox Coptic Church to Jamaica could hardly be expected to serve the interest of most Rastafarians.

Rastafarians and the Ethiopian Coptic Church

The name of this church was not unknown in Jamaica. In fact early in the 1960s the author saw a small church bearing the name 'Ethiopian Coptic Church' on the Spanish Town Road in an area called Four Miles. From all appearances, however, there was no similarity between this church and the Ethiopian church by the same name.

In keeping with the recommendation by the 1960 UCWI study, a branch of the Ethiopian Orthodox Church was officially introduced to Jamaica in 1970. Rastafarians and others with strong African orientation attended in great numbers initially. As was to be expected, the excited visitors had varying motives for attending. Some were impressed and became members, but others became suspicious of this old Christian institution.

It is worth noting that the official adoption of Christianity as Ethiopia's state religion dates back to somewhere between the years 341 and 346. The new religion received the blessing of Athanasius, the Egyptian Patriarch who also consecrated Frumentius, first bishop with the title Abuna of Axum under the name Abba Salama.[31] The Ethiopian Church later became involved in the controversy over the nature of Christ, which resulted in the formal division of the Christian believers at the Fourth General Council of the Church held at Calcedon in 451. The eastern and western branches of the church held the view that Christ was both human and divine, while the Coptic Church, including the Ethiopian Church, held the view referred to as monophysitism, that is, Christ is divine only. The Ethiopian Orthodox Church also differs from the Western Church in its rejection of such doctrines as purgatory and original sin, but accepts the Sacraments of Ordination, Holy Unction, Penance, Holy Matrimony, Confirmation, Baptism and the Eucharist. To what extent, one must ask, did Rastafarianism share a common belief with Ethiopian Christianity?

The Rastafarian movement is unstructured, lacking formal organization and centralized leadership. The movement developed around a number of charismatic leaders and there seems to have been no serious attempt to create a central organization. This means that there exists no single set of beliefs to which all Rastafarians are expected to subscribe. Not surprisingly then, different groups of brethren emphasize different themes. And although the Christian Bible is widely used among the Rasses, the only doctrine of the movement which can be considered universal is belief in the divinity of Haile Selassie I. Belief in the casual and/or ritualistic use of marijuana (ganga) as the source of wisdom is widely held, but some, such as Reverend Henry's group, came to discourage its use. Most Rastafarians believe that Blacks are the true Israelites and that the West is modern

Babylon. The belief system of Rastafarians is essentially based on the experience of Africans in the West cast in a biblical mold.

As Israelites, most Rastafarians seek to abide by the Livitical dietary laws. Many also worship on the seventh day sabbath rather than on the first day as do most Christians. In these regards Rastafarians share common beliefs and practices with the Ethiopian Falasha, but they have very little in common with the Ethiopian Orthodox Coptic Church. From all appearances, however, most Rastafarians were pleased with the gesture of the government to facilitate the establishment of the Ethiopian church on the island, but they were not going to conform to this alien institution. The following comment from one of the brethren, which was quoted by the scholar Leonard Barrett, is quite revealing:

> I joined the Ethiopian Orthodox because it's 'fi wi church' [our church]. We had a bishop but we drove him out. This man cut his hair and his wife straightened hers. This was too much and we 'blow him out'. . . . We Rastas now control the church and as soon as we get a man in the administration we will make it our church. Up to now things are not to our liking but 'wi a gwan bad' [we protest]. When the priest talk nonsense contrary to our doctrine we raise 'rass' [hell] in the church and stop him. The man is not a Rasta, so we can't have him as our preacher. One day the brethren asked him if he believed in Jah Rastafari and he could not give a definite answer. We can't have that.[32]

The Ethiopian church has little to do with Ethiopianism; therefore, if it is to be relevant to Jamaica its leaders must understand and embrace the vision of liberation. This might mean substantial changes on the part of this traditional and fairly conservative religion.

Rastafarianism and the Demise of Haile Selassie

To understand the response of the Rastafarian community in general to the death of Emperor Haile Selassie in 1975, we must remember that the emergence of the movement, as argued here, represents a form of cultural revitalization in response to the deprivation and repression of colonialism. We must also bear in mind that since Rastafarians could not see God through the image of the oppressive European colonizer they chose to see him through the Ethiopian Emperor. In other words, Haile Selassie is the Messiah of an oppressed, non-Western people and belief in him promises liberation from the West. The death of such a symbol would, therefore, mean an end to all hope of salvation.

Responses by Rasta men and women to the demise of Haile Selassie range from a simple denial to a fairly substantial theological explanation. There are those who consider reports of the Emperor's death to be another case of media distortion,[33] while others explain that the Messiah is in 'mastic' exile and that many individuals fail to understand this explanation because of a strong Western bias.[34] Despite the somewhat different explanations that can be expected from Rastafarians regarding the whereabouts of Haile Selassie, they all claim that their King of Kings and Lord of Lords is alive. He may be absent in the flesh, some contend, but his presence in the spirit endures forever. Many Christians find this response odd or even amusing, but they make identical claims regarding their Messiah, a claim which was evidently viewed by non-Christians with equal incredulity during and well after the first century.

The perspective presented here on Ethiopianism renders the matter of Haile Selassie's demise less important than it may at first appear. Rastafarians embrace Ethiopia as the symbol of liberation and Haile Selassie as the Messiah. But a distinction can be made between the mythical Haile Selassie who is divine and Haile Selassie the man. For Rastafarians, however, there existed and continues to exist only one perfect, immortal, omnipotent and omniscient Ras Tafari. Therefore, any suggestion that he has died is a demonstration of ignorance. In fact many Rastafarians take this concept a step further in claiming for themselves divinity.

Rastafarians frequently confound their Christian listeners by making statements such as, 'I and I' dwell, or 'I is God'. In essence they are saying what the Christian Messiah taught. 'I and my father are one.' 'If you see me you see the father.' Such statements were clearly meant to be an affirmation of the incarnation. In addition, the Christ expressed the desire for his followers to be one with him. Although many Christians teach about the 'indwelling of the Holy Spirit', they consider Rastafarians to be mad for articulating an identical concept.

Rastafarians discovered the importance of their roots as a means of creating their own self-image and rejecting that which was imposed upon them. They have demonstrated the potential of Ethiopianism as a force to liberate the mind from colonial bondage. Yet mental and spiritual freedom and a positive self-image may not be enough to release one from economic deprivation – a discussion that must wait for a subsequent study.

Notes

1. Albert Memmi, *The Colonizer and the Colonized,* Boston 1965, p. 20.
2. B. Sundkler, *Bantu Prophets in South Africa,* London 1961, p. 39.
3. Ibid., p. 38.
4. Ibid., p. 73–4.
5. Ibid., p. 278.
6. Leonard Barrett, *The Rastafarians: Sounds of Cultural Dissonance,* Boston 1977, p. 76.
7. Amy Garvey, *Philosophy and Opinions of Marcus Garvey,* London 1967, p. 34.
8. Ibid., pp. 60–61.
9. Quoted in Rupert Lewis, *Marcus Garvey: Anti-Colonial Champion,* Trenton, N.J. 1988, p. 172.
10. Ibid., p. 172.
11. Gersham Nelson, 'The Peasant and Working Class in the Jamaican Political Process', Ph.D. dissertation, University of Illinois at Chicago 1987, p. 36.
12. Collin Clarke, *Kingston: Jamaica Urban Development and Social Change, 1692–1962,* Los Angeles 1975, p. 120.
13. M.G. Smith, Roy Augier and Rex Nettleford, *The Rastafari Movement in Kingston, Jamaica,* Kingston 1960, p. 5.
14. Smith, Augier and Nettleford, *Rastafari Movement,* p. 6.
15. Ibid., pp. 6–7.
16. George Eaton Simpson of Oberlin College published the findings from his 1953 study of the Rastafarians in 1955. See 'Political Cultism in West Kingston, Jamaica' in *Social and Economic Studies,* June 1955, pp. 133–49.
17. Smith, Augier and Nettleford, *Rastafari Movement.*
18. When the British seized the island of Jamaica from Spain in 1655, African slaves, owned by the Spanish, fled to the hills and successfully fought the British to keep their freedom. Through treaties with the British their freedom and an internal system of government were guaranteed.
19. Smith, Augier and Nettleford, *Rastafari Movement,* p. 9.
20. Barrett, *The Rastafarians,* p. 89.
21. The Ethiopian World Federation Inc. was founded in New York in 1937 as a lobbying organization to solicit aid for the Ethiopian struggle against Italian occupation.
22. See the letter from the Ethiopian World Federation reproduced in Smith, Augier and Nettleford, *Rastafari Movement,* pp. 39–40.
23. *The Star,* Kingston, 6 March 1958, p. 1.
24. *Jamaican Times,* Kingston, 8 March 1958, p. 1.
25. *The Star,* Kingston, 24 March 1958, p. 1.
26. Smith, Augier and Nettleford, *Rastafari Movement,* pp. 15–16.
27. Barrett, *The Rastafarians,* p. 97.
28. Ibid., p. 98.
29. Smith, Augier and Nettleford, *Rastafari Movement,* p. 38.
30. Ibid., p. 17.
31. Jean Doresse, *Ethiopia,* New York 1969, p. 62.
32. Barrett, *The Rastafarians,* p. 208.

5

Renewed Traditions: Contrapuntal Voices in Haitian Social Organization

Patrick Bellegarde-Smith

The cultured leaders did not realize that the revolution had triumphed
because their words had unshackled the soul of a nation and that they had
to govern with that soul, and not against it or without it.

José Martí

In contrast to the traditionalism of the Luso-Hispanic states, Haitian traditionalism is rooted in a transplanted African tradition, amended by four
centuries of 'alien' rule. The dominant cultural and, by extension, economic and political forces are Western, and their Franco-Haitian variant
comprises perhaps 5 percent of the country's population.

The successful independence movement was largely the work of former
slaves – half of whom had been born in Africa. This struggle of forty-nine
years' duration, known as the Haitian Revolution, led to establishment of
Latin America's first independent state in 1804. Yet the former slaves failed
to hold and maintain control, to establish a 'proto-African' state similar to
that of Palmares in Brazil or of the Djuka people of Suriname. The state
founded by an incipient Haitian elite of former *affranchis* – people of color
owning slaves and property of their own, who asserted hegemonic control
after 1806 and strengthened that control in 1843 and 1915–34 – was pat-
terned after France. The ideologies and the social and cultural policies of
the elites in power were like those of the French *patron*.[1]

These three periods anchor this analysis. But also of great significance
were earlier massive slave revolts in 1691, 1697 and 1757 and their direct
connection with the movement for independence, which started in the

Vodun ceremony of Boïs-Caiman of 14 August 1791 and the general insurrection plotted for 22 August of that year.[2] Makandal, Plymouth, Boukman and other slave leaders were *houngans* and *manbos,* Vodun priests and priestesses. The leader of the 1757 revolt, Makandal, was an African-born Moslem, with an extensive knowledge of medicinal plants, as was Toussaint L'Ouverture. Makandal's sacred mission was to rid the colony of all whites and create an African kingdom. He died at the stake four years later in 1761. The Haitian historian Dantes Bellegarde (1877–1966), who was most unsympathetic to Vodun, wrote that the

> certainty [that Makandal survived death] played an important role in organizing later uprisings. It maintained the trust of the slaves who had found in the Vodun cult a particularly strong ferment to exalt their energies, since Vodun . . . had become less a religion than a political movement, a kind of '*black carbonarism*' whose objective was white extermination and Black liberation.[3]

Vodun remained a religion, but has also had profound significance for Haitian politics even to this day. It became a defining element of the Haitian nationality, as no other element could. The fact that it proved to be an alternative for social organization can be measured by colonial efforts to encourage conversion to Christianity and the harsh policies against Vodun adopted by Haitian elite governments – notably those of Toussaint and Christophe, despite their personal proclivities as believers – leading to full-fledged religious persecutions, such as the *campagne anti-superstitieuse* of the 1940s, whose bases were established much earlier by the Roman Catholic Church, the American military authorities of the occupation forces from 1915–34, and the elite.[4] The 1986 persecutions, in which several hundred Vodun priests were murdered 'in the name of Christ and civilization', were further evidence of the strength of Vodun and the fear it continues to elicit.

Haitian presidents have had to rule either by suppressing or by controlling Vodun. The alternative policy, that of ruling in conjunction with Vodun, did not occur, largely as the result of a colonial legacy of rigid class structure, a linguistic and cultural rift between slaves and *affranchis,* peasantry and elites, that led some scholars to argue the existence of two nations. Ultimately, however, westernization in Haiti as advocated by social thinkers like Beaubrun Ardouin (1796–1865), Demesvar Delorme (1881–1901) and Bellegarde depended upon the formation of new elites imitating French institutions, not just upon renewed commitment on the part of an older elite, which would have been demographically risky.[5] This process paralleled that described by Cesar Graña in which capitalist values could be acquired by co-option.[6]

While most elite writers were faithful to the West, Jean Price-Mars

(1876–1969) led a neo-African cultural challenge, seen by Léopold Sédar Senghor as the genesis for international *Négritude*. But the reassessment presented by *Indigénisme* – largely triggered by the US military occupation from 1915 to 1934, and the creation of a political left by such elite writers as Jacques Roumain (1907–44), was never truly complete, since their links with the peasantry were tenuous at best. This elite 'challenge' to the status quo does not qualify as 'Haitian traditionalism', largely because the class ascription of its protagonists ensured that their efforts would be rooted in Western ideological terms, positivism and Marxism, not in African concepts. The characterization by Price-Mars of elite thought and behavior as exhibiting a collective *bovarysme* may be too strong, but it contains elements of truth.[7]

The thread of traditionalism, pursued throughout Haitian history, did not require a connection to *Indigénisme*, although the latter was significant, particularly if it could lead to an intellectual integration or assimilation of the elite into the peasantry toward a *cause commune*. Interestingly, the ideologies and behavior of both the elite and the mass could be 'revolutionary', though arising from differing impulses. The elite was revolutionary in international terms in asserting the worth of persons of color (rather than people) in the context of contrary beliefs in the West.

The mass was revolutionary in its efforts to formulate the basis of a national culture and ethos. Both could be 'conservative': elite thought, by rationalizing the status quo, upper-class privileges and the oppression of the peasantry; the peasantry, by resisting *imposed* change seen as detrimental to its economic and social interests, as well as cultural obliteration. The one, indubitably would lead to a neocolonial framework in the sense that the judge and jury would be the West.[8] The other is more uncertain of its direction. This uncertainty led the United States to opt for the support of the Duvalier dictatorship (1957–86) to ship emergency weapons to the military government it helped install in 1986, and to help American Protestant groups in their efforts to eradicate Vodun and its priesthood.

Formed in struggle, Haitian traditionalism erupts on the national scene at key stages in history. Otherwise it lies dormant, following periods of political repression and religious persecution. Its persistence, under the circumstances, astounds researchers and is clearly illustrated by the 'staying power' of Vodun religion and the Kreyol language. Haitian traditionalism can be seen as communal survival, resistance to assimilation and nationalism, with portents for social and economic growth and development.

The dates mentioned earlier in this essay are critical to my analysis. The slave revolts of 1691, 1697, 1757 and 1791 were interdependent, and independent of the upheavals taking place in parallel movements espoused by other classes in colonial Saint-Domingue. These revolts hoped to abolish slavery and establish an 'African' state. The African-born leadership (*neg bosal* rather than *neg Kreyol*, creole blacks) was anathema to the white and brown colonists who, unlike their peers in Spanish America, failed to complete a grand alliance. The alliance between mostly black slaves and mostly brown *affranchis* – symbolized by the agreement between Jean-Jacques Dessalines and Alexandre Pétion, and by the blue-and-red-striped Haitian flag – was cynical and short-lived.[9] The Haitian Revolution ended effectively in October 1806 with the assassination of Dessalines, whose identification with the peasantry sealed his fate. This murder followed an earlier pattern whereby the original leadership was also silenced when Toussaint, Pétion, Christophe and Dessalines assumed control of the movement. A counter-revolution in fact occurred, despite Latin America's first agrarian reform by President Pétion. 'Normalization' was institutionalized, and diplomatic openings were made to the United States, France, the Holy See, the United Kingdom and Prussia.

The rural uprisings of the first decade of the twentieth century during which seven presidents in seven years came to power, parallel earlier periods: four presidents took office between 1844 and 1846, and five successive governments were installed during six months in 1956–57. In the first period, one observes the protracted dictatorship of Faustin Soulouque (1847–59). In the second, one sees the dictatorial rule established by the United States Marine Corps (1915–34) in which Haitian fascism blossomed under President Louis Borno.[10] The third period is the Duvalier dictatorship (1957–86). The eight governments during 1986–94 follow a similar pattern.

The consolidation of upper-class hegemony that occurred in the 1820s, during the long reign of President Jean-Pierre Boyer, led to the *Piquets* revolt in 1843. 'The Suffering Army', as these peasants called themselves, demanded that the rich be dispossessed, that the land be redistributed, and that a 'black' (rather than an elite mulatto) be named president. The *Piquets* were defeated, but a legacy was found in an untranslatable Haitian expression, the *politique de doublure*, which came to define the political system in which a non-elite, preferably illiterate black, a veteran of the wars of independence, would 'front' for elite interests.[11] This system remained in operation essentially until the American occupation, when elite rule, sustained by the US military, did not need a façade.

The slow dissolution of the political system may be said to start either in 1843 or in 1859 at the overthrow of Soulouque. Elite historians write that the period between 1859 and 1920 was one long *caco* war of sixty years' duration, in which 'peasant-bandits' fought a more enlightened (some brown, some black) European-trained leadership. These events are significant, since they encompass both a rebellion against the central authority and the resistance to US occupation. That Bellegarde chose to see them either as phases of one struggle or as eruptions of lawlessness indicates why the Haitian elites did not offer armed resistance to the US invasion in alliance with the peasantry, but allowed the suppression of that movement. Upper-class resistance, such as it was, could neither vanquish the United States nor crush the *cacos*, a commentary on its domestic power, divorced from the population. The United States, for its part, would not leave until it had trounced the 'bandits', 'gooks', or 'cockroaches', as the Americans called the *cacos*, and until it had secured the redirection of Haitian commerce towards the United States and consolidated its allies in Haiti, partly through the creation of a national guard, the Garde d'Haiti.

The creation of this constabulary, in the words of American anthropologist Sidney W. Mintz, made a peasant uprising against the central authority impossible.[12] Ideologically, the US occupation had the same goals as France, the Haitian elite, and the Church, including the persecution of Vodun.[13] The reorganization of the state, and the promotion of an efficient military in particular, consolidated power in Port-au-Prince to the detriment of provincial centers. It also reinforced the waning power of the elite vis-à-vis the peasantry, and the westernizing elements in Haitian society.

Peasant resistance to the US occupation had as its immediate cause the enforcement of an old law that had fallen into disuse, the *corvée*, which required peasants to supply gratis several days of labor per year for road construction. The *corvée* rapidly degenerated into forced labor, and the peasants felt, with some justification, that the whites were reinstituting slavery. Together with US agribusiness efforts to consolidate land parcels into plantations for commercial agriculture as had been done in the rest of the Caribbean, such measures were unbearable to the peasantry, who saw *corvée* and plantation as symbols of the dissolution of the highest achievements of the Haitian Revolution, the conversion from plantation to small landholdings, from slave to peasant.

In response to guerrilla warfare in the countryside, US reprisals were swift and drastic. That as many as 50,000 Haitian peasants may have died during the US occupation can be inferred from statistical evidence. As many as 600,000 peasants out of a population of 2 million may have left the country for US plantations in Cuba and the Dominican Republic as a result of land pressure, financial inducements and US massacres. The rebellion against US occupation may have involved one-fifth of the population.[14] Stringent policies were devised to suppress it: concentration camps, torture, forced labor, religious persecution. Vodun was to be eliminated, 'not only because it was a religion of the devil, but because it was immoral and uncivilized. Besides, it complicated the struggle against the *cacos*.'[15]

As usual, the military authorities saw the connection between politics and religion, the increased agribusiness and rebellion, even when these elements did not inform the analysis of social scientists.[16] To the economic dimension, a political element was added by the *cacos:* 'to overthrow the invaders into the ocean, and liberate the country'. This resurgence of nationalism and anti-Americanism was 'due directly to bad administration and to the cruelty of Marine Corps officers'.[17]

The entire leadership of the rebellion came from the peasantry: some were 'middle peasants' – for the lack of a better term – who formed a sort of rural middle class, and whose leadership was widely accepted by other peasants, while 'Dartiguenave [the US-sponsored president] would not live a day without [US] military protection', as an American officer testified.[18] The American writer James McCrocklin underlined the extraordinary stability of the rebellion and its rapid spread through the countryside.[19]

The two principal leaders of the insurrection were Charlemagne Péralt, (1885–1919) and Benoît Batraville, (circa. 1888–1920), *paysans aisés*. The first had occupied civil and military positions, while the second had been a school teacher. There is some evidence that both men were Vodun devotees, if not *houngans*. At any rate, their following thought so, and followed their lead enthusiastically based on the premise (and promise) of Vodun: these men were clearly seen as messiahs.[20] Both were murdered by US troops under conditions of high drama. However, American authors would write that the movement was sheer banditry, and that the peasants had been coerced into joining.

The *cacos* were defeated in 1920, and except for a resurgence in 1929 in southern Haiti, they were essentially eliminated. The peasantry had experienced a steady deterioration in both its economic life and its political clout since the early part of the nineteenth century: the revolts, indicating dissatisfaction, albeit without a 'plan', were attempts to provide solutions.[21] Instability in Haiti was, perhaps, not so much the result of stagnation as of a certain dynamism, resulting from an interaction between the polity, the economy, the political system, the class structure and exogenous factors.

The struggle between the dominant Franco-Haitian and the subordinate Afro-Haitian constructs and intellectual paradigms, part of the colonial legacy, has been relived by every generation. It has been too simplistically analyzed as the 'color question'. Color does play a role, but it is a 'shorthand' term for class and cultural differences. Some elements of a reassessment of this question occurred in the emergence of a middle class from the educational reforms of the 1920s, the *Indigénisme* of the 1930s and the socialist alternatives of the 1940s. These movements constituted a middle-class challenge to upper-class political power, as seen in the so-called 'revolutions' of 1946 and 1957, the governments of Estimé (center left) and Duvalier (extreme right). They argued that they were the vanguard of the peasantry, and they did achieve an 'opening' of the political system, at least for the middle class. The anguished cry of an upper-class ideologue: 'que deviendrait un îlot Dahoméen au coeur des Amériques?' [What would become of a Dahomean islet in the heart of the Americas?] articulated the international and domestic dilemmas.[22] Although addressing a power struggle between the upper and middle classes, all part of the elite, it prophetically announced the widening of the circle to include the peasantry.

The movement leading to the overthrow of the Duvalier dictatorship in February 1986 arose from the peasantry, spearheaded by the Vodun hierarchy. Though the Roman Catholic 'base communities', sectors of the army and foreign pressure are elements of the equation that need further research, it now appears that Vodun communities in Gonaives and elsewhere played the preponderant role. Therefore, one cannot merely say that the peasantry awoke from its customary lethargy: rather, as we have seen, such uprisings have been an essential feature of Haitian history.

Notes

1. *Patron* means both 'boss' and 'pattern' in the French language. The *jeu de mots* is deliberate here.

2. The number 22 seems to have a marked significance in Vodun numerology, and many events are made to occur on that date.

3. D. Bellegarde, *Histoire du peuple haïtien*, Port-au-Prince 1953, p. 59. 'Carbonarism' refers to a secret Italian society that met in the woods in the early nineteenth century to plot that country's unification.

4. See for instance, Mgr J.M. Jan, *Collecta*, Port-au-Prince 1955, and John H. Craige, *Cannibal Cousins*, New York 1934.

5. See P. Bellegarde-Smith, *In the Shadow of Powers: Dantes Bellegarde in Haitian Social Thought*, Atlantic Highlands, N.J. 1985.

6. Cesar Graña, *Bohemian Versus Bourgeois*, New York 1964, p. 107.

7. From Gustave Flaubert, *Madam Bovary*, Paris 1857: Emma Bovary pretends to be what she is not.

8. See P. Bellegarde-Smith, 'Race, Class, Ideology: Haitian Ideologies for Underdevelopment, 1806–1934', AIM, Occasional Papers 32, 1982.

9. This is the elite version of the creation of the flag; the peasantry has always assumed a much different significance to the colors based on Vodun color esoterism.

10. For an excellent study on these matters, see Rayford W. Logan, *The Diplomatic Relations of the United States with Haiti, 1776–1891*, Chapel Hill, N.C. 1941.

11. *Doublure* in French means the lining in a garment.

12. Sidney W. Mintz, 'Introduction', in James G. Leyburn, *The Haitian People*, New Haven, Conn. 1966 [1941], p. xvii.

13. In addition to the sources listed in note 4, see Suzy Castor, *La Ocupacion norteamericana de Haiti y sus consecuencias, 1915–1934*, Mexico City 1971, and Brenda Gayle Plummer, 'Black and White in the Caribbean: Haitian–American Relations, 1902–1934', Ph.D. thesis, Cornell University, 1981.

14. See the excellent work by Hans Schmidt, *The United States Occupation of Haiti, 1915–1934*, New Brunswick, N.J. 1971, Roger Gaillard, *Les Blancs débarquent*, Port-au-Prince 1973–83, and Kethly Millet, *Les Paysana haitiens et l'occupation Americaine, 1915–1930*, Montreal 1978.

15. John Dryer Kuser, *Haiti, Its Dawn of Progress after Years in a Night of Revolution*, Westport, Conn. 1921, cited by Millet, *Les Paysana Haitiens*, p. 70. Italics mine.

16. For more details see P. Bellegarde-Smith, 'The Peasant-Patriots: Haitian Resistance to United States Intervention; Preliminary Notes', unpublished paper delivered at the XII International Congress, Latin American Studies Association (LASA), 18 April 1985, Albuquerque, New Mexico.

17. US Congress, *Inquiry into the Occupation and Administration of Haiti and Santo Domingo. Hearings before a Select Committee on Haiti and Santo Domingo,* United States Senate, 67th Congress, 1st session, Washington, D.C. 1922, p. 183.

18. U.S.M.C. Commandant Lejeune to Secretary of the Navy Daniels, 1920, cited in Plummer, 'Black and White', pp. 591–2; *Hearings* hereafter.

19. James McCrocklin, *Garde d'Haiti, 1915–1934*, Annapolis, Md. 1956, p. 107.

20. See *Hearings,* p. 603, and Craige, *Cannibal Cousins*, pp. 64–5. The evidence holds despite what may be some self-serving exaggerations by Marine officers.

21. Celso Furtado, cited in Richard P. Schaedel, ed. *Research and Resources of Haiti*, New York 1969, p. 14.

22. D. Bellegarde, *Haiti et ses problèmes*, Montreal 1941, p. 17.

6

Sounds Authentic: Black Music, Ethnicity, and the Challenge of a *Changing* Same

Paul Gilroy

My nationality
is reality
Kool G Rap

Since the mid-nineteenth century a country's music has become
a political ideology by stressing national characteristics, appearing as a
representative of the nation, and everywhere confirming the national
principle ... Yet music, more than any other artistic medium, expresses
the national principle's antimonies as well.

T. W. Adorno

The basic labours of archaeological reconstruction and periodisation aside,
working on the contemporary forms of Black expressive culture involves
struggling with one problem in particular. It is the puzzle of what analytic
status should be given to variation within Black communities and between
Black culture. The tensions produced by attempts to compare or evaluate
differing Black cultural formations can be summed up in the following
question: How are we to think critically about artistic products and aesthetic codes which, though they may be traceable back to one distinct location, have been somehow changed either by the passage of time or by their
displacement, relocation or dissemination through wider networks of communication and cultural exchange? This question serves as a receptacle for
several even more awkward issues. They include the unity and differentiation of the creative Black self, the vexed matter of Black particularity and
the role of cultural expression in its formation and reproduction. These
problems are especially acute because Black thinkers have been unable to

appeal to the authoritative narratives of psychoanalysis as a means to ground the cross-cultural aspirations of their theories. With a few noble exceptions, critical accounts of the dynamics of Black subordination and resistance have been doggedly monocultural, national and ethnocentric.

The transnational structures which brought the Black Atlantic world into being have themselves developed and now articulate its myriad cultural forms into a system of global communications. This fundamental dislocation of Black cultural forms is especially important in the recent history of Black musics which, produced out of the racial slavery which made modern western civilisation possible, now dominate its popular cultures. In the face of the conspicuous differentiation and proliferation of Black cultural styles and genres, a new analytic orthodoxy has begun to grow. It suggests that since Black particularity is socially and historically constructed, the pursuit of any unifying dynamic or underlying structure of feeling in contemporary Black cultures is utterly misplaced. The attempt to locate the cultural practices, motifs or political agendas that might connect the people of the Pan-African diaspora with each other and even with Africa is therefore dismissed as essentialism or idealism or both.

The alternative sketched below offers a tentative rebuke to this position, which I regard as a careless and premature dismissal of the problem of theorising Black identity and Pan-Africanism. I suggest that weighing the similarities and differences between Black cultures remains an important element of some urgent concerns. This response relies crucially on the concept of diaspora (Glissant 1989; Drake 1987), which I believe is still indispensable in focusing on the political and ethical dynamics of the unfinished history of Blacks in the modern world.

The dangers of idealism and pastoralisation associated with this concept ought, by now, to be obvious but the very least that it offers is a heuristic means to focus on the relationship of identity and non-identity in Black political culture. It can also be employed to project the plural richness of Black cultures in different parts of the world in counterpoint to their common sensibilities – both those residually inherited from Africa and those generated from the special bitterness of New World racial slavery. This is not an easy matter. The baseline concept of Pan-Africanism, that is, the proposition that the post-slave cultures of the Atlantic world are in some significant way related to each other and to the African cultures from which they partly derive, has long been a matter of great controversy capable of arousing intense feeling that goes far beyond dispassionate scholastic contemplation. The situation is rendered even more complex by the fact that the fragile psychological, emotional and cultural correspondences that connect diaspora populations in spite of their manifest differences are often apprehended only fleetingly and in ways that persistently confound the protocols of academic orthodoxy.

There is, however, a great body of work which justifies the proposition that some cultural, religious and linguistic affiliations can be identified even if their contemporary political significance remains disputed. There are also valuable though underutilised philosophers who have formulated stimulating conceptions of the relationship between identity and difference in the context of advancing the political project of female emancipation (Flax 1990; Harding 1988; Butler 1990; Spelman 1988).

Precisely because some of the most idealised constructions of Blackness, Africanity and Pan-Africanity have ironically relied upon an absolute contempt for the lived complexities of Black vernacular culture in the New World, I want to propose that the possible commonality of post-slave, Black cultural forms be approached via several related problems that converge in the analysis of Black musics and their supporting social relations. One particularly valuable pathway is afforded by concern with the distinctive patterns of language use which characterise the contrasting populations of the modern African diaspora (Baugh 1983). The oral focus of the cultural settings in which diaspora musics have developed presupposes a distinctive relationship to the body – an idea expressed with exactly the right amount of impatience by Glissant (1989, p. 248):

> It is nothing new to declare that for us music, gesture, dance are forms of communications, just as important as the gift of speech. This is how we first managed to emerge from the plantation: aesthetic form in our cultures must be shaped from these oral structures.

The distinctive kinesis of the post-slave populations was the product of these brutal historical conditions. Though more usually raised by analysis of sports, athletics and dance it ought to contribute directly to the understanding of the traditions of performance which continue to characterise the production and reception of diaspora musics. This orientation to the specific dynamics of performance has a wider significance in the analysis of Black cultural forms than has so far been supposed. Its strengths are evident when it is contrasted with approaches to Black culture that have been premised on textuality and narrative rather than say dramaturgy, enunciation and gesture – the pre- and anti-discursive constituents of Black metacommunication.

Each of these areas merits detailed treatment in its own right (Farris Thompson 1983, 1990). All of them are marked by their compound and multiple origins in the mediation of African and other cultural forms sometimes referred to as 'creolisation'. However, my concern here is less with the formal attributes of these syncretic expressive cultures than with the

problem of how critical (anti)aesthetic judgements on them can be made
and with the place of ethnicity and authenticity within these judgements.
If, for example, a style, genre or performance of music is identified as
expressing the absolute essence of the group that produced it, what special
analytical problems arise? What contradictions appear in the transmission
and adaptation of this cultural expression by other diaspora populations
and how will they be resolved? How does the hemispheric displacement
and global dissemination of Black music get reflected in localised traditions
of critical writing and, once the music is perceived as a world phenomenon, what value is placed upon its origins in opposition to its contingent
loops and fractal trajectories? Where music is thought to be emblematic
and constitutive of racial difference rather than just associated with it, how
is music used to pinpoint general issues pertaining to the problem of racial
authenticity and the consequent self-identity of the racial group?

UK Blak

Born and Raised this way
Is a different game bi-culturally
Fresh Direction, new ideas
Opening our eyes and ears.

Caron Wheeler

All these questions have acquired a special historical and political significance in Britain. Black settlement in that country goes back many centuries. Indeed, affirming its continuity has become an important part of the
politics that strive to answer contemporary British racism. However, the
bulk of today's Black communities are of relatively recent origin dating
only from the post–World War II period. If these populations are unified
at all, it is more by the experience of migration rather than the memory of
slavery and the residues of plantation slavery. Until recently, this very new-
ness and conspicuous lack of rootedness in the 'indigenous' cultures of
Britain's inner cities conditioned the formation of syncretic racial subcultures that drew heavily from a range of 'raw materials' supplied by the
Caribbean and Black America. This was true even where these subcultures
also contributed to the unsteady equilibrium of antagonistic class relationships into which Britain's Black settlers found themselves inserted as racially subordinated migrant labourers but also as working-class Black
settlers.

The musics of the Black Atlantic world were the primary expressions of
cultural distinctiveness which this population seized upon and sought to

adapt to its new circumstances. It used the separate but converging musical traditions of the Black Atlantic world if not to create itself anew as a conglomeration of Black communities, then as a means to gauge the social progress of spontaneous self-creation, which was sedimented together by the endless pressures of economic exploitation, political racism, displacement and exile. This musical heritage gradually became an important factor in facilitating the transition of diverse settlers to a distinct mode of Blackness. It was instrumental in producing a constellation of subject positions that was openly indebted for its conditions of possibility to the Caribbean, the United States and even to Africa. It was also indelibly marked by the British conditions in which it grew and matured.

It is essential to appreciate that this type of process has not been confined to settlers of Afro-Caribbean descent. In re-inventing their own ethnicity (Sollors 1989), some of Britain's Asian settlers have also borrowed the Sound System culture of the Caribbean, the soul and hip hop styles of Afro-America, as well as techniques like mixing, scratching and sampling as part of their invention of a new mode of cultural production with an identity to match.[1] The experience of Caribbean migrants to Britain provides further examples of cultural exchange and of the ways in which a self-consciously syncretic culture can support some equally novel political identities. The cultural and political histories of Guyana, Jamaica, Barbados, Grenada, Trinidad and St Lucia, like the economic forces at work in generating their respective migrations to Europe, are widely dissimilar. Even if it were possible, let alone desirable, their synthesis into a single Black British culture could never have been guaranteed by the effects of racism alone.

Thus the role of external meanings around Blackness drawn, in particular, from Afro-America become important in the elaboration of a connective culture which drew these different 'national' groups together into a new pattern that was not ethnically marked in the way that their Caribbean cultural inheritances had been. Reggae provides a useful example here. Once its own hybrid origins in rhythm and blues were effectively concealed it ceased, in Britain, to conceal an exclusively ethnic, Jamaican style and derived a different kind of cultural power both from a new global status and from its expression of what might be termed a pan-Caribbean or Creole culture.

The style, rhetoric and moral authority of the Civil Rights movement and of Black Power suffered similar fates. They too were detached from their original ethnic markers and historical origins, exported and adapted with evident respect but little sentimentality to local needs and political climates. Appearing in Britain through a circulatory system that gave a central place to the musics that had both informed and recorded Black struggles in other places, they too were re-articulated in distinctively European conditions. How the appropriation of these forms, styles and histories of struggle was possible at such great physical and social distance is in itself an interesting question for cultural historians. It was facilitated by a common fund of urban experiences, by the effect of similar but by no means identical forms of racial segregation as well as by the memory of slavery, a legacy of Africanisms and a stock of religious experiences defined by them both. Dislocated from their original conditions of existence, the sound tracks to this African-American cultural renaissance fed a new metaphysics of Blackness elaborated and enacted within the underground, alternative public spaces constituted around an expressive culture that was dominated by music.

The inescapably political language of citizenship, racial justice and equality was one of several discourses which contributed to this transfer of cultural and political forms and structures of feeling. A commentary on the relationship of work to leisure and the respective forms of freedom with which these opposing worlds become identified provided a second linking principle. A 'folk historicism' animating a special fascination with history and the significance of its recovery by those who have been expelled from the official dramas of civilisation was a third component here. The representation of sexuality and gender identity, in particular the ritual public projection of the antagonistic relationship between Black women and men in ways that invited forms of identification strong enough to operate across the line of colour, was the fourth element within this vernacular cultural and philosophical formation reproduced by and through the music of the Black Atlantic world.

The conflictual representation of sexuality has vied with the discourse of racial emancipation to constitute the inner core of Black expressive culture. Common rhetorical strategies developed through the same repertory of 'enunciative procedures' have helped these discourses to become interlinked. Their association was pivotal, for example, in the massive secularization that produced soul out of rhythm and blues and persists today. It can be observed in the bitter conflict over the misogynist tone and masculinist direction of hip hop. The most significant recent illustration of this is provided by the complex issues stemming from the obscenity trial of the 2 Live Crew. This episode is also notable because it was the occasion for an important public intervention by Afro-America's best known cultural critic, Henry Louis Gates, Jr. Gates went beyond simply affirming the artistic status of this particular hip hop product, arguing in full effect that the Crew's material was a manifestation of distinctively Black cultural traditions that operated by particular satirical codes in which one man's misogyny turns out to be another man's parodic play. In dealing with the relationship of 'race' to class it has been commonplace to recall Stuart Hall's suggestive remark that the former is the modality in which the latter is lived. The tale of the 2 Live Crew and the central place of sexuality in the contemporary discourses of racial particularity points to an analogous formulation: gender is the modality in which 'race' is lived. Experiencing racial difference through particular definitions of gender has been eminently exportable. The forms of connectedness and identification it makes possible cannot be confined within the border of the nation-state. They create new conceptions of nationality in the conflictual interaction between the women who reproduce the Black national community and the men who aspire to be its soldier citizens.

These links show no sign of fading out, but the dependence of Blacks in Britain on Black cultures produced in the New World has recently begun to change. The current popularity of Jazzie B and Soul II Soul, Maxi Priest, Caron Wheeler and Monie Love in the US confirms that during the 1980s Black British cultures ceased to simply mimic or reproduce wholesale forms, styles and genres which had been lovingly borrowed, respectfully stolen or brazenly hijacked from Blacks elsewhere. Critical space/time cartography of the diaspora needs therefore to be readjusted so that the dynamics of dispersal and local autonomy can be shown alongside the unforeseen detours and circuits that mark the new journeys and new arrivals, which in turn prompt new political and cultural possibilities (Said, 1983).

At certain points during the recent past, British racism has generated turbulent economic, ideological and political forces that have seemed to act upon the people they oppressed by concentrating their cultural identities into a single powerful configuration. Whether these people were of African, Caribbean or Asian descent, their commonality was often defined by its reference to the central, irreducible sign of their common racial subordination – the colour Black. More recently, though, this fragile unity in action has fragmented and this self-conception has separated into its various constituent elements. The unifying notion of an 'open' Blackness has been largely rejected and replaced by more particularistic conceptions of cultural difference. This retreat from a politically constructed notion of racial solidarity has initiated a compensatory recovery of narrowly ethnic culture and identity. Indeed, the aura of authentic ethnicity supplies a special form of comfort in a situation where the very historicity of Black experience is constantly undermined. These political and historical shifts are registered in the cultural realm. The growth of religious fundamentalism among some Asian-descended populations is an obvious sign of their significance, and there may be similar processes at work among peoples of Caribbean descent, for whom a return to ethnicity has acquired pronounced generational features. Their desire to anchor themselves in racial particularity is not dominated by the longing to return to the 'Victorian' certainties and virtues of Caribbean cultural life. However, in conjunction with the pressure of economic recession and populist racism, this yearning has driven many older settlers to return to the lands in which they were born. Among their descendants, the same desire to withdraw has found a very different form of expression. It has moved toward an overarching 'Afrocentrism', which can be read as inventing its own totalising conception of Black culture.

This new ethnicity is all the more powerful because it corresponds to no actually existing Black communities. Its radical utopianism, often anchored in the ethical bedrock provided by the history of the Nile Valley civilisations, transcends the parochialism of Caribbean memories in favour of a heavily mythologised Africanity that is itself stamped by its origins not in Africa but in a variety of Pan-African ideology produced most recently by Afro-America. This complex and frequently radical sensibility has been recently fostered by the more pedagogic and self-consciously politicised elements within hip hop. The 'college boy rap' of groups like X Clan and Brand Nubian represents one pole in the field that reproduced it, while the assertive stance of hip hop's 'five percenters' (artists whose raps make explicit demands for support on behalf of the Nation of Islam) represents the other.

This political change can be registered in the deepening splits within hip hop over the language and symbols appropriate for Black self-designation and over the relative importance of opposing racism on the one hand, and elaborating cultural forms of Black identity on the other.[2] These necessary tasks are not synonymous or even coextensive. (This issue merits far more detailed treatment than I can give it here.) What is more significant for present purposes is that in Afrocentric discourse the idea of a diaspora tends to disappear somewhere between invocations of an African motherland and powerful critical commentaries on the immediate, local conditions in which this music originates. These complexities aside, hip hop culture (which is not neatly reducible to its Afrocentric components) is simply the latest export from Black America to have found favour in Black Britain. It is especially interesting then that its success has been built on structures of circulation and inter-cultural exchange established long ago.

From the Jubilee Singers to
The Jimi Hendrix Experience

The Hendrix Hairdo, frizzy and bountiful, was viewed by many cultural onlookers as one of the most truly remarkable visual revolts of London.

David Henderson

The distinctive patterns of cross-cultural circulation on which the rise of Afrocentric rap has relied precede the consolidation of coherent youth cultures and subcultures in the post–World War II world. They can be traced right back to the beginnings of Black music's entry into the public domain of late-nineteenth-century mass entertainment. The worldwide travels of The Fisk Jubilee Singers provide a little-known but nonetheless important example of the difficulties that, from the earliest point, attended the passage of African-American 'folk' forms into the emergent popular-cultural industries of the overdeveloped countries. At that time, in the late nineteenth century, the status of the Jubilee Singers' art was further complicated by the prominence and popularity of minstrelsy (Toll 1974; Boskin 1986). One review of the earliest performances by the group was headlined 'Negro Minstrelsy in Church – Novel Religious Exercise', while another made much of the fact that this band of Black minstrels were, in fact, 'genuine negroes' (Silveri 1989). Doug Seroff (1990, p. 4) quotes another contemporary American review of a concert by the group: 'Those who have only heard the burnt cork caricatures of negro minstrelsy have not the slightest conception of what it really is.' Similar problems arose in the response of European audiences:

> From the first the Jubilee music was more or less of a puzzle to the critics; and even among those who sympathised with their mission there was no little difference of opinion as to the artistic merit of their entertainments. Some could not understand the reason for enjoying so thoroughly as almost everyone did these simple unpretending songs. (Marsh 1875, p. 69)

The role of music and song within the abolitionist movement is an additional and equally little-known factor which must have pre-figured the Jubilees' eventual triumph (Dennison 1982). The choir, sent forth into the world with economic objectives that must have partially eclipsed their pursuit of aesthetic excellence in their musical performances, initially struggled to win an audience for Black music produced by Blacks from a constituency that had been created by fifty years of 'Blackface' entertainment. Needless to say, the aesthetic and political tensions involved in establishing the credibility and appeal of their own novel brand of Black cultural expression were not confined to the concert halls. Practical problems arose in the mechanics of touring when innkeepers would refuse the group lodgings having mistakenly assumed that they were a company of 'nigger minstrels' (that is, white). One landlord did not discover that 'their faces were coloured by their creator and not by burnt cork' (Marsh 1875, p. 36) until the singers were firmly established in their bedrooms. He still turned them into the street.

The choir's progress was dogged by controversies over the relative value of their work when compared to the output of white performers. The Fisk troupe also encountered the ambivalence and embarrassment of Black audiences unsure or uneasy about serious, sacred music being displayed to audiences conditioned by the hateful antics of Zip Coon, Jim Crow and their ilk. Understandably, Blacks were protective of their unique musical culture and fearful of how it might be changed by being forced to compete on the new terrain of popular culture against the absurd representations of Blackness offered by minstrelsy's dramatisation of white supremacy. The Fisk singers' own success spawned a host of other companies who took to the road offering a similar musical fare in the years after 1871.[3] (The meaning of this movement of Black singers for our understanding of Reconstruction remains to be explored. It will complement and extend work already done on representations of Blackness during this period [Gates 1988] and promises to go far beyond the basic argument.) I want to emphasise here: Black people singing slave songs as mass entertainment initiated and established new public standards of authenticity for Black cultural expression. The legitimacy of these new cultural forms was established precisely through their distance from the racial codes of minstrelsy. The Jubilee Singers' journey out of America was a critical stage in making this possible.[4]

Almost one hundred years after the Jubilee Singers set sail from Boston for England on the Cunard ship *Batavia,* another Black American musician made the same transatlantic journey to London. Jimi Hendrix's importance in the history of African-American popular music has increased since his untimely death in 1970. The European triumph which paved the way for Hendrix's American successes represents another interesting but rather different case of the political aesthetics implicated in representations of racial authenticity. A seasoned if ill-disciplined rhythm and blues sideman, Hendrix was re-invented as the essential image of what English audiences felt a Black American should be. Charles Shaar Murray quotes the following diagnosis of Hendrix's success by the rival guitarist Eric Clapton:

> You know English people have a very big thing towards a spade. They really love that magic thing. They all fall for that kind of thing. Everybody and his

brother in England still think that spades have big dicks. And Jimi came over and exploited that to the limit ... and everybody fell for it. (1990, p. 68)

Sexuality and authenticity have been intertwined in the history of Western culture for several hundred years. The overt sexuality of Hendrix's own 'minstrel' stance seems to have been received as a sign of his authentic Blackness by the white rock audiences on which his pop career was solidly based. Whether or not Hendrix's early performances were parodic of the minstrel role or simply confirmation of its enduring potency, his career points to the antagonism between different local definitions of what Blackness entails and to the combined and uneven character of Black cultural development. The complexity of his relationship to the blues and his fluctuating commitment to overt racial politics extend and underscore this point. The creative opposition in his work between blues-rooted tradition and an assertively hi-tech, futuristic spirituality distills a wider conflict not simply between pre-modern or anti-modern and the modern but between the contending definitions of authenticity which are appropriate to Black cultural creation on its passage into international pop commodification.

Music Criticism and the Politics of Racial Authenticity

> That [The 2 Live Crew situation] ain't my problem. Some people might
> think it's our problem because rap is one big happy family. When
> I make my bed, I lay on it. I don't say nothin' I can't stand up for, 'cause I
> seen one interview, where they asked him [Luther Campbell] a question
> and he started talkin' all this about Black culture. That made everybody
> on the rap tip look kinda dense. He was sayin', 'Yo this is my culture.'
> That's not culture at all.
>
> *Rakim*

The problem of cultural origins and authenticity to which these examples point has persisted and assumed an enhanced significance as mass culture has acquired new technological bases and Black music has become a truly global phenomenon. It has taken on greater proportions as original, folk or local expressions of Black culture were identified as authentic and positively evaluated for that reason, while subsequent hemispheric or global manifestations of the same cultural forms got dismissed as inauthentic and therefore lacking in cultural or aesthetic value precisely because of their distance (supposed or actual) from a readily identifiable point of origin. The fragmentation and subdivision of Black music into an ever-increasing proliferation of styles and genres has also contributed to a situation in which authenticity emerges as a highly charged and bitterly contested issue. The conflict between trumpeters Wynton Marsalis and Miles Davis is worth citing here. The former insists that jazz provides an essential repository for wider Black cultural values, while the latter insists upon prioritising the restless creative energies that can keep the corrosive processes of reification and commodification at bay. Marsalis's assertive, suit-wearing custodianship of 'jazz tradition' was thus dismissed by Davis as a 'safe', technically sophisticated pastiche of earlier styles. This was done not on the grounds that it was inauthentic, which had been Marsalis's critical charge against Davis's 'fusion' output, but because it was felt to be anachronistic:

> What's he doin' messing with the past? A player of his calibre should just wise up and realize it's over. The past is dead. Jazz is dead – Why get caught up on that old shit? . . . Don't nobody tell me the way it was. Hell, I was there – no one wanted to hear us when we were playing jazz – Jazz is dead, God damn it. That's it, finito! it's over and there's no point apeing the shit. (Davis interviewed by Kent, 1986, pp. 22–3)

There are many good reasons why Black cultures have had great difficulty in seeing that displacement and transformation are unavoidable and that the developmental processes regarded by conservatives as cultural contamination may be enriching. The effect of racism's denials not only of Black cultural integrity but of the capacity of Blacks to bear and reproduce any culture worthy of the name are clearly salient here. The place prepared for Black cultural expression in the hierarchy of creativity generated by the pernicious metaphysical dualism that identifies Blacks with the body and whites with the mind is a second significant factor, one that has roots in eighteenth- and nineteenth-century discussions of aesthetics. However, beyond these general questions lies the projection of a coherent and stable culture as a means to establish the political legitimacy of Black nationalism and the notions of ethnic particularity on which it has come to rely. This defensive reaction to racism can be said to have taken over its evident appetite for sameness and symmetry from the discourses of the oppressor.

European romanticism and cultural nationalism contributed directly to the development of modern Black nationalism. It can be traced back to the impact of European theories of nationhood, culture and civilisation on elite Afro-American intellectuals in the early and mid nineteenth century. Here, Alexander Crummell's endorsement of Lord Beaconsfield's views on the primary importance of race as 'the key to history' should sound a cautionary note to contemporary cultural critics who would give artists the job of refining the ethnic distinctiveness of the group or who are tempted to use the analogy of family to comprehend the meaning of race and the mechanics of racial identification:

> Races, like families are the organisms and the ordinance of God: and race feeling, like family feeling, is of divine origin. The extinction of race feeling is just as possible as the extinction of family feeling. Indeed race is family. The principle of continuity is as masterful in races as it is in families – as it is in nations. (1891, p. 46)

Today's absolutist varieties of Black nationalism have run into trouble when faced with the need to make sense of the increasingly distinct forms of Black culture produced from various diaspora populations. These are often forms that have deliberately reconstructed the cultural heritage of the Black Atlantic in novel ways that do not respect the boundaries of discrete nation-states or the supposedly authentic political communities they express or simply contain. My point here is that the unashamedly hybrid character of these Black cultures continually confounds any simplistic (essentialist or anti-essentialist) understanding of the relationship between racial identity and racial non-identity, between folk cultural authenticity and pop cultural betrayal.

Pop culture has been prepared to endorse the premium on authenticity. It supplements the appeal of selected cultural commodities and has become an important element in the mechanism of the mode of 'racialisation' necessary to making them acceptable items in the pop market. The discourse of authenticity has been a notable presence in the mass marketing of successive Black folk-cultural forms to white audiences. The distinction between rural and urban blues provides one good example of this, though similar arguments are still made about the relationship between authentic jazz and 'fusion' styles supposedly corroded by the illegitimate amalgamation of rock influences or the struggle between real instruments and digital emulators. Similar issues arise in the sale of so-called 'World Music' as a subgenre of pop. Paul Simon's borrowings from African, Latin and Caribbean sources have, for example, been licensed by the discourse of cultural authenticity as much as by simple commercial considerations. In all these cases, it is not enough for critics to point out that representing authenticity always involves artifice. This may be true, but it is not helpful when trying to evaluate or compare cultural forms, let alone in trying to make sense of their mutation. More important, this response also misses the opportunity to use music as a model that can break the deadlock between the two unsatisfactory positions that have dominated recent discussion of Black cultural politics.

Soul Music and Anti-anti-essentialism

> Rather than seeing [the modern soul] as the reactivated remnants of an
> ideology, one would see it as the present correlative of a certain technol-
> ogy of power over the body. It would be wrong to say that the soul is an
> illusion, or an ideological effect. On the contrary it exists, it has a reality,
> it is produced permanently around, on, within the body by the functioning
> of power that is exercised . . .
>
> *Michel Foucault*

Critical dialogue and debate on these questions of identity and culture
currently stages a confrontation between two loosely organised perspectives which, in opposing each other, have become locked in a symbiotic,
and entirely fruitless relationship of mutual interdependency. Both positions are represented in contemporary discussions of Black music and both
contribute to staging a conversation between those who see the music as
the primary means to critically explore and politically reproduce the necessary 'ethnic' essence of Blackness and those who dispute the existence of
any such unifying, organic phenomenon. Wherever the confrontation between these views is staged, it takes the basic form of conflict between a
tendency focused by some variety of exceptionalist claim (usually though
not always of a nationalist nature) and another more avowedly pluralistic
stance which is decidedly sceptical of the desire to totalise Black culture, let
alone to make the social dynamics of cultural integration synonymous with
the practice of nation building and the project of racial emancipation in
Africa and elsewhere.

The first option typically identifies music with tradition and cultural
continuity. Its conservatism is sometimes disguised by the radical nature of
its affirmative political rhetoric and by its laudable concern with the relationship between music and the memory of the past. It currently an-
nounces its interpretive intentions with the popular slogan 'It's a Black
thing; you wouldn't understand.' But it appears to have no great enthusiasm for the forbidding, racially prescriptive musical genres and styles that
could make this bold assertion plausible. There has been no contemporary
equivalent to the provocative, hermetic power of Dub, which supported the
radical Ethiopianism of the 1970s or the anti-assimilationist unintelligibility
of BeBop in the 1940s. The usually mystical 'Afrocentrism' which animates
this position perceives no problem in the 'internal' differentiation of Black
cultures. Any fragmentation in the cultural output of Africans at home and
abroad is only apparent rather than real and cannot therefore forestall the
power of the underlying racial aesthetic and its political correlates.

Elitism and contempt for Black popular culture are common to both this exceptionalist position and to the would-be postmodern pragmatism which routinely and inadequately opposes it. Something of the spirit of the second, 'anti-essentialist' perspective is captured in the earlier but equally historic Black vernacular phrase 'Different strokes for different folks.' This notional pluralism is misleading. Its distaste for uncomfortable questions of class and power make political calculation hazardous if not impossible.

This second position refers perjoratively to the first as 'racial essentialism'.[5] It moves towards its casual and arrogant deconstruction of Blackness while ignoring the appeal of the first position's powerful, populist affirmation of Black culture. The brand of elitism, which would, for example, advance the white noise of Washington, D.C.'s Rasta thrash punk band The Bad Brains as the last word in Black cultural expression is clearly itching to abandon the ground of the Black vernacular entirely. This abdication can only leave that space open to racial conservationists who veer between a volkish, even proto-fascist sensibility and the misty-eyed sentimentality of those who would shroud themselves in the supposed moral superiority that goes with victim status. It is tantamount to ignoring the undiminished power of racism itself and forsaking the mass of Black people who continue to comprehend their lived particularity through what it does to them. Needless to say, the lingering effects of racism institutionalised in the political field are overlooked just as its inscription in the cultural industries which provide the major vehicle for this exclusively aesthetic radicalism passes unremarked upon.

It is ironic, given the importance accorded to music in the habitus of diaspora Blacks that neither pole in this tense conversation takes the music very seriously. The narcissism which unites both standpoints is revealed by the way that they both forsake discussion of music and its attendant dramaturgy, performance, ritual and gesture in favor of an obsessive fascination with the bodies of the performers themselves. For the unashamed essentialists, Nelson George (1988) denounces Black musicians who have had facial surgery and wear blue or green contact lenses, while in the other camp Kobena Mercer (1986) steadily reduces Michael Jackson's voice first to his body, then to his hair and eventually to his emphatically disembodied 'parodic' image. I want to suggest that even though it may have once been an important factor in shaping the intellectual terrain on which politically engaged analysis of Black culture takes place, the opposition between these rigid perspectives has become an obstacle to critical theorising.

The syncretic complexity of Black expressive cultures alone supplies powerful reasons to resist the idea that an untouched, pristine Africanity resides inside these forms working a powerful magic of alterity in order to repeatedly trigger the perception of absolute identity. Following the lead established long ago by LeRoi Jones, I believe it is possible to approach the music as a *changing* rather than an unchanging same. Today, this involves the difficult task of striving to comprehend the reproduction of cultural traditions not in the unproblematic transmission of a fixed essence through time but in the breaks and interruptions which suggest that the invocation of tradition may itself be a distinct, though covert, response to the destabilising flux of the post-contemporary world. New 'traditions' are invented in the jaws of modern experience and new conceptions of modernity produced in the long shadow of our enduring traditions – the African ones and the ones forged from the slave experience which the Black vernacular so powerfully and actively remembers. This labour also necessitates far closer attention to the rituals of performance that provide prima facie evidence of linkage between Black cultures.

Because the self-identity, political culture and grounded aesthetics that distinguish Black communities have often been constructed through their music and the broader cultural and philosophical meanings that flow from its production, circulation and consumption, music is especially important in breaking the inertia which arises in the unhappy polar opposition between a squeamish, nationalist 'essentialism' and a sceptical, saturnalian, 'pluralism' which makes the impure world of politics literally unthinkable. The pre-eminence of music within the diverse Black communities of the Pan-African diaspora is itself an important element in their essential connectedness. But the histories of borrowing, displacement, transformation and continual re-inscription that the musical culture encloses are a living legacy that should not be reified in the primary symbol of the diaspora and then employed as an alternative to the recurrent appeal of fixity and rootedness.

Music and its rituals can be used to create a model whereby identity can be understood neither as a fixed essence nor as a vague and utterly contingent construction to be re-invented by the will and whim of aesthetes, symbolists and language gamers. Black identity is not simply a social and political category to be used or abandoned according to the extent to which the rhetoric that supports and legitimises it is persuasive or institutionally powerful. Whatever the radical constructionists may say, it is lived as a coherent (if not always stable) experiential sense of self. Though it is often felt to be natural and spontaneous, it remains the outcome of practical activity: language, gesture, bodily significations, desires. These significations are condensed in musical performance, though it does not, of course, monopolise them. In this context, they produce the imaginary effect of an internal racial core or essence by acting on the body through the specific mechanisms of identification and recognition that are produced in the intimate inter-action of performer and crowd. This reciprocal relationship serves as strategy and an ideal communicative situation even when the original makers of the music and its eventual consumers are separated in space and time or divided by the technologies of sound reproduction and the commodity form which their art has sought to resist (Gilroy 1982, 1987). The struggle against commodity status has been taken over into the very forms that Black mass cultural creation assumes. Negotiations with their status are revealed openly and have become a cornerstone in the anti-aesthetic which governs these forms (Gilroy 1990). The aridity of those three crucial terms – production, circulation and consumption – does scant justice to the convoluted transnational processes to which they now refer. Each of them, in contrasting ways, hosts a politics of 'race' which is hard to grasp, let alone fully appreciate, through the sometimes crude categories that political economy and European cultural criticism deploy in their tentative analyses of ethnicity and culture.

Some Black Works of Art in the Age of Digital Simulation

> Like law (one of its models), culture articulates conflicts and alternately legitimises, displaces or controls the superior force. It develops in an atmosphere of tensions, and often of violence, for which it provides symbolic balances, contracts of compatibility and compromises, all more or less temporary. The tactics of consumption, the ingenious ways in which the weak make use of the strong, thus lend a political dimension to everyday practices.
>
> *Michel de Certeau*

Hip hop culture grew out of the cross-fertilisation of African-American vernacular cultures with their Caribbean equivalents, the immediate catalyst for its development being the relocation of Clive 'Kool DJ Herc' Campbell from Kingston to 168th Street in the Bronx. The syncretic dynamics of the form were complicated further by a distinctly Latin input into the break dance moves, which helped to define the style in its early stages. But hip hop was not just the product of these different, though converging, Black cultural traditions. The centrality of 'the break' within it and the subsequent refinement of cutting and mixing techniques through digital sampling, which took the form far beyond the competence of hands on turntables, meant that the aesthetic rules which govern it are premised on a dialectic of rescuing, appropriation and recombination that creates special pleasures and is not limited to the technological complex in which it originated.

The deliberately fractured form of these musical pieces is worth considering for a moment. It recalls the characteristic flavour of Adorno's remarks in another, far distant context:

> They call [it] uncreative because [it] suspends their concept of creation itself. Everything with which [it] occupies itself is already there . . . in vulgarised form; its themes are expropriated ones. Nevertheless nothing sounds as it was wont to do; all things are diverted as if by a magnet. What is worn out yields pliantly to the improvising hand; the used parts win second life as variants. Just as the chauffeur's knowledge of his old second-hand car can enable him to drive it punctually and unrecognised to its intended destination, so can the expression of an up beat melody . . . arrive at places which the approved musical language could never safely reach. ([1938] 1978, p. 127)

Acoustic and electric instruments are disorganically combined with digital sound synthesis, a variety of found sounds: typically screams, pointed fragments of speech or singing, and samples from earlier recordings – both vocal and instrumental – whose open textuality is raided in playful affirmations of the insubordinate spirit that ties this radical form to one important definition of Blackness. The nonlinear approach which European cultural criticism refers to as montage is a useful principle of composition in trying to analyse all this. Indeed it is tempting to endorse the Brechtian suggestion that some version of 'montage' corresponds to an unprecedented type of realism, appropriate to the extreme historical conditions which form it. But these dense, implosive combinations of diverse and dis-similar sounds amount to more than the technique they employ in their joyously artificial reconstruction of the instability of lived, profane racial identity. An aesthetic stress is laid upon the sheer social and cultural distance which formerly separated the diverse elements now dislocated into novel meanings by their provocative aural juxtaposition.

Ronnie Laws's recent instrumental single release 'Identity' is worth mentioning here. Produced in a low-tech setting for an independent record company, the record is notable not just for its title, but as an up-to-date case of the more radical possibilities opened up by this new form of the old genre, which demands that the past is made audible in the present. The architect of the tune (the eccentric Californian guitar player Craig T. Cooper) has utilised an ambient style that recalls the oversmoked Dub of the Upsetter's Black Ark studio at its peak. The track combines a large number of samples from a wide range of sources: a sampled fragment from the chorus of the Average White Band's 'Pick Up the Pieces' (already a Scottish pastiche of the style of James Brown's JBs) struggles to be heard against a Gogo beat, half-audible screams and a steady, synthetic work-song rhythm reconstructed from the sampled sound of The Godfather's own forceful exhalation. Having stated an angular melody and playfully teased out its inner dynamics, Laws's soprano saxophone embellishes and punctuates the apparent chaos of the rhythm track. His horn has been phrased carefully so as to recall the human voice trained and disciplined by the antiphonal rituals of the Black church. 'Identity' is the product of all these influences. Its title offers an invitation to recognise that it can be experienced fleetingly in the relationship between improvisation and the ordered articulation of musical disorder. The chaos which will tear this fragile rendering of Black identity apart is forestalled for the duration of the piece by the insistent, inhuman pulse of the digital bass drum.

It bears repetition that the premium which all these Black diaspora styles place on the process of performance is emphasised by their radically unfinished forms – a characteristic which marks them indelibly, as the product of slavery (Hurston, 1933a). It can be glimpsed in the way that the basic units of commercial consumption in which music is fast frozen and sold have been systematically subverted by the practice of a racial politics that has colonised them and, in the process, accomplished what Baudrillard refers to as the passage from object to event:

> The work of art – a new and triumphant fetish and not a sad alienated one – should work to deconstruct its own traditional aura, its authority and power of illusion, in order to shine resplendent in the pure obscenity of the commodity. It must annihilate itself as familiar object and become monstrously foreign. But this foreignness is not the disquieting strangeness of the repressed or alienated object; this object does not shine from its being haunted or out of some secret dispossession; it glows with a veritable seduction that comes from elsewhere, having exceeded its own form and become pure object, pure event. (1990, p. 118)

From this perspective, the magical process whereby something like a twelve-inch single, released from the belly of the multinational beast, comes to anticipate, even demand, supplementary creative input in the hidden spheres of public political interaction that wait 'further on up the road' seems less mysterious. We do, however, need an enhanced sociology of consumption that can illuminate its inner workings and the relationships between rootedness and displacement, locality and dissemination that lend them vitality. The twelve-inch appeared as a market innovation during the late 1970s. It was part of the record companies' responding to the demands placed upon them by the dance subcultures congealed around the Black genres – Reggae and rhythm and blues. Those demands were met half-way by the creation of a new type of musical product that could maximise their own economic opportunities, but this had other, unintended consequences.

The additional time and increased volume made possible by the introduction of this format became powerful factors impelling restless subcultural creativity forwards. Once dubbing, scratching and mixing appeared as new elements in the deconstructive and reconstructive scheme that joined production and consumption together, twelve-inch releases begin to include a number of different mixes of the same song supposedly for different locations or purposes. A dance mix, a radio mix, an a cappella mix, a dub mix, a jazz mix, a bass mix and so on. On the most elementary level these plural forms make the concept of a changing same a living reality.

Record companies like this arrangement because it's cheaper to go on playing around with the same old song than to record more tracks, but different creative possibilities open out from it. The relationship of the listener to the text is changed by the proliferation of different versions. Which one is the original? How does the memory of one version transform the way in which subsequent versions are heard? The components of one mix separated and broken down can be more easily borrowed and blended to create further permutations of meaning. The twelve-inch single release of LL Cool J's current rhythm and blues/hip hop hybrid hit 'Round the Way Girl' comes in five different versions. The LP cut, built around a sample from The Mary Jane Girls' 1983 Motown pop soul hit 'All Night Long', and several re-mixes that extend and transform the meaning of the original rap and this first sample by annexing the rhythmic signature of Gwen McCrae's 'Funky Sensation'. This funky Southern soul record from 1981 was an original B. Boy cut, used by the old school DJ's and rappers who originated hip hop to make breaks. These borrowings are especially noteworthy because they have been orchestrated in pursuit of a means to signify Cool J's definition of authentic Black femininity. The record's mass appeal lies in the fact that his authenticity is measured by vernacular style reviled by the Afrocentrics as pre-conscious because it doesn't conform to the stately postures expected of the African queen, but also disavowed by the Black entertainment industry, in which bizarre, white-identified standards of feminine beauty have become dominant. To be inauthentic is, in this case, is to be real:

> I want a girl with extensions in her hair
> Bamboo earrings at least two pair
> A Friendly bag and a bad attitude
> That's what it takes to put me in a good mood.

The hybridity which is formally intrinsic to hip hop has not been able to prevent that style from being used as an especially potent sign and symbol of racial authenticity. It is significant that when this happens the term hip hop is often forsaken in favour of the alternative term 'rap', preferred precisely because it is more ethnically marked than the other. These issues can be examined further through the example of Quincy Jones, whose personal narrative has recently become something of a cipher for Black creativity in general and Black musical genius in particular. The figuration of Black genius constitutes an important cultural narrative which tells and re-tells not so much the story of the victory of the weak over the strong but explores the relative powers enjoyed by different types of strength. The story of intuitive Black creative development is personalised in the narratives of figures like Jones. It demonstrates the aesthetic fruits of pain and suffering and has a special significance because musicians have played a disproportionate part in the long struggle to represent Black creativity, innovation and excellence. Jones, an entrepreneur, pre-eminent music producer, record company executive, arranger of great skill, sometime Be-bopper, fundraiser for Jesse Jackson's campaigns and currently emergent TV magnate, is the latest 'role model' figure in a long sequence that stretches down the years from slavery.

He is untypical in that he has recently been the subject of a biographical film supported by a book, CD/tape soundtrack and single. In all these interlocking formats the 'Listen Up' initiative seeks to celebrate his life, endurance and creativity. Most of all, it affirms Black participation in the entertainment industry, an involvement that Jones has summed up through a surprising invocation of the British Broadcasting Company's distinctive corporate code: the three Es, 'Enlightenment, Education, Entertainment'. The process which culminated in this novel commemorative package was clearly encouraged by Jones's growing involvement with TV as producer of *The Fresh Prince of Bel Air* and *The Jesse Jackson Show*. But it began earlier with the release of his 1989 LP *Back on the Block*. This set made use of rap as its means to complete the circle of Jones's own odyssey from poverty on Chicago's South Side through Seattle, New York, Paris and thence to L.A. and mogulhood. The positive value of *Back on the Block* is its powerful and necessary argument for the seams of continuity which lie beneath the generational divisions in African-American musical culture. However, there were other, more problematic and even insidious elements at large in it. One track, a version of Austrian-American Joseph Zawinul's 'Birdland', typifies the spirit of the project as a whole by uniting the talents of old- and new-school rappers like Melle Mel, Kool Moe D, Ice T and Big Daddy Kane with singers and instrumentalists drawn from earlier generations. George Benson, Dizzy Gillespie, Sarah Vaughan, Miles Davis and Zawinul himself were among those whose vocal and instrumental input was synthesised by Jones into an exhilarating epic statement of the view that hip hop and Bebop shared the same fundamental spirit. Jones puts it like this:

Hip hop is in many ways the same as bebop, because it was renegade-type music. It came from a disenfranchised subculture that got thrown out of the way. They said, 'We'll make up our own life. We'll have our own language.'

Rap provided this montage (it is tempting to say mélange) with its articulating and framing principle. Rap was the cultural and political means through which Jones completed his return to the touchstone of authentic Black American creativity. Rapping on the record himself in the unlikely persona of 'The Dude', he explains that he wanted the project 'to incorporate the whole family of Black American music . . . everything from gospel to jazz that was part of my culture.' Brazilian and African musical patterns are annexed by and become continuous with his version of Afro-America's musical heritage. They are linked, says Jones, by the shared 'traditions of the African *griot* storyteller that are continued today by the rappers.' The delicate relationship between unity and differentiation gets lost at this point. Old and new, east and west, simply dissolve into each other or rather into the receptacle provided for their interaction by the grand narrative of African-American cultural strength and durability. However compelling they may be, Jones's appropriations of Brazilian rhythm and African language are subservient to a need to legitimate African-American particularity. The promise of a truly compound, diaspora or even global culture that could shift understanding of Black cultural production away from the narrow concerns of ethnic exceptionalism recedes rapidly. The potential signified in the inner hybridity of hip hop and the outer syncretism of musical forms that makes Jones's synthesis plausible comes to an abrupt and premature end. It terminates in a portrait of the boys, back on the block where they ride out the genocidal processes of the inner city through the redemptive power of their authentic racial art.

Young Black Teenagers Then and Now

The times are always contained in the rhythm.

Quincy Jones

Assuming for a moment that most Black cultural critics do not want to simply respond to 'the death of innocent notions of the Black subject' with festivities – whether they are wakes or baptisms: Do we attempt to specify some new conceptions of that subjectivity that are less innocent and less obviously open to the supposed treason that essentialism represents? Or do we cut ourselves off from the world where Black identities are made – even required – by the brutal mechanics of racial subordination and the varieties of political agency which strive to answer them?

As a child and a young man growing up in London, Black music provided me with a means to gain proximity to the sources of feeling from which our local conceptions of Blackness were assembled. The Caribbean, Africa, Latin America and above all, Black America, contributed to our lived sense of a racial self. The urban context in which these forms were encountered cemented their stylistic appeal and facilitated their solicitation of our identification. They were important also as a source for the discourses of Blackness with which we located our own struggles and experiences.

Twenty years later, with the soundtracks of my adolescence recirculating in the exhilaratingly damaged form of hip hop, I am walking down a street in New Haven, Connecticut – a Black city – looking for a record shop stocked with Black music. The desolation, poverty and misery encountered on that fruitless quest force me to confront the fact that I have come to America in pursuit of a musical culture that no longer exists. My scepticism towards the master narrative of family, race, culture and nation that stretches down the years from Crummell's chilling remarks means that I cannot share in Quincy Jones's mourning over its corpse nor his desire to rescue some democratic possibility in the wake of its disappearance. Looking back on the adolescent hours I spent trying to master the technical intricacies of Albert King and Jimi Hendrix; fathom the subtleties of James Jamerson, Larry Graham or Chuck Rainey; and comprehend how the screams of Sly, James and Aretha could punctuate and extend their metaphysical modes of address to the Black subject, I realise that the most important lesson music still has to teach us is that its inner secrets and its ethnic rules can be taught and learned. The spectral figures of half-known or half-remembered musicians like Bobby Eli, Steve Cropper, Tim Drummond, Andy Newmark, John Robinson and Rod Temperton appear at my shoulder to nod their mute assent to this verdict. Then they disappear into the dusk on Dixwell Avenue. Their contributions to rhythm and blues leave behind a whispered warning that Black music cannot be reduced to a fixed dialogue between a thinking racial self and a stable racial community. Apart from anything else, the globalisation of vernacular forms means that our understanding of antiphony will have to be changed. The calls and responses no longer converge in the patterns of secret, ethnically encoded dialogue. The original call is becoming harder to locate. If we privilege it over the subsequent sounds that compete with each other to make the most appropriate reply, we will have to remember that these communicative gestures are not expressive of an essence that exists outside of the acts which perform them and thereby transmit the structures of racial feeling to wider, as yet uncharted, worlds.

Notes

I would like to thank Vron Ware, Jim Clifford, Hazel Carby, Robert Reid Pharr, bell hooks, Kellie Jones, Robert Forbes, Rigo Vasquez and the members of my Yale graduate seminar during the fall of 1990 for the conversations that helped me to put this together. The staff of Integrity in Music in Weatherfield, Connecticut, were of great help to me. Long may they stay in the vinyl business.

1. These processes have been explored in Gurinder Chudha's film *I'm British But* (BFI, 1988). The adaptation of these forms by Hispanic hip hoppers in L.A. should also be recognised. Kid Frost's absorbing release 'La Raza' borrows the assertive techniques of Black nationalist rap, setting them to work in the construction of a Mexican-American equivalent.

2. The field of cultural forces that comprises this movement is triangulated by three sets of coordinates that can be ideal typically represented by Kool G Rap and DJ Polo's release 'Erase Racism' (Cold Chillin), the calculated and utterly insubstantial defiance of NWA's 'Hundred Miles and Running' (Ruthless) and the programmatic jive of King Sun's 'Be Black' (Profile).

3. Seroff's research lists over twenty choirs in the period between 1871 and 1878.

4. The musical authenticity of the Jubilee Singers has been explicitly challenged by Zora Neale Hurston, who refers to their work as 'a trick style of delivery' and a 'misconception of Negro Spirituals'.

5. This apparently serious insult was laced with some fraternal acid and gently lobbed in my direction by Kobbie Mercer. It appears in his 1990 *Third Text* article criticising my earlier attempts to discuss Black culture through the concept 'populist modernism'. My response to his position is formulated here, though I wish to emphasise that his reconstruction of my position fails to represent my thinking accurately.

Bibliography

Adorno, T.W (1938) 'On the Fetish Character in Music and the Regression of Listening', in A. Arato and E. Gebhardt, eds, *The Essential Frankfurt School Reader*, London 1978.

Baudrillard, J.(1990) *Fatal Strategies*, New York: Semiotext(e).

Baugh, John (1983) *Black Street Speech*. Austin: University of Texas Press.

Boskin, J. (1986) *Sambo: The Rise and Demise of an American Jester*. New York: Oxford University Press.

Butler, J. (1990) *Gender Trouble*. London: Routledge.

Crummell, A. (1891) *Africa and America*. New York: Wiley.

Dennison, S. (1982) *Scandalize My Name*. New York: Garland Press.

Drake, St. C. (1987) *Black Folks Here and There*. Los Angeles: CAAS Publications.

Flax, J. (1990) *Thinking in Fragments*. Berkeley, Calif.: University of California Press.

Gates, H.L., Jr.(1988) 'The Trope of the New Negro and the Reconstruction of the Image of the Black'. *Representations*, vol. 24, pp. 129–56.

George, N. (1988) *The Death of Rhythm and Blues*. New York: Omnibus.

Gilroy, P. (1982) 'Stepping Out of Babylon – Race, Class and Autonomy,' in CCCS, eds, *The Empire Strikes Back*. London: Hutchinson.

_____ (1987) *There Ain't No Black in the Union Jack*. London: Hutchinson.

_____ (1990) 'One Nation Under a Groove,' in D.T. Goldberg, ed., *Anatomy of Racism*, Minneapolis: University of Minnesota Press.

_____ (1991a) 'It Ain't Where You're from Its Where You're At: The Dialectics of Diaspora Identification'. *Callaloo*, Summer.

Glissant, E. (1989) *Caribbean Discourse*. Charlottesville, Va.: University Press of Virginia.

Harding, S. (1988) 'The Instability of Analytical Categories of Feminist Theory', in S. Harding and J. O'Barr, eds, *Sex and Scientific Inquiry*. Chicago: University of Chicago Press.

Henderson, D. (1983) *'Scuse Me While I Kiss The Sky*. New York: Bantam.

Hurston, Z.N. (1933a) 'Spirituals and Negro Spirituals'. In N. Cunard, ed., *Negro,* New York: Ungar 1970.

_____ (1933b) 'Characteristics of Negro Expression: Conversions and Visions. Shouting. The Sermon. Mother Catherine. Uncle Monday'. In N. Cunard, ed., *Negro.* New York: Ungar, 1970.

Jones, Q. (1990) *Listen Up – The Lives of Quincy Jones.* New York: Warner.

Kent, N. (1986) 'Miles Davis Interview'. *The Face,* vol. 78, pp. 18–128.

Marsh, J.B.T. (1875) *The Story of the Jubilee Singers with Their Songs.* New York: Hodder and Staughton.

Mercer, K. (1986) 'Monster Metaphors: Notes on Michael Jackson's "Thriller".' *Screen,* vol. 27, no. 1.

_____ (1990) 'Black Art and the Burden of Representation'. *Third Text,* vol. 10 (Spring), pp. 61–79.

Said, E. (1983) 'Travelling Theory', in *The World, The Text and The Critic.* London: Faber.

Seroff, D. (1990) 'The Original Fisk Jubilee Singers and The Spiritual Tradition', Pt 1. *Keskidee,* vol. 2, pp 4–9.

Shaar Murray, C. (1990) *Crosstown Traffic.* London: Faber.

Silveri, L.D. (1989) 'The Singing Tours of the Fisk Jubilee Singers: 1871–1874', in G.R. Keck and S.V. Martin, eds, *Feel the Spirit: Studies in Nineteenth-Century Afro-American Music,* New York: Greenwood.

Sollors, W. (1989) *The Invention of Ethnicity.* Oxford: Oxford University Press.

Spelman, E. (1988) *Inessential Woman.* Boston: Beacon Press.

Thompson, R.F. (1983) *Flash of the Spirit.* New York: Vintage.

_____ (1990) 'Kongo Influences on African-American Artistic Culture', in J.E. Holloway, ed., *Africanisms in American Culture.* Bloomington, Ind: Indiana University Press.

Toll, R.C. (1974) *Blacking Up: The Minstrel Show in Nineteenth-Century America.* New York: Oxford University Press.

Discography

Brand Nubian (1990) 'Wake Up'. Elektra 0-66597

Quincy Jones (1989) 'Back on the Block'. Qwest 26020-1

_____ (1990) 'Listen Up'. Qwest 926322-2

King Sun (1990) 'Be Black'. Profile PRO 7318A

Kool G Rap & DJ Polo(1990) 'Erase Racism'. Cold Chillin 218110

Ronnie Laws (1990) 'Identity'. Hype Mix LSNCD 30011

LL Cool J (1990) 'Round the Way Girl'. Def Jam 4473610

PART II

Contradictory Legacy:

Black Intellectuals and

Pan-Africanism

7

Pan-Africanism as Process: Adelaide Casely Hayford, Garveyism, and the Cultural Roots of Nationalism

Barbara Bair

> This cultural process [of the subordination of the colonized to the 'idea of white Christian Europe'] has to be seen if not as the origin and cause, then at least as the vital, informing, and invigorating counterpoint to the economic and political machinery that we all concur stands at the center of imperialism . . . The other problem is that the cultural horizons of nationalism are fatally limited by the common history of colonizer and colonized assumed by the nationalist movement itself. Imperialism after all is a cooperative venture.
>
> *Edward W. Said*

> . . . people and actions do move in multiple directions at once.
>
> *Elsa Barkley Brown*

In his essay 'Yeats and Decolonization', as in other works, Edward Said has argued that colonization, and the nationalist independence movements that arise in resistance to colonization, must be considered as not just political and economic processes, but cultural ones as well. This argument concerning the recognition of the political nature of culture allows us to recognize that nationalisms, by factors other than class consciousness and social change, are the formulated actions of specific political organizations and economies. It also raises the unhappy question of the complicity of some of the colonized in the exploitative process of imperialism. Or, as Said has put it, the idea that imperialism 'is a cooperative venture' as well as a repressive one; and that 'the accumulation on a world scale that gathered the colonial domains systematically into the world market economy was supported and enabled by a culture giving empire an ideological license'.[1] This latter quandary highlights collusion on the part of a westernized, colonized elite (who become leaders of nationalist independence movements), in effect discounting the experiences of the masses of colonized peoples, which perhaps could be better characterized by the twin realities of victimization and resistance (militant, cultural, spiritual, and ideological) to gross political force and to the imposition of economic and cultural hegemony. However, early-twentieth-century Pan-Africanism, both as a cross-cultural, middle-class political movement and as an intellectual enterprise, is representative of the collaborative process that Said describes. The vision of unity and independence fostered through Pan-Africanism was simultaneously counter-hegemonic in its aims and reflective of the very culture and system of domination against which it was reacting.

The exploitative and racist meanings behind territorial imperialism were ideologically masked by European policy makers through a discourse of social mission or uplift. Justification and realization of this ideological mission were sought through the creation of such colonial institutions as schools, missions, hospitals and systems of transportation, communication and capital exchange. The resulting development of an indigenous consumer culture and of a professional and bureaucratic African bourgeoisie was then used by colonizers to buttress, rather than question, the previous construction of Western culture as the locus of superiority/advancement/mortality/maturity, and thus to support the ongoing 'right' of Europeans to, as Said has said, 'rule, instruct, legislate, develop, and at the proper times, to discipline, war against, and occasionally exterminate non-Europeans'.[2] Pan-Africanism, as a response to such exploitation and control, was articulated primarily by the very Western-educated, middle-class African elite whose status had been created through participation in the colonial infrastructure.[3] Many of these Pan-African theorists and activists (along with their African-American and African–West Indian counterparts) did not question the basic colonial paradigm of 'advancement' – with its components of Christianity, monogamy, nuclear families, capitalistic modes of industrial development, transformation of landholding and international trade – but rather wanted greater control over those structures (and over the perceived benefits accrued from them) by Africans and peoples of the African diaspora.

Garveyism, as one manifestation of Pan-Africanism, is a case in point. Largely formulated by African–West Indians and African-Americans, Garveyism was also embraced by Africans, who added their own meanings to it. In Southern Africa, as in the Caribbean and Central America, the interest in Garveyism took on a millennial as well as a political foundation. In West Africa, the response from the elites was stirred less by Garveyism as a political platform and spiritual philosophy than by the Black Star Line as a Black-owned commercial venture that would counteract European monopolies on shipping and lead to greater African control over the development and distribution of resources in the international market.[4]

The study of Garveyism is also a crucial area in which culture must be considered in addition to political organization and economic enterprise. The Garvey movement did not fulfill its own goals in terms of its efforts to introduce separate political and economic institutions. UNIA enterprises such as the Black Star Line (an international commercial and passenger line), the African Commercial League/African Factories Corporation (the commercial wing of the UNIA, with small businesses in Harlem), the Liberian Construction Loan (a fund-raising scheme to finance UNIA development and eventual colonization in Liberia) and Liberty University (a high school–level educational institution in Virginia) failed financially under the weight of persistent undercapitalization, insider complaints over Garvey's autocratic administration and the cumulative effects of political surveillance, infiltration and repression by colonial and American authorities. Similarly, Garvey's People's Political Party, his effort to bring the UNIA directly into electoral politics, was short-lived. Garveyism in its cultural manifestations, on the other hand, was far-reaching and radical in its impact. In rhetoric, ritual and philosophy it succeeded in creating a powerful narrative of liberation that reshaped the political consciousness of its adherents, reversed white-defined constructions of value and influenced the actions of a new generation of Africans who made anti-colonial independence movements a reality.

In Africa, as in the United States and the Caribbean, the UNIA attracted grassroots members and local leaders who sometimes brought to the organization ideas, priorities and agendas that revised the articulation of racial and economic philosophy presented by Garvey himself. While some UNIA members remained active Garveyites throughout their lives, others spent a brief period of involvement in the movement and then left for other forms of organizing. Adelaide Casely Hayford is an example of the latter. Born into the elite Creole society of Sierra Leone, Adelaide Casely Hayford was educated in England and Germany, married the prominent Gold Coast Pan-Africanist Joseph E. Casely Hayford and served briefly as the lady president of the Freetown, Sierra Leone branch of the UNIA. She made two fund-raising tours of Black organizations in the United States in the 1920s and founded a school for African girls in Freetown. She participated in the 1927 Pan-African Congress in New York and remained connected to an international network of Black and white women activists. Her life is emblematic of the multiple consciousness and complicated cultural roots of Pan-Africanism, particularly of Pan-Africanism as lived and articulated from the viewpoint of a middle-class African woman socialized within the British Empire. The questions of relative radicalism and reaction, of complicity in – or criticism of – colonial structures that can be asked of Garveyism as a whole, can also be applied to Casely Hayford's particular experience. As an African and as a feminist, she added a different dimension to the notions of Pan-Africanism being articulated by Garvey and other male leaders.

Adelaide Casely Hayford: Feminist Pan-Africanist

Adelaide Smith (1868–1960) was born into the elite Creole society of colonial Freetown, Sierra Leone, a mixed society dominated by the descendants of Blacks repatriated to Africa from Britain and from the British Empire, particularly from Canada and the West Indies. Her father, William Smith, was a civil servant within the colonial bureaucracy. His world view, gleaned from the Westernized value structure created through his community's participation in the infrastructure developed by European imperialism, was a microcosmic example of the phenomenon described by Edward Said and Gayatri Spivak: colonialism as a bourgeois revolution, as the imposition of a consumer culture and of an imperial power structure which 'affected the detail and not just the large outlines of life' for the colonized.[5] As Spivak has pointed out, the direct colonial subjects of territorial imperialism were men; 'women accede[d] to it indirectly and through class- and caste-privilege'.[6] In nineteenth-century Sierra Leone, Creole men were prepared for entry into the colonial infrastructure through education at Fourah Bay College or in Europe; women either received no formal education or were prepared to be good wives to these civil servants through secondary educations abroad. By the 1870s, Creole culture in Freetown was predominantly British in detail as well as in its large outlines, with social life framed by Christian churches, cricket matches, choral societies, English-language newspapers, drama and social clubs and a strong sexual division of labor, with a domestic/consumer existence for women and a petty bourgeois work life for men. By the late nineteenth century, this broad outline began eroding as opportunities for socioeconomic mobility for Creole men gave way before the Europeanization of the colonial bureaucracy, producing status anxiety and a new brand of color consciousness.[7] Adelaide Casely Hayford's own life was profoundly shaped by her relational status to men within this colonized society, first as a daughter, then as a wife. Her experience was equally affected, however, by her relational status to women: as a sister and a mother, as a political activist in the woman's movement, as a believer in separate education for girls and as an individual politically conscious of her gender. While the first web of relations allowed her private status according to the norms of her community, the second formed the core of her woman-centered public politics. As a public speaker, a writer, an activist in a number of organizations (including the UNIA) and as an educator, Adelaide Casely Hayford centered her life around the question of women's status. She served as an advocate and personal prototype for a Third World brand of middle-class feminism that combined women's claim for Enlightenment standards of individual agency and rights with ideas of women's cultural separatism and domestic power. Her feminist consciousness amalgamated traditional African values with the ideas of the international women's movement, and was limited in scope by the class valuation and resulting racial parochialism of her colonial background. She thus becomes an example of what Spivak has described as a norm for the emergence of Third World feminism, a feminism formulated by a 'bourgeois indigenous nationalist elite ... making up its object in the tradition of benevolent imperialism'.[8]

Daughter and Wife: Westernization and Alienation

The first half of Adelaide Casely Hayford's life was shaped by her private roles as a daughter and a wife, and by her many years in England. Her family of origin was a large, extended, racially mixed network with African and European members. William Smith and his first wife had seven children; seven more children, including Adelaide, were born to him and his second wife, Anne Spilsbury. During the formation of this second wing of the family, William retired from the civil service in Sierra Leone and moved to England, settling in a community where the Smiths were the only Blacks. Adelaide's mother died when she was a small child, and when Adelaide was a teenager her father married for a third time, to a white Englishwoman. Adelaide was a schoolgirl in Jersey and went on to study as an exchange student in Germany, still the lone Black child among her peers. Her memories of her early family life are class conscious, with happy recollections of watching the adults play croquet on the lawn. They are also race conscious. In her memoirs, she recalls the favor shown to her sisters Emma and Nettie, with their 'light complexion and beautiful hair', and describes her mother, who she loved dearly, as 'dark – a real Sambo', while her father 'was exceptionally fair'. She also described her own position within this color-casting of the family: 'I was a hamite, so was very much left out in the cold'.[9]

As a young woman, Adelaide Smith briefly returned to Freetown with her sister Emma and taught school there. After coming of age in Europe, she recalled these two years in West Africa as a period of 'anguish of soul and disillusionment on our return to our native shores'.[10] They returned to England to care for their elderly and ailing father, and at his death, she and Emma, the two unmarried Smith sisters, were the primary inheritors of his property in Freetown.[11] Seven years after her father's death, Adelaide Smith married Joseph E. Casely Hayford, a distinguished Gold Coast lawyer and a leading Pan-Africanist intellectual. They met and married in England in 1903, when she was thirty-five years old.

Joseph Casely Hayford (1866–1930), a Fante lawyer, journalist, politician and political theorist, was interested in Garveyism in its early stages and was lauded by Garvey and the UNIA. His writings – including *Gold Coast Native Institutions* (1903) and *Ethiopia Unbound* (1911) – may have had an influence upon the young Garvey's thoughts.[12] Educated at Fourah Bay College in Freetown, he served as a principal of the Wesleyan Boys' High School in Accra before beginning his dual career in journalism and law. He was called to the bar in England in 1896. He served in the Gold Coast (now Ghana) Legislative Council from 1916 to 1926, and was the editor of the *Gold Coast Leader* from 1919 to his death in 1930. A prominent, if conservative, nationalist, he was a member of the Aborigines' Rights Protection Society and one of the founders and presidents of the National Congress of British West Africa (NCBWA), the first regional alliance of West African nationalists. He was well aware of Pan-African developments in the United States, and the speech he gave at the founding conference of the NCBWA in Accra in March 1920 included favorable reference to the UNIA's economic program. After the *Negro World* newspaper was banned in West Africa, he continued to obtain it through private correspondence with Garveyites in New York. Similarly, UNIA members in the United States followed his activities. In the early 1920s he was lauded in the pages of the *Negro World* and honored with a UNIA knighthood by Garvey.[13]

The Casely Hayfords left England in October 1903 for the Gold Coast, where Joseph Casely Hayford had a struggling law practice. Once back in Africa, this time without her sister, Adelaide again experienced extreme alienation, feeling no connection to the Gold Coast or to its people and their ways.[14] She suffered from malaria, became pregnant and had a difficult childbirth experience when her daughter, Gladys, was born premature and with a congenital hip defect.[15] Soon after giving birth, she took the baby to England. Although the trip was ostensibly for the baby's health, it seems more likely that Adelaide herself desired an escape from her life in Africa. In 1907 she returned to Africa with her toddler daughter and lived in Tarkwa. She complained of the poverty and rough conditions there, remembering that 'I was entirely surrounded by illiterate peasants who spoke a different language altogether' and that only 'one civilized woman' came to visit her.[16] Clearly oriented to a Eurocentric middle-class world view, she felt little identification with Africa or with African women, attributing the language barrier that existed between them to the peasant African women's lack of English education rather than to her own ignorance of their culture. She soon became pregnant for a second time and left with Gladys to have the baby in England. The infant was stillborn during the voyage; Adelaide continued on to England and enrolled her young daughter in school there. While she felt isolated and miserable in the Gold Coast, in England she became actively involved in middle-class charity work, church activities, and public speaking.[17]

Adelaide made a third attempt to adjust to married life in Africa ca. 1913–14, when she returned to live in Cape Coast while her husband practiced law in Sekondi. After a short time trying this arrangement, they agreed to a separation. She left him in May 1914 and joined her sisters in Freetown. The Casely Hayfords never formally divorced. Their marriage endured as a legal entity until Joseph's death in August 1930, and Adelaide spent much of the intervening years bitter over his lack of financial support for her and his daughter. On the first anniversary of his death, she wrote to an English acquaintance that 'I was married for 27 years and have been a neglected widow for 23'.[18]

The causes of the differences between Joseph and Adelaide Casely Hayford can only be surmised. Her biographer, Adelaide Cromwell, has conjectured that because Joseph Casely Hayford and his brothers had a reputation as philanderers, and many Gold Coast elites continued African kinship patterns of serial or polygamous marriage, one primary problem may have been Adelaide's resentment of her husband's sexual infidelity, in combination with her own Anglicized inability to accept the basic parameters of life as he led it. Rina Okonkwo has raised the issue of Adelaide Casely Hayford's relatively advanced age at marriage as an indication of her extremely independent personality. The account of the break-up given by Adelaide Casely Hayford's acquaintance, Anna Melissa Graves, supports this view. She surmised that 'the truth was probably that both were dominating characters and neither could bear the other's domination. At any rate Mrs. Hayford felt that she could not live with her husband and left.'[19]

Adelaide Casely Hayford's early life as a daughter and a wife illustrates the fact of kinship as an economic as well as a social relation; in Casely Hayford's situation, both roles served to reinforce her middle-class status, which in an African context was a Creole caste-status as well. The condition of dependency on male kin for support also underlined the consumer/privatized status of women under colonization and emphasized the cultural gulf between Westernized, urban, middle-class, mixed-race Africans and rural, nonwesternized Africans. However, the personal politics of Adelaide Casely Hayford's life had roots in precolonial African mores as well as in middle-class European norms.

Filomina Chioma Steady has identified the roots of African feminism in precolonial patterns of 'parallel autonomy, communalism, and cooperation' in which 'men and women in traditional African societies had spheres of autonomy – in economic, social, ritual, and political terms', performed productive work according to a sexual division of labor and placed a high value upon strategies of survival. Women, as cowives within polygamous systems, 'developed strong bonds with other women', shared child-raising responsibilities and work flow, and greatly valued motherhood. Childbirth was not only essential as part of the mode of survival, but 'a woman's role in reproduction often received supreme symbolic value' as the means by which culture and communal continuity were perpetuated. Sexual difference between women and men was viewed as complementary, with women balancing self-reliance and leadership within their own sphere in cooperation with men.[20]

Karen Sacks has used the kinship terms of 'sister' and 'wife' to encapsulate the kind of dual nature of African women's power before colonialism that Steady describes. In precolonial societies such as the ones Steady refers to, a wife was simultaneously a sister, defined by Sacks as a producer who acts in concert with other women as an 'owner, a decision-maker among others of the corporation, and a person who controls her own sexuality'. Sacks concurs that in the dual-sex political systems of precolonial villages, women and men operated with relative autonomy within their sex-segregated realms. She notes that in the precolonial context,

> one can speak of each sex being independently stratified and in control of its own sphere of authority. Men's authority derived ultimately from their place in the corporate patrilineal organization; women's from their association with other women through marital residence, from their lineage, and from trading cooperation.

In class-based societies, such as those imposed by colonialism, women's status is popularly assumed to be subsumed in the wife role, defined by Sacks as 'a subordinate in much the way Engels (1891) asserted for wives in families based on private property', whose primary task is the reproduction of class through childbearing.[21] Gayatri Spivak, in reference to Foucault and Chatterjee, has traced a similar narrowing of the sources of women's power within territorial colonialism, wherein the colonial state seeks to supplant communal forms of power (in which 'tribe, clan, kinship, affinity, consanguinity provide the sustaining underpinning of the flow of power') with bourgeois forms (in which women's status is derived from male upward class mobility and through her own individualism).[22] A purely privatized vision of colonial women obtaining status through male relations is inaccurate, however, for the majority of non-middle-class women who were peasants or working class, fulfilling both domestic roles of wife/mother and active roles in agricultural production, trade or the wage-work force. As both Steady and Sacks have pointed out, the imposition of a colonial economy actually subverted (rather than reinforced) the wife role for many peasant women because men became separated from village life through participation in migrant labor forces, in effect making the primary relationships of the women left behind those of sister and mother.

Recognition of the cultural retention of precolonial communal norms within the 'bourgeois revolution' of colonized societies is important. The dual-sex or parallel autonomy systems that Sacks and Steady describe as characterizing precolonial African life have their echoes, for example, in the twentieth-century organization of the Garvey movement, with its separate, largely autonomous hierarchies of women and men; with its very high valuation of motherhood and male–female complementarity as the means of unity and survival of the race; and with the dual role of Garveyite women as political and personal helpmates to husbands (wives) and as woman-centered activists in ladies' divisions and women's auxiliaries (sisters). They also have their parallels in Adelaide Casely Hayford's life. At first glance, Adelaide Casely Hayford would seem to have conceded completely to the modernization model offered by colonialism, spurning African modes of communalism in favor of bourgeois determinants of women's status. However, it was ultimately sisterhood, and not her status as a wife, which was the main determinant of her political outlook. Her communalist devotion to the construction of separate institutions for women, along with her individualistic arguments that women should play important roles in the bourgeois public sphere and employment sectors previously reserved for men, attracted her to the Garvey movement and led her along the path to cultural nationalism.

In the immediate sense, Adelaide Casely Hayford gained the status of wife and mother through her marriage to Joseph Casely Hayford. By leaving him, she lost the economic privileges/support she felt to be her due within a bourgeois contract; however, she also gained independence from the duties and obligations of the wifely role and greater autonomy to focus on sister/mother functions.[23]

Sisterhood and Self-Respect:
Feminist Pan-Africanism

Female Education and Involvement in the UNIA

When Adelaide Casely Hayford left her husband and returned to Freetown with her young daughter in the spring of 1914, she became a music teacher at the Annie Walsh Memorial School, where she had volunteered years before. In addition to finding work, she also became active in community affairs, much as she had been in England. Soon after her arrival she spoke at the Wesleyan church on 'the Rights of Women and Christian Marriage' and thereafter made 'frequent public addresses' in women's forums, including a talk to the Ladies Pastoral Aid Association on the 'social troubles in the family, industrial troubles (labor vs. capital), economic war (war between producers and consumers); disease, health problems and finally racial war'.[24]

By October 1919, she was president of the local YWCA and was teaching YWCA classes for young women along with her niece Kathleen Easmon.[25] During this period of her involvement in the YWCA, she also became a member of the local Freetown branch of the UNIA. There is no direct documentation of Casely Hayford's reasons for becoming a leader in the UNIA; however, her membership coincided with her desire to start a school for girls with a curriculum that stressed many of the same elements that were central to the educational program of Garveyism. Garvey had begun the UNIA as a benevolent association in Jamaica, with plans to begin an industrial training school for Blacks in the West Indies on the model of Booker T. Washington's Tuskegee Institute. When he traveled to the United States to raise funds for the UNIA and its proposed school, the organization took on broader economic and political goals. Although the Jamaican institute was not built, education remained a mainstay of the Garveyite platform. Unlike W.E.B. Du Bois and other advocates of a liberal or classical education for Blacks, Garvey endorsed a combination of industrial/vocational training and a curriculum that would heighten student awareness of African history and an appreciation of African arts. According to the UNIA Constitution, each local UNIA division would plan a series of classes for children, with mostly women from the ladies' wings of the divisions serving as teachers. The women's auxiliaries also sponsored classes, with Mothers' Clubs meetings, Black Cross Nurse instruction on home nursing and nutrition and the teaching of practical arts such as dressmaking and millinery. Women's divisions also sponsored exhibits of African art and clothing. UNIA division meetings and special events also relied heavily on the arts, with choral music, elocution performances, debates, drama events, pageants and dances among regular division activities. Music and oratory were also important functions within the UNIA's African Universal Church. The UNIA briefly opened the Booker T. Washington University, a classroom building in Harlem, and in the mid 1920s invested in Liberty University, a former high school in Virginia that was converted to a UNIA curriculum. In 1937 Garvey taught eleven students in the African School of Philosophy, a training course for UNIA organizers and officers. The lessons from Garvey's training sessions were later made available to Garveyite men and women as a home study correspondence course.[26]

While West African men were attracted to the UNIA's economic program, particularly to the promise of the Black-owned and -operated Black Star Line, it is likely that Adelaide Casely Hayford came to the organization because of its dual-sex structure, which afforded women a separate sphere of influence as well as leadership roles within the hierarchy of the women's wings of the divisions, and because of the divisions' cultural and educational programs. Explaining her desire to build the school, Casely Hayford wrote that she had come to a realization about the importance of appreciating and preserving African heritage, and of instilling the kind of firm race consciousness that Garvey preached to his followers. In her article 'A Girl's School in West Africa', she wrote a critique of colonial education as social control:

> the education meted out to us had, either consciously or unconsciously, taught us to despise ourselves, and that our immediate need was an education which would instill into us a love of country, a pride of race, an enthusiasm for the Black man's capabilities, and a genuine admiration for Africa's wonderful art work. We needed an education more adapted to our requirements, which while assimilating all that was good in European education, would help us to maintain our natural heritage of African individuality, and to become the best type of African we could be.[27]

In addition to this cultural nationalist agenda, which challenged the hegemony of Eurocentric teaching in colonial and missionary schools, Casely Hayford also had feminist reasons for beginning a school for girls. She envisioned that her school would train young adult women for positions in the work force previously reserved for men, particularly as white-collar and clerical workers within the civil service and in business enterprises. At the same time that she would better prepare girls to support themselves as producers in the labor force, she would also obey the class dictates of her own background, planning to train them in the domestic and fine arts in order to make them more companionate wives for well-educated husbands.

Rina Okonkwo has noted that Casely Hayford's ideas for the school grew out of her personal awareness of her need to support herself and her child, and by extension, the need for other women to learn a trade and to foster their talents and self-respect independent of their relationships with men. The educational curriculum advocated by Casely Hayford thus had a compensatory nature: it would overcome the cultural deprivation inflicted by colonial educational systems, and it would offer the same opportunities for advancement to girls that had been previously made available to boys.[28]

By the spring of 1919, Casely Hayford was the lady president of the Freetown UNIA division and as the leading female officer, had enlisted the women of the division in raising funds for her proposed school for girls. The plan was initially endorsed by both the ladies' division and the larger male and female membership. In April 1919 Casely Hayford delivered a UNIA address about the school, telling her audience that the 'purpose underlying the idea of the Technical Training School for Girls was to enable the female section of our country to get their livelihood by honourable means and independently'.[29] Kathleen Easmon devised a strategy for grass-roots campaigning on behalf of the school. Placards were posted in the streets and announcements about the school were read from Freetown pulpits. UNIA women went door-to-door with collection boxes to solicit funds; leading Europeans in the colonial infrastructure were also approached for financial support.[30] Controversy arose in Freetown when news spread that Casely Hayford had approached members of her husband's NCBWA for support and had not only been rebuffed, but reprimanded for beginning a scheme that would compete with the NCBWA's own limited ability to win financial support for its programs.[31] When Casely Hayford contacted a NCBWA member and told him of her plan to travel down the West African coast to raise funds for the school, he 'gave her distinctly to understand that any such move by her would be countered by him: that he would cable to the various centres down the coast, warning the people of her probable activities among them . . . . If, however, she would sit tight for a while and throw in her lot with the Congress', then perhaps 'she and her scheme would be favourably entertained in the near future'.[32] Soon after, the Freetown barrister C.D. Hotobah-During wrote a letter to the editor of the *Sierra Leone Weekly News* stating that the proposed school was unnecessary since there were no jobs for trained women. Kathleen Easmon replied that jobs would be created if there were skilled women to fill them and if the colonial Civil Service was opened to female employees.[33] Meanwhile, a dispute arose within UNIA ranks over Casely Hayford's management of the funds collected by female UNIA members and over the legal question of whether Casely Hayford or the UNIA leadership would have direct authority over the proposed school. In response to these internal politics and the recalcitrance of community members who opposed the training of girls, Casely Hayford resigned as lady president of the UNIA, returned the funds collected by women UNIA members, canceled the fund-raising trip down the coast and made alternative plans to travel to the United States with Kathleen Easmon. Having been stymied by African male Pan-Africanists, she turned instead to African-Americans, particularly to African-American women, for the aid and expertise she needed.[34]

Sisterhood as Cultural Education: The United States, 1920–22

Adelaide Casely Hayford and Kathleen Easmon arrived in the United States in August 1920.[35] They proceeded to make extensive speaking tours of African-American women's groups, organizations, conferences, churches, colleges and secondary schools. They spoke to innumerable audiences, toured institutions, displayed African arts and clothing and produced pageants about the African diaspora that were performed in several cities. Their American itinerary included a virtual Who's Who of leaders, organizations and institutions founded by the middle-class Black women's movement or by male and female African-American educators. Although they arrived in New York City in the midst of an international UNIA convention, there is no evidence that they attended it. Indeed, the trip of these former UNIA members is testimony to their successful networking with representatives of organizations that Garvey considered rivals or enemies, most notably the NAACP and the Phelps-Stokes Commission, and with individuals who drew Garvey's criticism, such as Paul Robeson and W.E.B. Du Bois.[36]

The political liaisons formed between the middle-class African fundraisers and their African-American counterparts were occasions for mutual education. Casely Hayford countered African-American stereotypes about, and attitudes of superiority toward, Africa. 'Having expected to see two semi-civilized illiterate uncouth women', she recalled, her African-American audiences were 'overwhelmed with enthusiasm, especially after they had listened to an address portraying the good points of our down-trodden race, instead of the usual fetish barbaric practices, and devil-worshipping rites to which they were accustomed'.[37] She also imparted her brand of relational feminism, telling her audiences how African women exercised their strong 'maternal instinct' and African men exhibited their 'spirit of chivalry' and asnwering that 'community life had its real birth in Africa'.[38] Casely Hayford left the United States with the satisfaction that she and Easmon had 'succeeded in giving the American Negro a very valuable education as to his ancestry'.[39]

On their side, Casely Hayford and Easmon were impressed by the standard of living of working- and middle-class African Americans. 'We were astonished by their number, their prosperity, their shops, their churches and their homes', Casely Hayford recalled, and also by their use of modern labor-saving technology, especially in relation to women's work: there were 'electric washers and irons, machines for washing dishes and hand vacuum cleaners', even buzzers to open downstairs doors. She admired the libraries, theaters and professional offices of Harlem, but the 'thing that impressed us most was the efficiency of the coloured girl':

> In every walk of life she takes her place beside the man. Now she has the vote she is likely to become a power in the land, because unfortunately the men have misused their privileges, and politics are very corrupt. The women intend to purify politics and have already organized several splendid clubs.[40]

The club movement not only impressed Casely Hayford with its 'social housekeeping/moral crusade' justification for women's entrance into public politics, but with a model for women's ability to organize and to occupy leadership positions with respect and dignity.[41] In addition to their work with women's organizations and churches, Easmon and Casely Hayford visited a number of institutions, including Morehouse, Spelman, Atlanta University, Lincoln, Hampton and Tuskegee. Casely Hayford found particular inspiration from prominent African-American educators Nannie Burroughs and Margaret Murray Washington.[42] Burroughs, Casely Hayford would later say, 'was the most outstanding Negro woman I met in America'.[43] NAACP and Baptist connections led to attendance at the National Association of Colored Women convention in Indianapolis in 1920 and an introduction to Burroughs, who invited Easmon and Casely Hayford to visit her National Training School for Women and Girls. There Casely Hayford found a working model of her desired curriculum for young women, which would combine vocational training with moral instruction.[44]

Beverly Guy-Sheftall has described the curriculum and goals of Nannie Burroughs's school, which had been in operation for thirteen years when Casely Hayford visited it. The National Training School for Women and Girls was founded

> for the purpose of producing missionaries, Sunday school teachers, stenographers, bookkeepers, musicians, cooks, laundresses, housemaids, and other skilled workers. Rigid moral codes were enforced by Burroughs, who wanted to develop strength of character in the women. Domestic training and the art of homemaking were also emphasized.[45]

Burroughs's involvement in the club movement also provided additional access to informal methods of teaching women. When Casely Hayford attended a State Federation of Negro Women's Clubs meeting in Pennsylvania, she was struck by the speeches on 'motherhood, religion, education, child welfare, temperance, literature, home economics, hygiene, citizenship, music, politics, business, young women, public health and athletics' and by the club women's community work with schools and in homes. Like the UNIA's Black Cross Nurses, the women gave instruction in hygiene, diet, food preparation and preservation, nursing, budgeting and child raising.

Casely Hayford was also strongly influenced by Margaret Murray Washington, head of the Women's Department and director of the Industries for Girls at Tuskegee Institute, founder of Mothers' Clubs and of the International Council of Women of the Darker Races of the World and a conservative voice within the woman's club movement. Tuskegee taught girls academic subjects combined with vocational training in sewing, cooking, agriculture and trades such as printing and upholstering. In a speech delivered during Casely Hayford's first few months in America, Washington explained that 'those of us who are teachers realize that our civilization depends upon the training we receive for the making of homes and for the carrying out of high home ideals'.[46] Casely Hayford visited Tuskegee with Nannie Burroughs and was very impressed with the domestic science program, which she described as Margaret Murray Washington's classes for 'brides-to-be'.[47] She felt that Washington's program was an excellent model 'for the uplift of our [African] womanhood' and for instilling the idea of the dignity of labor.[48]

By the end of her trip, Casely Hayford had formed an American advisory board for her school. It included individuals both friendly and antagonistic toward Garvey. Both Margaret Murray Washington and Nannie Burroughs were members, as were Dr R. R. Moton of Tuskegee and Dr J. E. Gregg of Hampton, and T. Jesse Jones and J.E.K. Aggrey of the Phelps-Stokes Commission. Aggrey served as treasurer for funds collected while Casely Hayford and Easmon were in the United States.[49]

Back to Africa

Adelaide Casely Hayford returned to Freetown, where she opened her Girls' Vocational and Industrial Training School in October 1923. Recalling her vision for the school, Casely Hayford wrote that:

> In my mind's eye I could see a school in which girls, instead of blindly copying European fashions, would be dressed in attractive native garments which would enhance their personal charms. I could see them sitting in homes which combined European order, method and cleanliness with the beauty of native basket

furniture, art work and draperies. I could see the young mothers teaching the little children on their knees that to be Black was not a curse nor a disgrace, that the color scheme of the races was part of God's divine plan, and that just as it was impossible to make a world without the primary colors, so it was impossible to make a world without the Negro. I could head the young mothers teaching their sons the glory of Black citizenship, rather than encouraging them to bewail the fact that they were not white. I could hear the native musical instruments, developed on scientific European lines discoursing sweet music in the place of wheezy harmoniums. I could imagine the artistic youth of the hereafter painting pictures depicting Black faces rather than white ones. I could visualize the listless, lethargic, educated town girl of today, through the medium of equipped gymnasiums and trained physical cultures enjoying the energy and vitality of her grandmother who thought nothing of spending days hoeing fields or of carrying a load as weighty as any man's. And then I could picture the sons and daughters of Africa's race 'looking the whole world in the face' without any apology whatsoever for the color of their skins, and with such self-respect as to command the respect of all nations.[50]

This dream of racial pride, moral motherhood and personal uplift through a curriculum based on Margaret Murray Washington's at Tuskegee withered when Casely Hayford failed to attract young adult women into her program. In reaction to this reality, she reconstituted the school as an elementary school for girls. The school was a social landmark, as one of the first African-owned and -run schools in Freetown, and one attempting to emphasize African arts, crafts and music.

The general community reaction, however, was recalcitrant. 'Had I been starting a brothel, the antagonism could not have been worse', Casely Hayford recalled, 'My own people were exceedingly hostile.'[51] The general feeling on the part of whites was to wonder if the education of women, or of Africans in general, was really necessary. 'Why ask such a question at all unless there be a large consensus of opinion against the enlightenment of the African, especially the girls?' Casely Hayford recounted. 'Such was the attitude towards our race at this period, so that I found myself walking on hot coals.'[52] Casely Hayford wrote to an English friend, 'It is quite evident that Sierra Leone educationists do not wish to see my type of Negro woman reproduced'.[53]

While spurned by her own community and treading softly around colonial officials, Casely Hayford also had to adjust her goals because of internal dissent in the school. After young adult women declined to attend altogether, the girls who did enroll refused to wear African dress, so Casely Hayford reserved this practice for a special 'Africa Day' with African history, folklore and songs.[54] The regular curriculum also veered away from vocational training and focused on domestic science and culture.

In 1926–27 Casely Hayford made a second trip to the United States. The 28 May 1927 *Negro World* reported that she had 'spoken before a great many gatherings in this country, including women's clubs, schools, the Horace Mann School, colleges and other representative groups'. Wearing African dress, she addressed the Harlem Committee members on African women, family life, community feeling, poetry and culture. 'My work is to get the women of the country to preserve these customs and all the native beauty of the African race', she told her audience, 'I want them to see that they have a contribution for the world, and to help them keep that contribution, so that civilization will not destroy it.'

During the trip she also became involved in the 1927 Pan-African Congress in New York. She was a member of the Black feminist Circle of Peace and Foreign Relations, headed by the Black Women's Club, the YWCA and the NAACP Suffrage Department activist Addie Hunton.[55] Drawing on the experience of turning to the National Association· of Colored Women as sponsors of the Third Pan-African Congress of 1923, W.E.B. Du Bois approached the Circle of Peace members, who had their headquarters in New York, for help in organizing what became the Fourth Pan-African Congress held 21–24 August 1927. According to Immanuel Geiss, 'This women's group was more or less responsible for organizing the fourth congress; they supplied the thirty-six members of the presidium, as well as the bulk of the nine committees (Education and Exhibits, Finance and Registration, Publicity and Press, Entertainment, Courtesies, Reception, Foreign Relations, Programme, Housing), which had a total of fifty-two members'.[56] Some two hundred delegates attended the Congress, with an overwhelming number from the Caribbean and the United States. Casely Hayford was one of a handful of Africans who participated. Issues discussed at the congress included two of Casely Hayford's fortes, African education and African art and literature.

Upon her return to Freetown, Casely Hayford operated the school until 1940, when, lacking assistance or an heir to her enterprise, she was forced to close because she was too frail to continue its operation on her own. When she prepared a speech on education for the Geneva Conference for the Welfare of the African Child in 1931, it was cultural nationalism rather than women's advancement that she emphasized. The themes of her speech serve as a description of the nationalist legacy of her school, its contribution to the construction of separate African institutions and the concept of intellectual freedom from Eurocentric cultural hegemony. In the speech, which was delivered by her daughter, Gladys, she stressed the importance of not denying native origins, of employing African teachers who understand African children, of using African-written and -produced textbooks, and having 'African-run, African-owned schools'. [57]

Conclusion: Inching towards Independence

Adelaide Casely Hayford's Pan-African brand of feminism was shaped equally by her pride in African culture and her socialization as a colonial subject within the British empire – by the communalism that she associated with the first and by the bourgeois privatism that she acquired from the second. Her pride in her African heritage was selective. While secure in her color,[58] and firm in her praise of the beauty of African arts and the importance of traditional African dress, she rejected much of African social history, including militant nationalism,[59] and substituted in its stead adherence to the middle-class European norms of monogamy, nuclear families, Christianity, the cult of domesticity and the ideas of moral motherhood and of extending female virtue from the private into the public sphere.[60] Her own sphere of influence in Africa, as in England and the United States, was distinctly middle class; she had little identification with or empathy for the lives of peasant Africans or lower-class African-Americans. Her focus of uplift was the bourgeois, westernized, African woman, and she reserved some of her highest praise for the European 'ladies' and 'gentlemen' who were her colonial rulers.

She eventually recognized her own failings in regard to class prejudice. In the last installment of her memoirs, she faulted herself and apologized for her 'tremendous conceit' and snobbery toward 'people of my own race', accused herself of political cowardice and admitted that she had been guilty of wielding a 'Napoleonic spirit of domination' towards others, including family members and coworkers.[61]

Her feminism was as multiplicitous as her Pan-Africanism. While she devoted her public life to relational politics – to the separate education of girls, which she saw as an extension of African communalism, and to participation in the international woman's movement – lauded moral motherhood (at a Freetown Mother's Day celebration she announced that 'the future of Africa depends on the African Mother'),[62] and spoke of the importance of the development of feminine African individuality, her personal family relations were fraught with discord. Her close ties with her sisters and with her niece, Kathleen Easmon, were central features of her life. Yet, as her biographer Adelaide Cromwell has pointed out, her public image as the wife of Joseph Casely Hayford and the mother of the Harlem Renaissance poet Gladys Casely Hayford 'is based on the denial or falsification of her true relationship with ... her husband and her daughter'.[63] Although technically lasting twenty-seven years, her marriage was in reality extremely short-lived. And the strong mother–daughter bond that existed between her and Gladys was forged to a great measure out of mutual disappointment and pain, as the mother wished to foster in her daughter the kind of life of individual achievement and devotion to relational politics and African uplift that she had chosen for herself; and the daughter, in turn, desired to assert her own individuality.[64]

Adelaide Cromwell has speculated that Adelaide Casely Hayford suffered from her improper fulfillment of the bourgeois role of wife, a situation that left her an 'unprotected woman . . . without a husband or son or brother' in a society that defined women through their relation to men, and thus left her open to patriarchal criticism.[65] I would surmise that her problems stemmed as much from the forces that kept her from full 'sisterhood' – from her own failure to identify with peasant and working-class African women, and from the lack of support she received from her own colonized Creole society for the modernized model of dual-sex communal relations and women's power that she had projected. Her intellectual vision of feminist Pan-Africanism, however, remains an important one. It represents one of those 'reflexive moments of consciousness' which Edward Said has described, that 'enabled the African, Caribbean, Irish, Latin American, or Asian citizen inching toward independence through decolonization to require a theoretical assertion of the end of Europe's cultural claim to guide and/or instruct the non-European or nonmainland individual'.[66]

Notes

1. Edward W. Said, 'Yeats and Decolonization' in Terry Eagleton, Fredric Jameson and Edward W. Said, *Nationalism, Colonialism, and Literature*, Minneapolis 1990, pp. 73, 74–5. These points about the cultural nature of class and of colonization/decolonization are, of course, not new; they have been particularly forwarded by social historians (especially in the fields of labor and women's history), anthropologists and literary theorists of the past two decades. Similar cultural analyses have been applied to race and gender. See, for example, Mari Jo Buhle and Paul Buhle's discussion of developments of new approaches to the study of class in 'The New Labor History at the Cultural Crossroads', *Journal of American History*, vol. 75, no. 1, June 1988, pp. 151–7, part of a *JAH* roundtable on 'Labor, Historical Pessimism, and Hegemony'. For recent examples of cultural approaches to questions of feminism and political economy, see Gayatri Chakravorty Spivak, 'The Political Economy of Women as Seen by a Literary Critic', in Elizabeth Weed, ed., *Coming to Terms: Feminism, Theory, Politics*, New York and London 1989, pp. 218–29, and *In Other Worlds: Essays in Cultural Politics*, New York 1988; Evelyn Brooks-Higginbotham, 'The Problem of Race in Women's History' in Weed, ed., *Coming to Terms*, pp. 122–33; and Catherine R. Stimpson, *Where the Meanings Are: Feminism and Cultural Spaces*, New York and London 1988.

2. Said, 'Yeats', p. 72.

3. Said has observed that 'at some stage in the antiresistance phase of nationalism there is a sort of dependence between the two sides of the contest, since after all many of the nationalist struggles were led by bourgeoisies that were partly formed and to some degree produced by the colonial power'. He points out that there lies within this phenomenon the potential for independence, but also for exploitation in a new guise: 'instead of liberation after decolonization one simply gets the old colonial structures replicated in new national terms'. There is the question of the status of the colonized elite within imperialism as well as their vision of a postcolonial state. Despite successful cooptation of Western education and modernization by

an African elite (or an Afro-American elite, for that matter), there remained what Said calls the 'imperial divide between native and Westerner' in social status and in the exercise of power within colonial/Western systems. In other words, African advancement according to overtly benevolent colonial terms did not dispel the racism that lay at the true heart of colonization (Said, 'Yeats', pp. 74, 75).

4. Gayatri Chakravorty Spivak has addressed this issue of Western-white cultural hegemony and the development of nationalist counterculture in the context of contemporary Third World feminism. As in earlier Pan-Africanism, current Third World feminist theory is coming from a 'bourgeois indigenous nationalist elite' who are largely 'making up its object in the tradition of benevolent imperialism' (Spivak, 'The Political Economy of Women', pp. 219, 228).

5. See Gregory Pirio, 'The Role of Garveyism in the Making of the Southern African Working Classes and Namibian Nationalism', paper presented at the South Africa in the Comparative Study of Class, Race, and Nation Conference, New York, September 1982. See also Robert A. Hill and Gregory Pirio, 'Africa for the Africans: The Garvey Movement in South Africa, 1920–1940', in Shula Marks and Stanley Trapido, eds, *The Politics of Race, Class and Nationalism in 20th-Century South Africa*, London 1987, pp. 209–53; and Rupert Lewis and Maureen Warner-Lewis, eds, *Garvey, Africa, Europe, the Americas*, Kingston 1986, especially Arnold Hughes, 'Africa and the Garvey Movement in the Interwar Years', pp. 111–35, and G.O. Olusanya, 'Garvey and Nigeria', pp. 137–51.

6. On the issue of Garveyism's appeal to an artisan/professional/intellectual westernized African elite who accepted the models of economic development propagated under colonialism, saw themselves as distinct from and in a leadership role vis à vis nonwesternized Africans, but were alienated by their increasing lack of power or advancement in white-controlled business and governmental bureaucracy, see Judith Stein, *The World of Marcus Garvey: Race and Class in Modern Society*, Baton Rouge, La. 1986, pp. 5, 7–23.

7. Said, 'Yeats', p. 71.

8. Spivak, 'The Political Economy of Women', pp. 223–4.

9. On Creole society in Sierra Leone and the Smith family as exemplary of it, see Adelaide Cromwell, *An African Victorian Feminist: The Life and Times of Adelaide Smith Casely Hayford, 1868–1960*, London 1986, pp. 1–17, 29–48. Cromwell's tribute to Adelaide Casely Hayford is both an interpretive biography and a documentary history, in that portions of many of Casely Hayford's writings are reprinted in the book.

10. Spivak, 'The Political Economy of Women', pp. 219, 228.

11. Adelaide Casely Hayford, 'The Life and Times of Adelaide Casely Hayford', *West Africa Review*, vol. 24, no. 313, October 1953, p. 1060.

12. *West Africa Review*, November 1953, p. 1169. Anna Melissa Graves, a white missionary and pacifist who became involved in Adelaide Casely Hayford's life in the 1930s, wrote simply of this period as a time when 'there was nothing for them to do there and they did not like it' (Graves, *Benvenuto Cellini Had No Prejudice Against Bronze: Letters from West Africans* [1943], p. 32). The Graves book is available at the Schomburg Center for Research on Black Culture, New York Public Library. In an amazingly patronizing and voyeuristic invasion of the privacy of Adelaide Casely Hayford and her daughter, Graves reprints and analyzes the mother's and daughter's personal correspondence of the 1930s, reveals intimate information about Gladys's sexual liaisons and institutionalization for mental illness and chronicles her own direct interference in the mother's and daughter's lives. As Adelaide Casely Hayford's biographer, Adelaide Cromwell, has noted, use of the Graves book as a source is distasteful; on the other hand, it offers glimpses into the Casely Hayfords' private lives that are impossible for a historian to ignore (see Cromwell, *An African Victorian Feminist*, p. 164).

13. See Cromwell, *An African Victorian Feminist*, Chs. 3 and 4.

14. See Arnold Hughes, 'Africa and the Garvey Movement', p. 117; see also Robert A. Hill, 'The First England Years and After' in John Henrik Clarke, ed., *Marcus Garvey and the Vision of Africa*, New York 1974, pp. 38–70.

15. On this, and other direct connections between the UNIA and African activists and intellectuals, see Tony Martin, *Race First: The Ideological and Organizational Struggles of Marcus Garvey and UNIA*, Dover, Mass. 1976, Ch. 7, 'Africa', pp. 110–50. J.E. Casely Hayford is discussed on p. 116. On Casely Hayford and the NCBWA, see J. Ayodele Langley, *Pan-Africanism and Na-*

tionalism in West Africa, 1900–1945, Oxford 1973. See also D.M. McFarland, *Historical Dictionary of Ghana*, Metuchen 1985, and Cromwell, *An African Victorian Feminist*, p. 120.

16. On this period of alienation, see Rina Okonkwo, 'Adelaide Casely Hayford: Cultural Nationalist and Feminist,' *Phylon*, vol. 42, no. 1, March 1981, p. 42. The Okonkwo article is an excellent overview of Casely Hayford's life and the feminist and nationalist aspects of her career.

17. Adelaide Casely Hayford was frequently ill; her perceptions of her own illness may be to some degree a part of her middle-class Victorian world view, which encouraged a cult of invalidism among women as an extension of the privatistic value placed upon their enforced leisure. However, a great deal of her illness was undoubtedly very real. Having lived much of her life in England, she had little resistance to many of the illnesses prevalent in Africa, including malaria and influenza. She had her first child at the advanced age of thirty-five, soon followed by a second difficult pregnancy that resulted in a stillbirth; the surgery she underwent in Freetown after she left Joseph Casely Hayford may have been connected to disability following these reproductive experiences. The reality and severity of illness as a factor in women's lives is highlighted by Casely Hayford's own family history: not only did her mother and two step-mothers die of illness in relative middle-age, her beloved niece, Kathleen Easmon, died of appendicitis at the age of 32 and her daughter, Gladys, suffered from mental illness and died of blackwater fever in her mid forties. Adelaide Cromwell has pointed out that despite Casely Hayford's many health problems and possible hypochondria, she lived a long life.

18. Cromwell, *An African Victorian Feminist*, p. 85.

19. Ibid., p. 88.

20. Graves, *Benvenuto Cellini*, p. 49.

21. Ibid., p. 34; Okonkwo, 'Adelaide Casely Hayford', p. 42. Graves also cited cultural differences, in that Creole society was more Anglo-oriented than the Gold Coast culture in which Joseph Casely Hayford lived, and Adelaide Casely Hayford 'would have none of these customs' that Joseph adhered to. Both Okonkwo and Graves see a political dimension to this cultural difference; Graves blamed Adelaide's favorable vision of the British Empire for her lack of understanding of and sympathy for Joseph's political nationalism (Graves, *Benvenuto Cellini*, pp. 33, 37; Okonkwo, 'Adelaide Casely Hayford', p. 42). The personality explanation for the separation is remarkably similar to that of Amy Ashwood Garvey in describing the reasons for the failure of her marriage to Marcus Garvey: each was assertive and domineering, and Ashwood refused to bend her own will and goals to serve the needs of her husband's.

22. Filomina Chioma Steady, 'African Feminism: A Worldwide Perspective', in R. Terborg-Penn, S. Harley, and A. Benton Rushing, eds, *Women in Africa and the African Diaspora*, Washington, D.C. 1987, pp. 3–24. Quotations are from pp. 8, 6, 7. See also Steady, 'The Black Woman Cross-Culturally: An Overview' in F.C. Steady, ed., *The Black Woman Cross-Culturally*, Cambridge 1981. Steady's somewhat idealized vision of the complementarity of male and female African life, which discounts severe patriarchy as a Western construction, is countered by viewpoints such as that of an African-American woman missionary in Southern Africa in the late 1800s, who was appalled by the seeming exploitation of women within the traditional African division of labor, in which 'the men and boys sit while the women and girls do the digging' (Nancy Jones, quoted in Sylvia M. Jacobs, 'Afro-American Women Missionaries Confront the African Way of Life' in Terborg-Penn, et al., *Women in Africa*, pp. 127–8). The novels of Nigerian author Buchi Emecheta and other African women writers also question the equity of male and female roles in traditional African life (see Emecheta's many novels and *Ngambika: Studies of Women in African Literature*, C. Boyce Daives and A. Adams Graves, eds, Trenton, N.J. 1986).

23. Karen Sacks, 'An Overview of Women and Power in Africa', in O'Barr, ed., *Perspectives on Power: Women in Africa, Asia and Latin America*, pp. 1–10. See also *Sisters and Wives*.

24. Spivak, 'The Political Economy of Women', p. 225.

25. Beverly Guy-Sheftall has commented on the differences in marital status between Black and white feminist activists. Whereas Nancy Cott has stated that most feminist leaders did the bulk of their political work when either widowed or single, Guy-Sheftall points out a large number of African-American women activists were married during the period of their greatest political productivity (see Guy-Sheftall, *Daughters of Sorrow: Attitudes toward Black Women, 1880–1920*, Brooklyn, N.Y. 1990, p. 174). This is not true for the Garvey movement, at least at the international and national levels. On the local divisional level, many married women were

active, sometimes as organizers or lady presidents. At the top of the movement's hierarchy, however, active women were either single or separated. Henrietta Vinton Davis (Fourth Assistant President General) and Ethel Collins (Secretary General) remained unmarried; the first marriage of M.L.T. De Mena (International Organizer) was very brief, and her second marriage came later in life. Amy Ashwood's marriage to Garvey was similarly brief and she never remarried; and Amy Jacques Garvey and Marcus Garvey lived separately for a great deal of their marriage, first because of his imprisonment and then because of his move to England. Adelaide Casely Hayford seems more representative than exceptional in this regard. On women in the Garvey movement, see Barbara Bair, 'True Women, Real Men: Gender, Ideology, and Social Roles in the Garvey Movement', in Susan Reverby and Dorothy O. Helly, eds, *Gendered Domains: Rethinking Public and Private in Women's History: Essays from the 7th Berkshire Conference on the History of Women*, Ithaca, N.Y. 1990.

26. Cromwell, *An African Victorian Feminist*, pp. 91, 95, 97; see also Okonkwo 'Adelaide Casely Hayford'.

27. Cromwell, *An African Victorian Feminist*, pp. 95–6.

28. For information about the numerous educational aspects of the Garvey movement, see volumes 1–7 of Robert A. Hill et al., eds, *The Marcus Garvey and UNIA Papers*, Berkeley, Calif. 1983–1990, and Hill and Barbara Bair, eds, *Marcus Garvey: Life and Lessons*, Berkeley, Calif. 1987.

29. Adelaide Casely Hayford, 'A Girls' School in West Africa', *Southern Workman*, October 1926, p. 450. See also Okonkwo, 'Adelaide Casely Hayford', p. 42, and Cromwell, *An African Victorian Feminist*, p. 102.

30. On Casely Hayford's educational philosophy, see her own writings and Okonkwo, 'Adelaide Casely Hayford', p. 42; Cromwell, *An African Victorian Feminist*, Ch. 2. Casely Hayford's ideas, though radical in the context of Freetown, were not unusual among female educators of her time. The main debate in women's education was similar to the industrial training/liberal arts debate within Black education, with educators split between those who believed in a 'sameness' doctrine, i.e. that women should be educated according to the same classical educational model as men; and those, like Casely Hayford, who believed in a 'difference' doctrine, i.e., that women should receive training different from that of men in order to prepare them for their separate social roles as mothers and wives, teachers and nurses. Sara Delamont has labeled the advocates of these two schools of thought the 'uncompromising and the separatists' (see Delamont, 'The Contradictions in Ladies' Education', in *The Nineteenth-Century Woman: Her Cultural and Physical World*, Sara Delamont and Lorna Duffin, eds, New York 1978, pp. 134–62; and Beverly Guy-Sheftall's discussion of Delamont's categories and of the debates over Black women's education in *Daughters of Sorrow*, pp. 130–158, and 201 n.124).

31. Cromwell, *An African Victorian Feminist*, pp. 59, 96–7.

32. *Sierra Leone Weekly News*, 12 June 1920.

33. Ibid.; see also Okonkwo, 'Adelaide Casely Hayford' p. 44; Cromwell, *An African Victorian Feminist*, p. 98.

34. *Sierra Leone Weekly News*, 12 June 1920.

35. Cromwell, *An African Victorian Feminist*, pp. 99, 100.

36. Okonkwo, 'Adelaide Casely Hayford', p. 43; Cromwell, *An African Victorian Feminist*, pp. 96–100.

37. Easmon never returned to Africa. During her time with Casely Hayford in America, she met and eventually married an East African educator, Kamba Simango, who had graduated from Hampton and was planning a career as a missionary and teacher in Portuguese East Africa. Easmon went with her husband to Lisbon to study Portuguese in preparation for teaching with him in Africa. She became ill and died after surgery in London in July 1924, at the age of thirty-two (see Cromwell, *An African Victorian Feminist*, pp. 118–19).

38. Adelaide Casely Hayford, 'American Journey', *West African Review*, January 1954, p. 57; see also Cromwell, *An African Victorian Feminist*, pp. 108–9.

39. Casely Hayford, 'American Journey', p. 54.

40. Cromwell, *An African Victorian Feminist*, p. 130.

41. Adelaide Casely Hayford, 'West Africa in America', *West Africa*, 7 January 1922.

42. Adelaide Casely Hayford, 'Sierra Leone Education Scheme: In Harlem – The Coloured Quarter', *West Africa*, 2 October 1920, p. 1273.

43. Adelaide Casely Hayford, 'Afro-American Clubland', *West Africa*, 19 November 1921, p. 1469.

44. Besides Burroughs and Washington, there were many other African-American women educators who believed in separatist forms of education for girls and who had developed successful programs for Casely Hayford to emulate. For example, Lucy Laney had founded the Haines Normal and Industrial Institute in Augusta, Ga. in 1886; Washington began as dean of the Women's Department at Tuskegee in 1889; Charlotte Hawkins Brown founded the Palmer Memorial Institute in Sedalia, N.C. in 1902; Mary McLeod Bethune began the Daytona Educational and Industrial Training School in Florida in 1904; and Burroughs had founded her National Training School for Women and Girls in Washington, D.C. in 1907. The writings and teaching example of Anna Julia Cooper at the M Street (Dunbar) High School offered models for the 'sameness' argument in favor of liberal education for African-American girls. Black women's education was also occurring through a full range of more informal Mother's Clubs and volunteer classes organized by a plethora of women's uplift organizations. See Guy-Sheftall, *Daughters of Sorrow*, pp. 29–30, 34, 74, 79, 95; see also Cynthia Neverdon-Morton, *Afro-American Women of the South and the Advancement of the Race, 1895–1925*, Knoxville, Tenn. 1989; and Dorothy Salem, *To Better Our World: Black Women in Organized Reform, 1890–1920*, Brooklyn, N.Y. 1990.

45. Graves, *Benvenuto Cellini*, p. 75.

46. *West Africa*, 24 July 1920 interview, 'Education of African Girls', p. 1002; see also Cromwell, *An African Victorian Feminist*, pp. 191, 192.

47. Guy-Sheftall, *Daughters of Sorrow*, p. 29.

48. Margaret Murray Washington, 'The Negro Home', speech delivered at the Interracial Conference held in Memphis, Tenn., October 1920 from the Tuskegee Institute Archives; quoted in Guy-Sheftall, *Daughters of Sorrow*, pp. 148, 204 n.168.

49. Cromwell, *An African Victorian Feminist*, pp. 111–12.

50. Adelaide Casely Hayford, 'American Journey', *West African Review*, February 1954, p. 153.

51. Cromwell, *An African Victorian Feminist*, p. 105. It is unclear exactly what kind of relationship Casely Hayford maintained with these key male members of the powerful Phelps-Stokes Commission. In an article in *West Africa* of 7 January 1922, Casely Hayford notes that she and Easmon met with Dr. Jesse Jones of the Phelps Stokes Commission 'and we are greatly indebted to him for using his influence on our behalf ... Dr. [James] Aggrey, too, has been our staunch supporter and has done all he could to hold up our hands'. But ten years later, Casely Hayford wrote to Anna Melissa Graves that her daughter Gladys had been refused educational aide by 'the Dr. Jesse Jones gang headed by Mr. K___ who was our Director of Education at the time, and who also belonged to the bunch. They simply didn't want to give her [Gladys] a helping hand, because they thought it would help *me* in the school' (Graves, *Benvenuto Cellini*, p. 48). Yet Casely Hayford wrote to Graves again on 24 May 1934 and said that Dr. Jesse Jones had visited her (Graves, *Benvenuto Cellini*, pp. 76–8). It seems that Casely Hayford had severe fallings-out with both her American and African advisory boards (Cromwell, *An African Victorian Feminist*, pp. 146–7).

52. Casely Hayford, 'A Girls' School'; also quoted in Cromwell, *An African Victorian Feminist*, pp. 102–3.

53. Adelaide Casely Hayford, *West Africa Review*, March 1954, p. 241.

54. Ibid., p. 239.

55. Graves, *Benvenuto Cellini*, p. 79.

56. Okonkwo, 'Adelaide Casely Hayford', p. 45.

57. See Addie Hunton, 'Negro Womanhood Defended' *Voice of the Negro*, vol. 1, July 1904, p. 280; see also Paula Giddings, *When and Where I Enter: The Impact of Black Women on Race and Sex in America*, New York 1984, pp. 87, 166–9.

58. Immanuel Geiss, *The Pan-African Movement*, New York 1974, p. 256. See also Elliott Rudwick, *W.E.B. Du Bois: Voice of the Black Protest Movement*, Urbana, Ill. 1982 [1960], p. 231.

59. Okonkwo, 'Adelaide Casely Hayford', p. 46; see also Graves, *Benvenuto Cellini*.

60. In her memoirs, she stated, 'My final word to subsequent torch-bearers is just this: NEVER be ashamed of your color. God *never* makes mistakes', *West African Review*, August

1954, p. 789, also quoted in Cromwell, *An African Victorian Feminist*, p. 202.

61. For example, she characterized the Bai Bureh Rising over hut taxes in the 1890s as 'a rebellion, not so much against white people, as against civilization generally', *West African Review*, June 1954.

62. Okonkwo deals very well with this internal contradiction in Casely Hayford's cultural nationalism.

63. Adelaide Casely Hayford, 'A Close-up . . . and a Close-down', *West African Review*, August 1954, p. 736. When Beth Torrey commented on her experience teaching at Casely Hayford's school, she said she felt it was an excellent project, but one that was 'the expression of *her* individuality and there was no possibility of anyone else expressing theirs, except to a very limited degree' (Graves, *Benvenuto Cellini*, p. 57). When Anna Melissa Graves inexplicably shared this letter with Casely Hayford without Torrey's permission, Casely Hayford responded, 'A woman cannot face life in Africa, *alone*, with great poverty, and a home to maintain, without acquiring a stern exterior; but no one yet has suggested that I am *terrifying*. . .' (Graves, *Benvenuto Cellini*, p. 60).

64. Cromwell, *An African Victorian Feminist*, p. 148.

65. Ibid., p. 161.

66. On Gladys Casely Hayford's life, see Cromwell, *An African Victorian Feminist*, Ch. 10, and the correspondence and analysis printed in Graves, *Benvenuto Cellini*. For discussion of Gladys Casely Hayford as a poet recognized by the Harlem Renaissance elite, see Gloria T. Hull, *Color, Sex, and Poetry: Three Women Writers of the Harlem Renaissance*, Bloomington, Ind. 1987, pp. 13–14.

67. Cromwell, *An African Victorian Feminist*, pp. 25, 28.

68. Said, 'Yeats', p. 76.

8

W.E.B. Du Bois

and Black Sovereignty

Cedric J. Robinson

I

The political and intellectual activities of W.E.B. Du Bois (1868–1963) span a critical period in world history. Among the developments most immediately pertinent to our inquiry into Du Bois's articulation with Liberia are colonialism and its concomitant formations of Black middle classes; the peculiar and unique history of the 'Americo-Liberian' elite; and the equally curious advent of the United States as a colonial power. By the early twentieth century, these elements were destined to collide when the United States and European states actively challenged the autonomy of Haiti, Liberia and Ethiopia.[1] How Du Bois responded to one of those challenges, the attempt to reduce Liberia to an American colony, is our concern. I shall contend that Du Bois, blinded by the elitism characteristic of his class prerogative, fell prey to American colonialism. More important, Du Bois's treatment of Liberia provides evidence of the ambiguous conjuncture of the discourses of race and class.

As what came to be known as 'the new imperialism' extended into the twentieth century, it provided unparalleled opportunities for the embryonic Black middle classes being nurtured in the Western hemisphere and in European colonies in Africa. As a class, their interests were identical to those of other 'middling' classes formed from professional service and intellectual and ideological functions rather than the domination of commerce and commodity production. Like their European predecessors in the eighteenth and nineteenth centuries, and their contemporaries in the twentieth century all over the world, the Black middle classes – that is, the

Black intelligentsias of the United States, the Caribbean and Africa – were captives of a dialectic: on the one hand, their continued development was structurally implicated in the continued domination of their societies by the Atlantic metropoles; on the other, the historic destiny of their class was linked to nationalism. Put bluntly, the future of the Black middle class was embedded in the contradictions of imperialism.

Margery Perham, a British anthropologist and colonial functionary, frankly described the projected role of the Black middle classes for an audience in attendance at a summer school training in colonial administration at Oxford University in 1938:

> The basic difficulty [in carrying out 'indirect rule'] . . . is (and here I speak especially of Africa) the great gap between the culture of rulers and ruled. In administration, reduced to its simplest terms, it means that for the most part the people do not understand what we want them to do, or, if they understand, do not want to do it . . . [therefore] we endeavor to instruct the leaders of the people in the objects of our policy, in the hope that they will, by their natural authority, at once diffuse the instruction and exact the necessary obedience.[2]

Imperialism and colonialism required a native base for their administration of so-called 'dependencies'. The consequence was a class of bureaucrats, militias, educators and professionally and technically trained factors whose existence and status hinged on its performance in the apparatus of domination. For this class the objective of national development had to supersede all else – even national liberation. Paradoxically for their imperial patrons, as the Black middle classes matured, their ideological predispositions towards elitism would scatter and fragment. Among those fragments were anti-imperialisms, costumed as either nationalism or radicalism. 'Ineluctably', in the twentieth century, 'the events which did most to shape their era – the crises of world capitalism, the destructive dialectic of imperialism, and the historical and ideological revelations or the naïvete of Western socialism – drove them into a deeper consciousness.'[3] Indeed, by the post–World War I period, a cohort of Black intellectuals drawn from the Black middle classes had evolved a political posture that required them to inspect closely the social legitimacy as well as the ideological presumptions of their own class.

II

In the late eighteenth century, when the modern bureaucratic and professional classes of Germany were first making their appearances, their intellectual representatives had created the notion of the 'universal class', a class whose nature and interests were commensurate with those of the society at large. Immanuel Kant, the first accomplished moral philosopher and theorist of this class, had privileged the bureaucratic class as the site of reason.[4] Hegel put the point even more strongly. In the context of a historical philosophy that posited humankind's ascent to a divinelike perfect reason, Hegel identified the bureaucracy – what he called the 'public class' – as 'necessity' itself.[5] It was this same concept, that of a 'universal class', which Marx would later appropriate for use in his construction of the historical proletariat.

At the root of the admiration Kant demonstrated for the bureaucracy and Hegel of his 'new public class' were their functions as apostolates to the modern State. As ideologues of a class that owed its very existence to the administrative needs of the emerging nation-state, it is not surprising that they would situate this new political institution at the hub of modern history. Hegel, we are told, went so far as to declare: 'It is the way of God in the world, that there should be the state.'[6] And Karl Mannheim observed: 'This bourgeois intellectualism expressly demanded a scientific politics . . .'[7] As we shall see, Du Bois and many other prominent intellectuals drawn from the Black middle class of the late nineteenth and early twentieth centuries recited from the same ideological catechism. With respect to Liberia, however, their most fundamental conceptual error was mistaking it for a nation-state.

III

The outlines of Liberia's history are already familiar. Founded in the early nineteenth century by Black émigrés from the United States (inspired by the earlier colonizing efforts of Paul Cuffe) and the American Colonization Society, Liberia acquired formal status and a republican constitution in 1847. Between 1822 and 1890, a steady stream of immigrants settled on the Liberian coast. Among them were nearly 20,000 Afro-Americans for whom the American Colonization Society took credit, joined by another 5,000 Africans aboard slave ships intercepted by the American navy.[8] These émigrés were the original Americo-Liberians.

For the next one hundred years following its formal independence, Liberia experienced the extremes of uneven development.[9] Writing in 1970 in defense of the leadership of the Americo-Liberians, Elliot Berg protested:

Until twenty-five years ago, Liberia could be called a 'country' or 'state' only in a strictly legal use of the term. It was in reality a collection of coastal communities, cut off from the hinterland and each other, and quite autonomous in most things that mattered. There existed almost no significant area of public activity which could give substance to the 'state'. The central government had at its disposal a few hundred thousand dollars annually, much of it periodically earmarked to pay off foreign loans. There were few schools, roads, or dispensaries. There were indeed almost no public goods and services at all. The administrative system could hardly be said to reach beyond Monrovia, so there was little knowledge and less control over happenings in the interior.[10]

The stagnation of Liberia, however, was not due to lack of interest or zeal on the part of Black leaders in the United States. 'In the 1890s [Reverend Henry McNeal] Turner became the leading advocate of emigration.'[11] Emphasizing the responsibility of American Blacks to the Christianizing mission were prominent figures such as Reverend Alexander Crummell; John Henry Smyth, the one-time US minister to Liberia; Reverend Charles S. Morris; Reverend John W. Gilbert, president of Miles Memorial College; and Reverend J.C. Price, president of Livingstone College. Others such as Thomas McCants Stewart (who had taught at Liberia College), Professor Richard T. Greener, Reverend Rufus Perry and Amanda Berry Smith (a former missionary in Liberia) encouraged American Blacks to provide 'scientific, technical and industrial education' to Liberians. Bishop Turner, while in Liberia, had written to American 'Black capitalists' that 'if they would start trading with Liberia they would be worth millions in a few years.'[12] Lenwood Davis reports:

> In 1904 came word of the formation of the African Trading Company which intended to facilitate commerce and emigration. About the same time the New York and Liberia Steamship Company announced its intention to start a ship to Africa. The American and West African Steamship Company also existed for a time. Later the Liberian Trading and Emigration Association of the U.S.A. was established. In 1907 a group of Blacks under the leadership of Walter F. Walker organized the Liberation Development Association ... In December 1913 a group of Blacks organized the African Union Company which proposed to handle African products on a large scale and establish mercantile operations between Africa and the markets of the world.[13]

Afro-American opinion on Liberia, however, was not always enthusiastic. In the mid nineteenth century, Martin Delaney had described Liberia as 'a poor miserable mockery – a burlesque of a government'.[14] And in 1886 Thomas McCants Stewart, the Afro-American lawyer who had taught in Liberia, observed: 'The natives of Liberia have been to the emigrants from America just what these ex-slaves were to the whites of the South. They have been defrauded, beaten with stripes, and made to feel that they were inferior beings.'[15] 'The motto of the republic, "The love of liberty brought us here", Stewart suggest[ed] ironically, ought really to read "To be free from labor we came here."'[16] Though largely understood as accurate, remarks such as Stewart's rankled Alexander Crummell, the former missionary to Liberia. Crummell focused on their potential political damage. According to Davis:

> [Crummell] was angry that Whites and Blacks were hostile to Liberia. This led him to say in 1891 that 'it is very common now-a-days to hear this little Republic referred to as evidencing the incapacity of the Negro for free government, and nothing is more constant, nothing more frequent than the declaration that 'Liberia is a failure!' . . . Nothing can be more ignorant, nothing more stupid than these utterances.'[17]

Immanuel Geiss, however, observes: 'Alexander Crummell, one of the most impressive Afro-American figures of the nineteenth century, never lost his balance vis-à-vis Liberia. Although he gave a positive appreciation of its function, he remained cool and "had nothing extravagant to say about Liberia".'[18]

IV

The same could not be said of Du Bois. As Geiss himself comments, Du Bois 'praised Liberia quite uncritically'.[19] Even after the Liberian slavery scandal of 1929–30 that had forced the 'retirement' of President C.D.B. King, Du Bois, at least in public, still minimized the injustices perpetrated by the Liberian ruling class and its foreign collaborators. Writing in *Foreign Affairs* in 1933, Du Bois concluded:

> Liberia is not faultless. She lacks training, experience and thrift. But her chief crime is to be black and poor in a rich, white world; and in precisely that portion of the world where color is ruthlessly exploited as a foundation for American and European wealth.[20]

This article is a particularly revealing sample of Du Bois's thought, and we shall return to it momentarily.

Du Bois's activities on behalf of 'Liberia', or more accurately on behalf of the ruling Americo-Liberians, took the forms of diplomacy, propaganda-publicism, and financial brokering. Among them four interventions by Du Bois assumed particular significance. First, as a special representative of President Calvin Coolidge – his title was Envoy Extraordinary and Minister Plenipotentiary – Du Bois had attended the inauguration of President C.D.B. King in January 1924. During his sojourn in Liberia, it is obvious that Du Bois became acquainted with the privileged social position enjoyed by the Liberian ruling class. In *Crisis* in April 1924, Du Bois described a Liberian senator as a 'curious blend of feudal lord and modern farmer'.[21] Another visit, twenty miles outside Monrovia, revealed 'a mansion of five generations with a compound of endless native servants and cows under the palm thatches.'[22] In absolute consonance with the colonial scenes in these word-paintings, Du Bois recorded that the native African Liberians sang in silly words, and 'gay with Christmas and a dash of gin, danced and sang and danced in the road.' Upon his return to the United States, Du Bois would report to Secretary of State Charles Evan Hughes

> ... of a country which had 'extended her democracy to include natives on the same terms as Liberians', had balanced her budget, and had 'never had a revolution or internal disturbance save in comparatively few cases, with the war-like native tribes.'[23]

Reflecting the preoccupations and imagination of his class, Du Bois 'recommended American economic and diplomatic support for Liberia's modernization'.[24] As he would confess nine years later, like many other members of the Black middle-class intelligentsia he had succumbed to a most terrible species of technocracy:

> I remember standing once in a West African forest where thin, silver trees loomed straight and smooth in the air. There were two men with me. One was a black man, Solomon Hood, United States Minister to Liberia; a man of utter devotion whose solicitude for the welfare of Liberia was like a sharp pain driving him on. And he thought he had found the solution. The solution was the white man beside us. He was a rubber expert sent by the Firestone Corporation . . .[25]

In this resolve, Du Bois and Hood were one. However, the seemingly perverse innocence of Du Bois's journalistic observations of Liberian manners and the technical emphases of his official report were quite likely accompaniments to a more sinister mission: to frustrate the plan of the Universal Negro Improvement Association to move its headquarters to Liberia and establish a new settlement of New World Blacks. This is the second (and more circumstantial) of Du Bois's interventions.

In January 1923, nearly a year before he was appointed Minister Plenipotentiary to Liberia, Du Bois had written Secretary of State Hughes suggesting that the US government undertake to 'aid or guide a plan of furnishing at least two ships [to Black American entrepreneurs] for the tentative beginning of direct commercial intercourse between Liberia and America.'[26] Du Bois further suggested that for this purpose the US government might secure the stock of the 'Bankrupt Black Star Line'. He informed Hughes that the failure of the Black Star Line was to be laid at the feet of Marcus Garvey: 'The difficulty ... was that its leader, Marcus Garvey, was not a business man and turned out to be a thoroughly impractical visionary, if not a criminal, with grandiose schemes of conquest.'[27] Herbert Aptheker, the editor of Du Bois's papers, comments: 'There appears to be no record of a response from the State Department.'[28] Nevertheless, ten months later Du Bois secured his State Department appointment, largely resulting from the persuasions of William Henry Lewis, 'a Boston Negro attorney and a leading Massachusetts Republican, who had served as assistant Attorney-General in the Taft administration', who warned President Coolidge of the imminent loss of Black votes in 1924.[29]

M.E. Akpan has documented rather conclusively that the State Department personnel in Monrovia were closely watching the progress of the UNIA mission with discrete hostility. He surmised:

> Although, so far as has been ascertained, the Department made no representation to the Liberian government against the Association, it is very probably that it was to indicate the attitude of the American Government towards the Association that President Calvin Coolidge appointed William E.B. Du Bois, Garvey's most formidable Afro-American opponent and critic, as United States representative at the inauguration of President King in January 1924.[30]

Akpan continues: '... the Liberian leaders could hardly have failed to seek Du Bois's opinion of the Association, which, it could be assumed, would be discreditable to the Association.'[31] In a letter to Azikiwe in 1932, Du Bois would deny even mentioning 'Garvey to Mr. King or to any Liberian official during my stay there.'[32] This denial is barely creditable in light of Du Bois's own assertion in 1933 that while in Liberia '... I did all I could to cooperate with Hood and Africa and Liberia and *tell them of the tremendous interest which American colored people had in them.*'[33] But whatever he might have said or not said in Liberia in January 1924, a few months later in a May 1924 editorial in the *Crisis,* Du Bois declared: 'Marcus Garvey is, without doubt, the most dangerous enemy of the Negro race in America and in the world. He is either a lunatic or a traitor.'[34]

Interestingly enough, during the same period in which Du Bois was quite evidently warning American officials and Black Americans of the 'visionary' schemes of Marcus Garvey, he was importuning the American government and American capital to support his own versions of Liberian development. To Secretary of State Hughes, Du Bois had inquired of federal protection for Black venture capital: 'If the matter were properly presented to black America, and if the colored people were safe-guarded from the exploitations which might arise in such a project, they could loan considerable money to Liberia.'[35] This, of course, was precisely the relationship between the State and private capital which had precipitated the occupation of Haiti which had begun in 1915.[36] Apparently, Du Bois's immersion in the ideology of the State had hidden this consequence from him.

Later, in 1925, Du Bois had followed up his Liberian discussions with Donald Ross, the representative of the Firestone Company. In 1924, Firestone had approached the Liberian government for a concession of one million acres for the cultivation of rubber coupled with a loan of $5,000,000. Largely on account of its perennial condition of bankruptcy, a fear of French and British designs on Liberian soil and pressure from the US State Department, the Americo-Liberians had finally agreed to Firestone's conditions in 1927.[37] In October 1925, Du Bois wrote to Harvey Firestone suggesting that in 'this experiment in Liberia' Firestone might employ among his 'industrial personnel' 'Colored Americans of education and experience.'[38] He encouraged Firestone:

> I believe that in this way you can inaugurate one of the greatest and far reaching reforms in the relations between white industrial countries like America and black, partly developed countries like Liberia if it can once be proven that industry can do the same thing in a black country like Liberia that it does in a white country like Australia: that is, invade it, reform it and uplift it by incorporating the native born into the imported industry and thus make the industry a part of the country.[39]

Here Du Bois exhibited a naïvete or at least an optimism with respect to capitalism which was more characteristic of the petty bourgeoisies of the mid nineteenth century than earlier or later.[40] After all, Hegel had observed that the mercantile and industrial classes '. . . base their subsistence on the misery of one class.'[41] To his credit, in 1933, just eight years after his approach to Firestone, Du Bois no longer suffered such illusions. Now as a radical Black intellectual, Du Bois confessed:

> I know what European imperialism has done to Asia and Africa; but, nevertheless, I had not then lost faith in the capitalist system, and I believed that it was possible for a great corporation, headed by a man of vision, to go into a country with something more than the mere ideal of profit.[42]

This is the Du Bois we find in *Black Reconstruction*.

There was, however, one more instance in which Du Bois held to the predilections of his class. Paradoxically, it came in 1933, precisely when Du Bois was acquiring the critical stance of a renegade petty bourgeois. The occasion was the most serious challenge to Americo-Liberian 'sovereignty' mounted by American and European interests.[43] I.K. Sundiata, one of the best students of the crisis, describes it in this way:

In June of 1929 the US State Department informed the Liberian government that there had come to its attention disturbing reports about 'the so-called "export" of labor from Liberia to Fernando Po ...' The reports indicated that the labor system in question was 'hardly distinguishable from organized slave trade, and that in the enforcement of this system the services of the Liberian Frontier Force, and the services and influences of certain high Government officials, are constantly and systematically used.' So began a scandal that would have worldwide repercussions.

An investigation of Liberia by the League of Nations in 1930 soon revealed that indigenous Liberian workers, mostly from the Kru and Grebo peoples, were being crudely exploited by the Americo-Liberian elite ...[44]

For the most part, Afro-American leaders rightly interpreted the crisis as an occasion for the Western powers to place Liberia under some sort of receivership. They were particularly concerned when President King was forced to retire in 1930 but the United States refused to recognize the regime of his successor, Edwin Barclay, King's former secretary of state. The issue came to a head in 1933 when the League of Nations debated the recommendation of its Liberia Committee that the reforms of the country be under the administration of a chief adviser and eight other foreign experts, and the counterproposal from the US government that the chief adviser assume autocratic powers:

The difficulty was increased by entreaties from Liberia itself. Americo-Liberia found itself poised between blacks in the Hinterland and blacks in the Diaspora. After 1930, in hopes of gaining support from overseas blacks, Liberia made a strong appeal to racial solidarity.[45]

Among the many Black leaders who responded sympathetically to the Americo-Liberian campaign, Du Bois and B.N. Azikiwe were by far the most passionate. Each used his genius to write ardent defenses of Liberia: Du Bois published his *Foreign Affairs* article in 1933 while privately proposing to the Liberian government that it secretly subsidize a book he would author.[46] Azikiwe published his own apology, *Liberia in World Politics,* in 1934. Sadly, too, both Du Bois and Azikiwe found reasons to justify the

153

'organized slave trade' documented by the League's investigation while trivializing the militant opposition of those subjected to forced labor. As far as the Liberian slave trade was concerned, Du Bois's argument sounded depressingly familiar. He wrote in 1933:

> Now labor supply for modern industry in Africa always tends to approximate slavery because it is bound up with the clan organization of the tribes . . . The Commission . . . proved that domestic slavery existed among the more primitive Liberian tribes . . .[47]

He was equally casual about the native resistance: 'There was trouble, serious trouble, with the Krus; but it was historical and administrative and connected with the present only in so far as the Krus thought the Liberian Government has been superseded by foreign control.'[48]

Nevertheless several divisions became apparent among Afro-American leadership: in support of the State Department were to be counted George Schuyler, Charles Johnson (one of the three members of the League's 1930 International Commission of Inquiry), President Robert Moton of Tuskegee, and Thomas Jesse Jones of the Phelps-Stokes Fund (aligned with the Firestone Company); among Du Bois's coterie were President Mordecai Johnson of Howard University, Rayford Logan of the Association for the Study of Negro Life and History, the historian Charles Wesley, and Emmett Scott (once Booker T. Washington's secretary but now secretary of Howard University).[49] The Black press also took up the cause of the Americo-Liberians.[50] On the radical left of the support for Liberian sovereignty stood intellectuals like George Padmore and T. Ras Makonnen:

> In 1941 Padmore wrote, 'I have always considered it my special duty to expose and denounce the misrule of the black governing classes in Haiti, Liberia, and Abyssinia, while at the same time defending these semi-colonial countries against imperialist aggression.'[51]

Padmore's characterization of his efforts is substantiated by reviewing his *The Life and Struggle of Negro Toilers,* published in 1931.[52]

In this difficult period, ending with the onset of World War II, Du Bois privately and publicly remained an uncritical supporter of the Americo-Liberian regimes. In 1941, the Liberian government belatedly recognized his efforts, bestowing on him the title of Knight Commander of the Order of African Redemption.[53]

V

Du Bois's encounters with Americo-Liberia in the 1920s and 1930s exposed a set of charactological weaknesses in his historical and social consciousness. These amounted to an envelope of petty bourgeois nationalism – an ideology grounded in the presumption that the State occupied a unique, rationalizing position in human history. At the root of this ideological limit in Du Bois's imagination was the class arrogance exhibited repeatedly by intellectuals of Du Bois's class, a class which made its initial appearance in the late eighteenth century. Fortunately, other, more radical and more renegade, representatives of the Black middle class began a systematic critique of their 'historical prerogatives' in the 1930s. Foremost among them was C.L.R. James in his monumental historical and theoretical work, *The Black Jacobins*.[54] In the postwar era, other Black radicals resumed the work, among them Frantz Fanon and Amilcar Cabral in their treatments of the 'national bourgeoisie'. Together, their works constitute the most comprehensive study and critique of the historical promise and political limitations of their class and the role of the State in the struggle for Black liberation.

Notes

1. See C.J. Robinson, 'The African Diaspora and the Italo-Ethiopian Crisis', *Race & Class*, vol. 27, no. 2 (Autumn 1985), pp. 51–65; Gayle Brenda Plummer, 'The Afro American Response to the Occupation of Haiti, 1915–1934', *Phylon*, vol. 43 (June 1982); and Fitz Baptiste, 'The United States and West Indian Unrest, 1918–1929', Working Paper No. 18, Institute of Social and Economic Research, University of the West Indies, Jamaica, 1978.
2. Quoted in C.J. Robinson, *Black Marxism*, London 1983, p. 254.
3. Ibid., p. 260.
4. See Michael J. Meyer, 'Kant's Concept of Dignity and Modern Political Thought', *History of European Ideas*, vol. 8, no. 3 (1987), pp. 326ff.
5. See Hegel's lectures on the Philosophy of Spirit in Leo Rauch, ed., *Hegel and the Human Spirit*, Detroit 1983, pp. 163–7.
6. Shlomo Avineri, *Hegel's Theory of the Modern State*, Cambridge 1972, p. 177.
7. Karl Mannheim, *Ideology and Utopia*, New York 1936, p. 122.
8. Raymond Leslie Buell, *Liberia: A Century of Survival*, Philadelphia 1947, p. 23; and Lenwood Davis, 'Black American Images of Liberia, *Liberian Studies Journal*, vol. 7, no. 1 (1975), p. 55.
9. See J. Gus Liebenow, *Liberia, the Evolution of Privilege*, Ithaca, N.Y. 1969.
10. Elliot J. Berg, 'Politics, Privilege and Progress in Liberia: A Review Article', *Liberian Studies Journal*, vol. 2, no. 2 (1970), p. 178.
11. Davis, 'Black American Images, p. 56.
12. Ibid., p. 66.
13. Ibid., pp. 66–7; and Edwin S. Redkey, *Black Exodus*, New Haven, Conn. 1969, p. 283.
14. Immanuel Geiss, *The Pan-African Movement*, London 1974, p. 124.
15. T. McCants Stewart, *Liberia: The Americo-African Republic*, New York 1886, p. 77; as quoted in Geiss, *The Pan-African Movement*, p. 125.

16. Ibid., p. 124. For an example of what Stewart was objecting to, see Gary Kuhn, 'Liberian Contract Labor in Panama, 1887–1897', *Liberian Studies Journal*, vol. 7, vol. 1 (1975), pp. 43–52.

17. Davis, *Black American Images*, p. 65.

18. Geiss, *The Pan-African Movement*, p. 126.

19. Ibid., p. 127.

20. W.E.B. Du Bois, 'Liberia, the League and the United States', *Foreign Affairs*, vol. 11, no. 4 (July 1933), p. 695.

21. Du Bois, 'Africa', *The Crisis*, vol. 27, no. 6 (April 1924), pp. 247–51, as republished in Julius Lester, *The Seventh Son: The Thought and Writings of W.E.B. Du Bois*, New York 1971, vol. 2, p. 345.

22. Ibid.

23. Frank Chalk, 'Du Bois and Garvey Confront Liberia', *Canadian Journal of African Studies*, vol. 1, no. 2 (November 1967), p. 138.

24. Ibid.

25. Du Bois, 'Liberia, the League and the United States', p. 682.

26. Du Bois to Hughes, 5 January 1923, in Herbert Aptheker, *The Correspondence of W.E.B. Du Bois*, Amherst, Mass. 1973, p. 261.

27. Ibid.

28. Ibid., p. 250.

29. Chalk, 'Du Bois and Garvey Confront Liberia', p. 137.

30. Akpan, 'Liberia and the Universal Negro Improvement Association: The Background to the Abortion of Garvey's Scheme for African Colonization', *Journal of African History*, vol. 14, no. 1 (1973), pp. 122–3.

31. Ibid., p. 123.

32. Aptheker, *The Correspondence of W.E.B. Du Bois*, vol. 1, p. 465.

33. Du Bois, 'Liberia, the League and the United States', p. 684, my emphasis.

34. Lester, *The Seventh Son,* p. 184.

35. Du Bois to Hughes, 5 January 1923, in Aptheker, *Correspondence of W.E.B. Du Bois*, vol. 1, p. 260.

36. Ernest Gruening, 'The Issue in Haiti', *Foreign Affairs*, vol. 11, no. 2 (January 1933).

37. Frank, Chalk, 'The Anatomy of an Investment: Firestone's 1927 Loan to Liberia', *Canadian Journal of African Studies*, vol. 1, no. 1 (March 1967), pp. 12–32.

38. Du Bois to Firestone, 26 October 1925, in Aptheker, *Correspondence of W.E.B. Du Bois*, vol. 1, p. 322.

39. Ibid., pp. 322–3.

40. This is an attitude towards 'bourgeois society' reminiscent of the naïvete of Marx and Engels found in *The Communist Manifesto*. For the ideology of the 'middle classes' of the nineteenth century, see E.J. Hobsbawm, *The Age of Revolution: 1789–1848*, New York 1962, p. 85.

41. Rauch, *Hegel and the Human Spirit*, p. 106.

42. Du Bois, 'Liberia, the League and the United States', p. 684. See the treatment of Du Bois in Robinson, *Black Marxism*, pp. 266ff.

43. Liberia's revenues had been under the control of European and American officials since receiving international loans in 1906 and 1912. Cf. Chalk, 'The Anatomy of an Investment', p. 12.

44. I.K. Sundiata, *Black Scandal*, Philadelphia 1980, p. 1.

45. Ibid., p. 108.

46. Aptheker, *Correspondence of W.E.B. Du Bois*, vol. 2, pp. 26–9.

47. Du Bois, 'Liberia, the League and the United States', pp. 686–7.

48. Ibid., p. 690. For similar arguments by Azikiwe, see his *Liberia in World Politics*, Westport, Conn. 1934, Chs 11 and 16.

49. Sundiata, *Black Scandal,* pp. 87ff.

50. J.R. Hooker, 'The Negro American Press and Africa in the Nineteen Thirties', *Canadian Journal of African Studies*, vol. 1, no. 1 (March 1967), p. 46.

51. Ibid., p. 110.

52. See George Padmore, *The Life and Struggles of Negro Toilers*, Hollywood 1971, pp. 68ff. Geiss observes, however, that 'in his last and most influential book [*Pan-Africanism or Communism?*]

Padmore devoted two chapters to the history of Liberia which were completely uncritical and almost amounted to eyewas': Geiss, *The Pan-African Movement*, p. 127.

53. Du Bois was originally nominated for the honor in 1908 but so too was Booker T. Washington. Du Bois believed the nomination was withdrawn upon the advice of Washington. Cf. Aptheker, *Correspondence of W.E.B. Du Bois*, vol. 2, pp. 287–90.

54. See Robinson, *Black Marxism*, pp. 349ff.

9

C.L.R. James:

Paradoxical Pan-Africanist

Paul Buhle

The monumental career of C.L.R. James, whose ideas and experiences reflect the complexities of Pan-African history, defies easy classification, but not primarily because of his own ambiguity. While exploring vastly different theoretical traditions, James attempted to produce a comprehensive international, political, and cultural solution to the intricate, contradictory developments in the nascent Pan-Africanist movement. An important figure in twentieth-century history, his visionary ideas have helped guide generations of politicians, agitators and scholars.

Any attempt to comprehend C.L.R. James must begin with his childhood in the West Indies and the complexities of the socioeconomic race codes he encountered there. In his first historical and political work, *The Life of Captain Cipriani* (1932), he provides an analysis of Black life in the West Indies:

> It has to be admitted that the West Indian Negro is ungracious enough to be far from perfect. He lives in the tropics, and he has the particular vices of all who live there, not excluding people of European blood. In one respect, indeed, the Negro in the tropics has an overwhelming superiority to all other races – the magnificent virility with which he overcomes the enervating influence of the climate. But otherwise the West Indian people are an easy-going people. Their life is not such as to breed in them the thrift, the care, and the almost equine docility to system and regulation which is characteristic of industrialized Europeans. If their comparative youth as a people saves them from the cramping effects of tradition, a useful handicap to be rid of in the swiftly changing world of today, yet they lack that valuable basis of education which is not so much taught or studied as breathed in from birth in countries where people have for

158

generation after generation lived settled and orderly lives. Quicker in intellect and spirit than the British, they pay for it by being less continent, less stable, less dependable. And this particular aspect of their character is intensified by certain social [racial – PB] prejudices peculiar to the West Indies, and which have never been given their full value by those observers from abroad who have devoted themselves to the problems of West Indian society and politics.[1]

But James's youth was not spent among the easy-going lower class. Both sides of his family, back two generations at least, had attempted to attain middle-class dignity: his father was a schoolteacher perpetually on the verge of financial ruin. He remembers his mother best 'sitting very straight with [a] book held high, her pince-nez on her Caucasian nose, reading till long after midnight'.[2] James internalized his parents' middle-class respect for culture, as well as their lack of emotional warmth; both factors greatly influenced his own development. His origins as a creative writer, as a social historian, as a political revolutionary and even as a Pan-Africanist may be traced to his resulting sensitivity to the cultural gap between Trinidadian classes, and his efforts to cross it.

James's education was based on the Bible, the Greek classics, Shakespeare and the great tradition of British (and to a lesser degree, French) literature; he insisted upon numerous occasions that in the West Indies, 'Everything depended formally upon European literature, European traditions'.[3] However, he *did* resist the assertion that Blacks could not appropriate these traditions, mix them with particular elements of folk and popular culture, and produce something culturally equal and politically superior to the original. We can trace this observation in the young James as a 'conversion' experience of awakening to Black selfhood within a multiracial culture.

A child prodigy of sorts, at age nine James seemed destined to become the lawyer, doctor or politician who brought glory and stability to his family. Within the British-style school system (and for some years after he left school) racism did not hinder him: schoolmasters encouraged him; his white and light-colored friends, the bulk of the privileged youth, admired him. Then suddenly, unexpectedly, psychic stress overtook him. He became a cricket fanatic with a total disregard for his studies. Neither parental beatings nor public humiliation brought him into line. According to Sylvia Wynter's shrewd reading of his semi-autobiographical cricket study, *Beyond a Boundary,* James had unknowingly broken with the racial and class 'code' of the dominant culture. Cricket brought him back to earth, in tune with the representative element of Trinidadian popular life.[4]

Through cricket, James first discovered his calling as a writer (he became a cricket correspondent to the local press) and his political destiny as a vociferous critic of racism. The emergence of West Indian world-class athletes, a consequence of England's relative decline after World War I, made it clear that the exclusion of Black cricketers from Test teams playing in Britain was inexcusable. For the first time, perhaps, the young intellectual sophisticate (by this time a schoolteacher himself) felt the rage of the common Trinidadian. *It wasn't fair.* Or again, in the code of the popular Western tradition: It wasn't cricket.

Various popular elements besides cricket broadened James's cultural awareness: he frequented calypso tents, forbidden by his parents during his youth; he listened to American jazz on gramophone records; and he conversed with people from diverse economic groups. But he did not develop the kind of political awareness that plunged his childhood friend, Malcolm Nurse, into early emigration and left political activity (as George Padmore). However, James enthused over the agitation of Arthur Cipriani, who reorganized the Trinidad Workingmen's Association and founded the Trinidad Labour Party; he gave an occasional speech for Cipriani and wrote an occasional essay for Cipriani's paper, *The Socialist.* By the time of his departure for England, James had collected enough material for his brief biography of Trinidad's foremost radical. But James did not then possess a burning political fire.

The early literary journal *Trinidad* (1929–30), co-edited by James, and its successor *The Beacon* (1931–33), rather expressed his combination of literary realism, nascent nationalism and middle-class aestheticism. He and his colleagues scrutinized Trinidadian society, but they approached it vicariously. Indeed, their greatest literary accomplishment was a detailed, sympathetic study of women in the slums, for which they had to cross class, gender and, for James's predominantly Creole literary comrades, racial barriers. James's own novel, *Minty Alley* (written in 1927 but published in 1936), follows a very James-ian protagonist who explores lower-class life, only to ultimately withdraw.[5]

One can make too much of a cultural and political figure's personal background, no doubt. But although the James who departed for England, still for all intents and purposes politically inactive, was already past thirty, his subsequent political work was greatly influenced by his unique background: the James family's socioeconomic position in the racially, culturally diverse Caribbean.

In England, the true harshness of empire and the ambiguities of race quickly became clear to him. He recalled that other West Indians in Britain looked upon their African counterparts as backward savages. Literature had prepared James to see otherwise. The English, on the other hand, regarded educated Blacks as cultural anomalies; neither Africans nor West

Indians were taken seriously in political terms, although (East) Indians, battle-scarred by the struggle for independence, were more respected.

These impressions help to account for James's response to subsequent events. On a personal level, he became almost overnight a noted cricket reporter for the *Manchester Guardian* and a popular public speaker on West Indian subjects. One could say that the English patronized him as had the colonial teachers and administrators in Trinidad. But James saw the real qualities of imperialism in European indifference to the plight of invaded Ethiopia. And he found, in small circles of comrades, the possibility of organizing a Pan-African liberation. He said that had George Padmore (then a leading figure in the Comintern's Black-oriented organizational force) asked him to go to Moscow to learn how to organize for national independence, he would have gone. A few years later, with Padmore himself no longer a member of the Comintern, the two of them set out to organize the revolution themselves.

But this formulation puts the matter too simply, diminishing once more the complexities of James's development. One is inclined to believe that the Communists' anti-intellectualism – slavish devotion to the crudest theories of art and culture – repelled him as much as their doctrines of Socialism in One Country. Perhaps, although he never said so, the *literary* quality of Leon Trotsky, the charismatic intellectual, appealed to him as well as Trotsky's less didactic vision of world transformation. At any rate, James's conversion to Marxism and to Trotskyism, in 1933–34, greatly influenced his understanding of all world issues. He combined theory, public speaking and literary activity, reviving Pan-Africanism of a certain type: as a Marxist he was wedded to the idea that the Western proletariat would play a crucial, perhaps *the* crucial, role in bringing about Third World independence and subsequent world socialism.

James's theoretical resolution of the apparent disparities between Pan-Africanism and Eurocentric Trotskyism can be found in *The Black Jacobins* (1938), one of the great historical studies in the English language, and the unsurpassed study of slave revolt (I believe) in any language. Here, the connection between events in France and Santo Domingo, the symbiotic relationship between two different forms of world revolution, suggested a pattern James believed could be fostered in the 1940s: the proletarian movements of the West, calling for solidarity from their brothers in the colonies, could stimulate rebellion in the non-white world. James continues to explore this theme, in a more general sense, in *A History of the Negro Revolt*, which explores the Black historical origins of this nascent uprising.

This sequence of events did not, of course, take place. Instead, we must examine James's subsequent activity in the light of unanticipated developments. On the one hand, Black national liberation movements assumed a predominantly constitutional character for some years; revolution in the Black Jacobin sense, for the most part, was no longer part of the agenda. On the other hand, the role of Black movements in the US, center of modern world empire, became increasingly critical to the fate of American and indeed world socialism. James, moving from England to the US in 1938, was geopolitically positioned to explore these developments. However, the resulting transition meant a temporary absence from the growing Pan-African movement during a critical era. (Although remaining on the executive committee of the International African Service Bureau, James played no apparent role in its function.) His contributions to Pan-African practical affairs, until the mid-1950s, must be measured in terms of the training he gave certain individuals: Eric Williams, an emerging scholar whom James paternally guided, and Kwame Nkrumah, whom James educated politically and sent on to Padmore in London. James's contributions to Pan-African theory during this time can be seen in his revision of Marxist (and Trotskyist) theories to highlight the Black role in American civilization.

During an era in which Communist party failures opened up real space on the political left, James became an enthusiastic convert to Trotskyism. Did Pan-Africanism, then, become a function of James's Trotskyism? The question cannot be answered decisively. He maintained in contact with a wide variety of Black intellectuals, and, in the mid-1940s, planned to publish a left-of-center popular Black monthly with various close friends including Richard Wright and Ralph Bunche. He even wrote a lengthy outline for a play in which he hoped Ethel Waters would star, a story of racial and sexual conflict in the era of Abolitionism.[6]

These last projects failed, perhaps because he could not put his whole self into them. However, he believed sufficiently in Trotskyism to attempt political approaches to the Black community through Trotskyist organizations: he wrote weekly newspaper columns on the 'Negro question'; a popular pamphlet urging Black resistance to world war; and many papers on the internal politics of Trotskyism. In 1941, he agitated in rural southwest Missouri, speaking to striking sharecroppers, mostly Black, and writing a remarkable pamphlet based on their thoughts. He also examined various questions of Marxist theory and practice, an effort resulting in an oeuvre at once philosophical, economic and cultural.[7]

James, one of the foremost Black Trotskyist theoreticians, led the development of the Johnson-Forest tendency, which became a small, independent organization. Singularly, it adopted the task of explaining the development of bureaucracy in the East and West as the consequence of a crisis in capital. It also distinguished mere nationalization, the control of resources by the state, from real socialism, the transformation of human social relations inside and outside the factory. Most important, however, the Johnson-Forest tendency suggested that the Black movement, just then emerging onto the political scene, could be used as the basis for a reorganization of the left. No one else had articulated this formulation before James's forceful argument with Trotsky in 1938; no one would again, after James's departure from the US in 1953, until the Black Power movement of the 1960s.

It may be objected that James and his comrades still presupposed the centrality of the proletarian revolution (and even, until the end of the 1940s, the Vanguard Party), in which Black workers would play only a small role. Black remained the color of the otherwise only heterodox Marxist prescription. But James had begun, at first more intuitively than analytically, to reason in a different direction. Living close to Harlem in the early 1940s, going to Cotton Club performances and even attending church, he recalls, 'I know that I said on one or two occasions, all the power is hidden in them there, it's waiting to come out, and the day when it comes out and takes a political form it is going to shake this nation as nothing before has shaken it.' No political or social movements as such, but the cultural signs he observed, reminded him of Du Bois's famous phrase about the Black surge towards equality: 'this is the last great battle of the West.'[8]

James records in his unpublished memoirs that, during his first years in the US, people would tell him he was 'no Black man' – skin color notwithstanding. Although the Communist movement was associated with an array of formidable Black political figures, James had few Black Trotskyist critics (Ernest McKinney, bitterly opposed to Black nationalism on any grounds, was the exception) and virtually no Black Trotskyist allies: he would later remark; 'I was the Third World within the Trotskyite party.' He worked out his formulations with the other members of the Johnson-Forest tendency, but on Black questions he clearly composed the theoretical prescriptions alone. They have a character not quite like any other political documents of the time. For example, at the close of a lengthy document tracing the centrality of Black influence in American life since the Civil War, James's resolution for a 1948 Trotskyist convention says this:

> Let us not forget that in the Negro people, there sleep and are now awakening passions of a violence exceeding, perhaps, as far as these things can be compared, anything among the tremendous forces that capitalism has created. Anyone who knows them, who knows their history, is able to talk to them intimately, watches them at their own theaters, watches them at their dances, watches them in their churches, reads their press with a discerning eye, must recognize that although their social force may not be able to compare with the social force of

a corresponding number of organized workers, the hatred of bourgeois society and the readiness to destroy it when the opportunity should present itself, rests among them to a degree greater than in any other section of the population of the United States . . . [9]

We see here the clearest premonition of the 1960s ghetto uprisings. James anticipated them, but *as if from the outside* – as the artist would see social events in preparation. Here, the artistic and intuitive James, the West Indian James and even the classist James re-emerge as if previously held in solution. Wilson Harris insists that James's intuitional analysis is such that, examined at close range, his views seem to cast a different light than at their first appearance. As usual, Wilson is acute. But there is more to the matter.

Government harassment in the early 1950s, for an earlier passport violation, heightened James's sense of isolation and stimulated the artist-critic in him. Even as the expulsion order arrived, he had written a remarkable text on Melville, *Mariners, Renegades and Castaways*, that placed the fate of society in the hands of the proletarians from all races (predominantly dark) and all corners of the globe who had come to work in capitalism's industrial centers. And he pinpointed in Captain Ahab ('abstract intellect, abstract technology, but blank, serving no purpose but the abstract purpose') the curse of the white world which – his friend Paul Robeson pointed out – Blacks would be fools to imitate.[10]

James was deported to England, now twenty years after he had ceased to be a British political personality. Characteristically, he did not remain inactive, turning his energies in three familiar directions: he surrounded himself with West Indian compatriots; he rediscovered cricket, tracing the trajectory of cultural nationalism in the rise of the Third World athlete; and he observed the revolution in Ghana, at a distance, with great intensity. He wrote variously on all these subjects. *Beyond a Boundary* (1963), one of the finest evocations of sports history and sports criticism anywhere, also presents West Indians as an independent factor in modern civilization. *Nkrumah and the Ghana Revolution* (1977), consisting partly of documents he had sent to Nkrumah decades earlier, is a close study of the revolutionary cultural and political process among Africans, and the bureaucratic leaders who abandoned this system. *Party Politics in the West Indies* (1962) examines, more through documents than narrative, a similar process in Trinidad, sidelighting the philistine middle class and the vital mass culture of the calypso.

In all of these works, the normal categories of the history of social analysis have been stretched to the breaking point. They are as much art criticism (or literary works) as they are analytical studies. The personal element, which becomes increasingly prevalent as James attempts to assess his role as a historical figure in the twentieth century, certifies his presence as subject and object.

James thus radiated a wholly individual, highly personalized Pan-Africanism. 'I think', says Harris, 'the essence of his being is rooted in an exploration of the building-blocks of his age seen through various windows and from different perspectives.'[11] In semiotic terms, James was 'de-centered' because, from the beginning, he had what Antiguan sociologist Paget Henry calls a 'floating center'. He was free to examine various perspectives, like a child raised among many languages, because the West Indies, *his* West Indies, allowed him to do so.[12]

What kind of Pan-Africanism is this? 'The behavioral sciences which colored Marxism', writes Wilson Harris, who might say the same of single-minded, development-oriented ideology of any kind, 'have underestimated the life of the psyche and of the intuitive imagination in its peculiar densities and cross-cultural values.'[13] C.L.R. James, even when he was not wholly conscious of his methodology, followed a unique process towards common goals. At one level, he repudiated the ideology of 'backwardness' through evoking the images of Greek civilization, powerful neither in empire nor numbers but mighty in the relation of philosophy, art and culture to the life of the citizen; this view represented the classics he learned in his youth. At another level, he demonstrated historically, from *The Black Jacobins* onward, that African cultures were by no means inferior to their European counterparts in the centuries before slavery, and that slavery made possible the West's economic-social leap forward *because* of the slaves' knowledge and culture; this view he gained through his training as a historian. And at a third level, he insisted that modern popular cultural phenomena, from calypso to reggae, demonstrate an immanent critique of the limits of Western civilization by those who have grown up in it but who refuse to be constrained by it. James developed this understanding through re-examining the thrill of the calypso tents (or the cricket pitch) illuminated by a lifetime of historical, anthropological and literary self-training.

Gregory Rigsby has called the underlying philosophical principle in James's the 'law of relation'.[14] James himself perhaps put it best in *Beyond a Boundary:* 'It is not a quality of goods and utility which matter, but movement; not where you are or what you have, but where you have come from, where you are going and the rate at which you are getting there.'[15]

Notes

1. Quoted in the revised edition of *The Life of Captain Cipriani, The Case for West Indian Self-Government*, London 1933, pp. 7–8.

2. James, letter to Constance Webb, n.d. 1945. Schomburg Collection, New York Public Library. Quoted with permission of Constance Webb.

3. 'West Indies: Microcosm – Interview', in Buhle, et al., eds, *Free Spirits,* San Francisco 1982, p. 93.

4. Sylvia Wynter, 'In Quest of Matthew Bondman: Some Cultural Notes on the Jamesian Journey', in Buhle, ed., *C.L.R. James: His Life and Work*, London 1986, pp. 131–3.

5. See James, *Minty Alley,* London 1971, and its introduction by Kenneth Ramchand.

6. This is treated at substantial length in Paul Buhle, *C.L.R. James: Artist as Revolutionary,* London 1988, Ch. 2.

7. Buhle, *C.L.R. James: Artist as Revolutionary*, Ch. 3.

8. Quoted from unpublished memoirs.

9. 'The Revolutionary Answer to the Negro Problem in the USA', reprinted in James, *The Future in the Present,* London 1977, pp. 126–7.

10. See Buhle, *C.L.R. James: Artist as Revolutionary*, Ch. 4, and 'Paul Robeson: Black Star', in *Spheres of Existence,* London 1980, pp. 256–64.

11. Wilson Harris, address at Hammersmith, London, 1986 (manuscript and permission to quote given by Harris).

12. See Paget Henry and Paul Buhle, 'Caliban as Deconstructionist: C.L.R. James and Post-Colonial Discourse', in Henry and Buhle, eds, *C.L.R. James's Caribbean,* Durham, N.C. 1992, pp. 111–14.

13. Wilson Harris, Hammersmith address.

14. Gregory Rigsby, 'The Gospel According to St. James', in Buhle, ed., *C.L.R. James: His Life and Work*, especially pp. 222, 228–9.

15. James, *Beyond a Boundary,* New York 1963, pp. 116–17.

10

Writers

and Assassinations

Barbara Harlow

You do not die because you are created or because you have a body.
You die because you are the face of the future.
Adonis, 'The Desert'

People who die for the freedom of others are, like women who die in
childbirth, difficult to explain except to those for whom they died.
Fawaz Turki, Soul in Exile

Everyone has the right to life, liberty and security of person.
Article 3: International Bill of Human Rights

On 22 July 1987, the Palestinian cartoonist Naji al-Ali was shot on a London street outside the offices of *al-Oabas*, a Kuwaiti newspaper for which he drew political caricatures. On 29 August 1987, some six weeks later, Naji al-Ali died without ever having regained consciousness. His last cartoon, drawn just before his assassination, was strangely ominous. In it, Hanzalla, the 'child of the camps' who appeared in all his drawings, back to the viewer, observing the corruption, exploitation and repression in and of the Arab world, lay face down on the ground, an arrow in his heel, killed perhaps by the same forces of oppression that for the last decade and a half the cartoonist had committed himself to exposing.

In the immediate aftermath of the shooting – the assailant has not yet been apprehended – writers, critics, ideologues and friends of the Arab artist raised the insistent question: Who killed Naji al-Ali? Univocal as the question might have been, however, the proffered answers, some tentative, others accusatory, were decidedly dissonant. *The Observer*, in London, on the day following the artist's death blamed the PLO. Reporting a phone call that Naji al-Ali had allegedly received from Yasser Arafat's organization warning him to 'correct his attitude', the *Observer* article went on to describe Naji al-Ali's subsequent cartoon critiquing the Palestinian resistance and its leadership, concluding from these details that 'the tone may have cost him his life'.

Various factions within the PLO, Iran, the Palestinian renegade-extremist Abu Nidal and Mossad, the Israeli secret service, were variously accused in the months that followed of assassination of the Arab world's most popular and well-known cartoonist. An editorial in the 14 September 1987 issue of *al-Hadaf*, the weekly magazine of the Popular Front for the Liberation of Palestine (PFLP), however, asked further, and with implications for the other question 'Who killed Naji al-Ali?', 'Why was Naji al-Ali buried in London?' Why, that is, was the Palestinian cartoonist buried in London and not in Palestine, where he was born, or in Ain al-Hilweh, the Palestinian refugee camp in southern Lebanon where he grew up? Two answers were suggested by the editorialist. The first explanation invoked reasons of security: Given the cartoonist's reputation and renown and the popular anger at his death, could state security forces contain, or even predict, the force of the people's reactions to the loss of this exemplar? The second response was more provocative still: Naji al-Ali's burial in London testified to his controversial independence, his contentious and critical ideological position vis-à-vis the Arab regimes and his insistent 'representation' of all the Arab people, who, like the Palestinians, were systematically exploited.

In a commemorative poem, one Palestinian poet, Murid Barghuti, seconded this indictment of the Arab regimes and their reactionary politics when, in an allusion to the Joseph story, he suggested that it was not the wolf who killed Joseph but his own brothers. For Mahmud Darwish, another Palestinian poet and head of the General Union of Palestinian Writers, Naji al-Ali's assassination provided an occasion to scrutinize the current political and cultural discourse of much of the Arab world. In an article in *al-Yawm al-Sabia'* on 3 August 1987 entitled 'No to Assassination by Bullets, No to Assassination with Words', Darwish wrote that 'for every bullet there is more than one killer and more than one victim'. Much as Israel has sought the mass assassination of the Palestinian people, so too, according to Darwish, has 'assassination come to characterize the dialogue of the Arabs with themselves'.

What was it that singled out Naji al-Ali for death by an assassin's bullet and assigned him a place in the pantheon of martyred artists? For Faysal Darraj, Radwa Ashur and Murid Barghuti in an article in the 17 August 1987 issue of *al-Hadaf*, 'The Tragedy and the Greatness of the Different

Artist', Naji al-Ali had distinguished himself by his very difference, his refusal to accept the dogma of any doctrine either aesthetic or political, and it was this tenacious indépendence that rendered the artist unacceptable, intolerable even, to regimes and systems that must, for their own self-preservation, suppress external opposition and internal contradiction. As an artist, the critics maintained, Naji al-Ali eschewed the structures of power as sanction for his work and chose instead to depict the arena of popular struggle in order to transform the existing distorted relations of power. His political practices too differed from those of the politicians themselves in that he scorned the maneuvers of tactics, calculation, brokering and bargaining. Naji al-Ali's concerns and priorities were elsewhere. But where? What, that is, is the task of the political artist/the artist politician? And why should it get him/her killed?

During the two trips to Africa he made in the last year of his life, and following his controversial departure from the ranks of Elijah.Muhammad's Nation of Islam, Malcolm X sought support from the African heads of state that he met with there for his proposal to bring the historical situation of African-Americans in the United States before the United Nations. That situation, like those in South Africa and Rhodesia, he argued, should be globally condemned as an abuse, flagrant and willful, of international covenants and agreements respecting the human rights of all peoples of the world. Malcolm X's work in Africa, like his activities in the United States, was meanwhile of considerable concern to the FBI, which included in its copious files on him a *New York Times* article from Cairo dated 14 July 1964 that reported: 'Malcolm X, the black nationalist leader said today that he had come to attend a meeting of the council of ministers of the Organization of African Unity as an observer. He arrived yesterday. He said he intended to acquaint African heads of state "with the true plight of America's Negroes and thus show them how our situation is as much a violation of the United Nations human rights charter as the situation in Africa and Mongolia."'[1] Malcolm X would, however, speak more challengingly – and decisively – to the issue on his return to the United States. In an interview on 2 December 1964 with talk show host Les Crane, he asserted that '[i]t's not a Negro problem or an American problem any longer. It's a world problem, it's a human problem. And so we're striving to lift it from the level of civil rights to the level of human rights. And at that level it's international. We can bring it into the United Nations and discuss it in the same tone and in the same language as the problems of people in other parts of the world also is (sic) discussed'.[2] And five days before he was assassinated in the Audabon Ballroom, Malcolm X returned to that transformative work that would link 'civil rights' with 'human rights' and make the United States accountable to international respect for those rights. He had concluded his Rochester speech of 16 February 1964 with this provocative admonition:

> All nations that signed the charter of the UN came up with the Declaration of Human Rights and anyone who classifies his grievances under the label of 'human rights' violations, those grievances can then be brought into the United Nations and be discussed by people all over the world. For as long as you call it 'civil rights' your only allies can be the people in the next community, many of whom are responsible for your grievance. But when you call it 'human rights' it becomes international. And then you can take your troubles to the World Court. You can take them before the world. And anybody anywhere on this earth can become your ally.[3]

Five days later Malcolm X's body was riddled by assassins' bullets as he rose to address a meeting of the newly formed Organization of Afro-American Unity, an attack that did succeed, temporarily at least, in halting the international inquiry that the Black leader had sought to initiate.

Much as the assassins – and it is still, a quarter of a century later, in dispute as to who and how many they were, and at whose behest(s) they had carried out the attack – shot down the man, the US Congress had for a decade and a half been engaged in obstructing the project of enforcing the United Nations Covenants on Human Rights in the US. While the United States had, with most other UN member nations, been among the signatories to the various charters, Congress had (and in most cases still has) yet to ratify them. Of particular concern to Congress was the Genocide Convention, the first such treaty to be forwarded to the Senate for approval. Congressional objections, as Natalie Kaufman has pointed out, were largely indicative of subsequent opposition to the other treaties as well, that is, that they would 'diminish basic rights', 'promote world government', 'enhance Soviet Communist influence', 'subject citizens to trial to abroad', and 'threaten the US form of government'. Senator H. Alexander Smith's (Rep.-N.J.) expression of concerns suggests that genocide might well be worth killing for, referring, as did others who endorsed a similar position, to the history of African-Americans, ratification of the Genocide Convention could mean that '[w]e may be charged with [genocide], that is the danger, and the Court of International Justice may say that there is a prima facie case made against the United States of genocide, and there you are, left, condemned in the eyes of the world.'[4] And that condemnation is precisely what Malcolm X, in linking the issues of 'civil rights' with the imperatives of 'human rights', was preparing to do when he was killed on 21 February 1965 by assassins' bullets.

Many are the questions that have been raised over the last quarter of a century concerning the circumstances of Malcolm X's death. For Malik Miah, writing in 1976, in the introduction to *The Assassination of Malcolm X*, 'Identifying the killers of Malcolm X, Martin Luther King, and Fred Hampton is not just a matter of historical interest. It is an urgent defensive measure for the Black movement, to prevent future assassinations of its leaders.'[5] Bruce Perry, more cynically, considers that '[r]evolutionaries are not required to succeed. Usually, they end up defeated or dead, martyrs to their chosen cause.'[6] For the FBI, the matter was rather different still. In a memorandum dated 25 February 1965, the Bureau wrote:

MALCOLM K. LITTLE
INTERNAL SECURITY – MMI

In view of the subject's death, his name is being removed from the Security Index at the Bureau and you should handle accordingly in your office.

Submit an appropriate memorandum noting his death, for dissemination at the Bureau,

Attention [BUREAU DELETION].

Cancel SI cards.[7]

The question, however, of who killed Malcolm X, like the inquiries on another continent into the death of Naji al-Ali decades later, is more than a defensive one, a cynical comment, or a 'security index' card. It is a systemic question, a historical one. What happens, that is, should genocide turn to assassination?

The very function of the author, at least in Western culture, according to Michel Foucault in 'What Is an Author?', is to 'limit, exclude, choose'. The author's self, in other words, provides the 'functional principle by which, in our culture, . . . one impedes the free circulation, the free manipulation, the free composition, decomposition and recomposition of fiction.' The author, maintains Foucault further, is 'the ideological figure by which one marks the manner in which we fear the proliferation of meaning'.[8] The critical convention governing the concept of 'author' presupposes the separation of the artist from the political conditions within which s/he writes, the ideological milieu within which s/he works. Such a separation between a self and an other, the rhetorical basis of a politics of identity and itself crucial to the definition of author as Foucault presents it, is a cordon that Naji al-Ali, for example, refutes, that his drawings confute. The collapse of the inherited distinction between culture and politics is, however, anathema to the dominant structures of power, which continue to insist on what Terry Eagleton has called the 'stalest of Arnoldian cliches, [that] the "poetic" as we have it today was, among other things, historically constructed to carry out just that of suppressing political conflict.[9] The guardians of cultural preserves must maintain the separation of culture and politics at least in so far as this separation underwrites their territorial elitism and the ideological mystification whereby their ascendancy remains unassailed. The politicians must, for their part, necessarily be wary lest culture be wrested from the control of the servitors they have appointed and whose services the state apparatus has enlisted -- lest, that is, culture begin to function in mobilizing popular opposition. The language of objectivity and transcendence cultivated by culture's keepers is thus designed to obscure its own antinomies, partisan positionings and the very sectarianism of the self/other divide.

The threat posed by the reassertion of the intersection of culture and politics, such as that argued in Naji al-Ali's cartoons, to a dominant ideology of authoritarian control is attested to by the violence and consistency of the policing reaction to such an intersection. Such policing is marked, for example, by the implementation of censorship both overt and covert, from the McCarthy hearings in the United States in the 1950s to the rhetoric of 'standards' and 'basics' that characterizes the Reagan/Bush regimes' education policy and makes it possible for one and the same man to qualify for the positions of both Secretary of Education and 'drug czar'. It includes the Israeli military occupation's repeated closings of Palestinian universities and schools in the West Bank and Gaza Strip, the official denial of a teaching post to the historian Walter Rodney when he returned to his native Guyana, and the Salvadoran army's four-year occupation of the University of El Salvador from 1980 to 1984, as well as the assassination by right-wing death squads in November 1989 of six Jesuit priests in El Salvador's Central American University. The control of what Foucault referred to as the 'circulation, manipulation and composition' of cultural production extends as well to the imprisonment of dissident intellectuals, and even, when necessary, the assassination of the authors.

The litany of committed intellectuals who have been the victims of political assassination bears witness, then, both to the coercive effectiveness of a dominant ideology of separatism and its need to eliminate those individuals in whose work a space is elaborated for 'the face of the future', the conjunction of culture and political struggle, as well as to the creative potential of such a conjunction and the collective possibilities across self/other divides that it entails. The violent deaths of these intellectuals delineate in turn a critical site for a self-critique from within the resistance movement to which they contributed through their work and a re-elaboration of strategies of resistance that emerges out of the inquiry into the circumstances of their deaths: Naji al-Ali (Palestinian, died 1987); Malcolm X (African-American, died 1965); Amilcar Cabral (Guinea Bissau, died 1973); Steve

Biko (South African, died 1977); Walter Rodney (Guyana, died 1980); Roque Dalton (Salvadoran, died 1975); Ghassan Kanafani (Palestinian, died 1972); and Ruth First (South African, died 1982).

The assassination of political writers, artists and intellectuals raises a number of significant questions with regard to the very nature of the investigation into their deaths. Beyond the most immediate question, 'who killed ...?', is located a further set of issues implied in the attempted responses to such a question, issues that challenge both the investigator and the research: 'what does it mean to ask, 'who killed ...?'' and what are the consequences that attend upon the asking of the question, 'who killed ...?'? What kind of examination is required in constructing an answer to these questions? The question posed in the terms of 'who killed ...? entails for the investigator a detective function, according to which a murderer-assassin must be identified, apprehended, and 'brought to justice'. The traditional 'whodunit' provides a literary model based on the structural prerequisites of 'law and order' for the narrative of such an investigation. The political or ideological function, by contrast, that asks not after the 'who', but into the 'how and why' that s/he was killed, not only redefines the 'crime' but reconstructs the very elements of history and agency that are constitutive of it. Unlike the detective function, the political or ideological response to political assassination involves an interrogation of the state apparatuses that determine the nature of crime itself, proposing thereby a narrative that challenges the past in its demands for a review of history and charts alternative possibilities for the future in its critical rethinking of the contradictions and conflicts of that past.

These two functions, the detective and the political or ideological, are differently assigned and alternatively defined in *Murder in Mexico*, the report on the investigation into the assassination of Leon Trotsky in Mexico City in 1940.[10] Its author, Leandro Sanchez Salazar, was at the time of Trotsky's death chief of Mexico's secret police, and in the introduction to his personal account of the police mission he describes his role in the investigation as well as his own investment in the work:

> Destiny ordained that there should be a gap in my long career as a soldier to allow me to occupy the post of Mexican Chief of Police. I threw myself into this work with great enthusiasm. Police investigations thrilled me. I realised that I had the makings of a good detective, and, with the loyal collaboration of my assistants, soon got used to the work and devoted all my energy to it. And thus it fell to my lot to investigate the final tragedy of Don Leon, as, with respect and admiration, I called Trotsky. (p. ix)

Julian Gorkin, by contrast, who assisted Sanchez Salazar in his narrative reconstruction of the police investigation, emphasizes rather the significance for him of the ideological opposition to Stalinism that such an inquiry enabled at the time. Gorkin's introduction to *Murder in Mexico,* which follows that of Sanchez Salazar, while not ignoring his own personal involvement in the investigation, nonetheless foregrounds instead the alternative possibilities of the hegemonic and the counter-hegemonic, contained in the question 'Who killed ...?:

> I have never been attracted by police work, for I have too often been its victim, but in these circumstances my disinterested aid was a duty. I took a deep interest in the enquiry. It was, in fact, really engrossing, for it consisted of a battle against Stalinism and its methods. I was only continuing a struggle started at the time of my break with the Comintern in 1929, a struggle which had already cost me so much bitterness. As will be seen, it was not yet finished. (pp. xv–xvi)

The subversive consequences of this combined investigation and report by both police chief (and albeit an exceptional one) and ideologue are further emphasized by the delay imposed on the publication of Sanchez Salazar's *Murder in Mexico* by the circumstances of World War II and Stalin's alliance at the time with the Western powers, a delay not unrelated to the deferral of the release of Trotsky's own book on Stalinism until, as Gorkin reports, a more 'opportune' moment. (p. xviii)

The controversy, then, surrounding the investigation and its published report of Trotsky's assassination – as much even as the assassination itself – makes manifest the critical enterprise and its political ramifications that inhere in the question, 'Who killed ...?' and its translations as 'How and Why?' The investigation becomes itself an intervention into the existing relationships of political power with consequences for the positioning of the investigators and their own political situation.

Assassination has been variously defined over the ages by political scientists, historians, and legal advisors to monarchs, rulers legitimate and illegitimate, and governments. The term itself, *assassination,* is generally traced to an Ismaili Shi'ite sect that operated in Syria and Iran in the eleventh and twelfth centuries. Known as the *hashishiyun* (whence the word *assassins*), the members of this group were reputed to slay their opponents with a bravado that was popularly attributed to their use of drugs. More recently, however, the legal and political definitions of assassination have been debated and refined in order to accommodate both the pressures of contemporary circumstances, and, just as significantly, the demands of a system that seeks to contain within its legal and political jurisdiction the challenges to its authority. The political scientists Havens, Leiden and Schmitt, for example, in *The Politics of Assassination* written in 1970 following upon a period of recurrent international assassinations, define *assassination* as the 'deliberate, extralegal killing of an individual for political purposes.'[11] The case studies they present range without distinction or qualification from Verwoerd in South Africa and Somoza in Nicaragua to Patrice Lumumba of the Congo and Martin Luther King, Jr in the United States, a collection designed presumably to demonstrate an their objective neutrality concerning the politics of assassination. That neutrality, however, betrays its own partisan positioning in the authors' expression of their abiding concern for the 'systemic impacts produced by assassination', their concern, that is, with assassination as an untoward, 'extralegal', disruption of the status quo.

Franklin Ford's more recent study, *Political Murder* (1985),[12] assumes a similarly 'neutral' position in its presentation of the history of assassination, from the regicides of ancient Egypt and Israel to contemporary acts of 'terrorism', Ford, however, locates his neutrality in that same historicizing of the phenomenon of 'political murder' and its centuries-long development, revealing in the volume's subtitle the political program that informs the ideological trajectory of his historical narrative: *From Tyrannicide to Terrorism*. Ford defines *assassination* as the 'intentional killing of a specified victim or group of victims, perpetrated for reasons related to his (her, their) public prominence and undertaken with a political purpose in view.' (p. 2) In his adjudication of contemporary assassinations, however, Ford marks a shift, 'from tyrannicide to terrorism', in what he has delineated in the history of assassination as 'political purpose' and concludes that 'what remains [today] is behavior, stripped of political trappings. And of behavior that is murderous, whatever its partisan claims, one must ask: 'What about political life?' (p. 240) In thus defining what counts as 'political' and what does not on what are claimed to be historical grounds, the 'political' itself becomes only that which can be accommodated within the parameters of the dominant ideology and its legislation of that 'political'. Ford's analysis of the modern world thus exempts from its purview assassinations carried out by the state or its paramilitary branches from political scrutiny and disallows investigation into the events of state-sponsored 'terror' and their legacy, a legacy of opposition and resistance that might serve to regenerate the very strategies that the state-committed assassination sought to eradicate.[12]

The much heralded 'death of the author', then, the assassination of writers and authors, cannot always be reduced, or sublimated, to a metaphorical, or even literary, phenomenon. Rather the assassination of the writer is a historical and political event with very tangible and material consequences for theorizing the subsequent participation in and reclamation of the work of intellectual figures who have been instrumental in organizing resistance to systems and discourses of domination.

In his essay, 'National Liberation and Culture', delivered at Syracuse University in 1970 as the first Eduardo Mondlane Memorial Lecture, Amilcar Cabral addressed his audience with the appeal, 'If we manage to persuade the African freedom fighters and all those concerned for freedom and progress of the African peoples of the conclusive importance of this question [of the relation between the national liberation struggle and culture] in the process of struggle, we shall have paid significant homage to Eduardo Mondlane.'[13] In concluding his address, Cabral returned to the assassination of the former president of Mozambique's resistance movement, FRELIMO, by agents of the Portuguese government in 1969:

> One might say that Eduardo Mondlane was *savagely* assassinated because he was capable of identifying with the culture of his people, with their deepest aspirations, through and against all attempts or temptations for the alienation of his personality as an African and a Mozambican. Because he had forged a new culture in the struggle, he fell as a combatant. (p. 154, Cabral's emphasis)

In this contextualization of his remarks on culture and struggle within the history of Mondlane's assassination, Cabral insists on the political and ideological significance of understanding the reconstruction of the resistance movement and recharting its agenda of liberation. While the essay, 'National Liberation and Culture', stands on its own as an important contribution to the complex debate on the function of national culture in organizing resistance to colonial domination, the narrative frame of Mondlane's assassination is itself critical to the essay's intervention into that debate. Amilcar Cabral, that is, historically grounds his already historicized theoretical formulations of the role of culture within that frame, developed from the specific material conditions of resistance, in the national liberation struggle.

Just four years after he delivered his homage to Eduardo Mondlane, Amilcar Cabral was himself assassinated in Conakry by members of his own Guinea-Bissau resistance organization, the PAIGC, working in collaboration with the Portuguese military regime. While Cabral had always maintained that 'we are all necessary to the struggle, but no one is indispensable',[13] his death was critical to the subsequent history of the national liberation struggle in Portugal's African colonies. Liberation would come to Guinea-Bissau a year later, in 1975, but the means to that liberation as well as to its developments in ensuing years were significantly conditioned by Cabral's leadership and his unanticipated death.

As Patrick Chabal wrote in his posthumous intellectual and political biography of the PAIGC leader, a study in which the fact of Cabral's untimely death provides a retrospective re-reading of the issues of 'revolutionary leadership and people's war',

> Revolutionary leaderships are sensitive to the deaths of party leaders both because leadership is usually a key to the success of their political action and because they often have no institutionalized mechanism to replace the leadership. In the early stages of a revolution, particularly, the loss of a strong leader may well change the unity and cohesion of the party itself. (p. 132)

Chabal goes on to examine the dynamics of the PAIGC on the eve of liberation and in the shadow of Cabral's death, as well as in the later developments of independence and postcolonial politics. Cabral's own philosophy of resistance becomes in this context crucial both to the enterprise of understanding the motivation for killing him and to the party's structural and theoretical capacity to sustain its strategy. Critical to Cabral's philosophy was the international vision of emancipation that he represented within Africa in the combined resistance movements of Cape Verde and Guinea-Bissau as well as globally in his emphasis on the necessarily collective struggle of Africans and the Portuguese working class against imperialist exploitation.

Basil Davidson, in his tribute to Cabral in 1980 on the tenth anniversary of the leader's death, reiterates that vision: 'The true vocation of these new nations – true in the sense of the capacity to yield a further process of development – was to overcome the colonial heritage by moving "beyond nationalism".'[15] Why, Davidson goes on to ask, 'should a revolutionary nationalism not grow in time, organically, regionally, into an internationalism?' (p. 43) Davidson's essay, 'On Revolutionary Nationalism: The Legacy of Cabral', focuses on Cabral's contributions to the First World's theorizing of resistance and in this it differs from Patrick Chabal's study, which focuses on the African context of the assassination of Amilcar Cabral. Davidson, however, reminds his audience that it is to Africa that the First World strategist must look in order to sustain Cabral's political and cultural legacy.

Davidson's reading of that legacy opens with two components of Cabral's thinking: the concept of a colonial petty bourgeois leadership which must commit 'class suicide' in its class consciousness (and class interests), and the argument that any real liberation must be a revolutionary process of revolution. These two directives taken from Cabral's strategy of resistance contribute as well to an understanding of Cabral's own death, revealing the failure of the colonial bourgeoisie to rethink and revise its own historical role. Davidson proposes rather to relocate Cabral's death through a re-examination of its significance in a 'process of revolution'. Significantly, then, it was Cabral's explicit acknowledgement of internationalism that Davidson sees as crucial to his legacy. Pointing to Cabral's work with regard to the Portuguese political situation, Davidson asks, 'Whenever before had revolutionary change in Africa helped to promote revolutionary change in Europe? Hadn't all the books declared that such a thing was impossible, even unthinkable? Yet it happened, and this was another part of the legacy of Cabral.' (p. 23)

At the trial in South Africa of Steve Biko in 1976, the leader of the Black Consciousness movement, on charges of 'alleged subversion by intent', a singular aspect of the prosecutor's examination of the defendant focused on the death by assassination of Nthuli Shezi, the vice president of the Black People's Convention (BPC). The prosecutor brought as incriminating evidence against Biko the wording of the tribute to Shezi issued by the BPC: 'The violent assassination was inflicted by an agent of protection of white racism, superiority and oppression on our Black brother. It should not be regarded as being directed towards him alone, but should be regarded as an assault on the entire Black community.'[16] More incriminating still as evidence of Biko's subversive intentions was the defendant's attendance at Shezi's funeral:

Attwell: Did you attend Shezi's funeral?

Biko: I was there, yes.

Attwell: Was it an emotional funeral?

Biko: All funerals are emotional.

Attwell: What sort of speeches were delivered?

Biko: There were speeches to encourage people to continue. It is the typical African situation, when anybody of note dies the normal theme of the speeches there is that what he was doing other people must continue with. That was the theme of the white minister who conducted the funeral.

Attwell: You say it was a white minister who conducted the funeral?

Biko: Yes it was.

Attwell: I submit to you that the speakers brought out all the good in Mr. Shezi, whatever good there may have been, and neglected any weak points that he may have had.

Biko: This is done.

Attwell: And brought out all the evil things they could about the whites, and ignored all the good there may or may not be. Would you agree with me?

Biko: I think they have not finished all the evil. (Woods, p. 202)

Steve Biko's own death in detention in 1977 has assisted in producing another kind of cross-examination, one designed to interrogate the South African apartheid system as a whole – as summed up in its prison apparatus. Because the official inquest into the causes and responsibility for Biko's death while in detention did not culminate in any indictment, much less punishment, of guilty parties in his assassination, because, as Donald Woods puts it, 'the State had not seen fit to indict anyone for the death of Steve Biko, it becomes necessary to indict the State' (p. 355). Following the inquest, however, and in response partly to international protest, the South African government did appoint a commission of inquiry headed by Justice Rabie to investigate the conditions of detention, and in particular political detention, in South Africa. The conclusions of the Rabie Report did expose some of the individual abuses of justice, but nonetheless upheld the overall authority of the legal system and its penal apparatus. The report furthermore carefully avoided the testimony or evidence of a single former detainee, but did make a number of recommendations that were eventually translated into law, including the Internal Security Act of 1982, which instituted four types of detention with trial.

In the meantime South African deaths in detention multiplied, including that of the trade unionist Neil Aggett in 1982, following which the Detainees' Parents Support Committee was established. Four years later, in 1986, three independent researchers from the University of Cape Town, Don Foster, Dennis Davis and Diane Sandler, published their own report on torture in South African prisons. Designed as a response to the Rabie Commission's official inquiry, *Detention and Torture in South Africa*.[17] is itself a kind of commemoration of Steve Biko's assassination in detention, the indictment of the State that Biko's comrades had called for. In the testimony of several former detainees cited in the report, the example of Steve Biko figures prominently, critically displaying the attempt on the part of the interrogators to appropriate once again from the popular narrative their own ultimate authority over the investigation into the circumstances of his death. According to one former prisoner,

> I was asked where I was going, and I told them that I was going to Sterkspruit for a holiday, and then I was taken to another office where there was a picture of Steve Biko. Then I was asked if I know this guy, and I say yes, that I know him. And they asked me where he is now, and I told them that he is dead. And they said that I will follow him if I don't speak the truth. (p. 130)

Another prisoner told a similar story of his experience of questioning: 'Because it was just after that Biko thing and they also told me, "You know how Biko died?" So we are going to take it seriously. After – they say people are trying to escape.' (p. 147)

In recontextualizing these excerpts of the prison system's interrogation of political prisoners within an investigation into the prison system itself, *Detention and Torture in South Africa* offers an alternative future, another legacy – if a posthumous one – of Biko's work and his death. That death then becomes a part of the investigation into conditions of political detention throughout the world. As Mario Hector wrote in *Death Row* from Jamaica in 1984, 'A new vibe emanated from this genesis of resistance . . .'[18]

In 1968, the Guyanese historian and theorist of Europe's underdevelopment of Africa, Walter Rodney, was barred from re-entering Jamaica where he had been teaching at the University of the West Indies following a two-year assignment in Tanzania. Twelve years later Walter Rodney was assassinated in his native Guyana where, as in Jamaica, he had been prevented from assuming the teaching post that he had returned from Africa to undertake. The actual circumstances of Rodney's death are not unknown, but the reasons for it remain controversial. According to Pierre Michel Fontaine, citing a sworn statement by Donald Rodney, Walter Rodney's brother, 'a government plant, Gregory Smith, an electronic expert and covert member of the Guyana Defense Force, had given Walter a two-way radio and advised him to go and test it in a particular area near the Georgetown prison. Apparently the bomb that the murderer(s) had placed inside the device being tested was triggered by a radio signal.'[19] The Guyanese government claimed for its part that it was Rodney's technological ignorance that caused his death.

If the government's account of the assassination is hardly credible, the death of the author of *How Europe Underdeveloped Africa* occasioned important reassessments among his comrades of Rodney's own historical significance and the history of counter-hegemonic resistance more generally. In investigating Rodney's death and its attendant injunctions for charting alternative trajectories, the historian's own admonitions, cited by Douglas Ferguson, are perhaps incumbent on his successors: 'Make certain the history you produce is the result of the application of the analytical tools and not the imposition of conclusions from elsewhere.'[129] If Patrick Chabal saw in Amilcar Cabral's assassination the fortuitous conjuncture of happenstance with the leader's 'personality and his style of leadership; the structure of the PAIGC as a whole', (Chabal, p. 135) C.L.R. James elicited a similar problematic from the conditions of Rodney's death. James asked not only 'Who?': 'The assassin, I believe, has disappeared. He was an agent of the Burnham government. Everyone has talked about the murder, but they have not talked about *that*' (p. 140; but also 'Why?' With this other question, James raised a further debate about Walter Rodney's assassination, one that summoned a larger political analysis of the structures of leadership and the collective responsibilities of the organization itself: 'Rodney', James claimed, 'should never have been there. No political leader had any right to be there. Not only should he never have been there, the people around him should have seen to it that he was not in any such position. That was a fundamental mistake, and it was a political mistake.'[21]

The task, then, that follows for researchers upon Walter Rodney's assassination is more than academic. According to Ewart Thomas, these inquirers into the manifold question of 'Who killed Walter Rodney?' are enjoined now to 'go into our various disciplines and attack the myths and distortions that result from the dominance of Eurocentric scholarship in these disciplines.'[22] This task involves, as C.L.R. James maintained, the research of politics as much as it does the politics of research: 'I hope somebody will make it his business to write a thesis on what happened in the Guyana revolution and the death of Walter Rodney, which is not just the death of a singular and remarkable individual. It is a whole political problem that is involved there, and I would like you to look at it that way.' (Alpers and Fontaine, p. 144)

'Who killed Naji Ali?' 'Who killed Walter Rodney?' What questions must be asked in order to begin an investigation into their assassinations. More important perhaps than the question 'Who?' are the issues of 'How?' and 'Why?' And when is the 'opportune moment' for the examination of these questions? Roque Dalton was a Salvadoran poet, writer and partisan in the Ejercito Revolucionario del Pueblo (ERP) within the Salvadoran resistance movement. In 1975 Dalton, who opposed the militaristic agenda of some of the members of the organization in favor of a prolonged people's war and more popular organizing on the ground prior to the undertaking of a major military operation, was ordered executed, in a decision whose consequences are still being played out, by those cadres with whom he had disagreed.

Three years earlier, in Beirut in July 1972, Ghassan Kanafani, a Palestinian writer, critic, novelist and journalist for the PFLP, was assassinated in a car-bomb explosion that also took the life of his twelve-year-old niece, Lamees. Mossad, the Israeli secret service, eventually claimed responsibility for the death of the 'commando who never fired a gun', as one obituary described the Palestinian intellectual. Mossad's claim, however, relieved the Palestinian resistance of the kind of self-scrutiny that had followed upon Naji al-Ali's assassination or Roque Dalton's execution. Kanafani's radical political theorizing on behalf of a 'democratic revolution' as the prerequisite for a 'democratic secular state', that had characterized his writing from the early novel *Men in the Sun* to his last essay on 'the case of Abu

Hamidu' raise again the question, 'If Ghassan Kanafani were alive today, would he be allowed to live?' Like Amilcar Cabral's internationalism, Steve Biko's Black consciousness, Walter Rodney's class analysis of the world capitalist system, and Roque Dalton's revisioning of militarism, Kanafani's critique of sectarianism was as anathema to recalcitrant forces in his own movement as it was to the Zionism of the state of Israel. The resistance movements themselves, the political and intellectual inheritors of these legacies, have assumed the task of elaborating answers to the questions posed by the 'deaths of their authors', the assassinations of their leadership.

Black Gold is a study of Mozambican migrant workers in the mines of South Africa, published in 1983 under the name of Ruth First, a white South African woman active in the ANC and the South African Communist party in the 1960s.[23] A journalist and a historian of Africa as well, Ruth First was arrested during the Rivonia raids on the African National Congress in 1963 in South Africa and sentenced under the Ninety Day Detention Law. Her prison memoir, *117 Days,* takes its title from this law, which allowed automatic renewal of detention at the discretion of the authorities. Eventually, following various banning orders and restrictions on her work, and later a period in England where she co-authored a biography of Olive Schreiner with Ann Scott, First went into her final exile in Mozambique. Her activities as a researcher at Eduardo Mondlane University in Maputo came to an end when she was assassinated by a parcel bomb in 1982. At Mondlane University, First had been part of a large research collective studying migrant labor patterns in the countries of Southern Africa and their effects on historical transformations in the indigenous social structures. The volume entitled *Black Gold* was part of that collaborative research effort and combines historical background and sociological analysis of the 'proletarianization of the peasantry', interviews with miners and their families and work songs composed and sung by male migrants as well as by those men, women and children who remained behind.

Black Gold was published posthumously in the year following Ruth First's death, posthumously, that is, only if one considers the function of 'author' according to the most limited definition of the word, as referring to the personal identity of the authorial individual. The contribution of *Black Gold,* however, to a reconstruction of political strategy and the ideology of literary critical practice is manifold and includes an implicit critique of authorship and the 'task of the intellectual' in the resistance struggle. The reformulation of genre, together with its textual analysis of class and race in the migrant labor movement, which confutes a sectarian definition of nationalism as an enabling paradigm, is reinscribed on a socio-political

182

level over the issue of authorial identity. The very circumstances of exile that conditioned First's participation in the research project require a particular construction of nationalism and departure from it. Unlike her compatriot Nadine Gordimer, for example, for whom exile from South Africa is construed either as escape to Europe, as in her novel *Burger's Daughter,* or as existential flight in the case of Maureen Smales's headlong plunge at the end of *July's People,* Ruth First would seem to have reworked the exile imposed by the South African state as continued participation in the popular history of African resistance. Ruth First's biographical narrative intersects with the labor history of the migrant worker, and *Black Gold* can be read critically as an active, indeed committed, conflation of the two modes, otherwise separated by disciplinary strictures and a cult of individual authorship. If *Black Gold* is read as the autobiography of the partisan intellectual subject in which a personal itinerary is assimilated into a larger historical narrative of resistance and struggle, then First's own exile becomes crucial as part of the means to the narration of the history of the migrant workers. Her political task as an intellectual is subsumed by the cooperative research project in which the laborers themselves acquire authorial voices and historical agency.

The issues of authorial identity and the work of the intellectual are reconstituted across national borders. Ruth First's identification, like that of other partisans, allows for an identification of the resistance movement within an expanded emancipatory agenda as well. It suggests multiple answers to the questions, 'Who killed ....?' and 'How?' and 'Why?' – answers to be located in a revisioning of the calculated antagonism of the dominant self/other paradigm into a collective struggle against sectarian exploitation.

A T-shirt popular in the occupied West Bank since the beginning of the Palestinian *intifada* carries on its back Naji al-Ali's 'child of the camps', Hanzalla. On the front of the T-shirt is a Naji al-Ali cartoon in which the Hanzalla figure with *nahnu,* or 'we', written on his back is shown reaping a field of wheat, whose shafts are drawn in the shape of the Arabic word for 'I'. All of these biographies/obituaries were written in blood prior to 1990–91, prior, that is, to the fall of the Berlin Wall, the Gulf War, the dissolution of the Soviet Union, crises which configure part of a conjectural closure to one era of 'national liberation'. That 'closure', however, enjoins at the same time a new urgency, perhaps a rewriting – if not in blood – a reprise of the radical secularist issues, the emancipatory and visionary linkage of 'civil rights' and 'human rights', that these writers/martyrs/revolutionaries lived – and died – for. Naji al-Ali, Malcolm X, Amilcar Cabral, Steve Biko, Walter Rodney, Roque Dalton, Ghassan Kanafani, Ruth First: If they were alive today, would their erstwhile enemies have made new allies, who in turn would find it no less necessary to assassinate them?

Notes

1. Cited in Clayborne Carson, *Malcolm X: The FBI File*, New York 1991, p. 330.
2. Bruce Perry, ed., *Malcolm X: The Last Speeches*, New York 1989, p. 89.
3. Ibid., p. 181.
4. Cited in Natalie Hevener Kaufman, *Human Rights Treaties and the Senate: A History of Opposition*, Chapel Hill, N.C. 1990, p. 45.
5. George Breitman et al., *The Assassination of Malcolm X*, New York 1976, p. 12.
6. Bruce Perry, *Malcolm X: The Life of a Man Who Changed Black America*, Barrytown, N.Y. 1991, p. 280.
7. Carson, *Malcolm X*, p. 383.
8. Michel Foucault, 'What Is an Author?' in Josue Harari, ed., *Textual Strategies*, Ithaca, N.Y. 1979, p. 159.
9. Terry Eagleton, 'Nationalism: Irony and Commitment', in Terry Eagleton, Fredric Jameson, Edward Said, eds, *Nationalism, Colonialism and Literature*, New York 1990, p. 33.
10. Gen. Leonardo A. Sanchez Salazar, *Murder in Mexico: The Assassination of Leon Trotsky*, with Julian Gorkin, Phyllis Hawley, trans., Westport, Conn. 1950.
11. M.C. Havens, C. Leiden and M.K. Schmitt, *The Politics of Assassination*, Englewood Cliffs, N.J. 1970, p. 4.
12. Franklin Ford, *Political Murder: From Tyrannicide to Terrorism*, Cambridge, Mass. 1985.
13. Amilcar Cabral, 'National Liberation and Culture' in *Unity and Struggle: Speeches and Writings of Amilcar Cabral*, Michael Wolfers, trans., New York 1979, p. 139.
14. Cited in Patrick Chabal, *Amilcar Cabral: Revolutionary Leadership and People's War*, Cambridge 1983, p. 142.
15. Basil Davidson, 'On Revolutionary Nationalism: The Legacy of Cabral', *Race and Class*, vol. 27, no. 3 (1986), p. 42.
16. Cited in Donald Woods, *Biko*, New York 1979, p. 201–2.
17. Don Foster, Dennis Davis and Diane Sandler, *Detention and Torture in South Africa: Psychological, Legal and Historical Studies*, New York 1987.
18. Mario Hector, *Death Row*, London 1984, p. 36.
19. Pierre Michel Fontaine, 'Walter Rodney: Revolutionary and Scholar in the Guyanese Political Cauldron' in Edward A. Alpers and Pierre Michel Fontaine, eds, *Walter Rodney: Revolutionary and Scholar: A Tribute*, Los Angeles 1982, p. 42.
20. E. Douglas Ferguson, 'Walter Rodney's Application of Marxist Theory to the African Past and Present' in Alpers and Fontaine, eds, *Walter Rodney*, p. 101.
21. C.L.R. James, 'Walter Rodney and the Question of Power' in Alpers and Fontaine, *Walter Rodney*, p. 139.
22. Ewart Thomas, 'Towards the Continuance of Walter Rodney's Work' in Alpers and Fontaine, eds, *Walter Rodney*, p. 40.
23. Ruth First, *Black Gold: The Mozambican Miner, Proletarian and Peasant*, New York 1983.

11

Max Yergan and South Africa:

A Transatlantic Interaction

David H. Anthony

Depression-era Black America gave rise to a number of local, regional and national leaders. One of these was Max Yergan, a one-time YMCA secretary in South Africa who became highly visible in the US left between 1936 and 1948. Yergan's work as a missionary in South Africa from 1921 to 1936 brought considerable acclaim.[1] In 1926, he received the Harmon Award for interracial service, and in 1933, the NAACP's coveted Spingarn Medal, that organization's highest honor. One distinctive feature of Yergan's career is the manner in which he channeled his South African expertise to further his advancement. No other African-American leader traveled a path quite like his, and few underwent ideological transformations as profoundly perplexing. This essay explores some of the dimensions of his particular brand of leadership, highlighting those historical elements that made it possible, and hopes to shed light upon his public and personal fate.

Max Yergan was born during the final decade of the nineteenth century in Raleigh, North Carolina. 'Mack' was one of several sons of a literate seamstress named Lizzie Yergan and a favored grandson of Frederick Yergan, a carpenter who had experienced and survived slavery.[2] The patriarch was an impassioned advocate of education as a vehicle of Black advancement, and shared the concerns of many of his contemporaries who sought to play a role in the 'Redemption of Africa' during the European imperial scramble for African colonies.[3] Max Yergan thus became one among many New World–based people of African descent who cultivated an interest in promoting African progress by means of a liberating interpretation of Christianity. His orientation was, therefore, similar to that of the early generations of Black Christians, often termed 'school people', who became influential social reformers fighting for betterment in *fin de siècle* South Africa.

Educated at two Protestant schools, the Episcopal St Ambrose Academy and the Baptist-funded Shaw University, Yergan's ethical sentiments found expression in the 'Colored Work' Department of the Young Men's Christian Association, an ostensibly nonpolitical vehicle for Christian cooperation, founded during the second half of the nineteenth century.[4] Like many institutions serving African-Americans in post-Reconstruction North America, the YMCA acquiesced in segregation. Therefore, those Black people who elected to participate in the 'Y' movement had to do so via its separate-but-equal Black branches.

Nevertheless, Black YMCA functionaries were often able to exert influence far out of proportion to their numbers. By the second decade of the twentieth century, they were seen as role models by the tiny but strategically placed Black intelligentsia. Their efforts frequently found support in the pages of *The Crisis,* the organ of the National Association for the Advancement of Colored People, then under the editorship of W.E.B. Du Bois. The existence of this alternative media network was later to prove invaluable to the development of Max Yergan's reputation.[5]

Yergan's relationship with the Black YMCA started during his student years, when he joined the Shaw University chapter of the movement. By his senior year, in 1914, Yergan was already nationally prominent among YMCA student secretaries. Even though Max Yergan's South African experiences provided him a vehicle with which to develop a radical approach to social and political oppression, he was already favorably disposed toward radical theory. Influenced by a social gospel–rooted brand of Christian radicalism as far back as 1915, Yergan welcomed left-wing ideas from the time he landed in South Africa during the early 1920s, slowly sharpening his awareness there. This is reflected in correspondence with friends and colleagues in North America, many of whom shared his openness to Christian radicalism as well as more secular types of socialist thinking.

The first area where this was true was within the YMCA itself. Outwardly apolitical, the YMCA nevertheless generated a surprising array of leaders either highly tolerant of or actively pursuing radical critiques of the status quo, within a broader, internationalist, context. Yergan had direct contact with several such men, dating from 1911, when he heard a talk given by social gospeler Robert Rauschenbush. Four short years later, Yergan responded to the vigorous exhortation of Edward C. 'Ned' Carter, director of YMCA war work in the East, by volunteering for service assisting Indian troops in World War I.[6]

He then went to Bangalore, India to serve Indian troops, later shifting to Dar es Salaam in German East Africa, where he served as a chaplain.

His transfer to East Africa provided Yergan with his first authentic African experience, as well as a bloody baptism in the horrors of war. There he ministered to the African porters assisting the British army in the East African campaign. The reputation Yergan gained as a result of his wartime activities was sufficient to warrant his recommendation for the post of first permanent YMCA secretary for British East Africa – a nomination that was not approved by the governor, Sir Edward Northey. In a devastating stroke, Northey minuted that he thought it inadvisable to introduce into East Africa 'negroes of a different calibre from those already present there'.[7]

Northey's suspicions were echoed in other parts of the British Empire during this period, as well as in the self-governing Dominions (including South Africa), which retained ties to Britain and British capital. This was especially evident in the wake of the Bolshevik Revolution of 1917 and in the emergence of nationalist movements in Africa and its vast overseas diaspora, particularly those in contact with the Garvey Movement or inspired by W.E.B. Du Bois and his disciples espousing Pan-Africanism from 1919 onward.[8]

Not surprisingly, then, following his exclusion from East Africa, Yergan found it impossible to secure another YMCA post elsewhere in British-ruled Africa, in spite of eloquent recommendations from some highly placed supervisors in the British National YMCA Council. Another possibility finally presented itself in 1921, in South Africa, when Yergan's name was placed in nomination for the newly vacant position of travelling secretary of the 'Native' branch of the Student Christian Association. If selected, Yergan would be expected to serve African youth and students, a job hitherto considered the exclusive responsibility of white officials. However, the old nagging suspicions concerning the potential dangers inherent in choosing an American 'Negro' again resurfaced as Yergan's candidacy was questioned by the European hierarchy of the South African YMCA.[9]

But this time Yergan's allies within and beyond the movement rallied to his side. Inside the missionary community, the famed Gold Coast educator James E. Kweggyir Aggrey lent support, while outside Du Bois marshalled the resources at his command as a key member of the NAACP executive and as editor of the *Crisis* to shape public opinion to convince the South African YMCA to reconsider its hasty and unpopular decision by the middle of 1921. Yergan was thus able to book sea passage for his wife and child in time for a December landing at Cape Town.[10]

Although Yergan initially attempted to domicile his family in Johannesburg, they eventually decided to relocate to Alice, near the Fort Hare campus.[11] Yergan's duties as SCA Travelling Secretary were to monitor the progress of duly constituted SCA branches in South Africa and its neighboring states, establishing new chapters where possible. His first months were marked by constant police surveillance, with informers transcribing each of his public statements verbatim before forwarding them to headquarters for further scrutiny.[12] Not only was Yergan the object of surveillance, his staff also suffered.[13]

In spite of these measures, however, Yergan forged friendships with staff colleagues, support personnel and students through his affable manner, fastidious appearance and inspirational appeals, offered both in the lecture hall and at the weekly Wednesday chapel meeting.[14] From his first day Yergan noted the staggering contradictions of South African life: the incomparable elegance of the landscape of the Eastern Cape; the opulence of the European-ruled 'Egoli', city of gold, Johannesburg, amid the abject penury of arid, rural 'locations' where ebony women eked out a living brewing beer and growing what they could, and the worker hostels where dark men languished in internal exile after selling their labor in mines, farms and white areas. Yet he also recognized that a tiny group of mission-educated Africans lived better lives, oppressed to be sure, but not very differently from their North American lynch law–era affines: jim crowed but unbowed. Somewhere between those two extremes stood the classical preacher, fuming and fulminating at the sins of this world and offering a vision of the prizes of the next, but never failing to gild himself in Joseph's coat of many colors.

Thus, ever mindful of the suffering and privation of the women, men and children around him, Yergan traveled widely and dined lavishly while in South Africa. Often in luxurious surroundings, he drove a Ford and wore the finest clothing he could purchase. His children were educated overseas, and the family invariably occupied what in colonial parlance would be styled a 'proper house'. This did not entirely insulate them from the scorn of jealous whites, but it did give the entire Yergan family a sense of social confidence, accompanied by a belief that Black Americans represented the most intellectually and materially advanced members of their race. In this sense, South Africa was a refuge for the Yergans. Even in the depths of a worldwide depression they still lived well.

During a stay in the US in 1927, Yergan struck up a friendship with Mary White Ovington, a wealthy white socialist-feminist who had been one of the prime movers of the NAACP. Returning to South Africa in March 1928, in his letters to her Yergan described in detail the political situation in the country and the circumstances under which the majority lived:

> You have doubtless learned that the Government has decided not to proceed with the proposed Native legislation which it had introduced in Parliament here this year. I am not yet able to say why this step was taken but I am inclined to

think that it is due to the tremendous protest made in this country as well as in Europe and America against such patently, [sic] inadequate and unfair legislation. I have reference to the segregation, franchise and land bills which have been before the Parliament of the county. I have not yet been able to gather up the threads of political developments but it does seem apparent that the Government realises more than it did two years ago a sense of responsibility towards the temporarily defenceless and largely voiceless Natives of this country.[15]

Stepping outside his role as missionary, Yergan shared with Ovington his thoughts about one local leader beginning to leave an imprint on South African society. Focusing on African trade unionists in the Industrial and Commercial Workers Union, led by Clements Kadalie, with whom he occasionally worked, he wrote:

Just now I am busy in preparation for a South African Missionary Conference which is to be held next week. This gathering will be watched by the country in general for its programme is certainly a departure from all previous gatherings of this nature. We are going to devote our whole time to a discussion of the full range of Native life. You may be interested in knowing that Mr Kadalie who is the efficient leader of a Native Labour Movement called the I.C.U. is to be one of the speakers at this gathering. I mention this because there was a very strong protest on the part of some missionaries and church leaders against appearing on the same platform with this man? [sic] I think it is a distinct advance to have made it possible for missionaries and church people to be exposed to the point of view of this very significant movement which Mr Kadalie is leading.[16]

By the end of the 1920s, Yergan had come to believe that the circumstances prevailing in South Africa for the social majority were so extreme that nothing short of a cathartic transformation of both society and economy could improve life. It would mean study, extraordinary discipline, militant organization, agitation and propaganda. While continuing to cultivate a low profile in his public activities, he privately began to support and encourage the construction of a new social order to destroy capitalist relations and to replace them with a more equitable system of redistribution of material wealth – the fruits of alienated labor.[17] This gradual, South African–rooted change of perspective influenced everything Yergan did during the ensuing two decades of his career.

With the coming of the Hertzog Bills of 1935, Yergan felt that South Africa had crossed the Rubicon, and he cultivated a coterie of disaffected students at Fort Hare. Many of these people are still alive, of whom the most notable was Govan Mbeki, released in 1987 after serving more than twenty years of a life sentence imposed at the monumental Rivonia treason trial of 1964. The bond between Yergan and Mbeki was close, perhaps because they shared several similarities. Both men came from profoundly religious backgrounds, were products of sectarian educational systems, and had lost faith in Christian theology as a vehicle for social liberation. Mbeki has credited Yergan with having given him his first glimpse of Lenin's *The State and Revolution,* and has described Yergan as having been 'utterly convincing' within their period of interaction at Fort Hare. Moreover, Mbeki emphasized that Max Yergan was the reason that he became a Communist, a conviction he retains today, a half-century after their first meeting.[18]

Had Mbeki been the only person influenced by Yergan in a left direction, his case might have been exceptional. But he also persuaded other students to adopt revolutionary politics during the interwar era and thereafter, although they did not always reveal their sentiments. Some joined other groups attempting to improve the quality of life for the social majority of South Africa. Notable among these were several militants associated with the Non-European Unity Movement and the All-African Convention, the latter a united front mounted in response to the threat posed by Hertzogism. Contact also may have been established between Yergan and a young Nelson Mandela, later prominent in the African National Congress Youth League, for Mandela is said to have been aware of Yergan in the 1940s during the Youth League's effort to revitalize the ANC.[19]

Given the necessarily clandestine character of Yergan's revolutionary work, it is unlikely that other instances of his radical mentoring will come to light. It may be stated with confidence, however, that the activities of this one YMCA secretary had far greater significance than may have been realized at the time. Alternatively, it may be argued that the initial suspicions of the South African authorities were completely justified. It is more plausible, however, that the South African government ensured that, whatever Yergan's views may have been when he arrived in the country, he would not leave it without being committed to smashing the state. In spite of painstaking and unrelenting spying by the CID and, it appears, his own inexperience, Yergan outmaneuvered the South African authorities. Even if the security apparatus had not then attained its present competence, the Special Branch was still capable of liquidating opponents of the regime at will, as seen in the murders of Johannes Nkosi and scores of other activists in the interwar period. It was no mean feat, then, for a Black man with a high public profile to operate in such a militant capacity for nearly a decade without being detected. That Yergan was not discovered is attested by several contemporaries, some of whom suggest that his true sympathies and covert teaching did not become public knowledge until well after his departure.[20]

The second stage of Yergan's relationship with South Africa began in 1937, the year following his resignation from the YMCA, when he and Paul Robeson co-founded an organization originally called the International Committee on African Affairs. It is probable that this name bore some relationship to Yergan's immediate past, as he had been a member of the board directing foreign missionary efforts in the North American YMCA, a body then known as its International Committee. The International Committee on African Affairs had been conceived as a vehicle through which to influence US policy toward Africa, and was openly sympathetic to anti-colonial agitation in imperial-ruled Africa and in the expatriate enclaves occupied by African students and other guest workers in the colonial capitals of Europe. By 1941 this group had become the Council on African Affairs and embraced intellectuals and working-class activists from various parts of the Black world, while also garnering support from liberal and left-wing white opponents of colonial oppression.[21]

Yergan's expertise in South African affairs had a strong impact on the activities of the Council on African Affairs; it was used to promote programs undertaken by representatives of organizations like the African National Congress, the Non-European Unity Movement and the All-African Convention, particularly during a period when the ANC and the NEUM sought to forge an alliance. The Council did this through the production of a monthly newsletter, first entitled *Spotlight on Africa* and later known as *New Africa,* and by sponsoring rallies, many conceived on a grand scale. These featured such luminaries as ANC leader Alfred Bitini Xuma; I.B. Tabata, doyen of the Unity Movement; AAC facilitator Professor D.D.T. Jabavu; and Indian National Congress head H.A. Naidoo.[22]

While Yergan was serving as the executive director of the Council on African Affairs, he was also elected president of the National Negro Congress. The NNC was a broadly based coalition that had been launched in 1935 under the aegis of Ralph Bunche in order to attain a greater level of coordination of anti-racist political action. Its primary aims were to end racial discrimination, lynching, and occupational, residential and other forms of segregation in the United States, as well as to improve working conditions for workers, irrespective of ethnicity.[23]

Both positions occupied the major part of Yergan's time during the World War II, with each organization supporting the claims of colonized peoples to greater democratic and economic rights. Yergan worked to promote a greater American awareness of the situation facing African miners in South Africa, and helped organize relief efforts during periods of famine and drought, like the Middledrift emergency of the mid 1940s. These concerns generated timely publications and personal appearances by militants from South Africa, and helped to sensitize certain sectors of North American opinion to African crises in general and South African problems in particular.

Campaigns mounted by the Council on African Affairs and the National Negro Congress also promoted the activities of leading figures representing movements associated with anti-colonial agitation in other areas as well. One of the beneficiaries of this concern was Nigerian politician Benjamin Nnamdi 'Zik' Azikiwe. After World War II, the Council on African Affairs became involved in supporting the cause of the people of Southwest Africa (now Namibia), who were defending themselves against annexation by South Africa by trying to secure a United Nations decision favorable to the majority of inhabitants of that UN Trust Territory.[24]

The Council on African Affairs and the National Negro Congress did not function in a vacuum, however. As time passed, both became casualties of Cold War policies and prejudices. Yergan, too, followed a similar path, and this is the key to his activities during the extraordinarily surprising final period of his life, for which he became notorious. This puzzling dimension of his biography may be explained by isolating the facets that led to the climax of his career and the volte-face that occurred.

Following his return from South Africa in August 1936, Max Yergan made no secret of his new left-wing ideological orientation. He soon became a highly visible member of the North American left and frequently participated in and was associated with organizations that identified with and were closely allied with the Communist Party USA. During his militant period, Yergan counted among his comrades many who belonged to the Party hierarchy, including Benjamin Davis, one of the two Party members elected to the New York City Council; Earl Browder, leader of the American Communist Party during World War II; and a number of other associates who were either 'card carrying' Party members or 'fellow travelers' with clearly socialist sympathies and fully supportive of the organization. Agent informants even alleged that meetings of the CP's Political Bureau were held at Yergan's residence, but this scarcely seems credible.[25]

A long-time contributing columnist to the Communist Party's newspaper, the *Daily Worker*, it was only a matter of time before Max Yergan came to the attention of the Federal Bureau of Investigation. Although the actual beginning date of its inquiry is uncertain, it was well under way within six months of US entry into World War II – but there are indications that it had started much earlier, for Yergan's public identification with the US left began around 1937, when, on an adjunct basis, he joined the faculty of the City College of New York, an institution known for left-wing activism.[26]

By 1942, FBI Director J. Edgar Hoover had taken a personal interest in Yergan's contacts and political activities, leading him to decide to initiate 'technical surveillance' – that is, wiretapping procedures – shortly thereafter. Yergan subsequently became one of many radical activists whose residences and offices were under electronic surveillance. Moreover, a file on him was prepared, and his movements monitored on a regular basis.[27] It is not known how long it took Yergan to become aware of this scrutiny, but he might have surmised it by the mid 1940s, because the awkward methods then used seem designed to arouse maximum paranoia on the part of the person under surveillance. 'Tailing' a suspect, for example, is often employed as much to intimidate as to gather data, and, unlike his 'double life' in South Africa, much of Yergan's political work in the US was undertaken openly.

It is possible that the surveillance of Yergan had begun as early as 1936, although this cannot yet be corroborated. 1936 was the year in which Yergan resigned from the YMCA, following a visit to the Soviet Union.[28] During this period, it was virtually impossible for any US passport holder to get into or out of the USSR without arousing the interest of the intelligence community. The mechanics of Yergan's tour are still shrouded in mystery, but the FBI would definitely have taken an active interest in such a sojourn. The Bureau certainly learned about it once surveillance of Yergan reached an advanced stage, for it was part of the file kept on him for future use by the FBI's Criminal Division.[29]

Although only a sketchy glimpse of Max Yergan's file was provided under the auspices of the Freedom of Information Act (FOIA), it is clear that it was extremely comprehensive. Consistent with the proclivities of the FBI's director, aspects of Yergan's political and personal activities were documented in painstaking and deliberately embarrassing detail. For one period of his life it is possible to chart virtually all his movements on a daily basis, even though Yergan's FBI file was heavily expurgated prior to its release, standard procedure in these matters. Researchers seeking to use such materials must, therefore, attempt to read between the (excised) lines. They cannot take any document at face value, because the files veritably brim with innuendo and obfuscation.[30]

The picture that thus emerges of Yergan is of a man seriously regarded by the FBI as a threat to the national security of the United States. Inasmuch as such cases were constructed against many members of the CP and their associates, there could have been some discussions among potential and actual targets of surveillance concerning the possible curtailment of their civil liberties. With the changing climate toward left and left-liberal activists following World War II, however, the dangers inherent in espousing socialism or communism became unmistakably evident.

This process of increasing intolerance for the left and leftists had both internal and external components. In the US itself there had been precedents, most ignobly the Red Scares of 1873 and 1919, but their lessons were not always heeded. Even when the signals were readily apparent, progressives could be so fragmented and subject to such divisive, sectarian rivalry that the necessary countermeasures were neither agreed-upon nor applied. During the early 1940s, for example, a series of left-wing activists were charged under the Smith Act with plotting to overthrow the government, a throwback to the 1798 Alien and and Sedition Acts. Similar statutes had been invoked to enforce conformity during World War I. The Smith Act, however, was first tested on Trotskyists and for this reason, the CP, guided by the dogmatic precepts of Stalin-era 'democratic centralism' did not oppose their prosecution. The dire precedent had, therefore, been set for subsequent action against the CP itself, which came in precisely the same manner later in the decade.[31]

The shifting national mood regarding left-wing politics was presaged by a number of significant indicators. One of the earliest occurred in 1947 when Attorney General Tom Clark published a list of subversive organizations. The list named several organizations with which Max Yergan had been closely connected, most notably the National Negro Congress and the Council on African Affairs. Shortly thereafter, testimony before the House Un-American Activities Committee alleged that the National Negro Congress, the Council on African Affairs and myriad other groups highly critical of the status quo were in actuality 'Communist front' organizations, in the course of which Yergan was implicated as one of many suspects charged with either wittingly or unwittingly furthering the cause of communism in the United States. Described as a 'Negro Communist leader in New York', Yergan was personally identified as having no less than seventy-eight Communist and so-called Communist front affiliations.[32]

The following year saw the enunciation of the Truman Doctrine and the establishment of loyalty oaths for government employees, each measure directed at isolating left-wingers from the ideological mainstream of American life, in a period characterized by escalating international tensions between the capitalist West and an increasingly socialist East. As the lines between these two camps became clearer, chiefly in the deepening competition between two systems as expressed in the evolution of two distinct spheres of influence and rival alliance networks (that is, NATO and the Warsaw Pact), the position of leftists in the US became ever more tenuous.[33] These external tensions affected internal forces arguing for either a socialist alternative or social reforms benefitting average working people in North America.

Nowhere was this clearer than in the American Communist Party. By the end of the 1940s, Earl Browder, who had served as the Party's guiding light during the turbulent war years, was suddenly purged. The reasons for this, while significant, are less immediately important than the fact that Max Yergan had been fond of Browder and appears to have felt his loss personally.[34] Browder subsequently began a gradual move to the right, having lost credibility among the orthodox left, a shift in political stance that Yergan must have noticed.

Yergan's subjective responses to these different stimuli were undoubtedly complex, but on the whole formed a pattern. In 1947, close on the heels of the publication of Attorney General Clark's wide-ranging report on subversive activities, Yergan resigned the presidency of the National Negro Congress. The following year he became embroiled in a messy, protracted, very public and ultimately unsuccessful faction fight dividing the Council on African Affairs, to counteract the accusation that the Council was a 'Communist front'.[35] Since Yergan operated in a rather heavy-handed manner, it is somewhat difficult to discover precisely what he had hoped to achieve, but there seem to have been two elements involved in his strategy.

First, he endeavored to get the Council's Executive Board to go on record as stating that the organization was non-Communist in action, composition and orientation. When this proposal failed, Yergan sought to purge those elements he had identified as being either Communist or friendly to the Party. This move also failed. These two abortive efforts at mollifying those who portrayed the Council in stereotypical 'red' terms convinced the remaining members of the executive that Yergan was no longer capable of contributing to the efforts of the group. He was, therefore, removed as executive director. The Council was then reorganized, eliminating the office that Yergan had held.[36]

Yergan interpreted his loss in the Council power struggle as a victory for communism. He subsequently mounted a vendetta against the very organization he had helped to create, attacking those within it who stood for a more tolerant attitude toward the left. Immediate targets were those whom he had felt had outmaneuvred him in his ill-fated coup attempt, Council Chairman Paul Robeson, Educational Director William Alphaeus Hunton, and the newest Council member, Yergan's former ally and advocate in his effort to gain entry into South Africa, that *eminence grise*, W.E.B. Du Bois.

There were several tragic ironies in this turnabout. Alphaeus Hunton was the son of Yergan's namesake, the first Black national director of the YMCA's 'Colored Work' Department, a role model, and an early Yergan mentor in the Black YMCA. Robeson had been among Yergan's closest friends and most intimate confidants throughout the previous decade and they had come to share the same vision for Africa and the African fight for freedom. The contributions of Du Bois to Yergan's career have already been detailed. Each of these individuals must have felt deeply betrayed.

It is likely that Yergan also felt betrayed, considering the vehemence of his reaction against the Council and its leadership. His response to the restructuring of the group was to use the newspapers to publicize his contention that Communists had mounted a successful coup in the organization.[37] To a certain degree this may have been influenced by the pattern of events taking shape within the new socialist camp. The period during which the Cold War took shape was also one in which reports of Stalin's 'excesses' began to have an impact on individuals who had earlier uncritically accepted his policies because they felt criticism might damage the cause. Yergan had clearly displayed this level of loyalty on numerous occasions by word and by deed. In retrospect, however, some of his contemporaries have recalled that Yergan had been beating a steady retreat from firmer ideological positions before 1948, albeit on a gradual basis.[38] By 1948, however, all of this simmering discontent exploded in an unusually public way.

In 1945, Yergan and his companion of twenty-five years, the former Susie Delores Wiseman, were divorced.[39] Shortly afterward, Yergan remarried, to a woman who had once been a Communist. This second marriage exerted a considerable degree of influence on Yergan, nurturing his ever-increasing impatience with radical ideas and left-wing people, despite having built a career on both.[40] It is even possible that this process of ideological reassessment and subsequent transformation may have had its roots in their union. If so, Yergan might have been harboring doubts about the left and his relationship to it from the end of World War II onward, only revealing them publicly in 1948. Having thus divested himself of his erstwhile left-wing constituency, Yergan then set about cultivating an alternative in the only quarter celebrating his defection: the right.

This political shift had extremely profound ramifications for Yergan's South African work. Yergan's anti-communism inevitably began to mesh with the orientation of the ruling Nationalist Party. Because Yergan's new emphasis was upon the perceived divisiveness of Communists, he found an ideological home within the monomaniacal pursuit of communism and Communists that characterized so much of South Africa's official stance toward the opposition activities of its most vocal critics. This view was also perilously close to that of such jaded observers of the American scene as FBI Director J. Edgar Hoover, who saw all dissent as Communist-inspired, particularly where 'Negroes' were involved, since he believed Blacks incapable of functioning on an organizational and political level without Communist direction.[41]

By the late 1940s Yergan had become a controversial but well-known public figure in the national Black community and within the international movement supporting the independence of Africa and other parts of the world still suffering under the yoke of colonialism. Capitalizing on his South African expertise, Yergan crafted a bully pulpit from which he spoke knowledgeably about political, social and economic conditions in Africa. His work as the executive director of the Council on African Affairs had put him in touch with several of the leading figures in the anti-colonial movement. Yergan's contacts in London kept him abreast of the maturing Pan-African movement. Today he might be the kind of 'expert' whose acumen could form the basis for a career as an African Studies or Third World development consultant. Yergan had ingeniously contrived a lucrative profession from his ability to explain the modalities of the African situation to both non-specialist and specialist audiencies, on the one hand, while dealing with women and men active in practical politics, on the other.

In the years he had left South Africa, Yergan had cultivated three distinct constituencies: the African-American intelligentsia, the North American left, and the international philanthropic and missionary establishment. During this period, Yergan carved out a niche that provided both social prominence and financial reward. Comprehending the wild contradictions of his era, Yergan managed to simultaneously assume a radical stance on all of the relevant issues of the day while maintaining a comfortable standard of living. Everything that he had struggled to build was inevitably jeopardized by the ideological shift that was taking shape in Cold War–era North America. He therefore allied himself with the right wing – the force that could guarantee his personal class position as a successful petty bourgeois professional. That he was also a Black convert to conservatism made him more attractive to them, given the Rooseveltian preference in African-American circles for New Deal–type Democratic leadership.

There was a devastating unity of purpose in this newly forged coalition, for it cut against Black American defense organizations such as the National Association for the Advancement of Colored People, the Congress of Racial Equality, the Urban League and the March on Washington Movement while undermining the activities of progressive forces fighting against apartheid in South Africa. Having dedicated himself to eradicating Communist influence wherever he detected or feared it, Yergan consciously courted allies among the most reactionary elements in both the United States and South Africa. He went on to redbait even the circumspect leadership of the NAACP, whose traditional anti-communism was an article of faith.[42]

Unquestionably the most profound impact of Yergan's about-face could be seen in regard to South Africa, especially in the wake of the National Party's victory in 1948. The Nationalist regime, advocating its far-reaching policy of 'separate development' or apartheid, greeted Yergan with open arms in 1949. So pleased were they with the enigmatic African-American that the South Africa Foundation, the public relations arm of government, would repeatedly serve as Yergan's hosts in the 1950s and 1960s. Granted the dubious distinction of 'honorary white' status, Yergan mouthed a plethora of pointless platitudes in praise of apartheid, seeing 'separate development' as the only realistic solution to a complex South African dilemma. By all indications, he had swallowed the Malan-Verwoerd thesis hook, line and sinker.[43]

The response to Yergan's final ideological transformation was swift and understandably severe. Not only was he denounced by his former comrades in the US, but among the progressive forces within South Africa as well.[44] So devastating was Yergan's turn that a few even called his mental state into question, but this, it seems, is a vast oversimplification. Yergan had apparently taken a number of calculated risks, acting in the hope that there would be some tangible benefit for him in both fiscal and geopolitical terms. When, for example, the key members of the Central Committee of the Communist Party USA were indicted under the Smith Act in 1948, including Eugene Dennis, Henry Winston and Benjamin J. Davis – all of whom were intimately acquainted with Yergan – he alone managed to escape prosecution, in spite of the case that had been prepared against him at the time. This case was ultimately dropped, but only after seven years of unrelenting scrutiny and interrogation.[45]

For the remainder of his life, Yergan continued to serve as a steadfast ally and unabashed apologist for the apartheid regime. His closest contacts in the US were among the counter-revolutionary coterie of right-wing intellectuals identified with William F. Buckley and William Rusher, editor and publisher, respectively, of the rightist *National Review*. The 1950s and 1960s saw Yergan's largest network of colleagues comprised of members of the South African diplomatic corps, men 'who admired him enormously'.[46] Yergan supported the Katanga secessionist movement of Moise Tshombe and the candidacy of Republican presidential nominee Barry Goldwater in 1964, and was a founding member of the ultra-conservative American African Affairs Association, which took consistently pro–South African government positions during the early 1960s; he also backed Ian Smith's Rhodesian outlaw regime in its unilateral declaration of independence in 1965.

Yergan thus moved from being an outspoken and principled critic of the South African regime to a willing tool of its propaganda apparatus. What remains to be studied is his precise role in that mechanism, though to be sure the full dimensions may never be known, given the South African government's penchant for secrecy. The question remains significant, however, for Yergan was only the first in a long line of Black apologists for South African oppression.

Yergan's political degeneration compromised his credibility as a would-be 'expert on African affairs', an honorific that appears to have meant a great deal to him.[47] Govan Mbeki, the most prominent convert from Yergan's radical days, became ashamed to tell anyone of the vital role Yergan had played in his own ideological development.[48] A youthful Nelson Mandela, who had heard Yergan speak during one of his visits to South Africa, declared him 'brilliant' and insightful in his analysis until he reached the subject of communism, upon which Yergan became fixated to such a myopic extent that it seriously undermined the strength of his presentation.[49]

Evaluation of a life of such wide-ranging scope is a daunting task. While at first glance the odyssey of Max Yergan may appear contradictory, closer consideration discloses elements of surprising consistency. Max Yergan was always an architect of the *cause célèbre:* wherever there was a cause of consequence, he was never far behind. His ideology appears to have been inspired by Manichaean conceptions of causation: whatever he supported he campaigned for wholeheartedly; whatever he hated, he strove to extirpate with comparable rhetorical intensity.

In his evangelical years (1910–31) he saw heathen ignorance as bedeviling, and he fought it uncompromisingly. In the radical years (1931–48), he viewed capitalist and racialist oppression as his enemies, vigorously struggling against them. In his anti-Communist phase (1948–75), he maligned socialism, communism and all their advocates as the bane of existence, opposing them unreservedly.

Yergan's Manichaeism, his division of the universe into moieties representing absolute good and irremediable evil, was an outgrowth of his Christianity. His major struggle with orthodox socialist theory in the Stalin era came not in 1948, when he broke with the left, but much earlier, almost at the outset of his flirtation with revolutionary Marxism-Leninism, over the question of the ostensibly 'atheistic' character of the ideology of materialism and the incompatibility of this aspect of the philosophy of praxis with his own deeply rooted spiritual beliefs. When he made his full-fledged conversion to ultra-conservatism, one of the chief elements of that belief was Yergan's rededication to Christianity after a period of intense doubt, and his refutation of socialism and communism as being fundamentally anti-Christian in conception and practice. This is especially evident in his letters to religious figures such as the cleric and philanthropist Anson Phelps-Stokes, who rejoiced at the prospect of seeing a prodigal son renounce his waywardness to return to the fold.[50]

There is nothing simple about this case, however. Yergan was no less spiritual during his socialist years, a time when he seems to have believed that socialism and Christianity were not necessarily incompatible, although there are indications that he became overtly and demonstrably hostile to religion during his final years in South Africa. Nor can we afford to ignore the factor of Yergan's own class standing, bearing and aspirations. Worth considering is the question of whether Yergan's identification with the 'moderates' of the postwar era was colored by his own patrician self-image. After his second marriage, to a woman of means, it was noted that Yergan gradually came to separate himself from others who could not or would not share his prosperity, and this may have led to a growing need to cultivate the company of those who could adopt an aristocratic bearing. It is logical, therefore, that this might lead him toward the defense of both property and a panoply of Republican ideological values. In fact, there are indications that this was the way at least some Africans perceived Yergan during his South African years.

While difficult to quantify, the weight of negative opinion among one section of the same African petty bourgeoisie who engaged in protest against the government at the same time that Yergan was radicalized cannot be ignored. Taken together, Yergan was said to have remained aloof from other Africans, including Professor D.D.T. Jabavu, the first Black academic to gain a reputation in the country, and a fellow member of the overwhelmingly white Fort Hare 'Native' College faculty. After Yergan had returned to the States, George Padmore cited unnamed South African doctors residing in England during the mid 1940s who claimed that Yergan had actually snubbed the accomplished Jabavu.[51] This does not square with the fact that Yergan named his second son Max Jabavu, however,[52] but remains worthy of note, especially in light of the fact that the Council on African Affairs failed to either respond to an invitation sent out advertising the Fifth Pan-African Congress in Manchester, or to participate in it,[53] arguably the single most significant African conclave of the postwar era – indeed, perhaps the signal gathering of colonial Africans in the entire twentieth century.

The final question of status is worth exploring because it recurs in the accounts of many of Yergan's former comrades on the left.[54] Benjamin Davis and Herbert Aptheker, for example, each suggested that what was most important for Yergan was a high level of physical comfort. Indeed he took great pains to retain ties with affluent humanitarians like Anson Phelps-Stokes and John R. Mott (under whom he served in the YMCA), throughout their lives. Little about the final trajectory of his life appears to have been inevitable; rather, it evolved in a conscious, deliberate fashion, as an angry response to a perceived series of slights and a desperate search for community. These slights may have triggered a vengeful streak in Yergan's personality. Financial success as a mode of retribution was a time-tested strategy for the Black middle class during the 1940s and 1950s. It was the logical extension of an attitude that had helped this fragile stratum survive the outrage of socio-economic marginalization.

Yergan's letters home regularly described humiliations of this kind in pathetic vignettes that readily brought empathic responses from his correspondents. Even casual white observers shared reminiscences that had this same tragic quality. J.W. Macquarrie, a lecturer at Fort Hare, recently cited a typical example of a wounding incident that he still recalled fifty years after its occurrence:

> My own recollection of Yergan was that he was well-built, well but quietly dressed and of dignified but modest bearing. When I first knew him he lived in Alice, among white neighbours, rather unusual but not against the law. He and his wife were well thought of, but had few if any social contacts with the Alice people, but plenty with the Fort Hare staff. In 1930 when on the point of marriage I bought some bedroom furniture and china ware from him as he was on the point of moving house to Fort Hare and, I presume, furnishing it even more luxuriously. I think his American associates kept him very comfortably off; certainly his house at Fort Hare was rivalled only by the Principal's.

His succession of cars was probably the most luxurious in the district:

> But he needed sound cars for he had to travel constantly over execrable roads, very seldom tarred and often muddy or pot-holed. Usually he had to eat and sleep in his car as few, if any, hotels or restaurants would have dared to defy regular patrons by accommodating a coloured man. On one occasion, when Yergan was driving some Fort Hare staff members to a meeting he stopped and asked a pedestrian the way. The pedestrian, a white man, looked at the luxurious car and well-groomed driver and cursed him viciously for speaking to a white man. Yergan's shocked colleagues apologized profusely but Yergan brushed the incident off. 'I'm used to this!' he said. I've no doubt that encounters of this kind helped to bring about his swing to communism.[55]

South Africa gave Yergan's career another curious consistency. Although he underwent profound transformations of consciousness at various stages of his life, each was motivated by experiences that had occurred during Yergan's period of service there. His first crisis of faith in Christianity, his conversion to socialism and his renunciation of Communist 'heresy' all bore a direct relationship to his years in Souh Africa. Clearly those were the most important years of his life. They facilitated the development of the reputation Yergan achieved on three continents as a missionary, and parlayed as the basis of a lucrative career as a scholar, activist, consultant and humanitarian.

Yergan's YMCA service in South Africa made him well known among Black college students during the 1920s and 1930s, and gave him a reputation within the Black press and among African-American professionals. From Fort Hare he was able to forge profitable bonds with the Rockefeller, Carnegie and Phelps-Stokes foundations and managed to manipulate public opinion well enough to allow him to assume the mantle of leadership within the African-American community upon returning from South Africa, in spite of the fact that most of his skills had been shaped by his fifteen years overseas. Yergan thus successfully cultivated three distinct constituencies: the African-American professional stratum, the liberal philanthropic establishment, and the radical left.

Yergan's connections with the left appear to have been made from South Africa, although they were certainly helped along by the incipient anti-imperialism of the interwar era, which brought fascists to Ethiopia and Spain, convincing radicals to connect with anti-fascist strategy. This facilitated his re-entry into Depression-era North America and granted him immediate acceptance and economic security.

When the cherished camaraderie of a progressive community was no longer available to him, he sought to synthesize it among others who shared his vision of anti-communism and his nostalgia for the South Africa of his youth. It is perhaps the most poignant paradox of Max Yergan's life that at its end he should derive his ultimate pleasure in the company of those social elements who bore direct responsibility for bringing the greatest pain to African people in South Africa, and to their dispersed descendants in North America: the capitalist class.

Yergan's story highlights not merely the odyssey of one enigmatic individual, but the contradictions of an entire stratum, the petty bourgeoisie. These incongruities have particularly troubling features for militants of color, and have long plagued American activists of varying backgrounds, whose dreams of a more perfect social order are nonetheless inseparable from a commodity-fetishism emanating from, animating and articulating with the powerful American Dream. With the erosion of an international socialist alternative in the wake of the collapse of the Union of Soviet Socialist Republics, these issues will continue to present profound problems for militants working for creative alternatives to class oppression, devoid of compromise. It is therefore necessary to confront the modalities of villainy in addition to celebrating present and past class heroes and heroines.

Notes

Note: A slightly different version of this article was delivered as a presentation before a seminar at the Institute of African Studies, the National University of Lesotho, in 1988. I wish to thank Robert Edgar, Hunt Davis, R.D. Ralston and Shula Marks for their aid. This article is dedicated to the memory of David H. Anthony, Jr, May 1921–January 1990.

1. Yergan's South African period is treated in D.H. Anthony, 'Max Yergan in South Africa: From Evangelical Pan-Africanist to Revolutionary Socialist', *African Studies Review*, vol. 34, no. 1 (September 1991), pp. 27–54.

2. Secretary's Record, Max Yergan File, YMCA Library, New York; Ralph W. Bullock, *In Spite of Handicaps*, New York 1927, p. 111.

3. Bullock, *In Spite of Handicaps*, p. 111. For other late-nineteenth-century manifestations of this sentiment, see Hollis R. Lynch, *Edward Wilmot Blyden, Pan Negro Patriot, 1832–1912*, New York 1967; Edwin S. Redkey, *Black Exodus: Black Nationalist and Back to Africa Movements, 1890–1910*, New Haven, Conn. 1970; Imanuel Geiss, *The Pan-African Movement*, New York 1974; J. G. St. Clair Drake, *The Redemption of Africa and Black Religion*, Chicago 1980; Walter L. Williams, *Black Americans and the Evangelization of Africa, 1877–1900*, Madison, Wis. 1980; Sylvia M. Jacobs, ed., *Black Americans and the Missionary Movement in Africa*, Westport, Conn. 1980; and J. Mutero Chirenje, *Ethiopianism and Afro-Americans in Southern Africa, 1883–1916*, Baton Rouge, La. 1988.

4. Secretary's Record, YMCA Library. The 'Colored YMCA', as it was known among its constituents, was seen as a vehicle for social and educational 'uplift' during the late nineteenth and early twentieth centuries. Although scrupulously avoiding any identification with politics, particularly radical politics, the Black YMCA did serve a useful function during the era of segregation in the United States. These 'colored' YMCAs, situated primarily on historically Black college campuses and in urban locales serving predominantly Black populations, not only provided accommodation but often served as regional community centers.

5. The *Crisis* promoted the activities of the Black YMCA on a consistent basis, maintaining close communication with the organization's national leadership.

6. Carter is an interesting figure in his own right. He played a shadowy role in the unfolding of Yergan's career, internationally as well as nationally. He was one of Yergan's staunchest YMCA advocates during the 1910s and 1920s, when British administrators sought to keep African-Americans out of colonial Africa. As it happened, Carter's spectre was to haunt Yergan for three decades.

7. Northey to McCowen, 24 September 1920, Max Yergan File, YMCA Library. The subject is also discussed in Kenneth J. King, 'The American Negro as Missionary to East Africa: A Critical Aspect of African Evangelism', *African Historical Studies*, vol. 3, no. 1 (1970), and King, *Pan-Africanism and Education: A Study of Race Philanthropy and Education in the Southern States of America and East Africa*, London 1971.

8. See W.T. Elkin, 'Unrest among the Negroes: A British Document of 1919', *Science and Society*, vol. 37, no. 1 (Winter 1968), pp. 66–79; J.M. Pawa, 'The Search for Black Radicals', *Labor History*, vol. 16, no. 2 (Spring 1975), pp. 272–84; Jervis Anderson, *A. Philip Randolph, A Biographical Portrait*, New York 1973; Tony Martin, *Race First: The Organizational and Ideological Struggles of Marcus Garvey and the Universal Negro Improvement Association*, Westport, Conn. 1975. Cf. Harry Haywood, *Black Bolshevik: The Autobiography of an Afro-American Communist*, Chicago 1978.

9. The copious correspondence treating this issue is found in the Max Yergan File in the YMCA Library. See Bridgman to Patton, 1 February 1921, File 'South Africa, 1906–27.' Bridgman, an American Board Missionary, wondered if Yergan had enough 'grace and grit' to endure life in Johannesburg, where he would not be allowed to use the streetcars unless he were a mulatto, in which case he would have the option of 'passing' as a Cape 'Coloured' man, although, Bridgman added, he might find this 'impracticable'. Arranging for the education for his children might also be difficult.

10. Secretary's Record, Max Yergan, YMCA Library.

11. Mary White Ovington, *Portraits in Color*, New York 1927, p. 39.

12. See File 'South Africa, 1906–27', YMCA Library.

13. 'Roch' Fanana Fobo, Interview, Roma, Lesotho, 8 February 1988.

14. J. M. Mohapeloa, Interview, Maseru, Lesotho, 16 May 1988.

15. Yergan to Ovington, 16 June 1928. NAACP Papers, Library of Congress. Ovington featured Yergan in her *Portraits of Color,* a series of biographies of notable Negro Americans (New York 1927).

16. Ibid.

17. Vincent G. (Joe) Matthews to author, 4 May 1985. This is also described in Gwendolen Carter and Thomas Karis, ed., *From Protest to Challenge: A Documentary History of African Politics in South Africa, 1884–1964,* Stanford, Calif. 1977, vol. 4, pp. 83, 168.

18. Thami Mkhwanazi, 'How a Schoolboy's Rage Turned Mbeki Toward Marxism', *Weekly Mail* (Johannesburg), 13–19 November, 1987, p. 6; Matthews to Anthony, 4 May 1985.

19. The question of Yergan's sui geneis radicalism, its origins and significance forms the subject of Anthony, 'Max Yergan in South Africa: From Evangelical Pan-Africanism to Revolutionary Socialism', *African Studies Review* September, 1991. It must be considered within the context of what Peter Walshe has described as an 'eclectic radicalism' that flourished within the Eastern Cape. *The Rise of African Nationalism in South Africa: The African National Congress, 1912–1971,* Berkeley, Calif. 1971. For a survey of the modalities of this activism see William Beinart and Colin Bundy, *Hidden Struggles in Rural South Africa: Politics and Popular Movements in the Transkei and Eastern Cape, 1890–1930,* Johannesburg 1987. For a more recent view of the emergence of African radicalism during the interwar years, see Robin D.G. Kelley, 'The Religious Odyssey of African Radicals: Notes on the Communist Party of South Africa, 1921–34', *Radical History Review,* vol. 51 (Fall 1991), pp. 5–24. Mandela's interest in Yergan is suggested in Matthews to the author, 4 May 1985.

20. W. M. Tsotsi, interview, Maseru, Lesotho, 19 October 1987; Matthews to author, 4 May 1985. It is true, however, that key YMCA officials knew about Yergan's politics, but seem to have taken every precaution to keep his secrets.

21. The Council on African Affairs has been discussed in Hollis Lynch, *Black American Radicals and the Liberation of Africa: The Council on African Affairs, 1937–1955,* Ithaca, N.Y. 1978, Cf. Clarence Contee, 'Black American Reds and African Liberation: A Case Study of the Council on African Affairs, 1937–1955', in Lorraine Williams, ed., *Proceedings of the Conference on Afro-Americans and Africans: Historical and Political Linkages. Howard University, June 13–14, 1974,* Washington, D. C., pp. 117–33. It is also examined in Anthony, 'Max Yergan: A Pan-African Enigma' (Master's Thesis, University of Wisconsin, Madison, 1975), especially Chapters 4 through 6. The Council is currently being investigated by Penny von Eschen, a dissertation student in history at Columbia University.

22. Council materials were widely distributed throughout the United States, and many of its events were well attended. Although extremely rare now, the voluminous publications that once appeared under Council auspices ranged from pamphlets to books authored by Council members. The best single source for Council materials was formerly the Paul Robeson Archives, which contains handbills, photographs, pamphlets, monographs and correspondence. Several documents and manuscript sources have been donated to Howard University. However, access to them requires direct permission from Mr Paul Robeson, Jr.

23. National Negro Congress File, Schomburg Collection, New York Public Library.

24. United Nations Archive Center, A.B. Xuma Papers, Hoover Institution, Stanford, Calif.

25. Max Yergan File, Criminal Division, Federal Bureau of Investigation. For evidence that the Party found Max Yergan a 'prize catch', see Mark Naison, *Communists in Harlem During the Depression,* Urbana, Ill. 1983, pp. 293–4. Also duly noted were Yergan's 'aristocratic' habits and predilections.

26. Max Yergan File, F.B.I.; YMCA Archives; Philip Foner to author, 1985.

27. Ibid.

28. This visit was apparently not discussed in any of Yergan's readily available correspondence, although material concerning it may well be sequestered in the restricted Yergan Papers at Howard University. He made reference to it in the 1950s, however, but these allusions are not particularly edifying. See 'The Communist Threat in Africa', in *Africa Today,* Charles Grove Haines, ed., New York 1955.

29. Memorandum, F.J. Younger to D.M. Ladd, 19 March 1942, Max Yergan File, FBI.

30. Some of the problems encountered by researchers using FOIA-generated materials are highlighted in David Garrow, *The FBI and Dr Martin Luther King, Jr., New York 1983.*

31. The literature on this subject is extensive, as it relates to the larger question of the fate of movements advocating Socialist alternatives for the United States. Several of these texts treat the issue as either a problem of 'decline' or 'failure', often rooted in the policies of the parties themselves, or as victimization at the hands of hostile government forces. At this juncture, it seems difficult not to argue that by reacting to this repression independently, the left conceded the floor to a regime then exercising its power in one of the most bellicose periods of its history. The results were so devastating that almost an entire generation was scarred by the scope and intensity of state repression.

32. Testimony of Walter S. Steele, House Un-American Activities Committee, 21 July 1947; Robert K. Carr, *The House Un-American Activities Committee*, New York 1952, pp. 52–5; Walter Goodman, *The Committee: The Extraordinary Career of the House Committee on Un-American Activities*, New York 1968, pp. 190–255. Steele made no attempt to distinguish between the 'innocent' and 'guilty'; all alleged participants in 'front' projects were judged culpable by the company they kept. Steele, originally a witness to HUAC in 1938 (the Dies Committee) implicated 122 publications or publishers as Communist-dominated. He was allowed to name scores of people related to these as editors or contributors.

33. This was evident in the Smith Act prosecutions of the mid and late 1940s. For a detailed overview, see Robert Justin Goldstein, *Political Repression in Modern America from 1870 to the Present*, Cambridge 1978, Chapter 9, 'Truman-McCarthyism, 1946–1954', pp. 287–396.

34. Yergan File, FBI.

35. Council on African Affairs File, Paul Robeson Archives.

36. Ibid.

37. 'African Affairs Splits over Red Issue', *New York Times*, 6 April 1948.

38. Personal Communication, Ernest Kaiser to author, July 1975.

39. 'Negro Red Leader Divorces in Reno', *New York World Telegram* 28 February 1945.

40. Ernest Kaiser to author, personal Communication; Yergan File, FBI.

41. See Garrow's introduction to *The FBI and Dr Martin Luther King, Jr.* On Hoover's instinctive hatred of Black protest, see Richard G. Powers, *Secrecy and Power: The Life of J. Edgar Hoover*, New York 1987, pp. 127–8.

42. On Yergan's estrangement from the traditional Black leadership, see the NAACP Papers, Library of Congress, Group II, General Office File, Box A675.

43. 'American Negro on Race Relations Mission', *The Friend*, 14 October 1948. For a later example, see 'Transkei Paper Asks: Why Not Matanzima? Negro 'White' Hotel Guest', *Rand Daily Mail*, 27 November 1964.

44. Professor Z.K. Matthews, an old associate of Yergan dating from their days together at Fort Hare College, was especially disappointed in this collaboration with pro-apartheid forces. See 'South African Leaders Blast Max Yergan', *Freedom*, vol. 2, no. 10 (October 1952); Z.K. Matthews, 'An African Leader Exposes Max Yergan', *Freedom*, vol. 3, no. 6 (June 1953); and Walter Sisulu, 'What Was Dr Max Yergan's Mission to Africa?' *African Lodestar*, November 1953, Carter-Karis Collection of Documents on South Africa, reel 2:DA 16/3:85/1. My thanks to R. Hunt Davis, Jr for sending me a photocopy of the latter, and to Robert Edgar for the references to *Freedom*.

45. Yergan File, FBI. An example of the kind of pressure Yergan was under well beyond the period of his recantation may be seen in the turning of Dorothy K. Funn. Funn, a former teacher in the New York City schools from 1923 to 1943, had resigned to become the National Negro Congress legislative representative from 1943 to 1946. At the height of the McCarthy period Funn appeared before the House Un-American Activities Committee, stating that she had been a member of the Communist Party in 1939–46, and naming twenty-four past and present school employees in New York plus forty-two other people in Baltimore and Washington, D.C. as known Communists. Among the latter was NNC President Max Yergan. See Peter Kihss, 'Artie Shaw Says He Was Red Dupe', *New York Times*, 5 May 1953. By then Yergan had already been contracted as an 'expert witness' for five years.

46. Rusher to author, 27 January 1987.

47. See Yergan's 'Africa: Next Goal of Communists', *U.S. News and World Report*, 1 May 1953, with copy proclaiming Yergan the 'foremost American authority on Africa'.

48. Matthews to author, 4 May 1985.

49. Ibid.

50. Yergan to Phelps Stokes, 1948, Anson Phelps Stokes Papers, Yale University.

51. Padmore to Du Bois, 9 August 1946, in Aptheker, ed., *The Correspondence of W.E.B. Du Bois*, vol. 3: *Selections, 1944–1963*, Amherst, Mass. 1973, pp. 146–8. I am grateful to Robert Hill and Herbert Aptheker for bringing this document to my attention.

52. Yergan to Moorland, 1926, Jesse Edward Moorland Papers, Box 126-65, Folder 1244, 'YMCA-Max Yergan', Moorland-Spingarn Research Center, Howard University.

53. Padmore to Du Bois, 5 August 1946.

54. See the appendix entitled 'Of Hypocrisy and the Like', in Benjamin J. Davis, *Communist Councilman from Harlem: Autobiographical Notes Written in a Federal Penitentiary*, New York 1969, pp. 199–202. Interview, Prof. Herbert Aptheker, 16 September 1988, San Jose, California. Interview, Louise Thompson Patterson, 11 November 1988, Oakland, California.

55. Macquarrie to author, personal communication, 27 August, 1991.

PART III

Southern Africa and the United States: Towards the Twenty-first Century

1 2

Apartheid

and the US South

Ann Seidman

Introduction: Pan-Africanism and the 1987 Africa Peace Tour

Fostering a rapidly changing international division of labor, the post–World War II technological revolution has imposed a whole new perspective on Pan-Africanism. This reality deeply impressed the nearly thirty African and American scholars who participated in the 1987 Africa Peace Tour throughout the southeastern United States. The tour aimed to help Americans understand why they should oppose expanding US military involvement in Africa, why, instead, they should support Africa's liberation and development.[1]

The tour became a kind of participatory research through which those involved came to realize that, behind the scenes, key actors are shaping the future of the Pan-African diaspora, indeed the full sweep of global relationships. The participants, together with the southern US audiences they addressed – Black and white – gathered evidence showing that the US military expansion in Africa during the 1980s represented an effort to open up the African continent much as, a century before, a Republican administration had wielded a big stick to enable US businesses to enter the Caribbean and Latin America.[2] Today, transnational corporations, taking advantage of the global technology revolution, put the wages and working conditions of American workers into direct competition with those of oppressed Third World peoples, not only in neighboring countries like Haiti, but throughout the vast continent of Africa.

With a land area three times and a population twice the size of the continental United States, Africa possesses vast, unexplored potential as a new source of raw materials, markets and profits. Expanding US military activity in Angola, Morocco, Zaire, Kenya, Somalia, Sudan, Liberia and Egypt seems directed at repeating the story of the penetration of the Caribbean – on a much larger scale.

Meeting and talking in schools, churches and union halls throughout the southeastern US, the Africa Peace Tour participants realized that, for the US military buildup and expansion in new regions like Africa, many Americans – Black and white – had to pay a high price in terms of growing unemployment and racism, and falling real incomes.[3] They learned about the consequences for Americans of the expanded transnational corporate investment fostered in oppressive conditions, particular those of South Africa, by US policies.

Several examples, from agriculture, mining, manufacturing and banking, illustrate the way, by the 1980s, transnationals put the wages, working and living conditions of southern US citizens in competition with those of the impoverished southern Africans.

African and Afro-American Tobacco Farmers

First, take agriculture, in particular the case of tobacco. On the one hand, until the 1970s in North Carolina and parts of Kentucky, tobacco remained the main agricultural crop for small farmers, especially small Black farmers.[4] On the other hand, a handful of tobacco companies, led by the British American Tobacco Company (BAT), handle most of the world's tobacco business. A transnational based in South Africa, Rothman Rembrandt is one of that handful. BAT, with major holdings in Africa and the United States remains, however, the world's largest tobacco company.[5]

BAT first invested in African tobacco in the 1920s in Southern Rhodesia (now Zimbabwe). There it taught the white settlers how to plant and cure tobacco – that is, how to make African workers plant and cure tobacco for them. Tobacco became a major cash crop, transforming Southern Rhodesia into the world's second largest tobacco exporter. To this day, tobacco makes up about a fourth of Zimbabwe's exports. In the early 1980s, some 1,200 white tobacco farmers still employed 76,000 Zimbabwean workers. Their annual income equalled almost twice their workers' total wages.[6] BAT and firms like Rothmans-Rembrandt, however, still dominated global tobacco marketing and manufacturing. They shipped most of Zimbabwe's leaf in crude form to factories in the United States or South Africa for processing.

From the mid 1970s to the mid 1980s, tobacco transnationals like BAT tripled their imports of tobacco into the United States. They maximized their profits by buying leaf at low prices made possible by the fact that commercial farmers in places like Rhodesia-turned-Zimbabwe paid their workers wages of about $25 a month.[7] Meanwhile, unable to compete, hundreds of small North Carolina farmers went out of business.

The returns for the tobacco transnationals far exceeded what they paid the growers in any country. A United Nations study showed that in the late 1970s about one dollar of every ten resulting from the final sale of cigarettes in the US actually went to tobacco growers. US state and local governments taxed away about half the companies' profits.[8] Reinvestment of those funds could have assisted farmers, both in the US southeast and Zimbabwe, to cultivate other crops as alternative sources of income and employment while reducing the sale of a harmful product to US consumers. Instead, the US government poured increasing amounts of tax revenues into its unparalleled peacetime military buildup.[9]

Mine Workers in Appalachia and South Africa

Mining and the associated iron and steel industries provide further examples of the way US government policies enabled US transnationals to pit South African wages and working conditions against those of workers in the US southeast. In the late nineteenth and early twentieth centuries, Appalachian mines produced the coal that fueled America's industrial revolution.[10] Coal-burning steam engines carried freight on steel rails that stretched across the country. Coal fired the furnaces as steel became the backbone of the nation's new industries. At the turn of the century, to take advantage of the South's coal deposits and low-waged Black workers, one of the world's largest steel companies, US Steel, built new plants in Birmingham, Alabama, transforming it into the Pittsburgh of the South.

After World War II, however, transnational investment decisions shifted basic iron and steel production and even the mining of coal to lower wage areas further south, fostering competition between unionized American workers and low-paid labor in countries like apartheid South Africa. By the 1960s, US steelmakers faced intensified competition from Japanese and German firms which, building more advanced steel production capacity, manufactured cheaper steel. Instead of investing in improved American steel technologies, however, US Steel and other big steelmakers reinvested their profits overseas or in other fields in the US. By the early 1980s, US Steel owned over $160 million worth of assets and employed almost 6,000 workers in South Africa where migrant contract labor worked for wages

that at most were a quarter of those earned by US workers.[11] Steel constituted about 13 percent of direct US imports from South Africa.[12] Even
after the imposition of sanctions in 1986, the Reagan and Bush administrations permitted ships to continue to freight cheap South African steel into
the country.[13] Several years earlier, after changing its name to USX, the
company had simply closed its Birmingham factories, leaving unemployed
thousands of frustrated workers who had dedicated their entire lives to
steel production.

US coal miners, too, suffered from the shift to low wage areas abroad,
including South Africa. As oil prices soared in the 1970s, business forecast-
ers anticipated a boom in the demand for coal.[14] Oil companies dipped into
their mounting profits to buy up most of the coal mines in Appalachia.
Many of them also held investments in South Africa.[15] Two companies in
partnership purchased control of the largest US coal producer, Peabody
Coal Mining Company.[16] One, Newmont, was affiliated with the South
Africa–based Anglo-American Corporation, estimated as the twenty-fifth
largest transnational corporation in the world.[17] The other partner, Bechtel,
had employed two of President Reagan's key advisors, George Schultz and
Casper Weinbeger.[18] This connection may help explain the support the
Reagan administration gave to the South African minority regime's con-
cerns.

To produce Appalachian coal at lower cost, the oil companies invested
in advanced technologies and laid off thousands of mine workers. Some
even imported coal from their South African mines. Under its new management, one company, A.T. Massey, took the lead in trying to break the
United Mine Workers Union, which over many decades had won improved wages and working conditions for US coal miners. One of A.T.
Massey's new owners, Shell BP, owned a 50 percent interest in the South
African Rietspruit mine. Managed by an Anglo-American Group firm,
Rietspruit in the 1980s annually exported over five million tons of coal.
Rietspruit's 1,050 migrant mine workers, living without their families in
company-owned barracks, earned wages a fraction of those earned by US
miners.[19] In 1985, Rietspruit's management revealed its anti-union bias
when, following a mine accident that killed two workers, it first fired union
representatives for organizing a two-hour prayer meeting and visits to the
miners' families, and then fired 86 of the 800 miners who walked out in
protest.[20] Another Shell BP affiliate co-owned a giant oil refinery and pet-
rochemicals firm in partnership with the South African government, assisting the import of oil into the country in violation of OPEC, United
Nations and, since 1987, US sanctions. A.T. Massey's second new owner,
Fluor, a California-based company, had engineered construction of three
sophisticated South African government-owned oil-from-coal plants. Pro-

ducing an estimated one-third of South Africa's oil needs from South African coal in the 1980s, these too helped ease the impact of international oil sanctions.

When Shell and Fluor took over A.T. Massey in the early 1980s, they rejected the United Mine Workers' agreement with the Bituminous Coal Operators Association. Instead, they insisted that the union must bargain separately with each of A.T. Massey's subsidiaries. In response, the union began selective strikes and peaceful picketing at several Massey mines in Virginia and Kentucky. The strikes dragged on for more than a year. Massey brought in strikebreakers and armed mercenaries as guards. An unknown assailant fired shots into the home of a local union president, and a bomb blew up a local union headquarters. A South African miners' union delegation, visiting the United Mine Workers Union in the area, remarked on the similarity of these tactics to those mining companies had employed in their efforts to break the South African miners' union. Massey's anti-union measures seemed a logical culmination of the company tactics that pitted the welfare of Appalachian miners against that of South Africa's migratory labor, forced by apartheid to work under slavery-like conditions.

Shifting Factory Employment

US investment in South Africa's manufacturing industry provides a third set of examples of the impact of intensified global competition on workers in the southeastern United States. As outright colonial rule collapsed in Africa after World War II, US manufacturing companies poured some three-fourths of all their investments into that continent, not into the newly politically independent countries, but into South Africa.[21] These investments contributed to building up significant aspects of the South African minority's military-industrial complex. First, US firms provided the advanced technologies which, as in Haiti,[22] served to perpetuate oppressive rule. They clearly contributed to the minority regime's goal of reducing dependence on Black labor. After the liberation of Mozambique and the 1976 Soweto uprising, the South African government and many businesses sought to replace Black workers with machinery and equipment, with computers and automation. This permitted a sharp reduction in migrant labor from neighboring countries.[23] At the same time, their capital-intensive character aggravated the problems of growing unemployment in South Africa. Apartheid laws forced growing numbers of Blacks to live in the bantustans – far from the cities where the whites lived – a cheap reserve of migratory labor, available when needed by white employers.

Although they provided a major share of foreign manufacturing investment in South Africa, US firms employed less than 2 percent of South Africa's labor force. One US conglomerate, the Celanese Corporation, for example, which produced chemicals and fibers required by textile industries in South and North Carolina,[24] invested some \$5.5 million and employed fifty workers in South Africa.[25] The relatively small size of its South African holdings suggests that it mainly sold fibers to South African textile manufacturer,s who in turn sold the finished goods in South Africa and abroad.

US high-tech investments in areas like transport, oil, computerization, electrical equipment and machinery and nuclear technologies, however, did facilitate the minority regime's control over its population at home and throughout southern Africa. They helped white troops attain the high levels of mobility required to move quickly from one 'trouble spot' to another to enforce apartheid laws within the country. They also strengthened South Africa's military capacity to destabilize neighboring countries. In the 1980s, South Africa launched lightning attacks on Mozambique, Swaziland, Lesotho and Botswana. It provided weapons and training for dissident forces in Mozambique, Angola and Zimbabwe. For years, tens of thousands of South African soldiers, backed by tanks, advanced weaponry and air power, remained mobilized in northern Namibia to block SWAPO's liberation forces. South African troops repeatedly crossed the border to disrupt neighboring Angola. In 1988, some 8,000 South African troops fought side by side with UNITA in an all-out effort defeated by the Angolan government forces.[26]

The shift of US investments to manufacturing in places like South Africa impacted the work and lives of folk in the southeastern US in two ways. First, it aggravated the trend towards growing unemployment. Starting in the 1920s, and accelerating in the 1950s and 1960s, the textile industry had moved south from the higher wage areas of New England. By the 1970s, North Carolina ranked higher in industrialization than the national average, even above that of the textile industry's original home, Massachusetts. In the mid 1980s, however, as textile firms closed down in the face of competition from imports manufactured by overseas firms still further south, including those in South Africa, North Carolina lost forty-three textile jobs a day.[27]

This trend reflected the US transnationals' response to the potentials of technological change. On the one hand, as transnational buying firms shipped in low-cost textiles produced abroad, major US-based textile companies succumbed to the wave of mergers manipulated by Wall Street financiers. The new conglomerates purchased sophisticated machinery and equipment to maintain output and laid off workers to cut costs. Ousting what used to be called 'mom and pop' textile plants in North Carolina, this process accelerated concentration, centralization and control.

On the other hand, US textile-marketing firms scoured the world for still cheaper textiles, buying from overseas manufacturers who found ways to reduce their wage costs still further. Taiwanese, Hong Kong and Israeli textile firms took advantage of the fact that apartheid forced unemployed South African Blacks to live in overcrowded, impoverished bantustans, desperate for jobs at any wage. Some seventy-five Taiwanese factories, established in the bantustans, paid their workers seven dollars a *week*. Workers in North Carolina earned five to seven dollars an *hour*.[28] US firms like Sears Roebuck and K-Mart could buy these textiles,[29] labeled 'made in Taiwan', or 'Hong Kong' or 'Israel' for sale in the United States. The Reagan-Bush administration's half-hearted monitoring of sanctions appeared unlikely to expose these kinds of violations of the 1986 sanctions. The shift of industry to places like South Africa also aggravated the dualistic pattern of growth alongside stagnation that, in the 1980s, increasingly characterized the US southeast. In the late 1970s and 1980s, as textile firms left and mining unemployment soared, the 'sunbelt's' vaunted prosperity bubble burst. The textile firms that closed down had mainly operated factories in rural areas where wages averaged a third less than in the cities. Husbands or wives and younger family members on small farms, especially among Black farm families, worked part-time in those plants to supplement their inadequate farm incomes. When the factories closed, cutting off that additional essential income, these families had to sell their farms, joining the region's growing pool of unemployed workers.[30]

The state governments sought a new approach to 'development' – if one could call it that. They joined the nationwide competition to attract high-tech industry, much of it associated with US military expansion.[31] New high-tech factories opened up in urban centers like the Durham Triangle in North Carolina; Huntsville, Alabama; and Atlanta, Georgia. These urban areas seemingly boomed while the rural areas stagnated.[32] A third of the high-tech labor force, however, comprised highly skilled engineers and professionals. Because the southern states' inadequate educational systems did not produce enough qualified graduates, many of these workers came from out of state.

The relatively unskilled southern workers, many of them women, mainly took the remaining two-thirds of high-tech jobs that paid little more than the minimum wage. This laid the basis for a new pattern of competition with the impoverished workers of places like South Africa. IBM, for example – the twelfth largest US investor in South Africa – had long done business there.[33] The extensive introduction of high tech to strengthen and perpetuate the military-industrial complex had made the white minority the world's most 'computerized' population – a sizable market for all kinds of computers. In the 1980s, IBM's managers widely publicized the sale of their South African assets to a South African company. They gave far less publicity to their continued supply of financial assistance and essential technologies that enabled the South African company to continue to sell computers to bolster minority rule.[34] In essence, they replaced their direct investments by a contractual system which permitted them to continue profiting from the South African market without risking their capital.

IBM had already experimented with a similar contract system in Huntsville, Alabama with SCI Systems, the city's largest employer with over 4,000 workers, to manufacture personal computers. The SCI workers' experiences illustrate how the system worked. A former SCI corporate counsel explained that, for three-fourths of the workers – mainly women earning minimum wage – who did relatively unskilled production work: 'You pay them as little as you can. . . .'[35] If the production employees joined a union, he added that IBM threatened to take away the company's contract.[36] Thus, like an increasing number of transnational manufacturers, IBM's managers introduced a global contract system to avoid tying its capital to any given location; this enabled them to shift production to whichever local company, in the US or abroad, kept labor costs the lowest.

The Role of Transnational Bankers

Banking and finance provide a fourth set of examples of how transnationals have taken advantage of new technologies to put the living and working conditions of US workers into competition with those of South Africa. In the 1970s, especially after the Soweto uprising, US investors in general no longer risked expanding their direct investments in South Africa. Instead, the bigger US banks began to lend more and more money, not only to the private sector, but also to South Africa's government, which required foreign exchange to finance its high-tech, oil and military imports. The transnational corporate managers increasingly recognized – as IBM finally realized in the 1980s – that, to gain access to South African markets and low-cost labor, they did not need to risk their capital by buying South African real estate. They could leave that risk to the South Africans, to the Anglo-American Group, to whoever proved willing to stay there. Frequently backed by both US and South African government guarantees, the banks could lend the needed funds to their long-time South African–based associates, reaping 15 to 20 percent profits in the form of interest.

By the mid 1980s, South Africa had run up a debt of close to $20 billion. The then biggest US bank, Citicorp, had provided the largest share, some $2.6 billion.[37] It also played a leading role in organizing consortia of other banks to extend loans. Citicorp owned offices in South Africa, and several directors on its board represented companies with South African investments.

Only in 1985, in response to anti-apartheid pressures, did US banks refused to roll over South Africa's maturing loans. Shortly thereafter, however, they rescheduled the loans on repayment terms that looked generous compared to those imposed on Latin American governments.[38] Although the 1986 US sanctions prohibited new bank loans to South Africa, the Mathias amendment permitted the US banks to continue providing suppliers credit to finance South African goods trade. Finally, in 1987, as US anti-apartheid pressures against bank support to South Africa mounted, Citicorp adopted the tactic of selling its South African holdings to the Anglo-American Group, with which it had long had links through MINORCO.[39] As in the case of IBM, this enabled it to retain its position in the South African financial market without the apparent complicity implied by direct investment.[40]

In the 1970s, at the same time that it expanded its South African business, Citicorp also sought to penetrate the banking market in the southeastern United States. It apparently aimed not to extend loans to southeast business, but to tap southeastern bank deposits in order to make more of its seemingly profitable loans abroad. However, it encountered stiff opposition from regional banks, which were protected by federal banking laws that hindered US banks from crossing state borders. Under the Reagan administration's 1980s deregulation thrust, the bigger southeastern banks pushed through state legislation that permitted them to merge across regional state lines, while further restricting the regional role of outsiders like Citicorp.[41]

Out of this financial turmoil, the North Carolina National Bank (NCNB) emerged as the southeast's leading regional bank. However, it reinvested a substantial share of regional depositors' funds, not to meet the small business, minority, housing or industrial needs of the US southeast, but in South Africa.[42] In the 1960s and 1970s, NCNB joined Citicorp as one of only three US commercial banks with offices in South Africa. By the mid-1980s, NCNB alone accounted for about one out of every seven dollars that US banks had loaned to the South African government and its agencies.[43] When pressed by church shareholders to withdraw from South Africa, Hugh McColl, NCNB's chairman, a former Marine officer, told his hometown paper:

> We're probably one of the best banks in South Africa. It's a different neighborhood, but I think we do a good job. . . . I love it [South Africa]. I think it's one

of the most wonderful countries in the world. . . . I've lived in a segregated society and that doesn't kill people. We ask for the impossible [majority rule], you see. . . . Should any rational and sane man believe that a group of people should deliver themselves of all their power?[44]

The Implications for Pan-Africanists

The wealth of evidence discovered in the course of the Africa Peace Tour tends to prove that, under the umbrella of the spread of US militarism throughout Africa, US transnational firms and banks took advantage of the technological revolution to shift major investments to South Africa as an opening wedge into the African continent's vast potential. In the process, they forced American workers, especially the poorest and most vulnerable – including Afro-Americans – to compete with the wages and working and living conditions of workers oppressed by apartheid.

This underscores another dimension of Pan-Africanism. It suggests that US Pan-Africanists should join with the peoples of Africa and South Africa to press for an end to the US government's military expenditures. It focuses, in particular, on the need to block US policies designed to open Africa to the penetration of transnationals' counterproductive business practices. This does not imply US investors should shun Africa; indeed all the independent African countries urge foreign investment that could increase their productive employment opportunities and raise their living standards. Pan-Africanists, however, should press for a global floor to protect and advance wages and working and living conditions throughout the diaspora. As a first step, they should demand a reduction of US military expenditures that tend to bolster counterproductive forces, not only in Angola and Southern Africa, but throughout the African continent.

Incorporating this element in the Pan-Africanist program could have two helpful consequences. First, in the US itself, it would strengthen efforts to redirect the billions of dollars made available by the end of the Cold War and the collapse of apartheid to provide jobs, homes, schools and higher living standards for all Americans, particularly the most oppressed: Afro-Americans. Second, in Africa, it would help create the conditions in which the peoples of that vast continent could attain self-reliant, self-sustainable development, increasing their productivity and raising their living standards, the only sound foundation for mutually beneficial trade with the US.[45]

Just consider the potentials of this approach in Southern Africa alone. The region's land area covers about the same amount of territory as the continental United States. It possesses extensive known mineral and agricultural resources. The regional population totals an estimated 100 million, over a third of that of the United States. Yet the United States normally sells about ten times as many goods per man, woman and child to Europe as it does to the peoples of Southern Africa.[46] Only when the peoples of southern Africa achieve full liberation (the dismantling of apartheid is only the beginning) will they be able to join those Americans willing to press for imposing an international floor to protect their mutual well-being. Only then will they be able to redirect and develop their valuable mineral and agricultural resources primarily to meet their own needs, but also for export at reasonable prices.[47] As incomes rise, they will want to sell products to the US to pay for expanded purchases of essential machinery, equipment and goods like those made in US factories, creating an expanding market that will contribute to increasing US output and employment.

In short, US Pan-Africanists today should assume leadership in the movement to end US militarism and adopt government measures to support the spread of productive employment opportunities and an improved quality of life both in the United States and Africa. This alone can lay the essential foundation for expanding mutually beneficial trade, contributing to the conditions necessary for peace and employment on both sides of the Atlantic.

Notes

1. For a full description and more extensive evidence for the following discussion, see Ann Seidman, *Apartheid, Militarism and the US Southeast*, Trenton, N.J. 1990.

2. See Chapter 5 on Haiti in this book.

3. The 1990 Census, as well as numerous studies, confirmed the 'devastating domestic effects' of this process in dichotomizing US society (see Robert Pear, 'US Reports Poverty Is Down But Inequality Is Up', *New York Times*, 27 Sept. 1990). While crises engulfed Africa and the Third World, in the United States growing numbers of blue-collar workers lost the high-paying jobs and fringe benefits they won in earlier decades. Union membership plummeted to roughly 15 percent of all wage workers (US Department of Commerce, *US Statistical Abstract*, Washington, D.C. 1989.). For the most part, only top managers in finance and business, especially in high-tech industries, spurred by expanding military-related R&D, experienced rising incomes. In twenty-six years, from 1947 to 1973, average US family incomes rose 111 percent. In contrast, from 1973 to 1989, family incomes edged up only 9 percent. More and more women, forced to take paid jobs to help support their families, accounted for most of that marginal increase (Lawrence Mishel and David Frankel, *The State of Working America*, Washington, D.C. 1990).

4. For details, see William D. Toussaint, 'Agriculture in the Southeast' (with particular attention to tobacco), study prepared for MDC, Inc., Raleigh, N.C. 1986.

5. For material relating to the tobacco transnationals, unless otherwise cited, see P. Taylor, *The Smoke Ring*, New York 1984; and the companies' annual reports.

6. Ann Seidman, *A Comparative Study of Three Tobacco-Exporting Countries: Kenya, Thailand and Zimbabwe*, prepared for the United Nations Transnational Corporate Centre, Harare 1983.

7. At independence, Zimbabwe raised the minimum agricultural wage to about US$50 a month, but, with International Monetary Fund advice, it devalued its currency, more than

halving the wages in US dollar terms: see International Monetary Fund, *International Financial Statistics*, Washington, D.C. January 1984.

8. United Nations Conference on Trade and Development, *Marketing and Distribution of Tobacco*, TD/BC 1/205, 1978, New York 1978, p. 72.

9. For the estimated consequences of US military spending on domestic welfare programs, 1986–91, see the report of the Center on Budget and Policy Priorities (*In These Times*, 19 Feb.–25 Feb. 1986). For the effect of the 1980–84 budget cuts on the southeastern states, see *Public Assistance and Poverty: A Special Report of the Southern Regional Council*, Atlanta 1985.

10. For this brief history, unless otherwise cited, see Francis J. Rivers, 'People and Jobs in the Southwestern Virginia Coalfields: A Report Prepared for the Commission on Religion in Appalachia and Community College Ministries', 1986.

11. See Ann Seidman, *The Roots of Crisis in Southern Africa*, Trenton, N.J. 1985, p. 50. In 1985, South African monetary authorities devalued the South African currency, the rand, reducing the average Black South African mine wage to about a tenth that of US miners'.

12. US Congress, House Committee on Ways and Means, *Monthly Reports on Status of the Steel Industry, Report to the Subcommittee on Trade*, Investigation no. 333-220 – under Section 332 of the Tariff Act of 1930 – US ITC Public 1852, Tables 8, 9, Washington, D.C. 1986.

13. Reported by American Friends Service Committee, Philadelphia 1987, and confirmed in 'Despite Curbs, South African Steel Is Entering US', *New York Times*, 15 April 1990. In addition to direct shipments, South African steel exporters, keeping the direction of their steel shipments a 'closely guarded secret', sought new export markets, and steel from Turkey, mainly rolled from semi-finished South African steel, flooded into the US.

14. Bruce Boyons, 'Development of Foreign Coal by American Corporations', *West Virginia Law Review*, vol. 87, no. 3 (Spring 1985).

15. See 'Unified List of US Companies with Investments or Loans in South Africa and Namibia', compiled by Pacific Northwest Research Center, Inc., New York 1985, in Seidman, *The Roots of Crisis in Southern Africa*, Appendix III. For additional information relating to US investment in South Africa, see the US Department of Commerce, *Survey of Current Business*, August or September issues, which annually report US foreign investments and returns by region and sector. These figures are understated to the extent that they exclude US investments in South Africa through US affiliates based in Europe or Canada.

16. Keystone Coal Industry Manual 1983, cited in *The United Mine Workers Journal*, October 1986.

17. For a detailed analysis of the Anglo-American Group in the early 1980s, see Duncan Innes, *Anglo-American and the Rise of Modern South Africa*, New York 1984.

18. *Who's Who in America*, Wilmette, Ill. 1986–7, vol. 2, 4th edn.

19. In 1982, African miners earned $1.67 per hour (calculated using the 1982 currency exchange rate from data published in the South Africa Institute of Race Relations, *Survey of Race Relations in South Africa, 1982*, Pietermaritzburg 1983).

20. Hans Hoffman, 'The Truth about Shell in South Africa', tr. from *Netherlands FNV Magazine*, 11 November 1986.

21. For a list of US manufacturing firms' assets and employment in South Africa in 1983, see 'Unified List'. The percentage of US direct investment is reported in Anne Newmann, 'The US Corporate State in South Africa', *Africa News*, vol. 24, no. 10, 20 May 1985.

22. See Chapter 5 on Haiti.

23. Before Mozambique won political independence in 1975, between 120,000 and 130,000 workers annually migrated to work on South African mines and farms. Both to reduce the drain on foreign exchange and to end any radical influence Mozambican workers could have on South African workers, the South African government proceeded to reduce this number dramatically.

24. See below for discussion of the impact of shifting US investments on the US textiles industry.

25. See 'Unified List'.

26. For a thorough analysis of UNITA, see William Minter, 'Savimbi and South Africa: No Casual Affair', Washington, D.C. 1987. Only two years after the conference at which this paper was presented, when the costs of its military mobilization imposed too great a drain on its resources, did the South African government finally agree to Namibian political inde-

pendence. Meanwhile, the US government more openly assumed the role of supplying military aid to UNITA.

27. Vic Rains, 'Annual Report 1986 of Announced Manufacturing Plant Closings and Permanent Layoffs', memorandum to Alton Skinner, North Carolina Department of Commerce, 30 January 1987.

28. Allister Sparks, 'Slave Wage Paid by Profiteers with Pretoria's Backing', *Observer* (London), 5 April 1987.

29. Sears, itself, had long had direct investments in South Africa; see 'Unified List'.

30. Stuart Rosenfield, *After the Factories: Changing Employment Patterns in the Rural South,* Durham, N.C. 1986.

31. An estimated three-fourths of US research is devoted to military-related activity.

32. Stuart Rosenfeld, 'A Divided South', and Marc Miler, 'The Lowdown on High Tech', in *Everybody's Business: A People's Guide to Economic Development,* a special issue of *Southern Exposure,* vol. 14, No. 5–6 (Sept.–Oct. 1986).

33. See 'Unified List' for IBM's 1985 assets and employment in South Africa.

34. 'Disinvestment and the Workers', *Sechaba,* London, February 1987.

35. In Miller, 'The Lowdown on High Tech'.

36. Ibid.

37. See 'Unified List', regarding US banks' known commitments. Because anti-apartheid critics increasingly focused their objections on growing bank loans, the amounts of additional short-term suppliers' credit the banks provided to South Africa remained difficult to determine.

38. Patrick Bond, based on interviews with South African bank officials as part of his research for a Ph.D. dissertation at Johns Hopkins University, in correspondence with the author, October 1987.

39. Anglo combined Citicorp's South African assets with those of Barclays Bank, in which it had held shares for years, to create the First National Bank of South Africa (Duncan Innes, paper presented to sanctions workshop, Gaborone Sun Hotel, Botswana, 7–8 November 1987).

40. MINORCO constituted Anglo's Bermuda-based affiliate through which, for a time, it became the second largest foreign investor in the United States (see Innes, *Anglo-American and the Rise of Modern South Africa*).

41. For this background information, see J.B. Moore, Jr, 'Regional Banks and Southern Markets', *The Southern Banker,* October 1985; A.S. Kilman, 'Regional Banking Grows Rapidly in Southeast', *Wall Street Journal,* 3 October 1985; 'Bankings' Balance of Power is Tilting Toward the Regionals: Some of the Money-Center Giants Are Going to Be Left Behind', *Business Week,* 7 April 1986.

42. See Maryland Alliance for Responsible Investment, *Comment on the Application of the NCNB Corporation of Charlotte, North Carolina, to Acquire Centrabank, Inc. of Baltimore Maryland and a Request for Public Hearing,* Baltimore 1987.

43. *Charlotte Observer,* 10 February 1985.

44. Ibid.

45. For a compilation of a growing body of research relating to how to attain these goals, see Ann Seidman and Fred Anang, eds, *Twenty-first Century Africa: Towards a New Vision of Self-Sustainable Development,* Trenton, N.J. 1992.

46. Calculated from United Nations, *Yearbook of International Trade Statesitics, 1979–80,* New York 1981, in the years before the deepening of the regional political economic and military crisis.

47. To call for the attainment of more balanced, integrated and self-reliant African political economies does not imply an end to participation in foreign trade; rather it requires restructuring that trade to facilitate acquisition of the necessary new techologies to increase productivity and raise the living standards of the African peoples: For discussion, see Seidman and Anang, *Twenty-first Century Africa,* Ch. 2.

13

Pan-Africanism and the Politics of Education: Towards a New Understanding

William H. Watkins

The exploration, colonization and partitioning of Africa has highlighted world affairs for nearly 400 years. Colonial powers have long recognized her value in their schemes to dominate industrial production, secure precious metals, exploit cheap labor, gain supplies of agricultural products and monopolize world markets. The 'scramble for Africa' has been at the heart of European and American foreign policy since the early 1800s. Africa not only represents the cradle of civilization but in many ways is both a barometer and a harbinger for the future of civilization.

The scattering of African people across the planet has been of the utmost social, political and economic consequence. Few doubt that the emergence of Western industrialization could have succeeded without the accumulations of wealth facilitated by slavery in the Americas. The indignities of brutal Western colonialism have left the world's richest continent on the brink of collapse.

The intense exploitation of Africa and her scattered peoples has spawned protest: oppositional and revolutionary ideologies and movements on both sides of the Atlantic. The separatist, Black nationalist and Pan-Africanist movements dating back two centuries represent these sentiments, emerging as a radical response to slavery and the debasement of Africa.[1]

Wilson Moses explains the origins of this outlook.[2] He points to the emergence of 'macro nationalist' theories evident in the emergence of 'Pan-Germanism' and 'Pan-Slavism', whose objective was to 'unite various independent ethnic groups under the banner of collective nationalism'. He traces the historical development of Pan-Africanism to the 'maroon revolutions of Haiti, Jamaica, and Surinam during the seventeenth and eighteenth centuries, and in the rebellions of Denmark Vesey and Nat Turner in the nineteenth'.

While strains of Pan-Africanist thought and practice range from identificationist to armed movements for national liberation, the central concepts remain to promote the interests that African people, regardless of their locus, have in common. In general those interests are against colonialism, for national liberation, for a united Africa, for the revitalization and promotion of African cultural ideals and for the betterment and uplift of Black people.

The examination of education takes on special importance within the Pan-African context. The colonial hegemonists understood from the outset that domination requires an ideological component to supplement rule by naked force. Education, more accurately miseducation, came to be an important weapon in the oppression of African people. Colonial education has come to be seen as cultural imperialism.[3] Interestingly, models of colonial education employed in 'British tropical' Africa were exported directly from accommodationist educational models piloted in the southern United States.[4] The study of the oppression of African peoples is incomplete without an understanding of the origins, rationale, personalities, sponsorship, objectives and long-term impact of a century and a half of that 'special kind of education'.[5] To undertake an examination of colonial education, some comments on the politicization of education may be useful in framing the discussion.

The Aims of Education: From Liberalism to Power Politics

Feudal Europe provided the historical circumstances for development of the notion of 'liberal' education. In many ways it was a reaction to the absolutism of the monarchy. David Sidorsky in his work on liberal education attributes it to the rise of a middle class critique in feudal Europe.[6] He associates liberal education with the rise of the 'new classes', that is, the mercantile and capitalist forces demanding a democratic world order. Democracy, more specifically, liberalization of authoritarian structures, was indispensable to the growth of the 'new classes'. The new philosophical liberalism demanded rationality, humanism, consistency and criticism. In Europe, Descartes and Kant came to represent the new liberalism. In England the political philosophies of Locke and Mill were indicative of such thinking.

Liberal education is directly associated with rational and political liberalism. Liberal education themes came to focus on unfettered human development. Sidney Hook's *Education for a Modern Man* described the educational objectives of the liberal philosophy.[7] Among the general aims were to develop the powers of critical independent thought, to promote sympathy and receptiveness to new ideas and to develop intelligent loyalty to democracy. Beyond societal goals the great strength of liberal education was believed to reside in its cultivation of individual self-actualization. Liberal education was supposed to strengthen inner resources, unlock human potential, facilitate growth, encourage reflection and strengthen individual resolve. Liberal education was to be inextricably connected to the democratic society. Inquiry, experientialism and naturalism were to replace imposition and rigidity.

The Civil War in the United States was a major political and educational watershed. Slavery gave way to free labor, agriculture yielded to industrialization and the rural community turned into the urban metropolis. Shielded by the watchwords *freedom* and *democracy*, the monopoly bankers and industrialists quickly usurped political and economic power. Democracy was to take on a specific and limited meaning in America. While expansionist capital would dominate the structures of power, electoral politics, civil liberties and the encouragement of individual human growth would become sacred tenets in the new political and social culture.

The nineteenth century found Western 'liberal' education combining this culture of democracy with the humanism inherited from the European, particularly German, child developmentalists.[8] These views became refined and institutionalized as common schooling spread in the early twentieth century. John Dewey's *Democracy and Education* and *Experience and Education* are examples of works widely accepted as the protocols of America's democratic humanistic education. To be far removed from the cauldrons of power and ideology, this education was to promote free inquiry, self-realization, community and freedom.[9,10]

Like much of America's democratic rhetoric, a duality quickly became evident in the grand pronouncements of humanistic education. People of color and the still dispossessed former slaves were not to participate in this blueprint for enlightenment. The opening years of the twentieth century witnessed the unfolding of colonial educational policies consistent with the political economy of unfettered industrialization and hegemonic national development.

There was little doubt from the Civil War onward that issues and questions surrounding Blacks would take on special importance. The victorious Northern industrialists were preoccupied with the re-annexation of the South. This would allow them a firm home base upon which to expand into overseas markets. Their chosen course of action was to aid Blacks without disturbing the racial and social class traditions in the South. The South with its fertile 'black belt' region would continue to exist as a colonial and semi-colonial region.[11]

The differentiated structures of Western industrial education had now taken shape. 'Liberal' themes would be promoted in the mainstream movement for popular education. For the colonial and subject peoples of the Black South, the Caribbean and colonial Africa the politics of control, containment and accommodation would define education. Imperial education was to draw from these themes within nineteenth-century sociological thought. Its theoreticians and practitioners were generously endowed by the corporate capitalists who were shaping the twentieth-century world order in their favor.

On Educating Negroes and Africans: The Search for Sociological Theory

Colonial foreign policy as well as educational policy sought rationale, justification and refinement from the academic and intellectual community.[12] While the seventeenth- and eighteenth-century traders and missionaries could talk of Christianizing their less fortunate dark-skinned brothers, the large-scale domination, plunder and commercially one-sided operations of the nineteenth century required more substantial justification. The 'social sciences' combined with the new theories of development and modernization quickly came to the rescue.

The latter half of the nineteenth century found a realignment of the 'social sciences' taking place in Western Europe and the United States. Herbert Spencer's work on Social Darwinism was gaining popularity as an explanation of social development. Racial and international interactions could now be explained with natural selection and evolution. Social scientists began to 'describe' the development of ethnic society. Theories of race hierarchy began to emerge.[13] Alleyne Ireland's work, *The Far Eastern Tropics*,[14] is indicative of an outlook that placed Europeans at the top of the evolutionary ladder.

Social Darwinism was soon supplemented by the notion of 'structural functionalism'. Refined by Talcott Parsons, the notion suggested that Western society was fundamentally sound and should be preserved at all costs. Where reform is needed it should be implemented but the system must be maintained.[15] The turn of the twentieth century found the social sciences in a period of realignment and ensconced in a battle for turf.[16] Spencer's significant contributions allowed the fledgling community of sociologists to make new claims. Franklin Giddings, professor and first chair of sociology at Columbia, declared that nineteenth-century approaches to generalized 'social science' were vague, inconsistent and clumsy. He argued for sociology as a scientific, logical and objective way to explain social and national development. He claimed it was sociology that could best describe social organization, kinship, class, demographics, education and social behavior.[17] Giddings and his sociological views soon gained acceptance and had significant impact on the education of both Africans and African-Americans.

In his general approach, Giddings was a social evolutionist. Nature and natural selection dealt the cards. Human beings had little ability to influence or better their circumstances. For Giddings inequality and human suffering were simply a natural part of evolutionary social development. He suggested that suffering was frequently a prelude to better circumstances.

Racial Classification and Education

As a part of his quest to make sociology an exact, quantitative science, Giddings was inclined to develop classification schemes. His schemes were typically hierarchies which labeled racial and ethnic groups. For example, he divided all people into 'vitality' classes. European and alpine people were described as vigorous, with high mental power, high birth rates and low death rates. The lower vitality groups, that is, people of color, were characterized as having low body vigor, low mental power, high birth rates and high death rates. Using this same conceptualization he divided people into 'personality' groups and 'moral' groups with a similar hierarchical rank ordering.

For Giddings, social populations were to be understood by their 'social mind'. The better developed (collective) social mind was given to intelligent, moral, reasoned and directed behavior, while the lesser developed social mind was inclined to 'impulsive' actions. Coincidentally, the impulsive people inhabited the warmer climates. It was they, gripped by ignorance, who had inclinations to act on fear, passion and irrationality. His view of homogeneity, that is, the like-mindedness of a people evolving together, meant that these qualities affected the common population. His endorsement of Ireland's ideas on the heat belt characterized his views on race and social development:

> Bearing in mind the elements which go to make up our own civilization – western civilization, so called – it is important to realize that during the past five hundred years, to go no further, the people of the heat belt have added nothing whatever to what we understand by human advancement. Those natives of the

tropics and subtropics who have not been under direct European influence have not during that time made a single contribution of the first importance to art, literature, science, manufacture, or inventions, they have not produced an engineer, or a chemist, or a biologist, or a historian, or a painter, or a musician of the first rank; and even if we include half-castes and such natives as have enjoyed European education, the list of eminent men in the domain of art, science, literature, and invention produced by the heat belt can be counted on the finger of one hand.[18]

Giddings's racial views easily transferred into anti-communism and anti-socialism, which he feared as the outstanding threats to uninterrupted capitalist development and the building of the Euro-American empire. Lybarger summarizes this outlook:

A profoundly conservative man, Giddings often voiced concern about 'proletarian madness'. Impulsive social action, the consequence of sympathetic like-mindedness, Giddings thought, played a role in all revolutions, and was always harmful. One manifestation of proletarian madness, socialism, Giddings thought especially pernicious, terming it 'nonsense': and a 'tremendous fallacy' . . . those who attribute economic exploitation to the wickedness and greed of a capital owning class commit a tissue of economic and sociological fallacies.[19]

Giddings's views on education were an extension of his outlooks on the nature of societal organization, control, maintenance, and the role of the individual within a dynamic world. His views were to become embedded in the foundations of colonial education. For him worthy citizenship should be at the heart of any educational program. Citizenship, he insisted, meant the individual adjusting himself to the existing social order. Arguing that the 'social mind' was at the heart of human development, education must understand the 'social mind' of the various racial groups. The 'social mind' of Black people could best be described as primitive. He wrote: 'The social disabilities of the negro and the social, legal and political disabilities of the Indian, show how far from perfect is the differentiation in our own nation, even now'.[20] Further,

Another race with little capacity for improvement is the surviving North American Indian. Though intellectually superior to the negro the Indian has shown less ability than the negro to adapt himself to new conditions. The negro is plastic. He yields easily to environing influences. Deprived of the support of strong races, he still relapses into savagery but kept in contact with the whites, he readily takes the external impress of civilization, and there is reason to hope that he will yet acquire a measure of its spirit.[21]

Giddings believed African peoples could be educated so long as they adhered to Euro-American developmental paradigms. Like social development, education was to be part of an evolutionary process. Black people were to be gradually but increasingly introduced to the Anglo-Saxon ideal.[22] Drawing from his broad sociological background, Giddings was able to present a rudimentary conceptualization of education for 'primitive' people. It was to be his protégé and doctoral student, Thomas Jesse Jones, who broadened and fine-tuned the ideological and practical program of colonial education for Negroes and Africans.

Thomas Jesse Jones: Architect of African and African-American Education

Early-twentieth-century colonial educational practices came to be indicative of the close link between Africa and the Black southern United States. Thomas Jesse Jones, more than any other individual, was responsible for the application of intercontinental educational practices. While Jones was skilled in using the language of racial uplift and social betterment, his role as 'evil genius of the Black race' demands examination.[23]

Jones was born in a small rural village in Wales in August 1873. In 1884, with his widowed mother and four siblings, the family emigrated to New York City. Seeking to escape the harsh working-class life of Liverpool and Wales, the Jones family was unprepared for the realities of immigrant life in late-nineteenth-century America. The family soon settled in Middleport, Ohio, an area then dominated by mining and the iron industry. Growing up in sympathy with the plight of the blue-collar workers of this area, Jones turned his intellectual attention to issues of pioneer settlement and societal formation.[24]

Upon graduation from Marietta College in Ohio, he returned to New York to take up graduate work at Columbia. Subsequent to receiving an M.A. in 1897, Jones began studying with Giddings who, as mentioned, was already deeply involved in the social science dialogue of the time. Giddings's views on the dynamics of racial and social development profoundly influenced Jones.

Jones's Ph.D. dissertation, 'The Sociology of a New York Block',[25] was written under Giddings's supervision. In this work, Jones employed Giddings's notions of hierarchical racial categorizing to the immigrant slum populations in New York's lower east side. Predictably, he found intellectual and character weaknesses in immigrants and people of color:

In the community under consideration there is great need of this assimilating process. Every possible agency should be used to change the numerous foreign types into the Anglo-Saxon ideal. The impulsiveness of the Italian must be curbed. The extreme individualism of the Jew must be modified. The shiftlessness of the Irish must give way to perseverance and frugality. And all must be shown the value of the spiritual in life.[26]

With his world view of socio-racial development consolidated, Jones began to establish linkages with his religious views, political conservatism, 'structural functionalism' and emerging anti-communism. While a graduate student, he began to conduct citizenship education classes for immigrants in the settlement houses of lower Manhattan.[27] This became the perfect platform for his political philosophy. Settlement house work directed Jones towards the teaching profession. The revolutionary social upheaval in Europe and Russia further convinced him that he could play a role in stabilizing America with its unstable ethnic populations.

Jones's elevation into prominence began with his appointment as professor of sociology and part-time chaplain at the Hampton Institute in 1902. By 1904 he had conceptualized and begun writing a social science curriculum for Hampton's predominantly Black and Native American students. It became America's first modern, that is twentieth-century, social studies curriculum. The Hampton Social Studies, as they came to be known, offered a model for educating subject and oppressed people. Although Jones declared that the Hampton Social Studies would proceed from the 'needs of the learner', it would unfold as both a developmentally and politically charged offering.

Developmentally, Jones was concerned with the socialization of the Negro. This socialization involved a minimalistic theme called the 'essentials'. Later written up in *Four Essentials of Education* and *Essentials of Civilization: A Study of Social Values*,[28,29] these essentials reflected basic education. For Jones, the four basics were to be added to the three R's. They were: knowledge of health and hygiene; knowledge of the physical environment; knowledge of domestic life and culture; and knowledge of recreation, the art of creating a sane and elastic personality, self-controlled and poised, serene of mind and capable of happiness. The Negro was to be humanized!

The political themes of the Hampton curriculum complemented Jones's political outlook, which was consistent with his views on social development. He believed natural forces would appropriately shape society. He saw little need for the government to impose itself into these natural processes. His lessons were, in effect, an ideological primer for political socialization and 'worthy' citizenship.

Courses in civics, political economy, civil government, mental and moral science, general history and Bible study all taught the triumph of Western civilization. Jones, an ordained minister,[30] saw his social studies as assisting in God's work. These studies would help the Negro 'acquire habits and ideals requisite for their development'.

More than mere school subjects, the accommodationist curriculum was to provide the socio-intellectual foundations elevating for a backward race. Economics material would establish a relationship between human toil and social progress. Government courses would contend that Western democracy provides optimum conditions for the evolution of human liberty, but could not be attempted by the ignorant or irresponsible. 'Race development' as a topic transcended many courses. Focus there was on evolutionary development, acceptance and *natural* order. Slavery was part of America's natural order and the government was repressive on account of the mixed ethnic population. If Blacks would only adopt white values all would be well.[31]

The physical and manual components of the curriculum consisted of perhaps six hours (daily) of agricultural and/or trades labor. It was here that Samuel Armstrong's influence would be felt. Armstrong believed that beyond developing marketable skills manual labor would build character, work habits and Christian morals.[32] Since much of Hampton's mission focused on the training of teachers, the notion of hard work as a character builder could be propagated in an educational rationale.

Jones, Phelps-Stokes and Accommodationism: African Connections

While early-twentieth-century Africa's social and political realities were very different from those of the southern United States, the dynamics of their kindred colonial status connected their destinies. The internationalization of capital through the multinational corporation had become a fledgling reality. The now familiar model of traditional western colonialism was in effect. The relationship worked thus: Western corporations procure cheap labor to extract precious metals and agricultural items, ship the raw materials to the 'mother country' for processing, sell the finished products to the world and repatriate profits to the Western corporations.[33] Most of Black Africa and the southern United States became linked as the objects and subjects of these colonial practices. The desire for imperial ideological containment through education was to grow in importance.[34]

Jones's early efforts were being matched by similar activities in Africa. Kenneth King documents the activities of both white and Black African accommodationist educators:

There had, of course, been missions, such as the Basel, and some of the South African institutions, which had had a thoroughly industrial character for a good part of the century, but it was particularly during the last decade that industrial department began to become fashionable. The year 1893 saw the start of the Hope-Wardell Institute in Calabar, designed by Dr Laws of Livinstonia; this was followed by Bishop Ingham's technical institute in Freetown in 1895, one in Brass in 1897, and another in Onitsha in 1898; the same year a technical department was opened in the government school at Accra, and in 1899 a separate government technical school was opened in Lagos. Meanwhile in East Africa following on the work of Krapf on the coast and Alexander Mackey in Uganda, the East African Scottish Mission began to [conduct] industrial experiments in Kilwezi in 1891.[35]

Other important individuals such as C.T. Loram and James Aggrey were active in the African chapters of the international missionary societies and attended certain Pan-African conferences where possibilities of 'Hampton in Africa' were discussed.[36,37] The commitment to Hampton/Tuskegee-style education grew, but lacked a force such as Jones, who was now well versed in political sociology, social studies, curriculum development, corporate administration and governmental relations.

Transatlantic accommodationist education became joined as a result of the entry of Jones and the Phelps-Stokes Fund into the international arena. The 'Africanization' of the Hampton/Tuskegee model dates from a visit to Tuskegee in 1912 by J.H. Oldham and Alek Fraser, both influential British missionary-educators who favored adoption and adaptation of Booker T. Washington's manual-vocational training program to Britain's African colonies.[38]

Oldham became a major proponent of the Hampton/Tuskegee model and is often credited with its implementation in Africa. From 1908 to 1910, Oldham was secretary of the World Missionary Conference in Edinburgh and subsequently secretary of the Continuation Committee from 1910 to 1921. In addition, he was editor of the *International Review of Missions,* an influential journal in the field of missionary education. Finally, in 1924, Oldham accepted a position at Phelps-Stokes' British office. Oldham was to vigorously pursue Jones's educational models in 'British' Africa.

Mention should be made of the Phelps-Stokes Fund, where Jones served as educational director for twenty-eight years.[39] The emergence of industrial and financial corporations in the post–Civil War period had a profound impact on political and educational processes. Corporate philanthropy, *private* money, influenced public policy as never before. Andrew Carnegie, industrial scion and author of *The Gospel of Wealth,* advocated of charitable giving and showed by his own donations how plutocrats could fund initiatives consistent with their socio-political vision of development.[40]

Following Carnegie's lead, the likes of the Peabody Educational Fund, John F. Slater Fund, Anna T. Jeanes Foundation, Rosenwald Fund, Rockefeller Memorial Fund and many others supported Hampton-style educational programs among their broader activities. Phelps-Stokes was one of these organizations. The Phelps-Stokes family with its New York banking interests became very involved in supporting Black education. Caroline Phelps-Stokes had decreed in her will that substantial funds be committed to educating the Negro in Africa, as well as the United States. Anson Phelps-Stokes was to manage the family's fund, develop its political outlook, expand its African operations and facilitate Jones's rise in his field.

Among the best examples of the collaboration between Jones, the philanthropic community, the industrial expansionists and local compradores was the Booker T. Washington Institute (BWI) established in Kakata, Liberia in the 1920s.[41] BWI was to emerge as a 'showpiece' demonstrating the benefits of international 'cooperation' in education. The expanding rubber empire of the Firestone family was to profoundly affect the political and economic relationships in this 'experimental' country founded by the American Colonization Society in 1822. The expansionist demands for cheap labor, an educated elite and a docile population reconciled to their plight made Liberia ripe for the proponents of industrial and agricultural education. With the strong backing of Olivia Phelps-Stokes, combined with the administrative savvy of Thomas Jesse Jones, the 'little Tuskegee in Africa' was established. BWI eventually came to exemplify the inequities and reactionary nature of such a program. Within a short period of time the school became the toy of special interests. While masquerading as the new symbol of American-Liberian friendship, the school was actually a recruitment station for cheap labor. Seeing little evidence of the promised educational program, students at BWI were instead instructed to flunkey for wealthy people and make furniture for the US military. Plagued by a corrupt administration, student unrest and manipulation by corporatists and philanthropists, BWI has served as a clear example of failed hegemonic educational policy.

Pan-Africans and Educational Self-Help

Jones and the accommodationist-corporate community were well aware of the early-twentieth-century popularity for common schooling. As in the United States, the entire world clamored for education to achieve technological advancement as well as social progress. In Africa and the rural south, the accommodationists exploited this heartfelt desire by providing their brand of schooling.

While the corporatists had little appetite for intercontinental cooperation and protest among African peoples, the nature of their oppressive policies certainly awakened consciousness of a common subjugation. In describing organized Pan-Africanism, Moses asserts:

> Pan-Africanism seems to have originated with the awareness of westernized Africans that all Black people were suffering from the slave trade which tended to confer an inferior status upon all Black people whether slave or free, and regardless of the continent upon which they lived.[42]

The very first Pan-African Congress was organized by Sylvester Williams, a lawyer from Trinidad, and Alexander Walters, a Black American bishop in the A.M.E. Zion Church. It was followed by the many subsequent conferences organized by W.E.B. Du Bois and other Pan-Africanists. Three factors seem to have contributed to increasing connections between Africans within the continent and those across the Atlantic. First, the activities of Jones required an administrative structure that was international in scope. The similarity of efforts in British colonial Africa and the American South meant an interchange of people, ideas and projects. Delegations frequently traveled back and forth across the Atlantic to collaborate, test pilot programs, plan and evaluate. Although delegations were primarily staffed by corporate people such as William Baldwin and Anson Phelps-Stokes, trusted American Blacks such as Max Yergan, a YMCA official, and trusted Africans, such as educator James Aggrey, participated.

Second, the missionary societies, though generally influenced by Jones, C.T. Loram and others, were international endeavors. Their charters were filled with the language of Christian charity, brotherhood, racial uplift and peace. Clearly not intended to promote radical or violent opposition to colonialism, they contributed to assembling scattered Africans to discuss uplift, social progress and self-help. The Le Zoute Conference was an example.[43] While its purpose was to ensure that Negroes and Africans worked in responsible, established Christian agencies for social improvement they, by the very nature of their gathering, assembled for important future work. King remarks:

> These early ventures in pan-Africanism failed to achieve their most concrete object, the introduction of American Negroes as the collaborators of the young politically-minded Africans. But no failure or proscription could prevent the slowly-growing consciousness of Negro unity that white prejudice had nurtured. The wiser of the missionaries in East Africa saw that these pan-African aspirations of the young Africans were modeled on the internationalism of the European and Indian communities in their midst.[44]

233

The third and most significant factor was the developing intellectual and political conceptualization of Pan-Africanism as a movement for unity, identity, anti-colonial protest and betterment. Major Black intellectual figures in both Africa and America took up the Pan-Africanist cause.

Moses believes that nineteenth-century Pan-Africanist ideology was popularized through the literary societies, the missionary organizations and the journals and magazines published by the Black intelligentsia. He examines the contributions of each of these avenues of thought, inquiry and protest, mainly within the United States. The literary societies arose primarily because interested Blacks were denied entry to white literary societies. Among the most well known was the Bethel Literary and Historical Association founded in 1881 by Bishop Daniel Payne. Its discussions, which included teachers and preachers, took up the study of ancient Egypt, Ethiopia and other racial matters linking Africa to the United States. It is known that luminaries such as Frederick Douglass, Alexander Crummell and Bishop Turner participated in these sessions. Another of the more well-known societies was the Saturday Circle, which also took up an interest in Pan-Africanism. Moses concludes that while the societies were not interest groups for Pan-Africanism, its advocates were welcome to participate.

As has been mentioned, the missionaries' societies were greatly influenced by corporate loyalists and functionaries at the top. The spirit of Christian brotherhood and humanism nevertheless remained an important force. Moses observes:

> Missionary activities were also a means by which Black Americans learned something of African brothers and sisters. Church magazines, such as the Baptist *Missionary Magazine* and the *A.M.E. Church Review* carried messages from Africa to America that were both educational and edifying. The *Missionary Review of the World* (June, 1904) carried an article on 'The Ethiopian Movement in South Africa'. . . . Such thought-provoking material was hardly inaccessible to Sunday School classes and 'Saturday circles', and for those whose consciousness had been raised by the likes of Blyden and Turner, it must have been enthusiastically received.[45]

African-American scholarship and literary expression raised important questions about African revitalization and its linkages to America. T. Thomas Fortune, sociologist and journalist, published the *New York Age*. Marcus Garvey's organization published the *Negro World*. Other secular Black magazines, including *The Colored American, Voice of the Negro,* and *Alexander's Magazine* explored the racial issues of the day.

Education in Africa and the Southern United States: Transatlantic Connections

It can be argued that self-help education was both a building block and a facilitator of Pan-Africanist thinking. Existing within the context of intellectual anti-colonial protest, education focused on the practical level. Cooperative efforts at education from both sides of the Atlantic inevitably generated interest and awareness in the common plight of African people. King comments on how transcontinental efforts in education contributed to developing an African consciousness:

> During this period, when Hampton and Tuskegee were gaining considerable popularity with missions and governments for their relevance to Africa, certain groups of Africans in Kenya and Uganda had been forming their own view of American Negroes. Indeed, a whole range of contacts with Negroes in America had been experienced by a small minority of East Africans in the years before the Phelps-Stokes Commission's second African tour of 1924, and its commendation of Tuskegee and Hampton. There were three most significant aspects of this East African interest in the American Negro: the pan-Africanism of the earliest nationalist movements in Kenya and Uganda; American Negro missionary activity in East Africa; and the part played by African students in American Negro colleges. Combined experience in these three areas had made some East Africans aware of the wide extent of potential aid from American Negroes before Aggrey and Jones pleaded for the specific adoption of Tuskegee's educational and political philosophy.[46]

Of the forces committed to the social betterment of all African people the YMCA was deeply involved. Long interested in altruistic activities, the post–Civil War Reconstruction period found the YM(W)CA assuming a prominent role in Christian-inspired human uplift projects. Alongside the Freedmen's Bureau and missionary societies, the YMCA adopted an active role. In the early years of the twentieth century Max Yergan, a college-educated American Black, became the inspirational leader and secretary. Under Yergan's tireless leadership, the Y was a significant part of educational self-help programs throughout Africa and the Black South. Yergan and the Y's worked to bring Africans and African-Americans together. King speaks about him:

> Yergan himself frequently drew attention to the educational opportunities in the Negro colleges of America, and he was probably in a small way responsible for encouraging East Africans to think of American Negroes as their brother, and to expect increased help from them.[47]

Yergan's sincerity, opposition to colonial domination, commitment to the liberal education and hope for true social justice often placed him at odds with the corporatist philosophy funding the 'philanthropic' efforts. Following World War I, Yergan's Pan-Africanist and anti-colonial views led to a gradual weakening of his organizational authority.

Beyond the altruistic and missionary activities of individuals such as Yergan, the work of more politically conscious and militant forces in promoting Pan-African protest should not be overlooked. The intellectual and organizational work of W.E.B. Du Bois is noteworthy in this respect.

W. E. B. Du Bois,
Pan-Africanist and Educator

While Du Bois courted many political ideologies and views during his long life, his significant support of Pan-Africanist ideals cannot be ignored.[48] A persistent critic of accommodationist education, Du Bois saw great possibilities in liberatory education for colonial and subject peoples. His Pan-Africanist activity as well as his polemics against Thomas Jesse Jones deserve attention.

Du Bois's interests in Pan-Africanism are evidenced as far back as his Ph.D. dissertation entitled 'The Suppression of the African Slave Trade'. Here he demonstrated an understanding of the complex connections that would impact African peoples in their social, economic and political development for the entire twentieth century. World War I dramatized for Du Bois the shifting balance of power to the West and the function of colonialism within that dynamic. Africa and Black America would continue to suffer mightily in the new world order. He wrote: 'The present war in Europe is one of the great disasters due to race and color prejudice and it but foreshadows greater disasters in the future . . . theory of the inferiority of the darker peoples.'[50]

Disturbed by the prospect of intensified exploitation of African peoples, Du Bois became a principal organizer of the Pan-African Congress in February 1919. His rhetoric of that period was of 'advancing the agenda of the colored peoples of the United States and of the world' and establishing political, economic and educational reforms in Africa, stating 'the African movement means to us what the Zionist movement must mean to the Jews.'[51]

The Congress, largely influenced by Du Bois, demanded that the Negro race of Africa be given a chance to develop unhindered; that certain African colonies be governed by international organizations; more humane governing of African peoples; regulation of resource exploitation and depletion in Africa; expanded education for Blacks; limited self-government; an end to all slavery; and the expansion of democracy.

Du Bois's influence was indelibly stamped on subsequent Pan-African Congresses. His writings, particularly in *The Crisis* magazine, highlighted the theory of the African diaspora, the aims of African liberation movements' labor unrest in South Africa and West Indian social protest.[52] Manning Marable argues that it was Du Bois who kept African awareness on the agenda for American Blacks. Marable writes:

> These Negroes felt themselves Americans, not Africans. They resented and feared any coupling with Africa. But Du Bois' theory of double consciousness dictated a strong affinity for the cultural and political links with African people. As Du Bois wrote in 1926 Africa appears as the Father of mankind. ... The sense of beauty of the last and best gift of Africa to the world and the true essence of the Black man's soul. Through the ideals of Pan-Africanism, Black Americans could rediscover and reaffirm themselves.[53]

Du Bois's Pan-African educational views and critiques surface in his little-known skirmishes with Jones.[54] Du Bois repeatedly expressed alarm at the spread of colonial education on both sides of the Atlantic by the corporatists. While Du Bois quietly observed Jones rise to power in Black education, Jones's two-volume report entitled *Negro Education* of 1917 was more than he could endure. It was (and remains) the largest study every undertaken.[55] Employing a large corps of researchers, it surveyed 747 public schools serving 1,055 counties. While the report acknowledged funding inequities, high illiteracy, poorly trained teachers, and lack of materials, it nevertheless supported the continuation of industrial training, character building and the continued themes of accommodationism.

Du Bois was passionate in his response to *Negro Education*. His *Crisis* article began by suggesting that the report was of limited usefulness:[56]

> The casual reader has greeted this study of Negro Education with pleasure. It is the first attempt to cover the field of secondary and higher education among colored Americans with anything like completeness. It is published with the sanction and prestige of the United States government and has many excellent points as, for instance, full statistics on such matters as the public expenditure for Negro school systems, the amount of philanthropy given private schools, Negro property, etc.: there is excellent and continued insistence upon the poor support which the colored public schools are receiving today. The need of continued philanthropic aid to private schools is emphasized and there are several good maps. Despite, then, some evidently careless proofreading, the ordinary reader unacquainted with the tremendous ramifications of the Negro problem will hail this report with unstinted praise.[57]

From there, Du Bois wastes little time assaulting Jones:

> Thinking Negroes, however, and other persons who know the problem of edu-
> cating the American Negro, will regard the Jones report, despite its many praise-
> worthy features, as a dangerous and in many respects unfortunate publication.[58]

Three contentions of the report evoked the ire of Du Bois: accommodationist education, cooperation with southern whites and a recommendation
for administrative cooperation between boards of education and corporate
foundations – all of which Du Bois viewed as retarding progressive Black
education. He felt that while declaring support for democracy, a republican
form of government and the rule of law the corporatists had only disputed
and manipulated the lives of oppressed people. Du Bois wanted to warn
them that the miseducation of African peoples not gone unnoticed.

Conclusion: Colonialism, Education and Modernization

The explanatory strength of the Pan-African analysis is its exposure of
colonial practices. The results of economic plunder are clear. Western
European and American business interests were able to accumulate tremendous profits and reserves from their African adventures. Slavery and subsequent imperialism guaranteed Western hegemony in the world for at
least three centuries – maybe longer. Africa and her scattered peoples have
been and will continue to be at the defining edge of the world's balance of
power, serving as a harbinger of what can happen given impeded social
development.

In addition, the Pan-African analysis illustrates commonalities in the development of African people on both sides of the Atlantic. This shared
legacy of toil, exploitation and resilience points to the potential impact of a
liberation movement bound to spread. It was beyond serendipity that the
modern civil rights movement of Alabama and Mississippi in the 1950s
and 1960s was accompanied by revolutions in Kenya, the Congo and the
Caribbean. Though unintended by the imperialists, the politics of colonialism have forever linked African peoples in protest and in their quest for
freedom.

While exploitation and the quest for profit have driven colonialism, the
ideological shaping of society has been an important companion factor. It
has been argued here that colonial education has played a key role in this
process. It is important to note the role that 'education' has played vis-à-vis
modernization theory, given that Jones and the philanthropists always

claimed to be acting in the interest of progress.

Operating behind the rhetoric of 'uplift', 'progress', 'planning', 'stability', 'betterment' and 'aid', the corporatists have demonstrated a political ideology developed along a parallel path with social science ideology.[59] Both were to be rooted in a 'scientific' understanding of social development. This 'scientific' view focuses on 'rationality' and posits that the social process should be managed, measured, and incremental; utilize manpower planning; and be consistent with the principles of Western democracy. Anti-communism has never been far from this corporate social theorizing.

The impact of foundation-sponsored modernization theory in the education of African peoples should not be understated. Edward Berman believed that World War II and the subsequent Cold War redoubled the efforts of foundation ideologists to guide the educational and political direction of subject people. He writes:

> The programs supported by the major foundations at home and abroad since 1945 have been conceived and implemented by a carefully selected and nurtured elite. This reliance on a few individuals for major policy decisions and program implementation is merely the continuation of long-established foundation procedure. In the mid 1930s and particularly after 1945, the major foundations began funding academic studies that tacitly, and frequently explicitly, supported the theory that elite dominance of American society was not inherently undemocratic. Support for this theory was clearly in the foundations' interests given ... their lack of accountability to any public body.[60]

Finally, we must conclude that Thomas Jesse Jones and the powerful corporate social theorists foresaw a common historical destiny for African peoples throughout the entire twentieth century. First, African people would continue as the 'beasts of burden' in the industrial and agricultural plantations. Assuming uninterrupted development, Western capital would continue its incessant demand for cheap and reserve labor. Second, African people would not soon obtain political or economic self-government, that is, control of their destiny. Such a change in status would ultimately deprive capital of its pool of cheap labor. Third, African people must be at least minimally socialized in their indigenous community lest they disrupt its peaceful development. As a corollary, it seems that the colonial educators understood the necessity for a compradore or indigenous middle class as a requisite to stability. Their educational policies moved decisively and successfully to train a cadre of ministers, clerks, teachers and cottage-level entrepreneurs for just such a purpose. At the end of the twentieth century, we can now witness the completion of that process. Both Africa and Black America offer a middle class estranged from the sufferings of their people and beholden to hegemonic interests. Last, the corporatist theorists have understood the power of ideological containment backed by the recourse to force. Colonial educational practices served them well in their schemes for domination. While favorable to those who have profited, the impact of colonial education on indigenous people has been devastating.

Africans on both sides of the Atlantic remain a conquered and divided people. Only their indomitable spirit allows them to survive and challenge the owners of the world, who are drunk with their own arrogance.

Notes

1. Wilson J. Moses, *The Golden Age of Black Nationalism, 1850–1925*, New York 1978, pp. 15–31, presents an extensive discussion on the historical evolution of Black nationalist and Pan-Africanist movements.

2. Ibid., pp. 197–219.

3. For further discussions of education as cultural imperialism, see Martin Carnoy, *Education as Cultural Imperialism*, New York 1974, and Robert F. Arnove, ed., *Philanthropy and Cultural Imperialism: The Foundations at Home and Abroad*, Bloomington, Ind. 1982.

4. An extensive discussion can be found in William H. Watkins, 'On Accommodationist Education: Booker T. Washington Goes to Africa', *International Third World Studies Journal and Review*, vol. 1 (1989), pp 137–43.

5. Henry Bullock, *A History of Negro Education in the South: From 1619 to Present*, Cambridge, Mass. 1967, uses the phrase to describe the peculiar features of Negro education.

6. David Sidorsky, 'On Liberalism and Liberal Education', in Paul Kurtz, ed., *Sidney Hook: Philosopher of Democracy and Humanism*, Buffalo, N.Y. 1983, pp. 97–112.

7. Sidney Hook, *Eduction for a Modern Man*, New York 1946.

8. This refers to Pestalozzi, Froebel, Herbart and other European educators, whose techniques were popularized by Francis W. Parker at Quincey, Mass., as well as spread throughout American public schools.

9. John Dewey, *Democracy and Education: An Introduction to the Philosophy of Education*, New York 1916.

10. John Dewey, *Experience and Education*, New York 1938.

11. For further discussion on the 'Black Belt' colony concept, see Nelson Peery, *The Negro National Colonial Question*, Chicago 1975, and William Z. Foster, *The Negro People in American History*, New York 1954, pp. 463–78.

12. An interesting discussion of how the academic community develops 'theories' which serve a corporate philosophy is in Donald Fisher, 'American Philanthropy and the Social Sciences: The Reproduction of a Conservative Ideology' as well as other essays found in Robert F. Arnove, ed., *Philanthropy and Cultural Imperialism*, pp. 233–68. Also see Edward H. Berman, *The Influence of the Carnegie, Ford, and Rockefeller Foundations on American Foreign Policy: The Ideology of Philanthropy*, Albany, N.Y. 1983.

13. See, for example, Joseph Arthur de Gobineau, *The Inequality of Human Races*, Torrance, Calif. 1983.

14. Alleyne Ireland, 'The Far Eastern Tropics' in Franklin H. Giddings, ed., *Readings in Descriptive and Historical Sociology*, New York 1906, pp. 68–70.

15. A summary of 'structural functionalism' can be found in Kathleen P. Bennett and Margaret D. LeCompte, *How Schools Work: A Sociological Analysis of Education*, New York 1990 pp. 5–7.

16. Michael B. Lybarger, 'Origins of the Social Studies Curriculum 1865–1916', Ph.D. dissertation, University of Wisconsin-Madison, 1981, pp. 89–122, offers an expanded discussion on the social science debates of the period.

17. Giddings wrote extensively about social organization. See Franklin H. Giddings, *Civilization and Society: An Account of the Development and Behavior of Human Society*, New York 1932; Giddings, *Perspectives in Social Inquiry: The Scientific Study of Human Society*, Chapel Hill, N.C. 1924; Giddings, *Studies in the Theory of Human Society*, New York 1922; Giddings, ed., *Readings in Descriptive and Historical Sociology*; and Giddings, *The Principles of Sociology: An Analysis of the Phenomena of Association and Social Organization*, New York 1896.

18. Ireland, 'The Far Eastern Tropics', pp. 2–4.

19. Lybarger, *Origins of the Social Studies Curriculum*, pp. 170–71.

20. Giddings, *The Principles of Sociology*, pp. 316–17.

21. Ibid., pp. 328–9.

22. For an expanded discussion, see Lybarger, *Origins of the Social Studies Curriculum*, pp. 138–80.

23. Following the issuance of *Negro Education* in 1917–18 under Jones's direction, Du Bois grew increasingly frustrated with Jones's growing influence on Black education. As his language became more strident he referred to Jones as the 'evil genius ...' in W.E.B. Du Bois, 'Returning Soldiers', *Crisis*, vol. 16 (May 1919).

24. Some information about Jones's undergraduate work and interests can be found in Stephen T. Correia and William H. Watkins, 'Thomas Jesse Jones: A Portrait', *History Chicago*, April 1991.

25. Thomas Jesse Jones, 'The Sociology of a New York City Block', Ph.D. dissertation, Colombia University 1904.

26. Ibid., p. 133.

27. In Jones's papers, now in the Hampton University archives, is a folder entitled 'Settlement Documents'. Noteworthy are several University Settlement Bulletins (circa 1900), several reports to the Committee of the Council of the University Settlement (1900–1902) and a 'University Settlement Who's Who' profiling Jones in 1901–1902. These documents offer a glimpse of Jones's activities during his employ there.

28. Thomas Jesse Jones, *Four Essentials of Education*, New York 1926.

29. Thomas Jesse Jones, *Essentials of Civilization: A Study in Social Values*, New York 1929.

30. Jones was devoutly religious. He managed to squeeze in theological studies alongside his graduate work. In 1900 he received the Bachelor of Divinity Degree from Union Theological Seminary in New York. His religious outlook played a significant part in his socio-political world view.

31. These are the abbreviated conclusions of the author after reading the Hampton Social Studies in their entirety. It is suggested that a reading of Lybarger, *Origins of the Social Studies Curriculum*, pp. 52–83, supports the author's summary.

32. James D. Anderson, *The Education of Blacks in the South, 1860–1935*, Chapel Hill, N.C. 1988, pp. 33–109, offers an extensive discussion of Armstrong's influence in accommodationist education.

33. A comprehensive discussion of colonialism can be found in Walter Rodney, *How Europe Underdeveloped Africa*, London 1974.

34. Both Martin Carnoy, *Education as Cultural Imperialism*, and Robert F. Arnove, ed., *Philanthropy and Cultural Imperialism*, have expansive discussions on colonialism and ideological containment.

35. Kenneth J. King, *Pan-Africanism and Education: A Study of Race Philanthropy and Education in the Southern States of America and East Africa*, Oxford 1971, p. 47.

36. C.T. Loram was active in promoting Hampton/Tuskegee-style education in South Africa. He worked closely with Jones in this objective. A more extensive understanding of Loram's work can be gained from King, *Pan-Africanism and Education*, pp. 21–57.

37. James Aggrey has been called the Booker T. Washington of Africa. King calls him the protégé of Jones. His role in spreading the Hampton/Tuskegee model of education throughout Black Africa was major. A more complete understanding of his contribution is included in many chapters of King, *Pan-Africanism and Education*.

38. More expansive discussion can be found in William H. Watkins, 'On Accommodationist Education: Booker T. Washington Goes to Africa'.

39. Further discussion of the Phelps-Stokes Fund can be found in Edward H. Berman,

'Education in Africa and America; A History of the Phelps-Stokes Fund', Ed.D. dissertation, Columbia University 1969.

40. Andrew Carnegie, *The.Gospel of Wealth and Other Timely Essays*, Edward C. Kirkland, ed., Cambridge, Mass. 1962.

41. For a detailed discussion of the Booker T. Washington Institute, see Donald Spivey, *The Politics of Miseducation: The Booker T. Washington Institute of Liberia, 1929–1984*, Lexington, Ky. 1984.

42. Moses, *The Golden Age*, p. 16.

43. The Le Zoute conference (1926) brought together Blacks from Africa and America to discuss Christian missions and education. It is described more fully in King, *Pan-Africanism and Education*.

44. Ibid.

46. King, *Pan-Africanism and Education*, p. 58.

47. Ibid., p. 62.

48. A detailed discussion of Du Bois's varied political activities can be found in Manning Marable, *W.E.B. Du Bois: Black Radical Democrat*, Boston 1986, pp. 1–120.

49. W.E.B. Du Bois, *The Suppression of the African Slave Trade to the United States of America 1638–1870*, Harvard Historical Studies No. 1, 1896.

50. W.E.B. Du Bois, 'World War and the Color Line', *Crisis*, vol. 9 (November 1914), pp. 28–30.

51. The author has condensed several themes which capture Du Bois's thinking and writing shortly following World War I. A detailed discussion of Du Bois's activities during this period can be found in Marable, *W.E.B. Du Bois*, pp. 75–120.

52. Many issues of *Crisis* magazine between 1919 and 1927 addressed issues of Pan-Africanism. It should be noted that Du Bois was the longtime editor of *Crisis*.

53. Marable, *W.E.B. Du Bois*, p. 107.

54. See William H. Watkins, 'W.E.B. Du Bois vs. Thomas Jesse Jones: The Forgotten Skirmishes', *Journal of the Midwest History of Education Society*, vol. 18, pp. 305–28.

55. Thomas Jesse Jones, *Negro Education: A Survey of the Private and Higher Schools for Colored People in the United States*, Washington, D.C. 1917.

56. W.E.B. Du Bois 'Negro Education', *Crisis*, February 1918.

57. Ibid., p. 161.

58. Ibid.

59. Edward H. Berman has written two essays that explore the development of corporate social science ideology as it relates to African and American education. One is entitled 'Educational Colonialism in Africa: The Role of American Foundations, 1910–1945'. The other is 'The Foundations' Role in American Foreign Policy: The Case of Africa, post 1945'. Both are found in Arnove, ed., *Philanthropy and Cultural Imperialism*.

60. Berman, *The Influence of the Carnegie, Ford and Rockefeller Foundations on American Foreign Policy*, p. 27.

14

Pan-Africanism and

Apartheid: African-American

Influence on US Foreign Policy

Lako Tongun

It is certainly fitting to open our discussion with a rather lengthy quote from 'The African-American "Manifesto" on Southern Africa' (henceforth 'Manifesto'), which was issued by the African-American leaders at the Black Leadership Conference on Southern Africa, on 25 September 1976.[1] The 'Manifesto' declares, in part:

> There comes a moment in the affairs of humankind when honor requires an unequivocal affirmation of a people's right to freedom with dignity and peace with justice. . . . Conscious of our duty to speak and recognizing our responsibilities to humanity and to the revolutionary ideals of our forebears, we, the descendants of Africa, meeting in Washington, D.C., on this 200th anniversary of the first modern war for independence, proclaim our unswerving commitment to immediate self-determination and majority rule in Southern Africa. We do this because we are African-Americans, and because we know that the destiny of blacks in America and blacks in Africa is inextricably intertwined, since racism and other forms of oppression respect no territories or boundaries.[2]

This quote elucidates several key points which will later provide the basis for our discussion: (1) the politics of symbolism (ideology) and rhetoric; (2) the politics of identity, manifested in various forms such as race and culture; and (3) the politics of cooperation or alliances.[3]

The politics of symbolism or rhetoric is significant and pervasive, for it permeates all levels of political discourse. For instance, it should be remembered that 1976 was a year of historical and symbolic significance for three reasons Insofar as the 'Manifesto' is concerned: the 16 June Soweto youth revolt in South Africa marked the galvanizing of a concerted resistance at home and widespread campaigns abroad against apartheid; the bicentennial of the United States was for some Americans an occasion for celebration and, for others, a solemn opportunity for reflection on historical reckonings and their relevance for contemporary contexts; the presidential elections marked the emergence of 'new Black politics', namely 'the politics of ballots' rather than 'the politics of protest'.[4] The conjuncture was evidently dramatic and revolutionary, and provided useful examples for those struggling against apartheid and other forms of oppression. It was in this context that the 'Manifesto' invoked 'the revolutionary ideals of our forebears' and 'the truth of the Revolution of 1776, which is also the truth of the Revolution of 1976 in Southern Africa'.[5]

Insofar as our discussion is concerned, the politics of symbolism or rhetoric in the 'Manifesto' represents the ideas expressed by a wide variety of African-American leaders at the Conference. It also embodies some forms of instrumentality, such as the need 'to formulate a national agenda for a progressive US policy toward Africa'.[6] A third relevant point is that the 'Manifesto' articulates significant aspects of Pan-Africanist thought, which will become clear later in our discussion.

The purpose of this essay is therefore twofold. Primarily, I want to isolate some of the structure within which Pan-Africanism, as a socio-cultural and political movement, is manifested in African-American identification with Africa and efforts to influence US policy toward Africa in general and Southern Africa in particular. I also want to discuss how these structures may or may not constrain the Pan-Africanist consciousness of African-Americans as well as the instrumental values of Pan-Africanism.

The gap between rhetoric and reality is often discernible in any socio-cultural and political movement, especially when discussing stated objectives and goals achieved. That gap usually draws skepticism and criticism, framed largely in terms of success or failure. Pan-Africanism, both in the past and in its contemporary manifestations, is no exception.[6] Indeed, the African-American 'Manifesto' on Southern Africa, noted above, will be evaluated in a similar manner: by weighing its symbolic claims against the nature of its commitment to the anti-apartheid struggle. The questions of expediency and opportunism may emerge while assessing the actions of the African-American leadership after the Conference.

However, one must go beyond a suspicion of symbolic politics in order to adequately understand the gap between rhetoric and concrete achievement. Other factors besides rhetoric need to be examined to provide satisfactory explanations for any apparent discrepancies between promises and deeds. This essay will focus on four core areas or factors that permeate the politics of Pan-Africanism. They are race, class, ideology and cooperation (alliance), each of which acts as an axis of socio-cultural and political articulation for African-Americans in their quest to achieve Pan-Africanist objectives. They constitute not only the decisive areas of the African-American experience at political, economic and socio-cultural levels, but also the explanatory factors that influence African-American relations with Africa, as well as the rationale for the formation of 'a progressive US policy toward Africa'.[7]

This essay is divided into two parts. The first part examines the role of African-Americans in the anti-apartheid movement. The burden of the discussion will be the period between the declaration of the African-American 'Manifesto' on Southern Africa (1976) and the passage of the Comprehensive Anti-Apartheid Act by the US Congress (1986). The focus will be on key activities and individuals during this period, in order to assess the African-American contributions to the anti-apartheid movement in the United States. This part of the discussion provides the basis for explaining and interpreting the interpenetrations of the politics of race, class, ideology and cooperation.

The second part analyzes conflicts that are apparent in the politics of race, class, ideology and cooperation. The analytical argument is that African-American actual and potential influence on US policy toward Africa is mediated, in a contradictory manner, by these important factors. That is, these elements form an essential overall context within which Pan-Africanist sentiments and instrumentalities are articulated, interpreted and understood.

While many studies have considered US policy toward Southern Africa in general and South Africa in particular from 1976 to 1986, few have dealt with the contradictions that confront the African-American role.[8] This essay hopes to provide a wider perspective, one that may furnish insights to enhance our understanding of the strategies a 'racial minority group' adopts to influence US foreign policy toward its ancestral homeland. It may also inspire us to wonder why, in a racialized and class-based hierarchical power structure, racial minority cultural groups tend to generate oppositional consciousness and counter-knowledge as responses to racism, both for internal and external reasons. This is the case with African-Americans, as it will be discussed in the following pages.

African-Americans and Apartheid

There are, historically speaking, two African issues that have attracted the most intense attention, outrage and active participation from African-Americans. The first is the invasion of Ethiopia by the Italian fascist army in 1935. The second is apartheid, especially between 1972 and 1986.[9] Both crises could be characterized as historical moments for African-Americans either to interrogate the sensitivity of US policy to their historical and emotional connections with their ancestral homeland or to influence that policy in Africa's favor. In the case of the Ethiopian crisis, it is not clear how much African-American protests contributed to the US response to Mussolini's invasion, a response which was basically coordinated by other European powers (Britain and France) to stop an increasingly assertive fascism in Europe and Japan. US interests were insensitive to African-Americans and more in concert with an established imperialist order; Mussolini's invasion of Ethiopia was seen as a threat to that order. For African-Americans, Ethiopia was a symbol of redemption and represented a movement of resistance and defiance byAfrican peoples to the European imperial and racial order. These perceptions of the historical significance of Ethiopia explain, to a large extent, the willingness of African-American volunteers to go to Ethiopia and fight against the Italian army.[10]

If the Ethiopian crisis represented the level and the significance of Pan-African consciousness in 1935, the apartheid issue has done the same in 1976. The mass killing of school pupils by the armed forces of the apartheid regime during the Soweto uprising provoked unprecedented global protests and a commitment by many to bring an end to that system. *Apartheid,* euphemistically called 'separate development' by its architects, the Afrikaners, who are mainly the descendants of Dutch, French and German settlers, was conceived and implemented in 1948 as an instrument of Afrikaner nationalism. While 'separate development' would imply segregation on the basis of horizontal relations amongst racial/ethnic and national groups, apartheid, in practice and indeed in theory, has to maintain *vertical* relations, constitutionally sanctioned and enforced by the instruments of the state's power of coercion and violence.[11] As an Afrikaner nationalist ideology, apartheid is a conceptual and operative strategy based on the dominant racial *minority's* fear of losing its hegemonic position and privileges. Although the strategy is clear, the struggle by the Afrikaners to maintain their dominance is concealed in the form of an appeal to the preservation of 'white Christian civilization' and Afrikaner 'national soul', *volksiel.*[12] That is, apartheid was designed to prevent, in the words of one Afrikaner, 'the end of Western Civilization in South Africa, in the political eclipse of whites and everything they have built up over a period of more than 300 years'.[13] Understandably, M.C. de Wet Nel does *not* take into account the contribution of cheap African labor for 300 years!

There is a fascinating conceptual edifice that underpins the Afrikaner argument for apartheid. The façade is, at the ideological level, an essential illusion for the Afrikaners to rationalize their hegemonic control over the majority. In reality, apartheid is simply a sophisticated power structure that is essential for a capitalist economy which is based on historically specific and peculiar conditions of racial exploitation. The constitutionalization of racism, in the form of apartheid, is what makes the South African capitalist economy (society) peculiar.[14] Coercion rather than consent is the mode of extracting labor from the African majority. But reliance on force is often a costly proposition for capitalism, in the long run. Also, the incongruent relationship between the political and the economic spheres creates constant tensions and conflicts which require an extraordinary deployment of brutal force, as well as other mechanisms of control and coercion, such as the pass system. Nevertheless, the extraordinary costs of coercion are magnificently offset by enormous short-term profits.[15] This profitability is one of the reasons why South Africa has been attractive to foreign capital, especially European and American investors.

But as we have recently witnessed, the profitable relationship between apartheid and capitalism was doomed to failure. For one thing, apartheid represented an extreme and antiquated mode of colonial exploitation, especially in light of the changed global circumstances of the post–World War II period. It is ironic and certainly an act of defiance that apartheid was instituted in 1948 when anti-colonial nationalists and intellectuals had begun, in earnest, to bring down the edifice of European colonial order through armed struggles and/or negotiated settlements. In the words of Frantz Fanon, the post–World War II period could be characterized as an era of 'dying colonialism'.[16]

The other aspect of the changed circumstances has to do with the position of the United Nations on issues of colonialism, racism and human rights. In 1948, the United Nations adopted the Universal Declaration of Human Rights.[17] The anti-colonial nationalists and intellectuals who were in a fierce struggle against colonialism and racism were largely responsible for steering the United Nations to adopt the declaration. It should also be noted that the most heinous crimes committed by the Nazi regime in Germany, in the name of racial supremacy, against millions of Jews and others, contributed to adoption of the UN position. It would appear obvious to the Afrikaner nationalists in the National Party that the codification of racism in the form of apartheid would be simply anachronistic and too blatant a policy of white supremacy in the postwar political climate, even for those who had practiced it in the previous period. It is in this changed context that apartheid has been roundly condemned by the United Nations as a 'crime against humanity'. That is to say, even at the rhetorical level, there is a recognition of something called 'humanity' which is a shared characteristic of all human beings. Hence, the UN Declaration of Human Rights represented more than a rhetorical embellishment of humanism in the UN. But, in spite of the UN condemnation, apartheid had enjoyed the support of powerful friends during this period, friends who denounced it as 'repugnant' and yet maintained its props.[18] This point will be elaborated later in this essay.

The above discussion of apartheid is intended to situate it in a global context. This is important for two reasons. First, the anti-apartheid movement, as noted earlier, has been universal, a reflection of shared perceptions of our common humanity, at least among some sectors of the world. Even if those who share these values have different agendas in participating in the anti-apartheid movement, nevertheless there has been space created for the politics of alliance and cooperation to bring down the apartheid edifice. The second reason for locating apartheid in a global context is to underscore the internationalism of Pan-Africanism, namely the spread of the Pan-Africanist consciousness among Africans on the continent and the diasporic Africans. It is worth noting the various themes which emphasize the internationalist character of Pan-Africanism:

- The global unity of Africans and Africans in the diaspora, at the level of racial solidarity, which is essential for liberation but not 'anti-others' nor racialist or imperialistic, in the sense of 'conquest or suppression of other people'.[19]

- Continental unity in the formation of Organization of African Unity, whose long-term objective of the unification of all African countries under one government and one economic organization – currently an illusive goal.

- A humanistic theme, which is, in the words of Maulana Karenga, a 'universal movement toward human freedom', whose emphasis is on shared human qualities which transcend racial identities.[20] The important point to note here is that these themes embody the internationalism of both Pan-Africanism and African-Americans in the context of the global struggle against apartheid and other forms of racial oppression.[21]

The internationalist sentiments of African-Americans arise from two main sources: Pan-Africanist consciousness, which by definition is global; and US domestic conditions, which constitute a set of complex relationships within the internal and external dimensions of the American political economy. At the internal level, African-Americans have been more aware of significant similarities between their own position in US society and the Africans' position under apartheid in South Africa. The American Constitution codified racism and slavery and retained that codification until after the Civil War. Frederick Engels made this useful observation on the subject. It is significant that the American Constitution, the first to recognize the rights of man, in the same breath confirmed the slavery of colored races existing in America. Class privileges are proscribed, race privileges are sanctioned.[22]

For Americans of African descent, the differences between apartheid South Africa and the US may be relative and time-framed, a sort of qualitative difference between a naked, brutal racial regime and the subtle racial structures of political-economic and social power in the global conditions of the post–World War II era, or even after the civil rights movement of the 1950s and 1960s. It is this internal dimension of US political economy that constantly informs and reminds African-Americans of their Pan-Africanist consciousness and its international sentiments.

The external dimension of US political economy involves foreign policy. It is evident that foreign policy is an extension of domestic policy, or to put it differently, domestic politics informs foreign policy.[23] The intersection of domestic and foreign policies formed a zone of contestation for African-Americans in their struggle against apartheid and in their attempts to influence US policy toward Africa and specifically South Africa. This is the point at which the 'Manifesto' entered the arena of US Africa policy. It developed from the historical fact that the 'ethnic factor' has been and continues to be an undeniable element in US foreign policy.[24] Charles C. Diggs, Jr, the former US congressman from Michigan, noted the connection between domestic and foreign political terrain for African-Americans. He writes:

> While expressions of Afro-American interest in Africa are hardly new, and have been well-documented, the current wave of interest drawn by Black Americans stems directly from the *domestic racial upheavals of the past decade* which revived intensely nationalistic race consciousness among our people. Out of this consciousness came an increased tendency to identify with Africa. To a considerable extent, this quest for identity with Africa was associated with predominantly cultural interests. However, growing awareness of the racial struggles in Southern Africa and the former Portuguese territories . . . inevitably gave more of a political expression to this interest. Not only did issues of African development and liberation become a part of the Congressional Black Caucus' initial program with respect to *US domestic and foreign policy* in 1971, but in 1972, the first African American National Conference on Africa . . . was convened at Howard University to begin a serious dialogue among Black Americans on how to mobilize our potential as a constituency for affecting political change in US African policy.[25]

Although Diggs's arguments are reflected in the 'Manifesto' (he was a key member of the conference that adopted it), there are clear connections here between the domestic and foreign policy concerns of African-Americans.

It is also clear from the quote that 1972 marked an important stage in African-American responses to and engagement in the anti-apartheid movement and US Africa policy. Prominent African-Americans and organizations, both at the grassroots level and at the center of national power, have been at the forefront of the anti-apartheid movement in the US. An eloquent opposition to various US positions on economic sanctions against South Africa drew support from prominent African-American leaders, such as Reverend Jesse Jackson, Representatives Ronald Dellums, John Conyers and William Gray III, among others, as well as from important organizations, such as TransAfrica, the first African-American lobbyist institution at the US Congress, and of course the Congressional Black Caucus. It was these efforts that convinced the US Congress and a reluctant Reagan administration to impose limited sanctions on South Africa in 1986.

Notwithstanding other American anti-apartheid movements (for example, the Washington office on Africa, numerous church and student organizations), apartheid has emerged as the single foreign policy issue that has provided the highest profile for African-Americans articulating their views on US policy toward Africa and, for our discussion here, South Africa. How does one explain the apparently intense commitment and involvement by African-Americans to the anti-apartheid movement? Three factors may provide the answer. First, intuitively and from 'lived experience', African-Americans have been, as noted earlier, fundamentally opposed to apartheid because of 'race' and 'racism' not only from 'kin and kith' and diasporic links but also from empathy. Second, since the 1960s (when both Africans and African-Americans were cutting the shackles of colonialism and Jim Crow laws, respectively), there emerged increasing Pan-Africanist interactions between Africa and the African diaspora. These transatlantic interactions have increased opportunities for African-Americans to play the 'ethnic card' in US policy toward Africa. They have used other ethnic groups as models: the Jews, concerned for the survival of Israel, the Poles, the Armenians, the Ukrainians, and so forth. Third, recent enfranchisement (as a result of the Civil Rights Act of 1964) has increased the electoral power of African-Americans, and hence their 'ethnic group' bargaining position on US foreign policy issues that concern their group interests.

African-American influence, both actual and potential, on US Africa policy has generally confronted problems that originate from the position of African-Americans in the US political economy. Martin Weil has identified three general areas through which ethnic influence over US foreign policy may be realized and enhanced: (1) an electoral threat, namely a bargaining position in which an ethnic group has the ability to provide a 'margin of victory' for a candidate, in presidential or congressional elections at the national level, and equally importantly at state and local levels; (2) a lobbying apparatus, namely an organization that represents special group interests and that engages in the craft of influencing elected or appointed individuals whose decisions can affect the group's special interests, either favorably or unfavorably; and (3) 'a successful appeal to the symbols of American nationhood', that is, an ethnic group must identify strongly with American ideals, both at the internal and external levels, in order to be effective in lobbying for support of the ethnic group's special interests.[26]

Weil's discussion of the three conditions as they apply to African-Americans is interesting, as well as insightful, and deserves some brief comment. Weil's arguments are that African-Americans are weak in all three conditions necessary for an effective ethnic influence on US policy. The sources of this weakness are internal as well as external to American society. In the former case, the weaknesses are located in the political-economic arena, but more importantly in the racism that keeps African-Americans from attaining political, economic and social power. Racism, in short, denies African-Americans the opportunity to acquire power and influence. In the latter case, Africa does not figure high in the priorities of the US foreign policy agenda. Weil discusses the reasons for the low priority accorded to Africa, which I do not want to repeat here. But what is equally important is the fact that racism and strategic interests influence US attitudes toward Africa.[27] Weil also argues that African-American allegiance to the US and its symbols of nationhood is always suspect, especially when the civil rights movement incorporates radical (read 'communist') ideological sympathy and support. The US obsession with anti-communism has been implicated in the general suspicion of African-American loyalties to America. The issue here is certainly complex and would divert attention from the limited objective of this essay. There is already well-documented evidence, for example, that the FBI wiretapped Reverend Martin Luther King, Jr's phone, especially when he began to speak out against the Vietnam War.[28]

In general, Weil's discussion of the weaknesses of African-American influence on US Africa policy was correct in 1974, the year his article was written. In fact, as Charles Diggs has noted, 1972 was the turning point for African-Americans to begin organizing as an electoral threat and a lobbying apparatus. The presidential elections of 1976 ushered into national politics the 'Black vote', which provided the margin of victory for Jimmy Carter and some congressional candidates in states or districts with a substantial African-American population.[29] Also, the Black Leadership Conference of 1976 led to the establishment of TransAfrica a year later, as the first African-American lobbying apparatus in Congress. Randall Robinson, a former aide to Charles Diggs, was selected as its first executive director. TransAfrica lobbies Congress for African and Caribbean interests, just as the Jewish lobby looks after Israeli interests. Indeed, under Robinson, TransAfrica, with the support of the Congressional Black Caucus, has played a critical role in mobilizing the anti-apartheid movement in the US Congress, as well as among the masses.

The third area that Weil identified, his contention that African-Americas lack 'an ideological harmony with the American psyche, an intense Americanism' which is essential to attract widespread support from the broad spectrum of American people,[29] touches on two issues. First, the question of how African-Americans relate to 'Americanism', a rather complex relationship to analyze and one that presents a paradoxical challenge to African-Americans. Even though African-Americans constitute one of the oldest ethnic groups in America, their commitment to American ideals is often suspect and in need of demonstration. Weil, for instance, asserts that '[a] black movement for reform of American policy toward Africa must be a vehicle for exporting *American* ideals'.[30]

The second issue touches on the question of ideology and identity, two areas of concern in this essay. American ideology, defined as constitutional ideals, has been at odds with the African-American presence in the US, constituting what Gunnar Myrdal termed an 'American dilemma'.[31] In practice, African-Americans have been excluded from the constitutional ideals and promises of the 'American dream'. It took some bitter struggles, in the form of the civil rights movement, to modify some of the most blatant aspects of the Jim Crow laws or 'petty apartheid'.[32] It is, historically speaking, this racial exclusion which, to some extent, casts a certain degree of ambiguity on African-American identity, sometimes on both sides of the hyphen. That is, racial exclusion may produce two unresolvable dialectical processes. In the case of African-Americans, the two processes are the de-Americanization and re-Africanization of identity, which occur simultaneously in times of increased racial oppression or despair. The reverse also occurs, namely, re-Americanization and de-Africanization when less unfavorable conditions prevail.[33] The relevant point here is that these processes of shifting identity may influence and explain the intensity of African-American attitudes toward Africa, as well as the quest for African identity or the prevalence of Pan-African consciousness.

The Politics of Race and the Anti-Apartheid Movement

Notwithstanding periodic bouts of ambiguity, race and racism provide the unifying factors for intense African-American involvement·in the anti-apartheid movement. For both Africans and peoples of African descent, apartheid is not an anomaly of the late twentieth century, nor a vestigial nuisance from the age of colonialism and slavery. Rather, it represents a continuous, stubborn historical reminder as well as an obstacle to a general African liberation from racial oppression. At the same time, apartheid presents a formidable challenge to Pan-Africanism. In this context, the struggle against apartheid creates a sense of unity in several ways. The anti-apartheid movement elevates the politics of race above all others, for example, class. This is necessarily the case because the politics of race has a consequent effect of 'political mobilization of identity' by producing group consciousness, as well as collective orientation and cooperation among group members.[34] The politics of race, at the level of cooperation, has not always been necessarily limited to African-Americans or Africans, especially in the struggle against racism or apartheid. Cooperation in both anti-racist and anti-apartheid movements has often transcended racial identities or class, even though it has sometimes created contradictions.

The prevalence of the politics of race in the spirited African-American engagement in the anti-apartheid movement requires further examination. In both the US and South Africa, where race has always defined group/personal identities, ordination and subordination play salient roles in the structuring of power at economic, political and socio-cultural levels. The significance of race, in this context, lies in its instrumentalist character, namely as a means to organize and structure social relations and political institutions which maintain and enforce 'a racially unjust social order', thus, giving rise to the politics of race.[35] The politics of race and racism is, therefore, a contested terrain where oppressive structures of power are opposed by forces of liberation. Insofar as race and racism define the identities and consciousnesses of the subordinated, there emerges a counter-knowledge and counter-consciousnesses that guide the politics of race. Similarly, Pan-African consciousness is liberatory and informed active African-American opposition to apartheid. It is worth quoting Magubane on this aspect of Pan-African consciousness:

> Pan-African consciousness has always been a determined effort on the part of black peoples to discover their shrines from the wreckage of history. It was a revolt against white man's ideological suzerainty in culture, politics and historiography. . . . The various manifestations of African consciousness among American blacks articulate an experience which goes beyond individual awareness. Pan-African consciousness which originated among black peoples in the Diaspora prepared a position in the African mind from which white hegemony was to be attacked. Pan-African consciousness proclaimed the idea of black emancipation as a necessary state for the full development of blacks everywhere.[36]

Magubane underscores three critical issues. First is the counter-knowledge which is essential for the liberating task of Pan-Africanism. Second is the importance of identity which serves a common sense of solidarity. Third is the idea of solidarity which implies a necessary cooperation in order to achieve the emancipation of the African peoples everywhere. Apartheid, in a fundamental sense, met the conditions which solidarity and cooperation demand of African peoples.

Identity is an important notion because it defines how race and racism construct the group. Anthony Smith's view of identity is interesting to note here: Smith defines identity as 'subjective feelings and valuations of any population which possesses common experiences and one or more shared cultural characteristic'. He goes on to add that identity does not imply a 'common denominator of patterns of life and activity, nor some average'.[37] By feelings and values, Smith suggests the importance of shared experiences, which consist of three parts: a transgenerational sense of continuity in the experiences of a people, shared memories which perpetuate the narratives of collective history or collective mentalities, and a sense of common destiny.[38] These three elements have been consistent themes in African-American interests in Africa since 1619, when the first Africans landed in Jamestown, Virginia. These elements also form the foundation of both real and imagined senses of the Pan-African consciousness and the 'intellectualization of the emotions' which bind Africa to the African diaspora.[39] Equally important here is the suggestion that subjective feelings and values explain active African-American involvement in the anti-apartheid movement. Let us now explore the level of that involvement, as well as the successful attempts to influence US policy toward South Africa.

The History of African-American Involvement in the Anti-Apartheid Movement

African-American involvement with Africa and African problems, such as liberation from colonialism and apartheid, is not new. It began at the dawn of African enslavement in the Americas. However, the consciousness of Africa in the minds and hearts of African-Americans, as well as the sense of a collective struggle against racism, slavery and colonialism, was heightened during periods of intense racial oppression and exploitation. For instance, the rise of the emigrationist impulse in the US was attributed to increased racial repression before and after the Civil War. Clearly, identification with Africa, at the level of consciousness, developed from an urgent need to be free – physically and psychologically – from racial repression. One of the most important moments in the history of emigrationist tendencies was the Garvey movement, which touched the raw nerves of African consciousness in the many African-Americans. This mass movement, which drew its support from the lower class, was also connected not only to Africa in general but more specifically to the South African struggle against colonial rule and the emerging apartheid system. A well-established link existed between the emergence of the African National Congress (ANC) in 1912 and the founding of the Universal Negro Improvement Association (UNIA) by Marcus Garvey. The Garvey movement also founded the *Negro World,* a popular newspaper in both the African diaspora and Africa. It was distributed by the ANC in South Africa. Because of the threat it posed to the colonial order, as a result of its agitation for liberation, unity and cooperation, the colonial powers in Africa banned not only the distribution of the *Negro World* but also any visit from Garvey himself, especially to South Africa. The banning explains why Garvey never set foot on the African continent, the land that was the *raison d'être* of Garveyism.[40]

Various missionary activities by African-Americans were equally important in the connections between the ANC and the African diaspora. African-American missionary work in South Africa was, to a great extent, motivated by 'spiritual brotherhood' as well as Pan-African consciousness. Some of the earlier leaders of the ANC received their formal education through the activities of African-American missionaries in the US. Many of these leaders attended predominantly Black universities and colleges. It should be noted, however, that African-American missionaries were engaged in activities which propagated Christianity. Yet Judeo-Christian values provided the ideological foundation for rationalizing and justifying imperialism and colonialism. It is not insignificant that European colonialism was imposed on Africa with two effective weapons in the European hand, the gun and the Bible, corresponds to the Gramscian notion of maintaining hegemonic control through the use of the twin instruments of coercion and consent.[41] The point here is that African-American missionaries, though motivated by 'spiritual brotherhood', were aiding imperialism in the manufacture of consent. Indeed, as we will note later, Christian influence has had a critical effect on the ANC strategy for national liberation, namely one that initially advocated a non-violent approach.

Mention should also be made of Sylvester Williams's visit to South Africa after World War I. Sylvester Williams was an African-Caribbean barrister, one of the founding fathers of modern Pan-Africanism. Williams's brief stay in South Africa was a personal fact-finding mission, significant in in establishing his Pan-Africanist connections. Even though apartheid was still in its early form as a 'color bar', Williams believed it was essential to experience and to see for himself the racial conditions in which the African people lived in South Africa. Presumably, such an experience would inform him of the nature of the beast that confronted Pan-African dreams, allowing him to develop strategies accordingly.[42] In a sense, Williams was the precursor of many African-American leaders who have visited apartheid South Africa for similar reasons. Prominent among them are the Reverend

Jesse Jackson, Andrew Young, and Reverend Leon Sullivan, all of whom have played significant roles in the anti-apartheid movement.

Garveyism, African-American missionary activities and Williams's visit thus represent the initial involvement of the African Diaspora in the South African struggle against apartheid. These activities are historically essential to the task of establishing the early Pan-Africanist consciousness and connections from which the contemporary anti-apartheid movement has learned some lessons: personal visits by prominent African-American leaders, for example. The US and South Africa share many characteristics as racially structured societies in which the politics of race and racism has always engendered oppression and resistance. A comparative perspective, in this respect, is essential to inform the strategies of counter-hegemonic knowledge and cooperation. That is, the strategies of racial repression and resistance can be clearly revealed and understood within given contexts. The precursors also provide a critical sense of historical continuity, which is important insofar as it performs the function of creating identity through history.

1976–1986: Sanctions, Divestment and Nonviolence

From the perspective of the domestic political agenda, the 1976 elections gave African-Americans a strong sense of optimism and a belief in their apparent electoral power.[43] At the same time, the 1976 elections also offered African-American elites the opportunity to play the 'ethnic factor' in the US Africa policy.[44] The preceding discussion has, so far, focused essentially on three questions: How have race and racism forged the basis of African identity, especially in the diaspora? How has this identity contributed to the formation of Pan-African consciousness as a necessary response? And how do race, racism and Pan-African consciousness define the 'Black constituency' in both the US political economy and its relations to Africa, within the context of 'ethnic group' interests in US foreign policy?[45] The important point here is that unity in action and purpose is assumed to be paramount in the 'Black constituency'. This is generally true, but not in all of the issues or crises that have often confronted the US Africa policy. We want to discuss why unity may or may not necessarily exist in the 'Black constituency', what issues are likely to create differences within the 'Black constituency' and what factors explain the divisions not only among African-Americans but also between Africans and African-Americans in the struggle against apartheid.

Three issues in the anti-apartheid movement constitute the terrain of contestation: sanctions, divestment and nonviolence. All three form the essential policy instruments that brought down the edifice of apartheid. They also define the policy choices made by Africans, African-Americans and others who participated in the anti-apartheid movements around the world. What is important here is that African-American choices in these three areas are likely to be shaped by class and ideology operating both inside and outside the African-American constituency. What follows is a correlation of class and ideological forces associated with the concerted African-American efforts to influence US South Africa policy between 1976 and 1986.

Prior to 1975, the issue of sanctions involved three countries in Southern Africa. Portugal refused to relinquish its colonial control over Mozambique, Angola and Guinea-Bissau, defying inevitable trends toward liberation and freedom from colonial rule. White minority settlers in the British colony of Southern Rhodesia, now Zimbabwe, declared unilateral independence in 1965 under the leadership of Ian Smith by severing their colonial ties with Britain à la the thirteen American colonies, the only difference being that in Zimbabwe an attempt was made to rule over and in defiance of the wishes of the majority (280,000 Europeans versus 8,000,000 Africans). And in South Africa, the heartland of apartheid, white minority rule was forcibly extended to Namibia (colonial name: Southwest Africa) in an arrogant defiance of the UN resolutions on illegitimate trusteeship, as well as the wishes of the Namibian people. The UN, under pressure from African and other Third World members, imposed graduated (calibrated) sanctions against the three recalcitrants, beginning with an arms embargo and trade and general economic sanctions, at different times for each country. Our interest here is to situate historically the evolution of African-American responses to US policy toward Southern Africa, which was clearly dominated by highly racialized white minority regimes. The region was radically transformed when Portuguese colonial rule collapsed in 1975 and independence was declared in Southern Rhodesia in 1980, removing the carefully constructed and well-maintained *cordon sanitaire* around the apartheid heartland.

Briefly, US policy toward the region was generally characterized by overt and covert support for white minority regimes. When many African countries attained political independence and membership in the United Nations in the 1960s, the pendulum gradually swung to covert support.[46] One explanation for the shift was an attempt by the US ruling class to reconcile two inconsistent policy choices at the domestic and foreign levels: the collapse of colonialism under the pressure of the African nationalist demand for independence, on the one hand, and the collapse of Jim Crow laws (petty apartheid) under the 'moral' weight of the civil rights movement, on the other. The threat of violence, as manifested in urban riots, was as important a factor as the non-violent and moral crusade against the

Jim Crow laws. The same tactics of moral persuasion, threats and violence, were used against colonialism and apartheid in Africa. Overt support by the US for the white minority regimes would unmistakably convey opposition to African rights to self-determination and the civil rights movement, which the Reverend Martin Luther King, Jr had invested with universal moral significance.

The Cold War competition between the US and the USSR was important insofar as it explained the moral stakes that civil rights and self-determination represented. The point is not of course to argue that morality, however defined, was an explanation for US policy choices, between overt and covert support for white minority regimes. Rather, the ideological competition between the 'socialist' world and the capitalist West embodied certain moral claims, especially in areas of individual equality and political and economic rights. Such claims could only be demonstrated by some policy representations at domestic and foreign sites. This was necessary, to some extent, because the Cold War was partly an ideological battle for the 'hearts and minds' of the newly liberated and articulate Third World leaders, intellectuals and societies. Capitalist hegemony over the Third World was losing ground to the socialist challenge in a number of countries in Asia (China, Vietnam, North Korea), Africa (Ghana, Mali, Egypt) and Latin America (Cuba, Grenada and later Nicaragua). This explains why the Cold War was fought in the Third World as a 'hot' war, with millions dead and devastating destruction. It was not basically meant to be fought in Europe because the white Russians and the white Americans and their allies would not annihilate themselves with nuclear weapons. This was unthinkable even though we know that two World Wars were started and largely fought in Europe.

This digression explains why the US tended to pursue a covert policy in support of white minority regimes in Southern Africa, especially in the 1960s. In the context of the Cold War, US ideological strategy was to win new friends in the Third World. Of course, winning 'friends' is not the aim of US business; rather, acquiring and maintaining new interests matters most. The US ruling class was thus compelled in the 1960s to reconcile the civil rights movement ('the American dilemma') at home with its foreign policy ideological claims. Thus, the independence movement in Africa and the civil rights movement were intimately linked. African independence was embarrassingly incompatible with Jim Crow laws.

The sudden influx of African and Third World ambassadors (who were people of color) into the United States after decolonization presented the most disconcerting challenge to the (white) American ruling class. Jim Crow laws became awkwardly inconsistent with diplomatic protocols. Some of the Third World ambassadors experienced petty apartheid acts:

discrimination and segregation in housing and restaurants were met with fierce and angry diplomatic protests. The Kennedy administration was particularly sensitive to African protests, because it understood how petty apartheid was undermining its efforts to cultivate US interests in the newly decolonized African and other Third World countries.

The strategy of the Kennedy administration in Africa was outlined in a document entitled 'Africa: Guidelines for United States Policy and Operation', which affirmed the administration's opposition to petty and grand apartheid in the US and abroad. It stated, in part:

> The most helpful things we could do to enhance our image and obtain the friendship of the African peoples are (a) to make our commitment to freedom in Africa clear without peradventure of doubt in such cases as Angola, Algeria and South Africa; and (b) to move more quickly to solve our problem of according dignity and equal opportunity to our own African-descended population.[47]

The vigor and commitment with which the Justice Department under Robert Kennedy pursued an end to Jim Crow laws may be partly explained by President Kennedy's attempts to remove the diplomatic embarrassment to his administration. Indeed, it was in 1963 that the civil rights movement gained enormous official recognition and visibility in the US, especially after the Washington march for freedom, in which the Reverend Martin Luther King, Jr delivered the most 'moral' challenge to the white racial regime.

There is also another historical relationship between the two episodes in Africa and the US that needs to be noted: the correspondence between European colonialism and imperialism in Africa, on the one hand, and Reconstruction after the Civil War in the US, on the other. Reconstruction policy aimed not only the physical rehabilitation of the newly emancipated African-Americans, but also, more importantly, the restoration and recovery of their humanity and civil rights through the bestowal of citizenship. Unfortunately, Reconstruction failed because it was incompatible with a global regime of racial exploitation and racist theories. It is in this context that the 'Manifesto' invokes the shared interests of Africans and African-Americans to cooperatively confront and end apartheid in Southern Africa.

Evidence of covert US support for the white minority regimes in Southern Africa came in 1969 when the Nixon administration authorized a secret study on US Southern Africa policy. Henry Kissinger, then national security adviser, directed the policy review. The result was the famous, or infamous, report, National Security Study Memorandum 39 (NSSM 39). The secret document was leaked to the US public by Jack Anderson, a syndicated columnist, in 1974.[48] Briefly, NSSM 39 was a reformulation of

US Southern Africa policy choices which consisted of five objectives and five options. It may be useful to list them, beginning with the objectives, which determined the options available to attain them, and more important, helped discern the policy 'tilt' toward the white minority regimes: in short, the racial has an ideological predilection. These were the objectives:

1. To improve the US standing in black Africa and internationally on the racial issue.

2. To minimize the likelihood of escalation of violence in the area and risk of US involvement.

3. To minimize the opportunities for the USSR and Communist China to exploit the racial issue in the region for propaganda advantage and to gain political influence with black governments and liberation movements.

4. To encourage moderation of the current rigid racial and colonial policies of the white regimes.

5. To protect economic, scientific and strategic interests and opportunities in the region, including the orderly marketing of South Africa's gold production.[49]

These objectives shaped the determination of the five policy options, which were:

Option One: Closer association with the white regimes to protect and enhance our economic, strategic and scientific interests.

Option Two: Broader association with both black and white states in an effort to encourage moderation in the white states, to enlist cooperation of the black states in reducing tensions and the likelihood of increasing cross-border violence, and to encourage improved relations among states in the area.

Option Three: Limited association with the white states and continuing association with blacks in an effort to retain some economic, scientific, and strategic interest in white states while maintaining a posture on racial issues which the blacks will accept, though opposing violent solutions to the problems of the region.

Option Four: Dissociation from the white regimes with closer relations with the black states in an effort to enhance our standing on the racial issue in Africa and internationally.

Option Five: Dissociation from both black and white states in an effort to limit our involvement in the problems of the area.[50]

After intense interdepartmental discussions and analysis, the Nixon administration chose option two, labeled by an observer as the 'tar baby' option.[51] The option was premised on the following:

> The blacks cannot gain political rights through violence. Constructive change can come only by acquiescence of the whites. We can by selective relaxation of our stance toward the white states and increased economic assistance to the black states in the region help to draw the groups together. Our tangible interests are a basis for contacts in the region and can be maintained at acceptable political costs.[52]

The thinking behind and the implications of the 'tar baby' option were arrogant and later proved historically incorrect by the collapse of Portuguese colonial rule and the Southern Rhodesian regime. Nevertheless, the Reagan administration's policy of 'constructive engagement' drew its inspiration from NSSM 39.[53]

Several points are of relevance to our discussion of NSSM 39: first, the historical context within which NSSM 39 was formulated; second, the reaction of African-Americans to the revelations and implications of the document; and third, the continuity and discontinuity of the US Southern Africa policy during different US administrations and the opportunities that were available to African-Americans. In the first instance, NSSM 39 was a component of the Nixon Doctrine, whose major objective was two-fold: a recognition of the global limits of US power, especially as a consequence of the costly and unwinnable Vietnam War; and a new global strategy in which the US would rely on regional powers in the Third World to maintain order on behalf of the US, that is, reliance on subimperialist states. South Africa was seen as a regional power in Southern Africa, for it exhibited the necessary conditions: apparent stability, preponderance of military and economic power and compatibility of interests at the ideological and economic levels.

The 'tilt' toward South Africa as a subimperialist state demonstrated by the 'tar baby' option, manifested the tacit US endorsement of the apartheid regime, in the eyes of both Africans and African-Americans. The revelations of NSSM 39 unambiguously confirmed the sympathy of the US government with the racial regime of repression and exploitation in Southern Africa. This perception was not lost on the few African-American members of the US Congress. There were some key political developments amongst African-Americans: the founding of the Congressional Black Caucus in 1971 by thirteen members; a few senior African-Americans were elected to the House of Representatives who could hold important positions on congressional committees and wield considerable influence on some issues, including those concerning US Africa policy; and some members of the CBC gradually developed keen interest in and gained remarkable knowledge about Africa. For example, Charles C. Diggs, Jr, was elected to Congress in 1955 and attended the 1958 All-African Peoples Conference in Accra, Ghana, organized by Kwame Nkrumah. Similarly, Adam Clayton Powell, Jr, who was elected earlier than Diggs, gained considerable insights into colonialism when he attended the Bandung Conference of African and Asian Nations in 1955. Indeed, Powell, on his return, tried to persuade the US to show strong opposition to colonialism and to pay greater attention to the Third World.[54] Diggs, who became an influential member of the House Foreign Relations Committee on African issues and later chair of the Foreign Relations subcommittee on Africa, played a critical role in galvanizing opposition to the Nixon administration's 'tar baby' option. For instance, Diggs strenuously opposed the sales of US arms to Portugal and South Africa, and championed congressional resistance to the Byrd Amendment, which allowed the US to import Rhodesian chrome in defiance of the UN's total economic embargo.[55]

Diggs's efforts were not successful. Nevertheless, these efforts laid the foundation for subsequent struggles against apartheid and for sanctions against South Africa. There are also two other points to note. First, Diggs and the other members of the CBC adopted what might be characterized as 'inside strategies', namely working within congressional channels, bargaining, compromising, influencing by utilizing 'standard operating procedures' in Congress.[56] Second, after recognizing the limitations of inside strategies, the CBC shifted to 'outside strategies', those which emphasized publicity and popular mobilization in order to influence the decision-makers and the policy-making institutions of the state.[57] The event that marked a profound shift to outside strategies was the National Black Political Convention, held in Gary, Indiana, in March 1972. Besides the politics of symbolism, the Convention set the stage for the 1976 'Manifesto' and the effective, combined strategies of inside and outside mobilization of African-American efforts to pursue US sanctions against South Africa from 1976 to 1986. Let us sketch out the forms which the campaign took.

Campaigns for sanctions against South Africa have generally followed a certain rhythm of internal crisis within the apartheid regime. The low and the high points of the crisis reflect the dynamics of repression and resistance. For example, the Sharpeville massacre in 1960, the Soweto rebellion in 1976, and the repression of anti-apartheid movements, especially the United Democratic Front (UDF) in 1983–86, point to periods of increased use of state terror to suppress African aspirations.

The Carter administration came to power in 1977 and for two reasons appeared sympathetic to the anti-apartheid movements and sanctions against South Africa. First, the Carter administration made human rights the thematic focus of its foreign policy. Regimes that consistently engaged in human rights abuses faced diplomatic criticism, isolation, threats of trade sanctions, cuts in US aid and other measures. Second, Andrew Young was appointed as US ambassador to the United Nations. It is important to note the 1976 elections as the context of Young's appointment. Southern Africa had figured prominently in the 1976 presidential elections, primarily as a result of the 'Black vote' and the increased visibility of African-American political leaders, especially the members of the CBC, a new breed of articulate, post–civil rights movement leaders who were becoming increasingly prominent in Democratic Party politics. Indeed, the Democratic Party platform made Africa, and Southern Africa in particular, one of the central issues of the party's foreign policy platform. There are, for example, interesting parallels between the Democratic Party platform on US Africa policy and the 'Manifesto'. The Carter administration's Africa policy reflected the two documents, especially during its first two years.[58] What were the prospects for economic sanctions against South Africa under the Carter administration? How effective was African-American influence on the Carter administration, especially through the agency of Andrew Young and the CBC, based on inside strategies?

To answer these questions, one needs to look at the pronouncements of candidate Carter, his thinking and administration regarding the issue of economic embargo against South Africa. Candidate Carter believed in the 'progressive' role of the US and Western transnational corporations in South Africa, as illustrated by his statement during the campaign: 'Our American businessmen can be a constructive force for achieving racial justice within South Africa' and 'economic development, investment commitment and use of economic leverage . . . seem to me the only way to achieve racial justice there . . . [and] I think . . . sanctions could be counter-productive'.[59] This line of argument was not and is not unfamiliar in US South Africa policy, but it was perhaps less expected from an American presidential candidate who appeared sympathetic to the call for sanctions against South Africa, as reflected in the Democratic Party platform. Once in power in 1977, Carter and his administration pursued US South Africa policy within the basic American assumption that US transnational corporations could play a progressive role in Southern Africa. Andrew Young was equally emphatic about the progressive role of US companies when he noted that 'the free market system can be the greatest force for constructive change now operating anywhere in the world'.[60] The belief that the Carter administration was more enlightened than its predecessors because of its pursuit of human rights in Southern Africa is therefore highly suspect.

A look at US positions at the United Nations epitomizes the Carter administration's duplicity on South Africa. For instance, in February 1977 the Carter administration engineered the formation of the 'Contact Group' (CG), composed of five Western powers: the US, the UK, France, (West) Germany and Canada. The purpose of the CG was to mediate the colonial conflict between the Namibian people, under the leadership of SWAPO, and the apartheid regime. The official argument of the Carter administration was basically that the CG was in a better position to mediate the dispute because South Africa was likely to trust the CG and hence be more forthcoming during negotiations. Trust stemmed from the understanding that the South African regime and the members of the CG shared common interests, both economic and strategic. The strategic interest here was the limitation of Soviet and socialist influences in Southern Africa, because many of the nationalist liberation movements espoused 'socialism' and some instituted regimes that proclaimed the principles of Marxism-Leninism as the basis of their development strategies. This was particularly the case in Mozambique and Angola after their triumph over Portuguese colonialism.

The response of South Africa to the perceived Soviet influence in Southern Africa was characterized by Pretoria as a 'total onslaught', an opportunistic claim, orchestrated vociferously after 1975–76 to win Western sympathy and support. To counter this alleged onslaught, Pretoria devised the 'total war strategy', which meant total mobilization of national resources in order to conduct undeclared wars against its neighbors and to eliminate anti-apartheid movements inside and outside the country.[61] But in Western capitals, the brutality of the 'total war strategy' in Angola and Mozambique won tacit approval and encouragement. For example, in April 1977, President Carter complimented the role of South Africa in the region when he noted that 'to a major degree the South African government is a stabilizing influence in the southern part of the continent'.[62] In the same month, Carter also carried out policy changes in his administration which sent different and encouraging signals to Pretoria. One important change was the replacement of Andrew Young, who initially coordinated US Africa policy, with Vice President Walter Mondale. Young lost his preeminent role because, among other things, he characterized the apartheid regime as illegitimate. It was not unrelated that in October 1977, nine conservative members of Congress introduced a resolution for the impeachment of Andrew Young for alleged sympathy with 'communist', 'Marxist' and 'terrorist' leaders in Africa.[63]

It has often been noted that events in South Africa tend to dictate the policy responses and actions of anti-apartheid movements.[64] In October 1977, the apartheid regime embarked on a savage policy of suppression of the anti-apartheid movements/organizations which were protesting the beating to death of Black Consciousness Movement leader Steve Biko by the police. The response of the Carter administration was to recall the US ambassador to Pretoria and other insignificant actions. But at the same time, the US joined the UK and France to veto UN resolutions calling for economic sanctions, an arms embargo, a ban on nuclear cooperation with Pretoria and a general condemnation of 'massive violence and repression against black people'.[65] A few months later the US Senate Africa subcommittee, chaired by Dick Clark (Dem.-Iowa) issued a report that called for an end to US investment in South Africa on the grounds that 'the net effect of American investment has been to strengthen the economic and military self-sufficiency of South Africa's apartheid regime.'[66] However, Carter rejected a recommendation that would have made it difficult for South Africa to export chrome alloys to the US. Other contrary actions by the Carter administration included military support for UNITA forces in Angola and Eritrean guerrilla movements in Ethiopia, in order to tie down the Cubans, and opposition to three bills calling for curtailment of US investment in South Africa. In fact, on 30 November 1978, while Carter met with South African Foreign Minister Pik Botha, Andrew Young delivered a speech in San Francisco arguing against economic sanctions. But just a month previously Carter had approved total economic sanctions against Uganda under Idi Amin. The Carter administration was perceived by critics of apartheid to be consistently hypocritical, as it tried 'to avoid precedent of cutting economic ties with non-Communist ally'.[67] Andrew Young was embarrassingly compelled to admit, in response to actions by the African representatives at the UN, that 'for good reason the African group does not trust the West – any of us, not even me – because they sense a long heritage of betrayal.'[68] In August 1979, Ambassador Young was forced to resign after coming under intense attack from the US establishment for a secret meeting with Zehdi Terzi, the chief PLO representative at the United Nations.

The above episodes and policy actions are intended to illustrate several points about our understanding of the Carter administration's policy toward South Africa and how African-American influence faired. It is clear that the Carter administration was against economic sanctions. In the words of a State Department official in 1977: 'nothing short of a South African invasion of the United States' would lead to the US imposition of 'real sanctions'.[69] Granted that this was perhaps a personal opinion, it nevertheless reflected the official attitude of the US government in general. The 'inside strategies' of African-Americans and other anti-apartheid groups had failed: the CBC could not muster legislation to win congressional support and presidential approval. The 'outside strategies' were weak and inadequately organized. For example, in 1978 the Executive Board of the NAACP called for 'total withdrawal of US firms from South

Africa', as a rejection of the Sullivan Principles of 1 March 1977, but to no avail.[70]

The Sullivan Principles were a code of conduct for US companies in South Africa formulated by the Reverend Leon Sullivan, an African-American civil rights leader in Philadelphia, and a member of the board of General Motors. Incidentally, GM was one of the 300 US corporations doing business in South Africa, providing an array of vehicles, including heavy trucks for the South African armed forces. The gist of the Sullivan Principles was a version of US affirmative action, which was to be implemented by the 300 US transnational corporations in South Africa. The code, which was voluntary and without enforcement mechanisms, consisted of the following: (1) desegregation of work facilities; (2) nondiscriminatory employment practices; (3) comparable worth pay policies for all workers; (4) training programs for non-whites to attain supervisory, administrative, technical and other career jobs; (5) creation of more management and supervisory positions for non-whites; and (6) contributions to the improvement of the quality of life for non-white employees at the community level, housing, schooling, recreation, health facilities, and so forth. These principles were not seriously implemented.[71]

The importance of the Sullivan Principles lies in two critical areas: the timing of the announcement and their effect on the pro-sanctions movement, both in the US and abroad. The timing was tactically brilliant. For one thing, the Soweto uprising and its brutal suppression had generated widespread revulsion and anger against the apartheid system and its vital props, especially foreign investments, transnationals and foreign (Western) government support. The announcement of the code thus came at a critical moment for transforming the widespread indignation and disapproval into concrete actions and demands for sanctions. But the code complicated the debate with the supporters of apartheid by introducing a powerful argument: namely that US corporations would play a progressive force in bringing about reform and 'peaceful change' in South Africa. The code consequently seemed to have placated the Carter administration and the US corporations, if only for a time. Equally important were the consequences of the code on African-American positions on sanctions. Foremost among the effects was the divisiveness the code engendered, which undermined solidarity on anti-apartheid sanctions. Moreover, the fact that an African-American civil rights activist authored the code to protect the apartheid regime from economic embargo lends itself to a sense of group betrayal or accusation of opportunism on the part of Leon Sullivan.[72]

The point about divisiveness here is not to suggest a monolithic view by African-Americans or any other group on a given issue, even one that is racialized. Schisms do occur in a larger political arena precisely because of differing ideological and economic interest. Even in South Africa, the anti-apartheid organizations differed on ideological and class tactics on the question of economic embargo – for instance, Bishop Desmond Tutu supported economic sanctions while Gatsha Buthelezi opposed them.

Another important aspect of Carter policy towards South Africa is the strategy behind the formation of the Contact Group. First, it was unlikely to effectively pressure South Africa to relinquish colonial control of Namibia. Second, the CG strategy basically neutralized the Socialist and the Third World blocs at the UN from exerting continuous pressure for sanctions against South Africa. Third, the CG amounted to a Western device whose objective was to postpone any immediate implementation of UN sanctions. Of course, sanctions could not work without the participation of the CG members. In the case of Namibia, the delaying tactics served the Western transnational corporations well by giving them more time to exploit the country's natural/mineral resources before independence. A SWAPO government was feared by the Western countries, since it was likely to restrict the exploitation of the country's natural resources.

The Carter administration thus took few steps to implement economic and arms embargoes against South Africa – contrary to the general perception that Carter was sympathetic to the implementation of tougher policies against the apartheid regime. He was surrounded by an equally supportive group of top African-American advisers at the State Department who could formulate and help supervise the implementation of such policies.[73] The initial fanfare about human rights remained at the level of rhetoric. James Petras has observed that morality is the recurring ideological expression of US imperialism in a period of crisis, and the aim of the liberal agenda of the Carter administration was to end the crisis of legitimacy in the US as a result of Watergate and its roots in the Vietnam syndrome.[74]

Two reasons explain this recourse to morality in periods of crisis. There is an attempt to curb disillusionment during a crisis of legitimacy in order to regain and stabilize the status quo ante. Morality is also used as a strategy to demobilize popular discontent and 'revolutionary' demands, which are unlikely to create ideological heterogeneity in the society; that is, a rise of many voices with different leaders or organizations, challenging state policies and power structures. The purpose of the 'new morality' was therefore to regain the initiative. Once that had been accomplished by the 'new morality', the ideological heterogeneity turned into mass confusion and inaction, and hence aided the restoration of the status quo.[75] In his book *Keeping Faith,* Carter talks about 'moral principles' as the 'best foundation for the exertion of American power and influence'.[76] One of the purposes of the human rights strategy was precisely to achieve US interests *not* to implement human rights.[77] A National Security Council staff memo

on human rights put the issue this way: 'If one ever tried to actually implement human rights, it would be a nightmare. Who would decide who is a
prisoner of conscience? Are the Wilmington 10?'[78]

The human rights strategy of the Carter administration toward South
Africa had the following effect on African-American efforts: it sowed the
seed of discord and confusion which, to some extent, paralyzed the African-American community. One reason was that the African-Americans relied heavily on 'inside strategies' since the Carter administration appeared
to support their interests and African-Americans were prominently represented in the administration. But in a fundamental sense, divisions in the
African-American community over interpretations of the real intentions of
the Carter administration toward Southern Africa represented class and
ideological differences and alliances, which were reflected in the form of
'inside' versus 'outside' strategies.[79]

The Reagan Administration

Reagan administration policy toward South Africa was known as 'constructive engagement', a phrase coined by Assistant Secretary of State for African Affairs Chester Crocker, who formulated and articulated the
arguments that underpinned the policy.[80] On close inspection, constructive
engagement was not an original formulation. It was, proverbially, old wine
in a new bottle, a repackaging of the 'tar baby' Option Two of NSSM 39,
but incorporating many aspects of the other options and premises. The
central argument of the policy consisted of a rejection of the Carter administration's façade of human rights commitment, which de-emphasized the
globalist policies of the United States, and the reassertion of Nixon and
Kissinger's *real politik*. Opposition to Soviet/Cuban influence in Southern
Africa was the core US policy in the region, precisely for the reason offered
by Alexander Haig, Reagan's first secretary of state: 'The enormous mineral wealth of Southern Africa' – was threatened by a 'resource war' fostered by 'Soviet proxy activity in the Third World'.[81] Another aspect of
constructive engagement included 'white-led change', advocated specifically
by the *verligte* ('enlightened') Afrikaners, a code word for a policy of tinker-
ing with apartheid at the margins, but offering no relief for the oppressed
majority in South Africa. Constructive engagement called for the re-estab-
lishment of a closer relationship with the apartheid regime in order to encourage 'peaceful' and 'nonviolent' change in Southern Africa; this was in
contradistinction to the rhetoric of the Carter administration, whose osten-
sible goal was to isolate Pretoria.

It is important for our purpose to locate constructive engagement within
the context of US ideology, which informed the Reagan administration.

Various characterizations of the ideology which differentiate the Reagan administration from the Carter administration included 'neo-conservatism' or 'new right conservatism'.[82] Insofar as foreign policy was concerned, the new form of conservatism was, for the Reagan administration, a vigorous and combative attempt to redefine and reassert US global hegemony and the role of the 'national security state' in its maintenance.[83] This conservative project was intended to reverse the decline of US global power, a decline that was perceived by the neoconservatives to have accelerated under the Carter administration. The essential elements of the conservative project were initially elaborated in the 1978 Senate Republican minority report, *Declaration on National Security and Foreign Policy*. It was followed by a series of secret documents, some regarding Africa and South Africa, which were leaked to the public by TransAfrica when the Reagan regime assumed power in January 1981.[84]

The core of the argument amounted to a Manichaean conception of the global relations amongst states and peoples. A Manichaean view of the world suffers from the 'angelic fallacy': according to American neoconservatives, any individual or state that opposes or criticizes US interests or policy is therefore on the side of the devil, but any individual or state that is supportive of US interests and policies enjoys the privilege of being on the side of the angels.[85] The ideological rigidity of the Reagan neoconservatives is critical for understanding the constructive engagement policy. It produced two consequences. First, it led to an arrogant defiance of an apparent international consensus, at least at the rhetorical level, on the brutality of the apartheid regime.

The second consequence of the ideological rigidity of constructive engagement was the manifestation of unambiguously racist elements in the policy, which, to a great extent, revealed an undisguised contempt for African-American and African feelings. For example, Jeanne Kirkpatrick, a Democratic turncoat and one of the intellectuals behind Reagan neoconservatism, made the following remark about apartheid: 'racial dictatorship is not as bad as Marxist dictatorship'.[86] This ideological blindness was equally demonstrated by President Reagan in a TV interview with Walter Cronkite on 3 March 1981. After defending constructive engagement, Reagan added this: 'Can we abandon a country that has stood beside us in every war we've ever fought, a country that is essential to the free world, that has minerals?'[87] Historical amnesia aside, it is well known that the architects of apartheid and the National Party were Nazi sympathizers during World War II. To complete the picture of the ideological rigidity of the constructive engagement policy, Reagan also argued that 'the African problem is a Russian weapon aimed at us'.[88] What do all these remarks mean?

The arguments of the Reagan administration for constructive engagement made its position on racism clear to everybody, and especially to African-American and Africans, in the following two senses: (1) that it was all right for the US and its corporations to conduct normal diplomatic and business relations with the apartheid regime, in spite of its heinous racial policies; while for many, any normalcy of relations, under the guise of subtle pressure for peaceful change, conferred dignity and comfort not only on the apartheid dictatorship but also on racism;[89] and (2) that it was still acceptable to injure, in a defiant and an unabashed manner, the feelings of 30 million African-Americans, as long as they did not constitute a significant political cost or electoral threat. Clearly, the explicitness of the Reagan administration had, in a strange way, created unity amongst the anti-apartheid movements in general and African-Americans in particular; that is, in some sense, the 'angelic fallacy' clearly delineated the terrain of contestation between the supporters and opponents of an evil system in a post–civil rights era, as well as in a postcolonial world. The correlation of forces was manifested along the following line: the emergence of combined 'inside' and 'outside' strategies, adopted by the anti-apartheid movements, on one hand, and the Reagan administration and its neoconservative supporters, on the other. What is interesting for us here is to sketch the dynamics of the struggle for sanctions during the Reagan administration and to show the prominent role played by African-Americans.

Two events reinvigorated both the inside and outside strategies: the Reagan administration's ideological 'tilt' toward the apartheid regime and the increasing internal crisis in South Africa itself, especially the rise in brutal repression of political opponents as well as the widening consequences of the 'total war strategy' on the neighboring countries. One of the first of the inside strategies was begun by the Congressional Black Caucus on 26 March 1981, when it called for the resignation of Jeanne Kirkpatrick, US ambassador to the UN, for having secretly met with five high-ranking South African military intelligence officers in Washington, D.C. The CBC apparently wanted to test the claim of American belief in equal treatment by drawing attention to the forced resignation of Andrew Young when he secretly met with a PLO representative in New York. The CBC was not surprised that Kirkpatrick was not forced to resign. However, the CBC followed this move by a bill, H.R. 3597, introduced by Rep. William Gray III (Dem-Penn.) to prohibit new US investments in South Africa. Although the bill did not pass, its introduction clearly defined the arena of confrontation between the Reagan administration and the anti-apartheid movements, both at the level of 'inside' and 'outside' strategies.

The Reagan administration's responses to CBC moves were articulated by Chester Crockers. In a series of speeches to pro–South African audiences, Crocker made clear the US position on sanctions, For example, in a speech to the American Legion in Honolulu, Crocker stated: 'South Africa is an integral and important element of the global economic system – the Reagan administration has no intention of destabilizing South Africa in order to curry favor elsewhere.'[90] Similarly, on 31 July 1981, the US broke with its European partners on the UN Security Council to veto a resolution which condemned the South African invasion of Angola. The CBC characterized the veto as 'a dastardly act . . . an all-time low in the morality of the Reagan administration foreign policy'.[91] In a sort of showdown, the Senate repealed the Clark Amendment, which prohibited clandestine CIA funds and support for UNITA in Angola. The repeal opened the door for the Reagan administration to pursue its policy of 'low-intensity warfare' (LIW) against Angola. Low-intensity warfare was the cornerstone of the Reagan administration strategy to 'roll back' socialism in the Third World by a brutal but slow process of killing and terrorizing civilians and destroying economies to render them utterly hopeless and destitute.[92]

Although the Reagan administration used a sophisticated propaganda machine to rationalize low-intensity warfare and support for South Africa on the basis of American anti-communism, there was an emerging popular discomfort with the consequences of its policies. Indeed, the CBC characterization of Reagan administration foreign policy as essentially immoral was indicative of the subsequent debate over the arrogance of the policies and the trampling of human decency and values in the name of anti-communism. Two developments emerged from the CBC's moral challenge. The CBC and its supporters in Congress shifted from inside to outside strategies. That is, popular sentiments were incorporated into the movement for sanctions in the US Congress and corporations. The arguments for sanctions were framed in moral terms, based on the same rhetoric as the civil rights movement. It is not unusual for the struggle for justice to evoke moral arguments that are ambiguous. This problematic of morality led to another development, namely the division between pro- and anti-sanctions supporters, highlighting more prominently than before the ideological character of the issue of sanctions, Insofar as the debate cohered around neoconservative and liberal positions. This sharp ideological definition was essential for the convergence of the inside and outside strategies pursued by the CBC and the African-American community. Let us illustrate the importance of the outside (popular) strategies in the struggle for sanctions.

The Reagan administration policy of constructive engagement provoked an equally committed response from prominent individuals and organizations outside the government, both in the African-American and other communities. The action-reaction dynamics produced, in a fundamental sense, a divisive and threatening politics of sanctions that cut across class and racial lines and assumed an important role in domestic US politics. This politicization was clearly noted by Senator Robert Dole (Rep.-Kans.) during a debate on sanctions against South Africa: 'Let's face it . . . there's a lot of politics involved . . . this has now become a civil rights issue.'[93] The perceived political threat was based on the fact that prominent religious organizations like the National Council of Churches, the AFL-CIO, the National League of Cities and African-American civil rights organizations (the NAACP, Urban League, and Operation PUSH) all registered their opposition to constructive engagement and strongly supported and worked for sanctions. Many universities and colleges added their opposition to apartheid because of student activism in the pro-sanctions movement. Divestment of their funds from companies doing business in South Africa showed the determination of these nongovernment organizations to confront the policy of constructive engagement and provided critical basis of support for the passage of the Comprehensive Anti-Apartheid Act of 1986. A certain reasonable level of consensus is considered essential for any administration in pursuing some specific foreign policy objectives. But the politics of sanctions was becoming increasingly discordant.

The passage of the Comprehensive Anti-Apartheid Act of 1986 was a culmination of the convergence of the inside and outside strategies. The CBC, which sponsored the bill in the House of Representatives, provided the critical leadership for public pressure on Congress to act as the Reagan administration arrogantly refused to respond to the plight of Africans under apartheid. At the popular level, TransAfrica in November 1984 initiated dramatic sit-ins and daily demonstrations at the South African embassy in Washington, D.C., which proved effective in mobilizing public opinion against the constructive engagement policy. This Free South Africa Movement gained unprecedented press coverage, which consequently inspired increasingly vocal anti-apartheid movements at grassroots levels, with effective national leadership provided by a number of well-known anti-apartheid organizations – for example, the American Committee on Africa, the Washington Committee on Africa, the Interfaith Center for Corporate Responsibility and the American Friends Service Committee.[94]

Although economic interests and strategic calculations underpinned the policy of constructive engagement, the charge of racism against the Reagan administration's South Africa policy proved a decisive emotional force for African-Americans and moderate and radical groups. The strategy of the Free South Africa Movement thus drew its inspiration from the symbolic politics of nonviolence that characterized the US civil rights movement, basically creating 'a broad-based rejection of racial division and injustice, a call to the US public to reaffirm opposition to racial oppression whether at home or abroad.'[95] This symbolic politics of nonviolence proved inspiring to the anti-apartheid movement and devastating to the neoconservative opportunism 'to exploit anti-communist sentiment in favor of a regional tilt to Pretoria'.[96]

The policy of constructive engagement was ended by the US Congress, on 2 October 1986, when the House overrode Reagan's veto of the comprehensive sanctions bill. The bill banned new US investments and loans, landing rights for South African Airways and imports of uranium, iron, coal, steel, textiles and agricultural products. But as Phyliss Johnson and David Martin have pointed out in *Frontline Southern Africa*, 'congressional intent' is one thing and the implementation of that intent, by an executive deeply opposed to it, is another. In spite of the weaknesses of the sanctions bill, the Reagan administration was reluctant to implement it. In addition, Johnson and Martin observed that the interpretation of the bill provided the Reagan administration with more opportunities to weaken the sanctions.[97] Despite the machinations by the administration, the message from the US Congress and the anti-apartheid movement to the apartheid regime seemed clear: no more *carte blanche* from a US administration for racist repression and brutalities. Even Reverend Leon Sullivan was finally compelled, in June 1987, to abandon his famous principles and to call for 'corporate withdrawal and comprehensive sanctions'.[98]

It is not the intention of this essay to fully evaluate the effects of the 1986 comprehensive sanctions bill on the apartheid regime. US sanctions clearly had some damaging consequences for the politics and the economy of South Africa. The collapse of the apartheid regime would not have occurred without US and European sanctions, as well as the divestment movement at the global level. All led to the isolation of the apartheid regime. Two key questions need to be raised in regards to the strategies of sanctions: (1) How effective were the sanctions, not only in ending the apartheid system but also in bringing about a meaningful majority rule that redistributes political and economic power in the long run? and (2) If sanctions provided a nonviolent strategy for dismantling apartheid, did they also foreclose a revolutionary alternative? These are complex empirical and theoretical questions which would require a lengthy exposition and analysis, neither of which is possible here. However, what follows in the final section of this essay is an attempt to briefly sketch out a conceptual framework within which to contextualize the problematic of the African-American position on African issues, as well as on apartheid.

Analytical Framework

This section analytically explores the interpenetrations of race, class, ideology and cooperation as explanatory factors in African-Americans' influence on US Africa policy in general and US South Africa policy in particular. Four elements constitute the essential building blocks from which solidarity is constructed at different levels of identity and interests. The social and political aspects of each factor define the basis of solidarity, which is manifested at two levels: internal and external. Internal solidarity refers to a feeling that arises in a group with a sense of identity derived from certain shared characteristics. External solidarity, on the other hand, simply applies to inter-group sharing of identified interests. The interaction of the two forms is essential for understanding the interpenetrations of race, class, ideology and cooperation, and the problematic of solidarity that is required for African-Americans to exercise considerable influence on US South Africa policy.

The notions of internal and external solidarity can be illustrated by focusing on the meanings of race, class, ideology and cooperation in the following senses. Race, for African-Americans, is a focused core whose characteristics are alleged to be internal to a racial group. This means that race, as a concept, claims to categorize humans into groups that are defined by certain shared physical characteristics, for example, skin color or hair texture. These phenotypical characteristics are claimed to correlate with the cultural, social, mental and even moral properties of a given social group.[99] The characteristics that define race have no scientific or biological basis justifying socio-cultural conclusions. Thus, race is a social construction which structures and organizes political power by favoring racial claims to superiority, which is manifested in the form of racism. From the perspective of the subordinated, race and racism define their identities and consciousness. Indeed, as noted earlier, Pan-Africanism was a response to racism or the racial exploitation and oppression of diasporic Africans. In this respect, the raison d'être for Pan-Africanism is race and racism. It may sound paradoxical for Pan-Africanism to confer recognition of race as an immutable, legitimate, scientific category: for example, W.E.B. Du Bois argued for 'the conservation of races' in 1897.[100] However, as Anthony Appiah has suggested, Du Bois's argument in 'The Conservation of Races' was basically a reaction to racism or racial prejudice. That is, race and racism create the 'dialectic of denial and acceptance of difference' precisely as a means of protection against racial oppression and brutalization.[101] Du Bois, in *The Souls of Black Folk*, resolved the 'dialectic of denial and acceptance of difference' by suggesting that African-Americans possess 'double consciousness': an American and an African consciousness in one body.[102] Pan-Africanism represents the sentiments of 'kin and kith' for African-

American struggle against apartheid. Hence, race and racism constitute a focused core which defines and sustains the imperatives of Pan-Africanism. This is not to argue that the idea of 'kin and kith' is not problematic. There are enormous differences between Africans and diasporic Africans. However, racial oppression and prejudice, and racialized imperialism and colonial rule, have been a shared historical experience, thus mitigating differences of racial oppression and liberation tht could undermine internal solidarity.

If the 'racial problematic' produces the ideological unity of African and African-American, class creates internal differentiation and disunity. This is because class is a category that locates an individual in relation to the structure of economic production relations. Class also manifests two elements within a group: it has an internal aspect, that is, African-Americans and Africans are divided along class lines, and an external manifestation, which cuts across racially defined groups. Unlike race, which is exclusivist by virtue of its imagined identities, class is inclusivist, insofar as it is defined by real economic production relations. Thus, for African-Americans, or any other racial group in the US, class structure and class conflicts are both internal and external.

Although class and race present a difficult dialogue in the African-American experience, it is undeniable that both constitute the reality of that experience – that is to say, race and class conflate the sites of social and political struggle for African-Americans. Thus, it is not so much the question of stressing race over class or class over race that is crucial but rather the need to understand their historical contingencies both analytically and experientially.[103] The importance of class in the African-American community lies in its role as a divisive force, as well as a defining structure of interests in the anti-apartheid movement. In a capitalist or class-based society, class is grounded in ideology, which is essential for class hegemony.

Like race or class, ideology is a complex concept to define precisely. For example, one author has identified more than twenty-seven senses in which the concept of ideology is used.[104] For Marx, Engels and some Marxists, ideology constitutes the 'ruling ideas' in a given society and epoch. These ruling ideas are performative and purposeful for the reproduction of power relations. Terry Eagleton defines ideology as 'the articulation of discourses and power . . . a set of discourses which wrestle over interests which are in some way relevant to the maintenance of power structures, central to a whole force of social and historical life'.[105] Ideology is 'life experienced in which individuals are constituted in such a way that they more or less submit to the existing order'.[106] On the other hand, an anthropologist sees ideology as a derivative of 'socially established structures of meaning'.[107] From these senses of ideology, one would agree with Terry

Eagleton's point that 'ideologies are by no means always the property of dominant classes'.[108] For example, Black nationalism is not necessarily an ideology of the dominant class.

These definitions clarify two aspects of ideology's role in the life of the African-American community. One aspect pertains to internal manifestations in the forms of nationalism, cultural nationalism, group consciousness, philosophy and Pan-Africanism. These forms are internal to African-Americans and are elements of self-definition or, on the left side of the hyphen, *African*. The other feature is external, namely, the universal American ideology which defines the right side of the hyphen, *American*. Hence, ideology, for African-Americans, operates both internally and externally, just like class structure. The implication is that ideology assumes a contradictory role when African-Americans deal with African and US interests – according to the dialectic of 'double consciousness'. Unresolved tension exists between being African and American, as noted earlier in the essay. Playing up Americanism and American symbols is as important as asserting Africanism and African symbols while influencing US policy toward Africa. Indeed, as we have seen, the success of any influence depends on a judicious balance of the two often contradictory identities. This is particularly poignant for two reasons: racism has been a significant element in US foreign policy and has pervaded US Africa policy, and US interests in Africa are those of the dominant white majority. The two present an unpalatable choice for African-Americans, especially those who have a strong Pan-African consciousness. It is a challenge that was evident in the anti-apartheid movement. The answer involves three options: cooperation on the basis of class or economic interests, for example, the case of Reverend Leon Sullivan; and cooperation with others, by appealing to the symbols and values of American society, for example, the inside and outside strategies that emphasiz moral arguments. In this second instance, cooperation operates at the level of shared values, symbols and history, real or imagined. Without cooperation from other Americans, African-American success in the sanctions movement would have been more difficult to achieve.

The third option is the rejection of appeals to Americanism and US interests. This is the radical option, attractive especially to separatists and cultural nationalists, who desire a fundamental break with US values and interests in Africa and the Third World. For them, apartheid is 'not an irrational race prejudice' but a structure of class and racial domination.[109] They would find an end to apartheid, not in reform but in an armed struggle, which is essential for national liberation. This option is informed by the articulate arguments of Frantz Fanon and Amilcar Cabral, who viewed the use of violence as a necessary requirement for national liberation, especially from imperialism and colonialism. For Fanon, violence is essential for psychological catharsis, that is, psychological liberation for the colonized, while Cabral's notion of the role of violence is a forceful re-entry into history.[110] Similarly, Malcolm X and George Padmore would concur with 'international racial solidarity and cooperation', which puts violence at the center of the anti-apartheid movement, precisely to deal with national liberation from both racial and class domination. For instance, Padmore, who was a prominent Pan-Africanist from Trinidad, observed that 'exploitation knows no color'.[111] He rejected any class compromise or nonviolent change that preserves class domination.

The nationalist position challenges the integrationist option, which rejects a revolutionary strategy for national liberation. Some scholars have labeled the nonviolent argument the 'Atlanta model', which is basically characterized by 'Martin Luther King, Jr's non-violent approach in enlisting the support of white American liberals and business folk in putting an end to racial segregation in the Southern States in the 1960s'.[112] The Atlanta model represents two additional characteristics: (1) it is seen as a 'final compromise between the black petty bourgeoisie and the white ruling class'; and (2) it shows an 'ideological flux' within the African-American community. African-Americans are influenced ontologically by the US core ideology, capitalism and its economic, political and cultural values.[113] W.E.B. Du Bois saw this influence in the 'double consciousness' of the African-American, although the 'American' aspect exerts overwhelming leverage. Du Bois lamented it in 1955 when he noted: 'The new leadership [of Black businessmen, bureaucrats, and white-collar employees] had no interest in Africa. It was aggressively American.'[114] Indeed, H.E. Newsum and Olayiwola Abegunrin fault Andrew Young's role in the Carter administration and his failure to advocate sanctions against apartheid, first because he was more committed to US interests than to relieving the plight of the Africans under apartheid, and second, because he was more interested in exporting the 'Atlanta Model' to South Africa, which would be compatible with American interests.[115]

It is clear that interpenetrations of race, class, ideology and cooperation make reconciliation of nationalist and integrationist arguments problematic. What the anti-apartheid movement demonstrates is that African-Americans confront a more complex political situation than any other 'racial' group in their attempt to influence US foreign policy, without class and ideological compromise. The essay has attempted to show the complexity of the history and the economics that have defined the African-American position. But the modest success in passing the 1986 Anti-Apartheid Act is a victory to relish, and a source of lessons for the campaigns that will engage coming generations of Pan-Africanists, both on the continent and in the diaspora.

Imagining Home

Notes

1. This is a revised version of a discussion presented at the conference 'Pan-Africanism Revisited' (April 1988). It was also presented at the Joint Center for African Studies at the University of California, Berkeley, May 1989. Personal note: I would like to note here that my interest in the issue of apartheid, Pan-Africanism, African-Americans and US policy toward Africa has been inspired and conditioned by my academic and personal involvement in anti-apartheid movements ever since my refugee life in Kenya in 1965 and subsequently in the US.

2. The Black Leadership Conference was organized by the Congressional Black Caucus and included 120 Black leaders from labor, business, civil rights, church, government, and other organizations, as well as individuals. The purpose of the conference was 'to formulate a national agenda for a progressive US policy toward Africa'. See the Congressional Black Caucus, 'The African-American Manifesto on Southern Africa' in *The Black Scholar,* January/February 1987, pp. 27–32.

3. Ibid., p. 32.

4. See Marguerite Ross Barnett, 'The Congressional Black Caucus: Symbol, Myth, and Reality', *The Black Scholar,* vol. 8, no. 4 (January/February 1977), p. 17.

5. 'Manifesto', p. 28.

6. Ibid., p. 27.

7. Ibid., p. 27

8. For a recent critical analysis, see H.E. Newsum and Olayiwola Abegunrin, *United States Foreign Policy Towards Southern Africa: Andrew Young and Beyond,* London 1987.

9. For a discussion of grassroots sentiments on African issues, see Minion K.C. Morrison, 'Afro-Americans and Africa: Grass Roots Afro-American Opinion and Attitudes Toward Africa', *Comparative Study of Society and History,* 1987, pp. 269–92.

10. See Bernard M. Magubane, *The Ties That Bind: African-American Consciousness of Africa,* Trenton, N.J. 1987, especially Ch. 7 for reactions to the Italo-European War; Richard Payne and Eddie Ganaway, 'The Influence of Black Americans on US Policy Toward Southern Africa', *African Affairs,* vol. 39, no. 317 (October 1980), pp. 585–98.

11. My discussion of apartheid here is drawn from Hermann Giliomee and Lawrence Schlemmer, *From Apartheid to Nation-Building,* Cape Town 1989, Ch. 2.

12. D. F. Malan, quoted in Giliomee and Schlemmer, *From Apartheid,* p. 42.

13. M. C. de Wet Nel, quoted in Giliomee and Schlemmer, *From Apartheid,* p. 42.

14. For a discussion of the peculiarity of the apartheid capitalist economy in South Africa, see Hillel Ticktin, *The Politics of Race: Discrimination in South Africa,* London 1991, especially Ch. 8; Harold Wolpe, 'Capitalism and Cheap Labor Power in South Africa', *Economy and Society,* vol. 1 no. 4 (1972).

15. For the rates of profit, see Ian Mackler, *Pattern for Profit in Southern Africa,* Lexington, Mass. 1972, Ch. 3; and Richard W. Hull, *American Enterprise in South Africa: Historical Dimensions of Engagement and Disengagement,* New York 1990, especially Appendix Table 12, p. 371.

16. Frantz Fanon, *A Dying Colonialism,* New York 1965.

17. The United States had not ratified the Declaration of Human Rights until very recently.

18. The Reagan administration consistently referred to apartheid as 'repugnant'; see Pauline H. Baker, *The United States and South Africa: The Reagan Years,* New York 1989.

19. Colin Legum, *Pan-Africanism: A Short Political Guide,* New York 1961, p. 33, quoted in Magubane, *The Ties That Bind,* p. 145.

20. Maulana R. Karenga, 'Which Road: Nationalism, Pan-Africanism, Socialism?' *The Black Scholar,* vol. 16, no. 2 (October 1974), p. 26; Karenga also formulated the three themes of Pan-Africanism.

21. See Frances M. Beal and Ty de Pass, 'The Historical Black Presence in the Struggle for Peace' *The Black Scholar* (January/February 1986), pp. 2–7, and also C.L.R. James et al., *Fighting Racism in World War II,* New York 1980.

22. Frederick Engels, *Anti-Duhring,* New York 1939, p. 127, quoted in Magubane, *The Ties That Bind,* p. 214. For a comparative analysis of South Africa and the US, see Stanley B. Green-

berg, *Race and State in Capitalist Development*, New Haven, Conn. 1980; George M. Frederickson, *White Supremacy: A Comparative Study in American and South African History*, New York 1981.

23. See James Rosenau, *Domestic Sources of Foreign Policy*, New York 1967. See also Julian Lider, *Correlation of Forces*, Aldershot 1986, Chs 5–6.

24. See 'African Policy and Black Americans', *Foreign Policy*, no. 15, Summer 1974, p. 108.

25. Charles C. Diggs, Jr, 'The Afro-American Stake in Africa', *The Black World*, January 1976, p. 6; my emphasis.

26. Michael Weil, 'Can the Blacks Do for Africa What the Jews Did for Israel?', *Foreign Policy*, no. 15 (Summer 1974), pp. 109–22.

27. See Michael H. Hunt, *Ideology and US Foreign Policy*, New Haven, Conn. 1987. See also George Shepard, Jr, ed., *Racial Influences on American Foreign Policy*, New York 1971.

28. On the FBI and the civil rights movement and Reverend Martin Luther King, Jr, see Mark Lane and Dick Gregory, *Code Name Zorro: The Murder of Martin Luther King, Jr*, New York 1977; and Ward Churchill and Jim Vander Wall, *The Cointelpro Papers: Documents from the FBI's Secret Wars Against Dissent in the United States*, Boston 1990, Ch. 5.

29. For the importance of the 'Black vote' in Carter's election, see Chuck Stone, 'Black Political Power in the Carter Era', *The Black Scholar*, vol. 8, no. 4 (January/February 1977), pp. 6–15.

30. Weil, 'Can the Blacks Do What the Jews Did for Israel?', p. 119. Emphasis in the original.

31. Gunnar Myrdal, *An American Dilemma: The Negro Problem and Modern Democracy*, New York 1944.

32. In South Africa, 'petty apartheid' refers to segregation in the use of public facilities and spaces, restaurants, restrooms, etc.

33. The emigration impulse as well as separatist tendencies represent processes of re-Africanization and de-Americanization, while integrationist inclinations generate de-Africanization and re-Americanization; 'The Last Alternative for Black America', *Phylon*, vol. 37, no. 2 (June 1977), pp. 203–10; and Martin Kilson, 'What Is Africa to Me: Dilemmas of Transnational Ethnicity', *Dissent* (Fall 1984), pp. 410–33.

34. For a discussion on the formation of race identity among African-Americans, see James S. Jackson, ed., *Life in Black America*, Ch. 12.

35. See Michael Omi and Howard Winant, *Racial Formation in the United States: From the 1960s to the 1980s*, London 1986, Ch. 5. See also Barrington Moore, *Injustice: The Social Basis of Obedience and Revolt*, White Plains, N.Y. 1978.

36. Magubane, *The Ties That Bind*, p. 230.

37. Anthony D. Smith, 'Toward a Global Culture', in Mike Featherstone, ed., *Global Culture*, 1990, p. 179.

38. Ibid., p. 179.

39. Magubane, *The Ties That Bind*, p. 145.

40. Ibid., Ch. 5.

41. For those who want to read more on the two concepts, see Antonio Gramsci, *Prison Notebooks*, New York 1971, part 2, Ch. 2. For an excellent exposition, see John Hoffman, *The Gramscian Challenge: Coercion and Consent in Marxist Political Theory*, Oxford 1984, especially Ch. 4.

42. See Tony Martin, *The Pan African Connection: From Slavery to Garvey and Beyond*, Dover, Mass. 1976, Chs 1–3.

43. According to one count, there was an increase from thirteen in 1971. See Marguerite Ross Barnett, 'The Congressional Black Caucus', p. 25; Bruce A. Ragsdale and Joel D. Treese, *Black Americans in Congress, 1870–1989*, Washington, D.C. 1990.

44. See Stone, 'Black Political Power', and Payne and Ganaway, 'The Influence of Black Americans', pp. 585–98.

45. See Philip V. White, 'The Black American Constituency for Southern Africa, 1940–1980', in Alfred O. Hero, Jr and John Barratt, eds, *The American People and South Africa: Publics, Elites and Policy Processes*, Lexington, Mass. 1981, pp. 83–101, and also Abdul Aziz Said, ed., *Ethnicity and US Foreign Policy*, New York 1981.

46. On US overt and covert support, see John Stockwell, *In Search of Enemies: A CIA Story*, New York 1978.

47. From a document cited in Edgar Lockwood, 'The Future of the Carter Policy Toward Southern Africa', *Issue*, vol. 7, no. 4 (1977), p. 11.

48. The NSSM 39 is reproduced in *The Kissinger Study of Southern Africa: National Security Study Memorandum 39*, Mohamed A. El-Khawas and Barry Cohen, eds, Westport, Conn. 1976. The existence of the secret document was originally revealed in cryptic reports in 1970 by Kevin Owen, the Washington correspondent for the *Johannesburg Star*. See Anthony Lake, *The 'Tar Baby' Option: American Policy Toward Southern Rhodesia*, New York 1976.

49. El-Khawas and Cohen, *The Kissinger Study*, p. 82.

50. Ibid., pp. 84–5.

51. Ken Owen coined the phrase in February 1971; see Lake, *The 'Tar Baby' Option.*, p. 271.

52. El-Khawas and Cohen, *The Kissinger Study*, p. 84.

53. See Chester Crocker, the main architect of 'constructive engagement', 'South Africa: Strategy for Change', *Foreign Affairs*, vol. 59 (1980).

54. See Ragsdale and Treese, *Black Americans in Congress*, pp. 113–15.

55. Ibid., pp. 39–45. For more on Charles Diggs, Jr's efforts, see Steven Metz, 'The Anti-Apartheid Movement and the Populist Instinct in American Politics', *Political Science Quarterly*, vol. 101, no. 3 (1986), pp. 379–95.

56. Metz, 'The Anti-Apartheid Movement', p. 380.

57. Ibid., p. 380.

58. For more discussion of the parallels, see White, 'The Black American Constituency', pp. 92–4.

59. 'Carter Speaks on South Africa', *The Financial Mail* (South Africa), 5 November 1976, p. 501, quoted in K. Danaher, *In Whose Interest? A Guide to US-South Africa Relations*, Washington, D.C. 1985, p. 42.

60. *Sevendays*, 20 June 1977 p. 10, quoted in Danaher, *In Whose Interest?*

61. On tacit US support of South Africa's 'total war strategy', see Christopher Coker, *The United States and South Africa, 1968–1985: Constructive Engagement and Its Critics*, Durham, N.C. 1986, pp. 227–41, and V.M. Nyathi, 'South African Imperialism in Southern Africa', *African Review*, vol. 5, no. 4 (1975), and also Ben Turok, ed., *Witness from the Frontline Aggression and Resistance in Southern Africa*, London 1990.

62. Danaher, *In Whose Interest?*, p. 123. The reference was to the peaceful resolution of the war of liberation in Zimbabwe/Rhodesia.

63. Danaher, *In Whose Interest?*, pp. 125–7.

64. See, for example, Coker, *The United States and South Africa*, Ch. 13.

65. Danaher, *In Whose Interest?*, p. 128.

66. Ibid., p. 130.

67. Ibid., p. 135.

68. Department of State Bulletin, 5 December 1977, p. 792, quoted in Kevin Danaher, *The Political Economy of US Policy Toward South Africa*, Boulder, Colo. 1985, p. 171.

69. Danaher, *The Political Economy*, p. 170.

70. Ibid., pp. 123 and 130.

71. For a detailed discussion of the Sullivan Principles, see Elizabeth Schmidt, *Decoding Corporate Camouflage: US Business Support for Apartheid*, Washington, D.C. 1980.

72. There is some evidence that Sullivan did not author the principles alone. The code was essentially formulated by US corporate interests in South Africa. Sullivan was a strategic front and received praise from official quarters for that role. See Schmidt, *Decoding Corporation Camoflage*, p. 17.

73. For a discussion of senior African-American advisers at the US State Dept., see Danaher, *The Political Economy*, Ch. 5.

74. James Petras, 'President Carter and the New Morality', *Monthly Review*, (1977), p. 38.

75. For more discussion on the strategy of the 'new morality' and the human rights crusade, see John Dumbrele, *The Making of United States Foreign Policy*, Manchester 1990.

76. Jimmy Carter, *Keeping Faith: Memoirs of a President*, New York 1982, p. 143.

77. For example, Edmund Muskie, Carter's secretary of state, asserted that 'emphasis on human rights serves our national interests', quoted in A. Glenn Mower, Jr, *Human Rights and*

American Foreign Policy: The Carter and Reagan Experience, New York 1987, p. 241.

78. J. Tuchman Mathews and L. G. Defend, memo for Brzezinski, 20 November 1978, cited in T. Dumbrele, *The Making*, p. 234.

79. See Newsum and Abegunrin, *United States Foreign Policy;* Raymond S. Franklin, *Shadows of Race and Class*, Minneapolis, Minn. 1991, Chs 1 and 7; and for a discussion of 'inside' and 'outside' strategies, see Steven Metz, 'The Anti-Apartheid Movement'.

80. See Chester Crocker, 'South Africa: Strategy for Change', pp. 323–51.

81. Quoted by William Minter, 'Destructive Engagement: The United States and South Africa in the Reagan Era', in Phyllis Johnson and David Martin, eds, *Frontline Southern Africa: Destructive Engagement*, New York 1988, p. 400.

82. Paul Rich, 'United States Containment Policy, South Africa and the Apartheid Dilemma', *Review of International Studies*, vol. 14 (1988), p. 187.

83. For an insightful discussion of the notion of 'national security', see Saul Landau, *The Dangerous Doctrine: National Security and US Foreign Policy*, Boulder, Colo. 1988.

84. Danaher, *In Whose Interest?*, p. 154.

85. The notion of the 'angelic fallacy' is attributed to Lionel Trilling.

86. *Economist*, 29 May 1981, p. 34.

87. Danaher, *In Whose Interest?*, p. 150.

88. *Africa*, no. 111 (November 1980), p. 50.

89. It was not coincidental that Pretoria responded to the Reagan inauguration by commando raids into Mozambique and later invasion of Angola in what was seen asa US *carte blanche* for the apartheid regime to destroy the two countries, through 'total war strategy', or euphemistically, 'destabilization': see Coker, *The United States and South Africa*, Ch. 13.

90. Danaher, *In Whose Interest?*, p. 157.

91. Cited by Danaher, *In Whose Interest?*, p. 158.

92. For a thorough discussion of LIW as a new form of US intervention in the Third World, see Michael T. Klare and Peter Kornbluh, eds, *Low-Intensity Warfare: Counterinsurgency, Proinsurgency, and Antiterrorism in the Eighties*, New York 1987. See also Alexander George, ed., *Western State Terrorism*, New York 1991.

93. Quoted in Pauline H. Baker, 'The Sanctions Vote: A GOP Milestone', *New York Times*, 26 August 1986, cited by Peter Schraeder, 'Speaking with Many Voices', p. 404.

94. For futher discussion, see Peter Schraeder, 'Speaking with Many Voices'; and Constantine C. Menges, 'Sanctions '86: How the State Department Prevailed', *The National Interest*, no. 13 (Fall 1988), pp. 65–77.

95. Johnson and Martin, *Frontline Southern Africa*, p. 423.

96. Ibid., p. 424.

97. Ibid., p. 430–33.

98. Johnson and Martin noted consistent 'incoherence in US Southern Africa policy', as illustrated by a US veto of a UN Security Council resolution calling for similar sanctions in February 1987, *Frontline Southern Africa*, pp. 433–9.

99. Anthony Appiah, 'Racisms', in David T. Goldberg, ed., *Anatomy of Racism*, Minneapolis, Minn. 1990, Ch. 1.

100. W.E.B. Du Bois, 'The Conservation of Races' in *W.E.B. Du Bois Speaks: Speeches and Addresses, 1890–1919*, Philip S. Foner, ed., New York 1970.

101. Anthony Appiah, 'The Uncompleted Argument: Du Bois and the Illusion of Race', *Critical Inquiry*, vol. 12, no. 1 (Autumn 1985), p. 25.

102. W.E.B. Du Bois, *The Souls of Black Folk*, New York 1969 [1903].

103. For a discussion of the debate over race and class in African-American experience, see Kinfe Abraham, *From Race to Class: Links and Parallels in African and Black American Protest Expression*, London 1982; Bernard R. Boxill, 'The Race-Class Questions', and Lucius T. Outlaw, 'Race and Class in the Theory and Practice of Emancipatory Social Transformation', in Leonard Harris, ed., *Philosophy Born of Struggle: Anthology of Afro-American Philosophy from 1917*, Dubuque, Iowa 1983, pp. 107–29.

104. See David S. McLellan, *Ideology*, Minneapolis, Minn. 1986.

105. Terry Eagleton, 'Ideology and Scholarship' in Jerome J. McGann, ed., *Historical Studies and Literary Criticism*, Madison, Wis. 1985, pp. 114–15.

106. Terry E. Boswell, et al., 'Recent Developments in Marxist Theories of Ideology', *The Insurgent Sociologist*, vol. 13, no. 4 (Summer 1986), p. 7.

107. Clifford Geertz, *The Interpretation of Cultures*, New York 1973, p. 12.

108. Eagleton, 'Ideology and Scholorship', p. 114. This is in response to the 'dominant ideology thesis'. See Nicholas Abercrombie et al., *The Dominant Ideology Thesis*, Boston 1980.

109. See Kevin Danaher, 'South Africa, US Policy and Anti-Apartheid Movement', *The Review of Radical Political Economics*, vol. 2, no. 3 (Fall 1979), p. 54.

110. See Magubane, *The Ties That Bind.*

111. Quoted in Beal and de Pass, 'The Historical Black Presence in the Struggle for Peace', p. 5.

112. Newsum and Abegunrin, *United States Foreign Policy*, p. 63.

113. Ibid., p. 2.

114. Cited by White, 'The Black American Constituency', p. 84.

115. Newsum and Abegunrin, *United States Foreign Policy*, Chs 1 and 3.

PART IV

Theory of Liberation,

or Liberation from Theory?:

Rethinking Pan-Africanism

15

Pan-Africanism

and African Liberation

Horace Campbell

Pan-Africanism is at once an exercise in consciousness and resistance. It reflects the self-expression and self-organization of the African peoples and expresses their resistance to Eurocentrism. Walter Rodney, in his attempt to grasp the content of Pan-Africanism at the time of the Sixth Pan-African Congress in Tanzania in 1974, wrote:

> Any 'Pan' concept is an exercise in self-definition by a people, aimed at establishing a broader redefinition of themselves than that which had so far been permitted by those in power. Invariably, however, the exercise is undertaken by a specific social group or class which speaks on behalf of the population as a whole. This is always the case with respect to national movements. Consequently, certain questions must be placed on the agenda, notably, the following:
>
> Which class leads the national movement?
>
> How capable is this class of carrying out the historic tasks of national liberation?
>
> Which are the silent classes on whose behalf 'national' claims are being articulated?[1]

As an exercise in self-definition, the Pan-Africanist project has been sharpened by resistance to Eurocentrism. Pan-African self-definition has taken many forms, but it has been most clearly articulated in the project of achieving the liberation of the continent of Africa and the dignity and self-respect of all Africans. For most of the century, political independence was seen as the key to achieving liberation and self-respect. But after more than thirty years of African independence, it has become clear that the social forces that led the independence movement were incapable of carrying out the historic tasks of social emancipation.

The assumption of power by African leaders in Africa, and by Black mayors and governors in the US and Afro-Caribbean prime ministers in the Caribbean, has not significantly improved the quality of life of the African peoples nor ended the impact of racism. It is now possible to say that the content of independence must be deepened to guarantee new relations of production. As part of the struggle for human emancipation, the struggle of the African peoples for a decent livelihood and for social justice has asserted itself as part of the struggle for social transformation and dignity. It is in this sense that Pan-Africanists such as Eusi Kwayana, who struggle in societies alongside other oppressed groups, embrace a concept of Pan-African humanism.

This new conceptualization of Pan-Africanism arose concretely out of the experiences of Pan-Africanists such as Walter Rodney, who had to clarify the real meaning of Pan-Africanism (in opposition to leaders like Forbes Burnham, who exploited the subjective forms of self-assertion to pit poor African workers against Indian workers in order to keep a small clique in power). At the intellectual level this new conceptual thrust is also an attempt to rescue the search for emancipation from the cultural vision of Europe, for example, in the Afrocentric approach to history.

Pan-Africanism, in its North American manifestations, remains constrained by the intellectual poverty of the United States and its ideological stress on great men of history. The historical record of the Pan-African movement in the West links the movement to great heroes (mostly males) such as W.E.B. Du Bois, Marcus Garvey, C.L.R. James, George Padmore, Kwame Nkrumah, Patrice Lumumba, Cheik Anta Diop, Nelson Mandela and Bob Marley. The individualism of the Afrocentric conception of history seeks to abstract these men from the social movement of which they were a part. If European power was seen as built on the genius of white males, the response must be to posit great African males. Both approaches to history denigrate the role of women.

In one sense, the intellectual poverty of the great-man-in-history approach has trapped some Africans in a search for positive role models in racist societies. It is this search for role models in response to the imperial arrogance of Europe that forced the early Pan-African writers to celebrate the great African empires of the past. Yet the depth of the economic crisis in Africa and among Africans overseas dictates that, however much Egypt was a great center of civilization in the past, the challenge of today's concrete reality is to change the wretchedness of the conditions of existence of the Egyptian and other African peoples.

Pan-African liberation at the end of the decade confronts both the falsification of African history and the intense ideological campaign manifest in the media images of Africans dying of famine and AIDS. The recolonization of the African continent in the period of the push for a united Europe (1992) and a common European home has clarified the fact that political independence and the unity of states as inscribed in the Organization of African Unity cannot be the basis of African liberation. Building a federation of Africa based on the cultural unity of the continent and the harnessing of the knowledge and skills developed by Africans over the centuries are some of the challenges that face the African peoples in the next century.

For those concerned with social transformation, the crisis has presented an opportunity to raise new questions in conceptualizing liberation in terms of real changes in human relations. After the period of guerrilla struggles in Africa there was the effort to develop the ideas of socialism as the ideology of liberation. But those states that embraced socialism used this ideology as a dogma that demobilized the producers. Ideas of modernization, though conceived of as Pan-African/Afrocentric, have emphasized catching up with Europe on European terms, and have thus left the African peoples alienated from the states established during decolonization.

All over the African world the search for cultural transformation and cultural freedom has inserted into the Pan-African struggle a new emphasis. Cultural resistance and cultural expressions reflect the deep ferment in the world of the African peoples. This ferment is manifest in a variety of religious forms that resist the consumerism of capitalist culture. In this sense the producers in Africa have challenged the intellectuals to conceptualize Pan-Africanism in ways that transcend their previous philosophical preoccupation with Europe and European standards, so that Pan-African humanism can be part of the new universal culture of emancipation.

This chapter traces the objective conditions out of which Pan-Africanism emerged in this century. The dismantling of apartheid opens possibilities for new conceptions of Pan-African liberation, and the prospect of a new political confederation in Southern Africa to organize reconstruction offers possibilities for a new kind of union based on popular groups.

Pan-Africanism in the Era of the Partitioning of Africa

The concept of Pan-Africanism has undergone many changes during this century in the face of the objective conditions of the underdevelopment of Africa and racial oppression in the West. Decisive periods in this progression are the era of the partitioning of Africa, the impact of the two world wars, the depression of the 1930s and the Italian invasion of Abyssinia, the period of political independence, the period of recolonization under the management of the International Monetary Fund and the battles to dismantle apartheid. Given the conditions facing African people, the forms of Pan-Africanist organization changed over time, with the intellectuals being the leading spokespersons in the period before political independence. In this sense, the record of the Pan-African movement has been dominated by the reports of meetings and congresses held since 1900.[3]

Pan-African ideas have always existed at different levels, and a new task facing scholars is to organize the research necessary to understand Pan-African consciousness as it has manifested itself in village communities and been disseminated through oral history, songs, stories, dances and other cultural media. Cheikh Anta Diop, in his study of linguistics, opened one window onto the cultural unity of Africa. This unity, which was ignored by colonial scholarship, proved to be the fountain of resistance to European domination and inspired all the social movements in Africa and overseas.

From the outset, those Africans educated and literate in European languages sought to use whatever tools necessary to give expression to this unity. One of the first forms of this expression was Ethiopianism, which was invoked by African preachers both on the continent and in the diaspora to reflect African continuities via the quest for independent religious reflection. This Ethiopianism can now be analyzed in the context of the impact of the missionaries, who were paving the way for colonial expansion and partition. Christianity in its European form carried with it the cultural arrogance of Europe, in that missionaries believed that they were civilizing non-whites even if this salvation justified the slave trade and slavery. In response, preachers in Southern Africa, the Caribbean and North America articulated Ethiopianism as one of the earliest overt forms of Pan-Africanism in an effort to tap the resentment of the African masses.

This response was not, however, adequate to meet the ideological assault of capitalism in the era of monopoly. The struggle against the political, economic and cultural imperatives of imperialism sharpened the philosophical basis of Pan-Africanism in the twentieth century. And for much of the century the thrust has been to unite the subjective reservoir of African identity into a social form capable of confronting imperialism in all its forms.

Modern imperialism has its roots in the tremendous technological changes in the organization of production in Western Europe and its extension in North America. The application of science and technology to production linked factory conditions in Europe and North America to resources of raw materials and labor around the world. The expansion, domination and partition of the world that ensued in the latter half of the nineteenth century led to the partitioning of the African continent.[4] Formal division was sealed at the Congress of Berlin in 1884–85 and was part of a larger enterprise in which the European and North American powers dominated the economies of Asia, North America, Africa and Australasia. These economic changes were accompanied in the ideological sphere by ideas of Western progress, free enterprise, democracy, Christian salvation and white superiority, packaged together and claimed as universal truths by European ideologues. This ideological project set the intellectual agenda of the twentieth century by falsifying the role played by Africans and ignoring their contributions to science, culture, philosophy and religion. A 'scientific' racism that was embryonic at the time of the slave trade was deepened to justify military expansion in Africa and to legitimate the brutal massacre of Africans and other non-whites. The ideation system of Eurocentrism was thus built on both the concrete conditions of the technical advances of capitalism and on the distortions of human development that imprisoned Africans everywhere in the cell of inferiority and insult.

The first Pan-Africanist intellectuals at the turn of the century took up the challenge to reverse the falsifications that were reproduced in European languages and culture.[5] Africans such as W.E.B. Du Bois, Edward Blyden, Robert Love and Sylvester Williams challenged the Eurocentric cultural assault, but did not have the resources to link their intellectual resistance to the cultural resistance of the African peoples. Even with this limitation, these Pan-Africanists made a fundamental contribution to the intellectual culture of Pan-African liberation.[6] W.E.B. Du Bois set a standard for intellectual inquiry and research linking Africans in America to other Africans in the West and to the African continent that has yet to be matched within the institutions of African-American studies in North America.

The first Pan-African Congresses, beginning in 1900, were marked by the appeals of intellectuals to the European powers to act more humanely towards Africans. But the impact of World War I on Europe and Africa demonstrated that the imperatives of capital accumulation wrought destruction and violence, and that the colonial metropoles would be unresponsive to appeals to reason and morality.[7] World War I also deepened the integration of African societies into the world economy and unleashed a major population movement of Africans in the West, especially in North America. The war thus brought about a dislocation by capital of the self-organization and self-mobilization of the African masses in all parts of the globe.[8]

Garveyism as Pan-Africanism Among the Producers

While intellectuals responded to the contradictions within the social system as they engaged in the reproduction of knowledge, Garveyism was the profound response of the masses to racism, war, lynching and the imperialist partition of Africa. How to confront the ideology of white supremacy, with its military and economic consequences for the African peoples, was the challenge taken up by the Garvey movement. Thus far the nature of intellectual work in North America, with its emphasis on the role of great men in history, has studied the Garvey movement with a focus on the strengths and weaknesses of Marcus Garvey, the Jamaican immigrant who was the titular head of the movement. But closer studies of this Pan-African response would demonstrate that this movement was not the creation of an individual, but the response of a people searching for self-discovery.[9]

The nature of the Garveyite response reflected how opposition to racism and racial domination had internalized the intellectual culture of the West. Though Garveyism was one brand of Pan-African thought seeking to build a tradition of liberation on the African cultural roots of the masses, the Universal Negro Improvement Association in its very nomenclature accepted the philosophical tenets of Western Europe and North America. Nevertheless, Garveyism was the most advanced conception of Pan-Africanism in the period after World War I.

The cultural outpouring of the oppressed Blacks in the US during this massive dislocation was one of the high points of American culture this century, for it was a period when the spirit of liberation opened up the appetite of the oppressed for self-discovery. Garveyism was one component of this process, and the vibrancy of the UNIA was apparent in the way in which Garveyites brought together diverse social forces, essentially the most oppressed sections of the Black community: working people, independent trade unionists, pacifists, cultural nationalists, women liberation fighters, militant self-help groups, socialists, church organizations and a whole host of unorganized Black folk. Black workers in the US had acquired the social weight and organizational experience to push forward the claims of African liberation and Black dignity.

Garveyism used the propaganda and organizational techniques available at that time to give meaning to the claim that the UNIA spoke for the liberation of all Blacks and for the liberation of the African continent. Through the *Negro World,* whose unique brand of radical journalism reached even those unable to read and write in English, the UNIA reached Africa and became the first Pan-African movement embracing Africans both on the continent and overseas. Garveyism and the UNIA instilled in the minds of the Africans of the West the principle that their freedom was inextricably bound up with the freedom of the African continent.

In Africa itself, the objective conditions of colonial rule ensured that the UNIA did not have the mass following that it had in the US or the Caribbean, though it was one of the first organizations to have branches and adherents all across the continent.[10] The spontaneous rebellions in Africa were still linked to the old precolonial ruling class, who resisted colonialism in order to restore their former economic and military positions. The spontaneous resistance of the Ashanti, Bambaata, Maji Maji, Nyabingi and other revolts was not then able to conceptualize resistance as a continental problem. It was in South Africa, where exploitation of mineral resources had organized segregation on a scale similar to that in the US, that the program of African redemption took root. The African National Congress, which was formed in the Union of South Africa in 1912, was one of the first organizations to emphasize the liberation of Africa as part of its political mobilization.

Whatever the weaknesses of the UNIA, its conception of African redemption spoke a language that the poor understood and the colonial overlords feared. France and Britain moved decisively to derail Pan-African linkages, and the leadership of the movement splintered when the US government moved to prosecute Marcus Garvey. But as revolutionary as the UNIA program was at the time, particularly in calling for the liberation of Africa by force, African workers and small farmers did not then have the organizational capacity then to give meaning to the call for independence. However, Garveyism planted a seed, and the urban workers, the seamen, small traders and a few intellectuals were attracted to the UNIA's symbols of racial pride. The Garvey appeal for redemption served as a beacon for a generation of Africans that used the ideas of the UNIA as a reference point in the struggle for political independence, but this struggle had to await the maturation of the social forces most capable of confronting the colonial state machinery.

The question posed earlier by Rodney in the formulation of Pan-African liberation is here relevant: Which were the silent classes in Africa on whose behalf the claims of Pan-African liberation were being made?

Pan-Africanism and Popular Resistance

By the end of World War I, after the structures of colonial administration and economic production had been established, the balance between humans, domesticated animals and agricultural land on the one hand, and wild game, tsetse flies and untamed forests, on the other, had shifted in favor of the latter.[11] One of the major problems exacerbated by colonialism was ecological imbalance, which is now being compounded by desertification, the results of soil exhaustion and in some cases overgrazing. Henceforth Pan-African liberation would have to cope with not only the absence of political independence, but also with the environmental degradation caused by the colonial mining corporations and plantations.

After the military reverses following open revolts in the period up to 1920, African resistance went underground and then took on religious/cultural forms. Or, in the words of Amilcar Cabral, African culture went underground like a seed awaiting germination. These seeds showed themselves as independent African religions, because other cultural forms were persecuted as witchcraft. Overt opposition took spiritual forms in what is now called in academic literature the African Independent Church Movement. These movements, the Mourides in West Africa, the John Chilembwe movement in Malawi, the Ethiopian movement in South Africa, Harry Thuku in Kenya or Simon Kimbangu in the Congo sought recourse to African cultural forms to develop forms of religious expression to oppose colonial rule.

Kimbangism and other forms of resistance represented the search for a conceptual framework outside of the ideation system of the European views of reason, progress and individual accumulation. The symbols and spiritual autonomy invoked by these movements were sophisticated forms of opposition to European domination. Like the Rastafari movement in the Caribbean, these movements were revolts against oppression and part of the sociopolitical protest engendered by the presence of Europeans and the system of colonialism.[12] Current scholarship in Africa distinguishes between the form and the content of the early phase of resistance. For though the protests were couched in the language of tradition and religion, they sprang from the oppressive conditions of forced labor, land alienation, racial discrimination and colonial taxation.

As Walter Rodney wrote, 'A people's consciousness is heightened by knowledge of the dignity and determination of their foreparents.'[13] In this sense the nationalist protest of the postwar period in Africa formed a common thread with earlier resistance by those who have been derided as millenarians. It is now acknowledged that the nationalism of the anticolonial revolts that ushered in independence had its roots deep in the African past, 'and that the political parties that won independence in so many countries were only the end product of a continuous process of resistance which took diverse forms: notably, armed struggle, independent churches, welfare associations, peasant crop hold ups and strikes by wage earners.'[14]

The opposition of the popular masses to Eurocentrism and colonial rule represented a profound response, but this kind of resistance could not at that time take political leadership in the struggle for independence. The intellectual and organizational tasks necessary for the conquest of political independence were undertaken by the Pan-African intelligentsia, which had developed in the period after Garveyism. At this time Pan-African liberation was equated with political independence. This position was articulated most clearly in the words of Kwame Nkrumah: 'Seek ye first the Political Kingdom and all will be added to thee.'

Pan-Africanism and Eurocentrism

The Pan-African intellectuals who emerged during the interwar period were confronted with a dominant European culture that centralized the changes in Europe during the Renaissance and that did not acknowledge Europe's debt to the cultures and transformations that had taken place in Africa, China and India for 4,000 years before the period of the industrial revolution in Europe. These intellectuals were therefore concerned with this distortion of human history, and, since they lacked an organic link to popular cultural resistance, they resisted Eurocentrism by pointing to the glories of the great kingdoms of Africa. The Pan-Africanists thus implicitly accepted the Eurocentric ideation system: If Europe had kings and emperors, it was necessary to draw attention to Egypt, Songhai, Zimbabwe, Ghana and Benin. Such a recollection of African greatness was a liberating experience in the era of colonialism, and served to mobilize anticolonial consciousness. This could be seen concretely in the Caribbean, where the African masses rejected the English king in favor of the African Emperor of Ethiopia. It was therefore not insignificant that the Rastafari as one form of cultural expression arose in the context of the Italian invasion of Abyssinia in 1935.

The invasion of Abyssinia was also a rallying point for Pan-Africanists everywhere, because Abyssinia was the oldest independent African society. Positive references to Ethiopia in the Bible had struck a responsive chord among Christianized Africans, so much so that when peasants in Southern Africa heard about the invasion they began to march up the continent to help to liberate Abyssinia, only to be turned back by the British. Poor and rural Africans thus responded to this invasion in ways that increased the spiritual, political and cultural bonds between Africans.[16]

The response of educated Africans all over the continent and beyond precipitated the formation of social movements calling for independence. The pre-eminent organization at this time was the International African Service Bureau in London. The group mobilized support for Emperor Haile Selassie and articulated demands for self-determination in Africa and the Caribbean. The group had a major influence on West African students, and luminaries such as George Padmore, C.L.R. James and Jomo Kenyatta were prominent. Their intellectual output proved a major inspiration to the national liberation movement. Padmore, James, Du Bois and many others contributed to the creation of a brand of Pan-African scholarship that sought to correct some of the Eurocentric falsifications of history. It was in this anticolonial intellectual and political climate that the Fifth Pan-African Congress was held in Manchester in 1945.

The spiritual and cultural bonds of the African peoples transcended the language barriers imposed by the French, Belgians, English and the Portuguese.[17] Pan-African liberation was articulated by many intellectuals, and the Négritude movement among Caribbean and French-speaking Africans also exalted the African past and the 'African Personality'. Négritude as an important component of Pan-African thought sought to grasp the cultural unity of Africa as reflected in the cultural personality of the African peoples. However, the more far-sighted of those scholars whose work embraced Négritude were aware that 'the restoration of the cultural personality of the African and black peoples in general can only be achieved through *struggle*'.[18]

At the philosophical level, unfortunately, the richness of the contributions of Pan-African/Négritude scholars has been overshadowed by those who accepted racialism by replacing one set of myths of the inferiority of the Africans with another set of myths that accepted the fundamental distinction between the races that had become a part of European culture. The centrality of history, of material conditions and the cultural expressions that formed the basis of the writings of intellectuals such as Aimé Césaire and Frantz Fanon were replaced by the concept of the 'existential African'. They accepted the vaunted rationality of Europe and argued that 'if Europeans were rational, then Africans had rhythm and emotion.' One set of myths replaced another set of myths as they reified the concept of race and gave it a place in historical terms which reinforced Eurocentrism.

The unscientific assumptions about race and the romantic outlook of some exponents of Négritude became clearer when the bearers of these ideas became a stumbling block to African liberation in Haiti and in Senegal. In Haiti, the Négritude of 'Papa Doc' Duvalier was the intellectual cover for brutal exploitation. This exploitation continued for more than two decades, with this history making it clear that the artificial classification of the division between Blacks, whites and mulattos imposes a distortion on human history.

Pan-African Liberation and the Struggle Against Racism

By the beginning of the twentieth century the exploitation of Africa and the racism of Europe had become so entrenched that race was given pseudo-scientific and theological justification. Racist philosophy produced not only a society of individual racists but a society in which white racism was so all-pervasive that it seemed a natural fact. Societies that developed on the basis of the trade in Africans had to develop a literature to justify the slave trade and slavery. In particular, English literature laid the basis for the general European conception of Black people; 'for the Dutch, the French and the Germans did not lag behind their English counterparts in providing the stereotypes and distortions which comprise racism.'

When television and other visual media carried this distortion into film and other modern forms, racism and anti-Black ideas were given visual images of the rational white and the irrational, shuffling, docile and uncivilized African. Tarzan and his heirs thus ensured that race consciousness would be an aspect of Pan-African consciousness. This trend was clear to the far-sighted. At the turn of the twentieth century, W.E.B. Du Bois had declared that the 'problem of the twentieth century was the problem of the color line.' Du Bois was an internationalist and Pan-Africanist who linked the question of African liberation to the emancipation of oppressed peoples in Asia, Latin America and the Caribbean. His concept of the battle against racism was a far cry from the kind of Afrocentric scholarship that accepts the unscientific classification of the races.

As one component of the battle against oppression, the struggle around the race question occupied a significant place in the struggles of the century. Yet the category of race was itself created in the process of exploitation. It required a materialist intellectual framework to be able to perceive that the division of the world into races has been one way of justifying unequal human relations. Individual Pan-Africanists attempted to understand this limitation with the preoccupation with race, but such a breakthrough was not possible at the level of individual enlightenment: it was only possible given the maturation of the social forces most able to generate the intellectual framework of the materialist history of humanity.

Such a materialist history, one that rises above the limitations of a Eurocentric vision of historical materialism, is now possible, for not only have the African peoples retaken their place in history and are in the process of closing the last laboratory of racism in South Africa, but there is enough evidence, documents and scientific breakthroughs in all fields to write a clear history of humanity. In the words of Diop: 'The West is fully aware of this, but it lacks the intellectual and moral courage required, and this is why the textbooks are deliberately muddled. It then devolves on us as Africans to rewrite the entire history of mankind for our own edification and that of others.'[19] Diop's challenge is now being taken up by African scholars, for this task had to await the decolonization of the continent.

Pan-Africanism and Independence

The quest for political independence marked the high point of the African liberation struggle during this century. During World War II the political and social consciousness of the African poor was transformed as the war increased the demand for labor and the compulsion of the colonial state intensified. Out of this process of intensified exploitation, new social forces emerged in Africa to chart the path of Pan-African liberation. It was the spontaneous and organized activities of the workers, the poor peasants, the school teachers and traders that sped the process of political independence in Africa. The push for sovereignty even within the confines of the states carved out at ythe 1884–85 Berlin conference brought a social movement embracing all classes and strata. Whether through armed struggles in Algeria, Kenya, Zimbabwe, South Africa, Mozambique, Guinea-Bissau, Angola and the Cameroon or the general strikes by workers and holding back cash crops by farmers, the formation of a political alliance to achieve political independence marked a watershed in African history. In turn this process sharpened the anti-racist struggles in the US. During this period the view was that African liberation was coterminous with political independence. But it was only for a brief moment, for the mass of producers learned that independence could not be built on the basis of the old colonial economy within the old colonial boundaries, and that liberation would have to be redefined.

When Ghana became independent in 1957, the French and the Portuguese were then not even thinking of giving up their overt form of colonialism in Africa. But the winds of change swept the continent and clarified the new tasks of liberation. These tasks and the links between African peoples were articulated at the All-African Peoples Congress, which was held in Ghana in 1958. This was one of the most important Pan-African congresses, for it brought together movements involved in the actual fight for independence. The armed struggles in Kenya had pushed this conference from calling for peaceful struggle for independence to the call for independence by any means. It was here also that Patrice Lumumba and the Congolese movement were able to make concrete links with other movements in struggle.[20]

Movements in struggle and parties in government in newly independent countries began to clarify the distinctions between different social forces. The leaders who had articulated a brand of Pan-Africanism/Négritude but had internalized the concepts of European development demobilized the popular masses after independence.[21] Outstanding leaders of the Fifth Pan-African Congress (in the English-speaking world) and the Rassemblement Democratique Africaine (which advocated self-rule for the whole of French

West Africa) who had formulated militant declarations they returned home to power, carrying with them the conception of modernization based on Western European consumption models.

Independence for many of these leaders meant catching up with Europe and strengthening the old institutions of the colonial state, which were built for repression. Expanding the armed forces and the bureaucracy and building prestige projects such as airports to link themselves to the West became the barometers of progress. Because history to many of these leaders was the history of kings and kingdoms, they conceptualized development based not on the knowledge and skills of the producers but on creating the equivalent of a new ruling dynasty. One of the more crude among these leaders even crowned himself emperor.

Modernization theory and the myth of the free market became the new salvation in the era of independence. Modernization was presented in both socialist and capitalist guises, depending on the rhetoric of the leadership. This approach looked on the producers as 'traditional', as obstacles standing in the path of nation building and developing the productive forces. It was not part of the calculation of this new leadership that the collective knowledge of the people accumulated over 10,000 years should be the basis for the launching of a new society in Africa.

Recent Egyptian history provides an excellent example of how the leadership of the independence movement failed to mobilize the people on the basis of their history and collective experience. For a short while, the leadership under Nasser provided a radical alternative, partly because of the confrontation with the West over the Suez and over the question of Israel, the rights of the Palestinians and the question of African liberation. However, despite his militancy Nasser did not fully mobilize the people to the point where the social aspirations of the Egyptian revolution could carry them to new stages of social emancipation. Nasser talked about socialist construction, but he did not entrust this task to the workers and small farmers; instead he deepened his dependence on external forces while building new monuments of modernization, a large army, a huge dam and industrial projects depending on foreign expertise. Without a coherent social and political plan, Nasserism did not survive Nasser, in spite of the positive legacy of anti-imperialism under his leadership. Nasser's political heirs demonstrated that dependence on capitalist or socialist states was equal to underdevelopment and depoliticization of the poor. While it was important to show that Egypt was the cradle of human transformation, this was not sufficient to build a new society. Political retrogression and the Islamic fundamentalism prevailing in North Africa today are manifestations of the spiritual void left by the development ideology of the leaders of the independence movement.

African Independence and African Unity

At the height of the Pan-African movement, its leading spokespersons examined the question of the political union of Africa to redress the creation of ministates at the Berlin Congress. A political union based on the cultural unity of African peoples was to be the framework for a new mode of economic development. Kwame Nkrumah addressed this issue very early when he said that the independence of Ghana was meaningless outside the context of the full liberation of the continent. The imperatives of popular consciousness pushed the leaders of the new states to the formation of the Organization of African Unity. Vincent B. Thompson, in his excellent study *Africa and Unity,* detailed the compromises that went into the formation of this organization, and Walter Rodney grasped the deep roots which the concept of Pan-African unity had taken among the masses when he observed:

> It is a tribute to the momentum of Pan-Africanism that the OAU had to be formed. The idea of Pan-Africanism had taken deep roots, and it had to be given expression, if only in the form of a consultative international assembly. This indicates a higher level of continental political coordination than was to be found in Latin America during the period when the old colonial regimes there were demolished. It is also true that no imperialist power is a voting member of the organization, in the way that the United States is entrenched within the Organization of American States. Nevertheless, the OAU does far more to frustrate than to realize the concept of African Unity.[22]

The OAU as a union of states continues to support the OAU Liberation Committee, but in the main African leaders place more emphasis on the annual meeting between France and her allies in Africa than on the OAU meetings.

The various European powers in fact not only divided Africa according to regional spheres of influence, but even within African states they carve out areas for 'development': this has especially been the case in the Congo, which was stabilized to become Zaire. From the outset, the issue of the Congo was clearly a test for whether those who conceptualized liberation would stand up to external manipulation and subversion. The manipulation of the African ministates and the United Nations in the process of assassinating Patrice Lumumba is part of the historical record. Zaire became a base for subversion of African independence from the era of the assassination of Lumumba and continued to play this role up to the time of the decolonization of Angola.[23] When the white South Africans were finally defeated in Angola,[24] external forces (primarily the US) continued to use Kamina in Zaire as a base for undermining struggles for liberation in Southern Africa. The OAU has, however, been unable to challenge the establishment of foreign military bases in Africa. The African leadership has also been silent on the conditions of racism and segregation in Europe and North America.

Not only has the OAU been committed to the inherited colonial boundaries and structures, it also buttresses the exploitative social systems that prevail across the continent. The clause of non-interference in the internal affairs of member states has been used to silence opposition in Africa to dictators who have killed large numbers of Africans. Leaders such as Idi Amin, Jean Bokassa and Sékou Touré gained international notoriety for their brutal treatment of Africans, yet African peoples on the continent could not protest. When the destruction in Uganda spilled over into Tanzania and the Tanzanians intervened, the OAU equivocated, and many African leaders gave political and moral support to Idi Amin. Many of those who theorize Pan-Africanism have forgotten a central point made by Walter Rodney: 'One of the cardinal principles of Pan-Africanism is that the people of one part of Africa are responsible for the freedom and liberation of their brothers and sisters in other parts of Africa; and indeed black people everywhere were to accept the same responsibility.'[25]

The OAU was organized to help speed the anti-colonial struggle, but the class divisions on the continent became clear as some African leaders attempted to colonize other African states. Morocco, which had supported the Algerian struggle for independence, tried to colonize the Western Sahara. This brazen form of colonialism was too much for some members of the OAU to remain silent, and when the OAU recognized the rights of the Saharwi Arab Democratic Republic, Morocco left the OAU.

The breakdown of all-class unity in the new African states was even more clear in the field of economic cooperation. Many forms of informal trade continue across borders, but this kind of trade is frowned upon by the leaders and their imperial overlords because the revenue from this informal trade circulates among the people instead of among the ruling classes and the transnational banking system. International financial institutions such as the World Bank talk about the development of market forces but discourage African markets and trade to ensure that Africans continue to produce raw materials and food for Europe and North America. Experiments in African unity such as the East African Community and the Economic Confederation of West African States foundered, because they were conceived not as instruments for political unity but as entities to facilitate greater control by transnational capital.

All over the continent the producers searched for new sources of livelihood. However, one-party rule and state control robbed the producers of the right to organize as workers, peasants, women, students, intellectuals or traders. This form of political leadership fomented internal divisions to the point of civil wars engulfed the continent. The politicization of region, religion and ethnicity accelerated as economic retrogression was compounded by political authoritarianism.

In the absence of real forums for democratic expression and participation, the people lost the political experience that they had gained in the period after World War II. With this demobilization and depoliticization, thinking became subversive to the point where some of the foremost intellectuals were forced to leave the continent as exiles. However, repression did not stifle their search for intellectual freedom as a component of their people's freedom. Meeting in the midst of war-torn Chad in 1989, African intellectuals assigned themselves the task of linking historical research to the democratization of knowledge and social commitment.[26]

Pan-African Liberation and the Dispersed Africans

In the midst of the contemporary economic crisis, when images of famine, war and epidemic dominate the world news, there has been a conscious effort to cut the progressive links that developed in the era of Malcolm X between African organizations and groups in the Caribbean and the US. The relations between African states and the neocolonial leaders in the Caribbean were nowhere clearer than in the context of the Sixth Pan-African Congress.

Progressive Pan-Africanists had called for a meeting of Pan-Africanists to chart a new course for liberation in the 1970s. The euphoria surrounding the congress soon abated when it became clear that the meeting was to be another OAU-type gathering with elements representing leaders like Forbes Burnham and Eric Gairy. Those Pan-Africanists carrying out the struggle for liberation in the Caribbean were excluded from the meeting, and in an act of solidarity C.L.R. James boycotted it.

This episode helped to clarify to many Pan-Africanists in the US that a line had to be drawn between those who served the interests of the working people and those who manipulated the symbols and language of Pan-Africanism to perpetuate exploitation. Inside the African-American delegation to the Sixth Pan-African Congress, the fissures over crude nationalism were about to erupt as the government of the United States sought to mobilize the negative aspects of race consciousness to support one ethnic faction in Angola. Inside the United States the popular outpouring of the civil rights movement and the positive identification with Africa was slowly domesticated when the more internationalist elements of the civil rights movement were silenced. The elevation of Black elected representatives inside the established political structures was positive in the short run, but in the long run negative in that many of these leaders supported US policies towards Africa. A small core of Pan-African activists organized African Liberation Day to keep African issues alive and used the few resources available to combat falsifications of African history and contemporary African realities.

Pan-Africanism in the Caribbean also had to deal with leaders who had reached the summit of their ambition with their occupation of the seat of power. Moreover, in Guyana and Trinidad, the Pan-African consciousness of the working people was exploited to divide the Indian and African workers. It was in this struggle that Walter Rodney, a Pan-African, Pan-Caribbean thinker, began to conceptualize the kind of internationalism that underlay Pan-African humanism. His commitment to democratic practice and the self-organization of the African poor was a threat to those who manipulated the slogans of Pan-African unity, and he was assassinated by a government that claimed to be in the forefront of the struggle for African liberation.

In reaction to this betrayal, ordinary working people in the Caribbean sought other means of expressing Pan-African culture and politics. The retention of African spiritual values since the time of colonialism had prevented Europe from destroying the rich cultural values of the African population in the West. Whether in Cuba, Brazil, Surinam or Haiti, African religious forms survived, though persecuted by officialdom and dismissed as millenarian by anthropologists. African religious thought and practice was frowned upon all over the Americas, but this was one concrete form of resistance to Eurocentric ideas and a resource from which people of African descent could draw.

The Rastafari movement in the Caribbean exploded in religious and cultural forms to confront the social decay in the Caribbean and the alienation of the youth. Starting as a rebellion against Babylon (a word that signified oppression by both white and Black) Rastafarianism inspired an international campaign against injustice by calling on peoples everywhere to 'Get up, stand up for their rights.' Cultural spokespersons such as Bob Marley sang of the need for a new kind of African unity, and it was through the popularity of reggae music that the Pan-African ideas of a new era were spread. Reggae found a fertile base among a section of the African youth that was mobile, alert and groping for new ways to understand contemporary realities. They were aware of the cultural assault of the West and the promotion of consumer values packaged in films and music. It was part of a paradoxical unity of opposites that it was through the same Western media complex that artists like Bob Marley and Alpha Blondy took their message to the youth.

The North American media had long used the cultural reservoir of Africans in the Americas to further the cause of cultural imperialism – as evident in the ways in which the United States Information Agency uses the creativity of the African-American population to sell the dream of the enterprising nature of capitalism and the myth of progress. Hence the memories of slavery, like those recounted in Alex Haley's novel *Roots,* or the essential unity of the struggles of African women, as depicted in the Alice Walker's *The Color Purple,* are packaged as products of the culture of capital. But as in all areas of cultural reproduction – art, music, poetry, dance, film and the novel – the anti-capitalist and anti-racist component of Black American music, theater and film forced itself onto the world stage and became an important aspect of Pan-African expression in the struggle of humanity to transcend racial classifications. It was in this complex of information and disinformation that cultural figures such as Stevie Wonder, Fela Ransome Kuti, Mbilia Bel, Alpha Blondy and countless others maintained the traditions of militant resistance.

Bob Marley thus inspired a generation of African youths, singing songs to mobilize freedom fighters everywhere and conveying the message of self-emancipation with the simple words:

> Emancipate yourself from Mental Slavery
> None but ourselves can free our minds.
> Have no fear for atomic energy
> For none of them can stop the time.

Pan-Africanists who kept abreast of the popular culture recognized the contribution of the Rastafari despite the contradictions inherent in deifying a deposed African monarch. In the words of one of the foremost Caribbean Pan-Africanists, Eusi Kwayana, 'The power of art that Bob Marley's music represented [did] more to popularize the real issues of African liberation than several decades of backbreaking work by Pan-Africanists and international revolutionaries.'

Pan-African Liberation and the Struggle Against Apartheid

By the closing decade of the century, South African apartheid stood as a major stumbling block to the liberation and political development of Africa. South African expansion and military intervention challenged Africa and humanity to resist the last vestiges of white supremacy, but in order for this challenge to register as part of the thrust for a new universalism, it was the task of African people to take up the struggle for liberation. And indeed, Africans in their daily struggles to affirm their dignity ensured that the questions that kept Pan-African liberation alive were the questions of social transformation of the region after apartheid was ended and the full independence of Africa achieved. The politicization and mobilization of the South African youth represented the pivot of the repoliticization of the oppressed masses in Africa.

That the question of apartheid was internationalized beyond the Pan-African constituency was in no small measure because of the spread of the self-organization and self-mobilization of the youth, workers, clergy, and women. The rise of grassroots governance dictated that the conception of liberation had gone beyond the question of majority rule or the issue of Africans replacing whites in the old state apparatus. Political struggles, ideological debates, armed confrontation and the international campaign for sanctions against South Africa sharpened the internationalist tenets of Pan-Africanism and exposed the negative brand of a nationalism based on a narrow all-class appeal. For this reason those who articulated a limited vision of Pan-Africanism were sidelined in one of the most important Pan-African struggles this century.

Pan-Africanism continues to be a potent force for mobilizing the poor, and this can be seen in small instances such as in the aftermath of the death of Samora Machel of Mozambique, when the cultural outpourings of the masses pushed the leadership to withstand apartheid. This Pan-Africanism from below is different from the intellectual and philosophical formulations of modernization, which condemn the producers to poverty. The failure of the International Monetary Fund and its African allies has shown that an alternate mode of economic development is necessary to achieve the social emancipation of Africa.

The South African resistance, in struggling to assert the dignity and self-worth of Africans, embraced the kind of race consciousness promoted by early Pan-African scholars, but developed beyond that point when those in the struggle saw that what was necessary was the creation of a democratic, nonracial society. This was, and remains, a challenge to humanity, because no models for this kind of democracy exist. The ideological and political tools necessary for creating this kind of society were instead being sharpened in the midst of the worst repression. So profound was the political transformation of this process that all the slogans and forms of struggle of previous eras had to be reevaluated. This necessity emerged all the more clearly after those movements that fought for independence retreated from the power of the popular masses once in power. Guerrilla movements, whether in Mozambique, Zimbabwe, Angola or Uganda, had been able to win military victories, but these victories did not empower the mass of the producers. The espousal of Marxism-Leninism as a state ideology remained empty because these attempts at following 'scientific' doctrine were not based on the history and culture of Africa.

The crisis in Africa with famine, war and destabilization enabled those in the forefront of African liberation to analyze the pitfalls of the leaders of the independence era. It required an understanding of the transformation of the cultural values so that the knowledge of the producers could be harnessed the new forms of association would be based on their capabilities. The dynamics of destabilization, disinformation, war, IMF management, external subversion and psychological warfare existed all over the African world, and the people showed by their collective resistance that the African liberation struggle can advance the liberation of humanity. In this search for a new social order Pan-African liberation was part of a new universalism and Pan-African humanism.

The Challenges Ahead

The tasks of African liberation are formidable and require a new theory of social reality. Small steps are being made with the social commitment of those African intellectuals who see liberation not as the work of individual leaders but as part of the process of self-mobilization and self-organization of the African peoples. New forms of consciousness have appeared at each period in the struggle for African liberation – often taking the form of attempts to hold on to the precolonial cosmic world. This kind of consciousness by itself cannot take the people forward, and an urgent task is to link the development of science and technology to the skills and knowledge of the African peoples. Cheik Anta Diop, as a nuclear physicist, was most sensitive to the dialectic of the positive and the negative in the traditional African forms of transmitting knowledge. He drew attention to the need to harness the positive without reinforcing the negative:

> The system of initiation whereby knowledge is transmitted in African societies is typically Egyptian. Yet this system which is generalized in African societies is not the best way to transmit or generalize scientific knowledge. Nor does this system allow for critical examination of scientific theories. This has been extremely harmful to the technological and social development of traditional black societies.[28]

This challenge was posed in the face of the scientific 'rationality' of capitalism, which has been used to justify the irrational destruction of human beings and the natural environment. Diop's work was part of a larger discussion of African cultures in relation to social transformation, but unfortunately the domestication of African-American scholarship in North America seeks to cut off young African-Americans from the study of Africa. The study of Africa in Africa and overseas will be part of the effort to galvanize the African peoples to make an original statement on social emancipation.

The lessons of the past century are that even the most advanced Pan-African thinkers had tended to despise African cultural expressions, whose content was equated with the ignorance and superstition of the Periphery, while viewing knowledge as being transferred from the European Center. Wamba dia Wamba, in his analysis of the relationship between culture and revolution in the African world, has observed:

> It seems like none of the modernizers in Africa has dared to learn from the surviving communities of gatherers and hunters: what had made the latter able to defy all the processes – since the agricultural revolution – which give rise to despotic communities? The whole dynamics of ameliorative therapy, i.e. man taking over nature to struggle and transform it, has been taken for granted. The whole knowledge process, in imperialist-dominated Africa, has been organized through a social epistemology emphasizing mimetism (mimicry) of the West or the East, routine mechanical learning through diffusionism. One of the results is that even institutions and practices that generate famine, chronic disease, desertifications are seen as developmental. Problems, shortcomings, crises, etc., experienced elsewhere, become not only difficult to avoid, but impossible to perceive ahead of time.[29]

Wamba dia Wamba has thus joined Frantz Fanon, Amilcar Cabral, Eusi Kwayana and Ngugi wa Thiongo, who understood that cultural transformations were at the core of liberation. These individuals, though trained in Western institutions, were part of the embryo of a new intellectual culture which strove for the emancipation of Africans and all oppressed peoples. They form a link with a new intellectual culture that is trying to transcend the ideological constraints of Eurocentrism and Afrocentrism, understanding that 'African paraphrases of models developed elsewhere, and intended to be Afrocentric, have not been discontinuous with, for example, Western civilization.'[30]

The experiences of this century have sharpened the concept of liberation beyond the achievement of independence. With the defeat of apartheid, the major stumbling block to African political unity and social development has been removed. Popular participation, cultural freedom and the development of new forms of social existence remain part of the task to place Africa on the road to alternative forms of economic organization. The political unity of Africa is an elementary precondition for the task of economic change so that the African peoples everywhere can draw strength from the freedom and cultural strength of Africa.

This task is also sharpened by the economic and social marginalization of African peoples in South America. The cultural resistance of African peoples in Brazil, Cuba, Haiti and the rest of the region provide a fertile base for real multiracial democracy. Thus far, however, even those social movements aspiring to achieve democracy continue to predicate development on catching up with Europe and North America. But the models of consumption of the culture of capitalism reserve this mode of consumption for a small minority of humanity in Europe, North America and Japan.

Pan-African liberation in the twenty-first century is thus inscribed in the struggle beyond the culture of capital and the effort to lobotomize humanity into mindless consumers. The liberation of the African peoples is linked to the liberation of other oppressed peoples and sharpens the elements of Pan-African humanism. A Pan-Africanism that seeks to reproduce the chauvinism of European racial categorization has been unable to inspire the kind of humanism necessary for emancipation from racism: the battle against racism cannot continue to accept the unscientific category of race.

Pan-African liberation is not only linked to the quest for a new social system, but also one in which the development of the productive forces is not simply linked to the production of goods but also the creation of new human beings. This perspective of free men and women, of cultural freedom, of harnessing the positive knowledge of the African past, now forms part of the conception of the struggle for Pan-African liberation in the twenty-first century.

Notes

1. Walter Rodney, 'Towards the Sixth Pan African Congress,' in Horace Campbell, ed., *Pan-Africanism,* Toronto 1975.

2. This challenge has been taken up in part by the new direction of research in Africa. See notes of 'A Working Group on the Cultural Dimension of Development in Africa', Bulletin of the Third World Forum, African Office, Dakar, Senegal 1987. See also Samir Amin, *Eurocentrism,* New York 1989.

3. Immanuel Geiss, *The Pan African Movement,* London 1974. See also Vincent B. Thompson, *Africa and Unity: The Revolution of Pan Africanism,* London 1969.

4. The element of racism in the process of partition is analyzed in Walter Rodney, 'The Imperialist Partition of Africa,' *Monthly Review,* (April 1970), pp. 103–14.

5. The images of Africa among African intellectuals in the West are analyzed by Bernard Magubane, *The Ties That Bind: African-American Consciousness of Africa,* Trenton, N. J. 1987.

6. Mildred Fierce, 'African American Interest in Africa and the Interaction with West Africa: The Origins of the Pan African Idea in the USA', Ph.D. thesis, Columbia University, 1976.

7. W.E.B. Du Bois, 'The African Roots of the War', published in *On the Importance of Africa to World History,* New York 1978. This pamphlet, written in 1915, predated Lenin's theses on imperialism and drew attention to the way in which the competition over Africa helped the precipitate World War I.

8. Tony Martin, *The Pan-African Connection: From Slavery to Garvey and Beyond,* Dover, Mass. 1984.

9. For an elaboration of the social forces involved in the Garvey movement, see Tony Martin, *Race First: the Ideological and Organizational Struggles of Marcus Garvey and the Universal Negro Improvement Association,* Westport, Conn. 1976.

10. Robert Hill and Gregory A. Pirio, 'Africa for the Africans: The Garvey Movement in South Africa, 1920–1940,' in Shula Marks and Stanley Trapido, eds, *The Politics of Race, Class and Nationalism in Twentieth-Century South Africa,* London 1987.

11. Helge Kjekshus, *Ecology Control and Economic Development in East African History,* London, 1977.

12. The themes are explored in my book *Rasta and Resistance: From Marcus Garvey to Walter Rodney,* Trenton, N.J. 1987.

13. Walter Rodney, 'The African Revolution', in Paul Buhle, ed., *C.L.R. James: His Life and Work,* Detroit 1981.

14. Ibid.

15. These themes are developed at length in the book *Eurocentrism* by Samir Amin, New York 1989.

16. S.K.B. Asante, *Pan-African Protest: West Africa and the Italo-Ethiopian War, 1934–1941,* London 1971.

17. Eunice Charles, 'Pan-Africanism in French-Speaking West Africa 1945-1960', African Studies Center, Boston University.

18. Quoted from an interview with Cheikh Anta Diop, in Ivan Van Sertima, ed., *Great African Thinkers,* New Brunswick, N.J. 1989.

19. Cheikh Anta Diop, *The African Origin of Civilization: Myth or Reality?,* Mercer Cook, ed., 1974, p. 115.

20. Interview with A.M. Babu on how Tom Mboya was made the chair of the All African Peoples Conference in 1958. Babu related the impact of the Kenyan and Algerian struggles on the deliberations of this conference and the influence of Frantz Fanon as a diplomatic representative of the FLN at this meeting. That the Kenya Land and Freedom Movement was a Pan-African movement and saw itself as such is only now being recorded. See Maina wa Kinyatti, *Kenya's Freedom Struggle: The Dedan Kimathi Papers,* London 1987.

21. Frantz Fanon, *The Wretched of the Earth,* New York 1961.

22. Walter Rodney, 'Towards the Sixth Pan-African Congress', p. 26.

23. Kwame Nkrumah's book of the same name gave some indication of the levels of external involvement in the Congo when the West landed paratroopers to prop up puppet rulers. The importance that the US placed on Zaire can be seen from the book by B. Kaib, *The Congo Cables,* London 1982.

24. The relationship between Cuba and the sovereignty of Angola has to be written in the context of the historic defeat of the South Africans at Cuito Cuanavale. See one short essay by this author in *Monthly Review,* April 1989. The relationship between Cuba and Africa has received both negative and positive responses in the Pan-African movement. For a detailed position from the point of view of an exiled Afro-Cuban, see Carlos Moore, *Castro, the Blacks and Africa,* Berkeley, Calif. 1989.

25. Walter Rodney, p. 12.

26. Report of the seminar Methodological Issues Facing African Historians, CODESRIA Bulletin, Volume 1, 1989.

27. W. Ofuatey-Kudjoe, *PanAfricanism: New Directions in Strategy,* Washington, D.C. 1986.

28. Quoted in Van Sertima, ed., *Great African Thinkers: Cheikh Anta Diop,* p. 245.

29. Wamba dia Wamba, 'Some Remarks on Culture, Development and Revolution in Africa', Mimeo, Dar es Salaam 1989, p. 2.

30. Ibid., p. 1.

16

Pan-Africanism or

Classical African Marxism?

Ntongela Masilela

> For it is perfectly consistent with the spirit of Marxism – with the
> principle that thought reflects its concrete social situation – that
> there should exist several different Marxisms in the world today, each
> answering the specific needs and problems of its own socio-economic
> system: thus one corresponds to the postrevolutionary industrial
> countries of the socialist bloc, another – a kind of peasant Marxism –
> to China and Cuba and the countries of the Third World, while yet
> another tries to deal theoretically with the unique questions raised
> by monopoly capitalism in the West.
>
> *Fredric Jameson, Marxism and Form*

The development in Africa in recent years of an intellectual system known
as Classical African Marxism, historically originating and logically finding
legitimacy in Classical Marxism, is a phenomenon that has fundamentally
transformed the structure of African intellectual history as well as altered
our understanding of African history. Although its mutations and meta-
morphoses have taken place within the historical coordinates of the African
revolution, principally the Algerian Revolution (1954–62) and the Guinean
revolution (1961–74), the historical lineages of Classical African Marxism
traverse the whole twentieth century from their origins in the African diaspora (the Americas, North and South, and the Caribbean).

The formation of Classical African Marxism thus bespeaks of the spiritual unity of the Black world, stretching from Soweto to Dakar, and from
Georgetown through Havana to Atlanta; that is, the movement of the historical forces behind the formation of Classical African Marxism has been
in the opposite and oppositional direction to imperialism, which politically,
culturally and economically devastated Africa.

We can thus trace the intellectual inspiration of Classical African Marxism in Pan-Africanist philosophy, but without doubt the structure of this materialist philosophy was determined by the opening to investigation of the continent of African history by African Marxist historians. It was the aim of Classical Pan-Africanism, which originated in the Americas in the late nineteenth century, to liberate Africa from imperialist domination. It also sought to bring about the historical unity of African people in Africa and in the African diaspora. The emergence of Classical Pan-Africanism was thus a direct response to the Berlin Conference of 1885, at which Africa was divided among various imperial powers. From the moment of its founding, Classical Pan-Africanism waged an unrelenting war to defeat colonialism.

The greatest triumph of Classical Pan-Africanism came in 1960, when nearly half the countries on the African continent attained their political independence. This victory was an outcome of a century-long political and cultural struggle. Yet paradoxically, at the very moment of its greatest triumph Classical Pan-Africanism suffered its fatal defeat, which was to destroy the political legitimacy of this philosophy on the African continent. This defeat was the Congo Crisis of 1960–61, which resulted in three things: the murder of the great African patriot, Patrice Lumumba, whom Jean-Paul Sartre was to memorialize as a Black Jacobin and as a revolutionary without a revolution in his brilliant essay on the crisis. This crisis was also the signal that classical colonialism has assumed a new form, that of neocolonialism, which was even more vicious than its predecessor. And it was the first humiliating defeat of the newly independent African countries, signaling the historical imperative of their political unification. From this moment onwards, Classical Pan-Africanism was superseded by the development of Classical African Marxism.

The aim of Classical Pan-Africanist philosophers and political leaders, among whom were C.L.R. James (Trinidad), George Padmore (Trinidad), Kwame Nkrumah (Ghana) and W.E.B. Du Bois (United States of America) was to expel European imperialism and its various forms of colonialism from Africa, which meant also the expulsion of European history (and all its national variations) that had superimposed itself, intellectually, ideologically and culturally, on African national histories. The fundamental issue for classical Pan-Africanists was to intellectually dynamize the movement of African history and resurrect its past glories. The effect of European imperialism and colonialism had been to break the dialectical movement of African history. In other words, European domination had rendered African history static and petrified, and the task of the Classical Pan-Africanists was to render it more dynamic again. But for this intellectual task to be achievable, colonialism had to be combatted politically on the material plane of social existence. We see, then, that unity of theory and practice was essential for the success of Classical Pan-Africanist philosopy.

It was in this historical circumstance of theoretically interconnecting the various components of African history and politically combatting the presence of colonialism in Africa that Classical Pan-Africanist philosophy encountered Classical Marxism. It was historically impossible for Classical Pan-Africanism to avoid coming to an understanding with Classical Marxism, for after all historical materialism was and is the only science of history, as well as the only philosophy that unites theory and practice in a dialectical movement. And it is only historical materialism that postulates the concrete structural forces and agents or subjects, the working class, through which capitalism can be defeated and as it has been defeated in the great Russian Revolution of 1917. To articulate the forms of African history and implement the means by which colonialism and imperialism could be defeated, Classical Pan-Africanism felt compelled to utilize the intellectual and political instruments available in the historical materialism of Classical Marxism. The Classical Pan-Africanist thinkers thus discovered Classical Marxism as what Jean-Paul Sartre thirty years ago called the living philosophy of our time, or the 'unsurpassable horizon'.

Having discovered historical materialism, all the Classical Pan-Africanist philosophers to a man embraced Classical Marxism. But at the moment they adopted historical materialism, Classical Marxism was deeply imbricated in the complications of European history, where in the Soviet Union Marxism broke into the dominant factions of Stalinism and Trotskyism. This violent factionalism in the interpretation of Classical Marxism was to affect an understanding of Marxism for generations. In Europe, for instance, while Georg Lukàcs gravitated towards Stalinism, Karl Korsch vacillated in between, hoping to formulate an independent position free from Stalinism and Trotskyism. Within the galaxy of Classical Pan-Africanist thinkers and political leaders, C.L.R. James moved in the direction of Trotskyism, while George Padmore moved in counterdirection towards Stalinism.

It was at the moment of this attempted synthesis of Classical Pan-Africanism and Classical Marxism that two of these brilliant thinkers produced two great historical works: C.L.R. James's *The Black Jacobins* and W.E.B. Du Bois's *Black Reconstruction*. In *The Black Jacobins,* James analyzed the success of one of the slave revolts in the context of the history of slave rebellions from antiquity to the present. Much more concretely, he sought to draw historical lessons from the Haitian Revolution for the then continuing resistance to colonialism and imperialism. It should be remembered that the Haitian Revolution (1791–1804) was one of the few defeats of Napoleon Bonaparte before 1815. In other words, the first great defeat of bourgeois France was at the hands of its Black slaves. Bonapartism, which was the mixture of bourgeois democracy and French imperialism and colonialism, was then terrorizing the whole of Europe from Spain to Russia. That Napoleon was disseminating the achievements of the French revolution throughout Europe by the sword cannot be doubted, but he was also the defender of French colonialism. C.L.R. James sought to explain the success of the Haitian Revolution in defeating France where Europe had for some time failed. In a later book, *The History of Pan-African Revolt,* James interconnected the series of Black revolts and rebellions against European imperialism from the Haitian Revolution through the slave revolts in Brazil and America in the nineteenth century, passing through the Bambaata rebellion of 1906 in South Africa and the Maji-Maji rebellion in 1907 in Tanganyika against German imperialism to the Algerian Revolution in the 1950s. James's task was thus to trace the configurations of the forms of African history through the moments of armed resistance to European domination and imperialism. It was a new way of writing a Marxist African history.

Du Bois's book *Black Reconstruction,* one of the monuments of American historiography, explained the failure of the attempt to incorporate black Americans into democratic institutions following the American Civil War of 1860–65. There can be little doubt that the construction of capitalist America was on the basis of the exploitation of Black labor and on the dead bodies of Native Americans. Du Bois put the blame for the continuing discrimination against the people of African ancestry and for their continued exploitation on the failure of the unity of the African-American working class and the European-American working class; this failure was the result of the latter's racism. On the international plane, Du Bois emphasized the need of the Black working class in America to identify and solidarize with the Black working classes in other parts of the African world, particularly in South Africa. In one of his later books, *The World and Africa,* Du Bois convincingly argued through empirical evidence and brilliant theoretical formulations that Egyptian civilization had been constructed by Black Africans, notwithstanding European historiography's racist attempt to incorporate it within 'white civilization'. Without doubt, Egyptian civilization had been the creation of the African genius. Greek civilization, which is the basis of European culture, had schooled itself in Egyptian civilization.

Simultaneous with the publication of these two books, which attempted to give coherence to the mutifariousness of Africa history, Classical Pan-Africanism at the intellectual level split into two wings, one moving in the direction of Stalinism and the other in the direction of Trotskyism. Between them, within an international African context, there was never any hostility, since both aimed to bring about the liberation of Africa from European

colonial domination. James embraced Trotskyism in search of possible socialist democratic forms within an African context. Padmore embraced
Stalinism in order to bring the power of the Communist International into
service on behalf of African peoples in their attempt to overthrow colonialism and imperialism. Both these versions of Marxism were governed by a
particular historical principle, first formulated by Aimé Césaire on the occasion of his resignation from the French Communist Party in dispute over
the latter's refusal to support the Algerian Revolution: 'Marxism should be
put into serving the historical needs of black people, and not that black
people should serve Marxism.' When both James and Padmore recognized
that the institutional forms of Marxism to which each had pledged allegiance no longer served the interests of African people, they broke with
those institutional forms. Padmore confused Communism with Stalinism,
which led eventually to his abandonment of historical materialism. On the
other hand, James never forsook Marxism despite his eventual rejection of
Trotskyism.

Meanwhile, there emerged the first serious attempt by African historians
to map the social geography and conceptual structure of African history.
This process of unveiling, in new and innovative ways, the continent of
African history, was made all the more politically imperative by imperialist
domination, which had broken the structure of African history and covered
in darkness some of Africa's contributions to human culture and civilization. These two great African historians, the Senegalese Marxist historian,
Cheikh Anta Diop, and the Burkina Fasian historian, Joseph Ki-Zerbo,
scientifically revolutionized the structure of African history and ideologically enriched our understanding of it.

To understand the significance of Diop's contribution, recall that from
the time of the Renaissance, and especially since the Romantic era, European historians had systematically denied that Egyptian civilization was in
fact an African civilization – that is, a 'Black civilization'. Philosophers and
historians such as David Hume, Immanuel Kant, Hegel and Ranke took
the view that Egyptian civilization was a 'white civilization' and could not
be an African civilization because, according to them, we Africans had no
concept of history and were living outside history. Cheikh Anta Diop in his
book *The African Origin of Civilization,* which was originally presented as a
doctoral dissertation at the Sorbonne in 1955 and rejected by that institution, argued forcefully with empirical evidence gathered from the writings
of Aristotle, Herodotus, Euclid and others, that Egyptian civilization was
an African civilization. What was self-evidently a historical fact during the
era of Greek civilization, that Egyptian civilization was an African civilization and that without Egyptian civilization Greek civilization would have
been impossible, in the bourgeois era of the Enlightenment and Romanti-

cism, because of racism and the emergence of the modern forms of imperialism, was controverted into a denial of the contribution of the African genius to human civilization. The Marxist praxis of Diop in writing this book was forcefully to reintroduce the contribution of the African genius to human history. In other words, it was a Marxist rectification of a racist bourgeois legacy.

That Cheikh Anta Diop was correct in his critique of the European bourgeois legacy stretching from Hume to Hegel and Ranke has been recently confirmed by Martin Bernal in his book *Black Athena*. This English historian, employing Western scholarly protocols, confirms the thesis of Cheikh Anta Diop that Egyptian civilization was a 'Black civilization'. He shows systematically that Greeks such as Herodotus and Aristotle accepted as in the natural order of things that Egyptian civilization was an African civilization. It is only with the emergence of bourgeois culture that the African was displaced from history. Upon the publication of *Black Athena* in London, a controversy concerning the historical authenticity of its thesis broke out. (By the way, Martin Bernal is the son of the English Marxist historian of science, J. Desmond Bernal.)

Among the various responses to *Black Athena*, the most interesting for us is that of Perry Anderson, the English historian, arguably the most important Marxist historian alive today. In an important review of *Black Athena* in *The Guardian Weekly*, Perry Anderson developed an ingenious thesis that is not as innocent as it appears. Though accepting the arguments of this book as plausible, that Egyptian civilization was instrumental in the emergence of Greek civilization, Anderson argues that the contribution of the former to the latter was not in those fields that went into the making of Western civilization transmitted through the Renaissance leading to the Enlightenment up to the present. Now this is a polite way of denying the contribution of the African genius to the making of human civilization. In other words, Perry Anderson's position is a continuation of the myth of the bourgeois Enlightenment legacy, though in Marxist coloration.

To understand the real meaning of what Anderson is saying it is necessary to look, however rapidly and schematically, at the argument presented in his two great historical works, *Lineages of the Absolutist State* and *Passages from Antiquity to Feudalism*. In both texts, Anderson attempted to answer the question initially posed by Max Weber: Why did capitalism emerge in the Occident – that is, in Europe and not elsewhere?

> Marxism aspires in principle to be a *universal* science – no more
> amenable to merely national or continental ascriptions than any other
> objective cognition of reality.
>
> *Perry Anderson, Considerations on Western Marxism*

Anderson reposed this Weberian question in relation to his observation
about Marxism. The other place where capitalism could have emerged
from feudalism was Japan, a possibility that did not materialize. Anderson
argues that it was the synthesis of the Greco-Roman tradition (democracy,
philosophy and law), transmitted and transformed by the Renaissance, that
made possible the emergence of capitalism and bourgeois civilization. It is
to be supposed, then, that in these fundamental spheres Greek civilization
learned nothing from Egyptian civilization. In other words, in what was
fundamental to 'white civilization', 'Black civilization' contributed nothing.
The whole tenor of Anderson's argument in this review is profoundly
questionable. After all, what follows is presupposed, prefigures, finds gesta-
tion and genesis in what precedes it. Even if these spheres may not have
been important in Egyptian civilization, the very fact that they became the
predominant legacy of Greek civilization to human culture today is also
partly because of the nature of the contribution of 'Black civilization' to
'white civilization' – just as many of the things that are best in Africa today
are the contribution of bourgeois European culture. In saying this, we do
not therefore seek to minimize the tragedy of imperialist intervention in
Africa. We seek only to indicate the Janus-faced nature of the historical
dialectic. A crucial point to stress here is that beyond class societies and
class struggles, that is, in true communism, the distinctions between white
and black will lose their historical significance and content; consequently
those categories will remain as empty shells.

If we have dwelt so long on Perry Anderson, it is because my Marxist
intellectual formation was and is still profoundly influenced by him, and
paradoxically, against Trotskyism. Besides being a great historian, he is
also a master of the English language. The other reason is that, by this
prolonged example, we seek to forestall the possible denial of the contribution of African Marxist culture to international Marxist culture, and the
denial of the existence of Classical African Marxism itself.

The other great African historian we mentioned was Joseph Ki-Zerbo.
Although he is not a Marxist, Ki-Zerbo's contribution to African historiography has been formidable. His book *Die Geschichte Schwarz-Afrikas* and
many of his methodological and historical essays in volume one of the
UNESCO General History of Africa have formulated new periodizations, configurations and conceptual forms of African history. To indicate his impor-

tance in African historiography, it would not be far from the truth to call him the African Ranke. Ki-Zerbo's work is thus a fundamental reference point of African cultural history.

It is clear from what we have said so far that one of the central aims of Classical African Marxism has been to reconstitute the structure of African history, which had been shattered by European imperialism. In other words, the shattering of African history was a dialectical consequence of European capitalist accumulation, which was based on the slave economies in the Caribbean and in the Americas. It is estimated that about 70 million Africans were taken from Africa in the three centuries of modern slavery. About 35 million of these Africans perished in one form or another. This holocaust is hardly mentioned with any seriousness in the historical works of European scholars, even in the works of European Marxists. In the past thirty years certain forms of European Marxism, especially in the English-speaking world, have tirelessly preoccupied themselves with the transition from feudalism to capitalism without fundamentally theorizing the forms of capitalist accumulation. The fact of the matter is that modern European bourgeois civilization was constructed on the dead bodies of 70 million Africans. This is an incontrovertible historical fact. In this context, Walter Benjamin's observation that culture is a product of barbarism and civilization takes on a profound historical truth. Those who doubt the veracity of what we are saying should consult the book *How Europe Underdeveloped Africa,* the work of the Guyanese Marxist Walter Rodney. This text graphically analyzes the forms of European destruction of African civilization, following which the major European bourgeois states occupied the continent and divided it among themselves. To be sure, we African Marxists have still to explain why Africa was incapable of resisting this European penetration.

The preoccupation of Classical Pan-Africanism with the task of constituting a new social geography of African history and its attempted synthesis with Classical Marxism was in many ways a great intellectual achievement. With the achievement of independence by many African countries in 1960, Classical Pan-Africanism had achieved its greatest political aim: the elimination of classical European colonialism from the African continent. But it would be naive and foolish to have expected that European imperialisms and American imperialism would accept this defeat without a historical response. After all, imperialism is a historical process. When its classical form of colonialism was defeated, imperialism responded with a new form, neocolonialism. This, as already stated, Classical Pan-Africanism was unable to defeat. The failure and demise of Classical Pan-Africanism as a *living philosophy* was its defeat by neoimperialism in the Congo Crisis of 1960. Without doubt, the defeat of Africa in the

Congo Crisis was an incalculable catastrophe whose consequences are still present with us in Africa today. One has only to look at the unending chain of neocolonialist regimes stretching from Senegal to Zambia. Kwame Nkrumah's book *Neo-Colonialism: The Last Stage of Imperialism*, published in 1964, not only announced a new phase in African history but also voiced the historical impracticability of Classical Pan-Africanism in a new historical phase. Nkrumah is an important transitional figure from the attempted synthesis of Classical Pan-Africanism and Classical Marxism to the emergence of Classical African Marxism. If Pan-Africanism, the legacy of its classical forms, still has any significance today, it is the attempt to forge a spiritual unification of all Black people in the world.

Classical African Marxism thus emerged to combat the then rapidly developing forms of neo-colonialism on the African continent. Within the international context of Marxist culture, Classical African Marxism emerged at the time when Western Marxism was in the process of exhausting itself as a philosophical system. This intellectual tradition, which is a legacy of Lukàcs, Gramsci, Bloch and many others ran aground in the May Rebellion of 1968. In South America, Latin American Marxism, founded by the Peruvian Marxist, José Carlos Mariategui, was transforming itself into Guevarism, whose aim was to liberate Latin America from neocolonial strangulation and possibly bring about the unity of Simon Bolívar's nations. In Asia, Maoism was gathering towards its crisis point in the Cultural Revolution, and the Vietnamese Revolution was in the process of defeating American imperialism. In the USSR, the conservatism of the Brezhnev regime was in the process of blanketing the Soviet republics in a cesspool of corruption and pessimism. In the United States itself, the civil rights movement and the student rebellion were joining forces to fight for new democratic positions. The formation of Classical African Marxism belongs to this historical conjuncture of political and cultural forces.

> Colonialism and its derivatives do not, as a matter of fact, constitute the present enemies of Africa. In a short time this continent will be liberated. For my part, the deeper I enter into the cultures and the political circles the surer I am that the great danger that threatens Africa is the absence of ideology.
>
> *Frantz Fanon, Toward the African Revolution*

Classical African Marxism, which is articulated in the writings of Frantz Fanon and Amilcar Cabral, is the product of both the Algerian Revolution and the Guinean Revolution within the context of the African Revolution.

Taking Perry Anderson's *Considerations on Western Marxism* as the classical summary of the tradition of Western Marxism, if we compare Western Marxism with Classical African Marxism we find the following historical contrasts: whereas the former was a product of defeat, the latter was a product of victory; whereas the former largely occupied the domain of philosophy, the latter concerned itself with the dialectics of politics; whereas the former separated theory and praxis, the latter was the very expression of its profound consummation; and whereas the former theorized aesthetics, the latter theorized a new sphere of history. In many ways, Classical African Marxism, more than Western Marxism, is a continuation of the themes of Classical Marxism. But it is necessary here to look at the specific concepts and distinctive characteristics of Classical African Marxism.

It was Frantz Fanon who mapped the political landscape within which Classical African Marxism achieved a revolutionary transformation in our understanding of African history by widening the perspective of Classical Pan-Africanism into a political unity of both Arabs and Africans on the continent, against the primacy given by both Pan-Africanism and Pan-Arabism. The very nature of Fanon's theoretical and political praxis within the Algerian Revolution was the forging of this North (Arab) – South (Black Africa) unity. For Fanon the Algerian Revolution was the first and primary dialectical process towards the unfolding of the African Revolution. According to him, or at least in accordance with the logic of his political position, Pan-Arabism and Pan-Africanism were to find their historical expression within the concept of the Third World. It was Fanon who articulated the concept of the Third World into a serious political category, giving it a fundamentally rich historical content. The Third World, which encompasses Africa, Asia and Latin America, was to be understood and analyzed in relation to the capitalist West, designated by Fanon as the First World, and in relation to the socialist East, which Fanon theorized as the Second World. At the moment of the formation of Classical African Marxism in the late 1950s and the early 1960s, this concept of the Third World was instrumental in forging a political consciousness among the dispossessed people of the world.

Although Fanon's advocacy and political practice of Arab-African unity were historically correct and salutary, he lacked the sociological categories and coordinates within which it could be achieved. In other words, Fanon never possessed a rich and original historical imagination. His articulation of historical categories was never solid. On the other hand, Fanon's critique of the intellectual mediocrity, economic bankruptcy and political immaturity of the African national bourgeoisies, which were then emerging, was profoundly deep and is still unsurpassed. It was the bankruptcy of this class and its alignment with imperialism that led Fanon to argue that socialism was the only way to the collective development of Third World peoples. But he was to add an important proviso, which with the passage of time has taken on greater significance, given the historical crisis of 'actually existing socialism': that Third World countries should not define their particular form of socialism in accordance with that defined by other peoples, in other continents, and in other historical circumstances. This was the context of Fanon's argument that the application of Classical Marxism within colonial contexts should always be stretched and made more elastic. This should not be taken to mean that Fanon advocated a form of African Socialism; for him there was only one form of socialism, Marx's socialism, which had to be specified in relation to the historical particularity of each Third World country. Unquestionably this is an issue of enormous complexity.

Fanon's stretching of Classical Marxism within the colonial context was to lead him to argue that the peasantry was the only revolutionary class, whereas the proletariat was privileged and conservative. In this way Fanonism can be compared to Maoism, even if within a limited historical space. Mao also emphasized the revolutionary role of the peasant class. But the real difference between the two is that, whereas Maoism argued for the primacy of the peasantry because of the small historical weight of the proletariat within the evolving Chinese social structure, Fanonism foreclosed any possibility of the working class being revolutionary because of its corruptibility within the colonial context. And whereas Maoism offered an ingenious reading of a complicated historical terrain, Fanonism misread a convoluted political space. Cabral was to provide, within the historical space of Classical African Marxism, an epistemological and political corrective to Fanonian historical misperception. It is this dialectical reciprocity and exchange between Fanonism and Cabralism that constitutes the unity of Classical African Marxism.

Whatever the historical misperceptions of Fanonism within Classical African Marxism – for instance, its belief that the Algerian Revolution had emancipated Algerian women – its great merit is that it expressed the inseparability of theory and practice within the Algerian Revolution. It should be remembered that Fanonism was the ideology of the Algerian Revolution, however much today for reactionary reasons Fanonism is disowned by certain elements within Algeria. This particular version of Classical African Marxism was superior to Western Marxism because it insisted on the unity of theory and practice, one of the cardinal points of Classical Marxism, while the illusions of Classical African Marxism as practiced by Fanon were no more debilitating than those of the tradition of Adorno, Althusser and Gramsci. The other merit of Fanonism is that it brought into being a successful political revolution against French imperialism, especially against its classically colonial forms, however much the Algerian Revolution later proved incapable of extricating itself from its own contradictions. Is Leninism in any way negated by the serious limitations that have been apparent in the results of the October Revolution since its inception?

There can be little doubt that *The Wretched of the Earth* implanted a revolutionary ideology in Africa, especially where ideology had been absent. Among its various salient characteristics, the following are perhaps the most important: first, that it is historically correct and politically wise to counterpose the revolutionary violence of the oppressed and the dispossessed against the counterrevolutionary violence of imperialism and colonialism; second, that the historical moment of the national bourgeois classes in the Third World is always a culturally useless and economically unproductive phase, in which national interests are always subordinated to the wishes of imperialism and neocolonialism; third, that only the peasant class is a revolutionary class within a colonial context; fourth, that culture should be an instrument in the national liberation struggle; fifth, that culture and politics are inseparable; and last, that the Third World should constitute itself as a historical entity. The impact of Fanon's ideology on African historical and political consciousness has been extremely uneven, leaving whole stretches of the African cultural imagination untouched, while simultaneously informing Steve Biko's Black Consciousness Movement in South Africa in its struggle against South African white fascism in the 1970s, and the struggle of Mulelism against the neocolonialist politics of Mobuto.

Alhough Fanonism has been an extremely fruitful source in the formation of Classical African Marxism, it has to be seen in light of its complimentariness to the other wing of African materialist philosophy, namely Cabralism. Amilcar Cabral is, without question, one of the great Marxist intellectuals produced by our deeply troubled century. His theoretical formulations constitute the fundamental base of Classical African Marxism – Classical, because African Marxism is a direct continuation of the Classical Marxism of Marx, Lenin and Engels. The many intellectual breakthroughs that are still to come in Africa during the next centuries can only be on the basis of Classical African Marxism, for this materialist theory of history is Africa's living philosophy today. There can be no going beyond it until all the historical tasks it calls forth have been fulfilled by the African peoples.

> The ideological deficiency, not to say the total lack of ideology, within
> the national liberation movements – which is basically due to ignorance
> of the historical reality which these movements claim to transform –
> constitutes one of the greatest weaknesses of our struggle against
> imperialism, if not the greatest weakness of all.
>
> *Amilcar Cabral, 'The Weapon of Theory'*

In a way beyond intellectual estimation and epistemological measurement, Cabral effected a revolution in redrawing the conceptual structure of African history and in formulating an ideology in accordance with Africa's historical specificity. Further, he has posed fundamental questions as to the intellectual structure of Classical Marxism. Cabral postulated Classical African Marxism as a response to the ideological deficiencies he encountered in Africa. It is perhaps necessary to make clear that when we talk of Classical African Marxism we are more concerned with its coordinates as an intellectual system and a political tradition. For Cabral, the whole historical period from World War II to the present, the era in which the African Revolution was unfolding in all its complex variations and mutations, is characterized by *national liberation struggles* on the three continents of the Third World, much more than by the *class struggles* in the late capitalist countries, and much more than by the struggle between *capitalism and socialism*. It is these national liberation struggles that he considered to be the prime motive force of our historical moment. The importance he accords them is in dialectical relation to the fact that for Cabral, and also for Fanon, national liberation struggles were the central means by which the oppressed, the dispossessed and the wretched peoples of the Third World could re-enter their own national histories, from which they had been expelled by imperialism, colonialism and capitalism. In short, armed revolutionary struggle is a fundamental method of re-entering and rewriting history.

In a great essay, 'The Weapon of Theory', which he delivered as a speech in Havana in 1966 at a celebration of the Cuban Revolution, Cabral argued for a new conception of Marxist history, especially in relation to the continent of African history. Since what Cabral was theorizing in 'The Weapon of Theory' reflected the developing process of the Guinean Revolution, of which he was the principal theorist, it can be said that it confirms the Marxist axiom that there can be no successful revolution without revolutionary theory. Cabral thus sought to theorize the nature of history in those African societies that were characterized by the absence of classes or class struggles. Since he did acknowledge that class struggle is the motive force of history, he went on to ask: Does it mean therefore that in those societies where this motive factor is absent those people live outside history? This is a crucial question, for when imperialism penetrated African societies it was on the pretext that these societies lived outside history and civilization. For Cabral, the intrusion of imperialism into Africa forced its peoples to leave African history and enter European imperial history. It is in this sense that armed struggle is a process of exit from colonial and imperial history, and a re-entry into African history (national histories) and peoples' history. For Cabral, both *before* and *after* class struggle, it is the mode of production that is the motive force of history. With this conceptualization of a new Marxist understanding of history, he sought to establish the patterns, lineages and forms of continuity within African history from antiquity to the present. Even during the era of colonial domination, we lived and experienced our African history in a particular way.

In arguing that, in particular circumstances, the mode of production rather than class struggle is a motive force of history, Cabral sought to articulate the process of the elimination of the concept of class and class struggle by socialism and communism. How would history be experienced and lived in truly communist societies, far beyond the contradictions of capitalism and imperialism? Cabral writes: 'Eternity is not of this world, but man will outlive classes and will continue to produce and make history, since he can never free himself from the burden of his needs, both of mind and of body, which are the basis of the development of the forces of production.'

Theorizing the progression of history, Cabral articulates three stages through which human history passes, that is, the progressive complication of the complex structure of the mode of production. The first stage is characterized by a low level of productive forces, in which there is no private appropriation and classes are absent. In the second stage there develops private appropriation of the means of production, and the subsequent appearance of social and economic contradictions that lead to the appearance of classes. In the third stage there is elimination of the private means of appropriation and the subsequent elimination of the concept of class and the class struggle. The formation of social structures corresponds to these stages, that is, from horizontality (absence of the state) through verticality (formation of the state) back to horizontality (abolition of the state). Cabral was here not merely articulating an abstract concept of social structures and history, but their actual imbrication in the complexity of social reality. In other words, Cabral was tracing the social determinants of history and the historical relationship between the abstract and the real. Indirectly, in the sense that it was not his central object of concern, Cabral was polemicizing against the theorists of so-called African Socialism, who postulate the absence of class formation in African history prior to imperial intrusion.

In this essay Cabral also sought to understand the process of bypassing the stages of development in historical progression – whether African societies could move directly from the feudal stage to socialism, bypassing capitalism. This question was related to the role of imperialism in African history. These theoretical questions were imposed on Cabral by the nature of the national liberation struggle in Guinea-Bissau, and by the political and armed practice of the African peoples in Guinea. Here we see a profound unity between theory and practice in the central process of Classical African Marxism, a unity whose absence profoundly debilitated Western Marxism after the 1920s, after the collapse of the Hungarian Soviet Republic, the defeat of the Turin workers' councils under the leadership of Antonio Gramsci, and the failure of the German Revolution led by Rosa Luxemburg. For Cabral, European imperialism in African history succeeded in its historical mission: in increasing the differentiation between classes, in accelerating the development of the productive forces, and in enriching the cultural text of the African peoples. One of the failures of imperialism was in not allowing the accumulation of capital on the part of the then incipient African bourgeois class.

To fight against the imperialist distortion of African history, national liberation struggle is the necessary political instrument. As Amilcar Cabral writes: 'In the national liberation of a people is the regaining of the historical personality of that people, its return to history through the destruction of the imperialist domination to which it was subjected.' In this sense, national liberation struggle is for Cabral not only a struggle against neocolonialism and the resurrection of the process of the development of the productive forces, it is also a revolution. The entrance of African peoples into history has the effect of potentially eliminating tribalism and of overcoming their social and cultural backwardness. Cabral agreed with Fanon on the necessity of employing revolutionary violence: of counterposing the liberating violence of nationalist forces against the criminal violence of the agents of imperialism. Through the process of armed struggle, the African peoples develop and attain revolutionary consciousness; and the attainment of revolutionary consciousness varies from class to class.

The nature of this revolutionary consciousness corresponds to the position of the various classes in the social structure. It was this awareness on the part of Cabral which led him to analyze the social structure of Guinea. In an essay, 'Brief Analysis of the Social Structure in Guinea', which was presented in a seminar at the Frantz Fanon Center in Milan in 1964 and established the credentials of Classical African Marxism, Amilcar Cabral analyzed the processes of structuration of an African social formation. The object of critique was also neocolonialism, the very historical process that necessitated the emergence of African materialist philosophy. There can be no doubt that this essay is one of the great documents of African intellectual and political history in the twentieth century. Here the problematics of Marxist analysis, which Perry Anderson in *Arguments Within English Marxism* saw as informing the polemic between Louis Althusser and E.P. Thompson, are employed in a profound way: the concept of mode of production as a category through which the dialectical movement of history can be periodized; the presence and existence of a plurality of modes of production within a particular social formation; the differential historical temporality of the various interconnected and hierarchical levels within society; and the dialectic between agency (social classes) and determination (structural process).

Though this essay takes as its empirical object the social structure of Guinea, the abstract theoretical structure of this object has universal applicability, particularly in Africa. One can only schematically indicate the complexity of the historical and social relationships analyzed in this text. What this analysis empirically proves is that long before the intrusion of imperialism in the domain of African history, African societies were already in a state of class stratification. Cabral distinguishes and interrelates to each other segmentations within a particular social formation: the patterns of property ownership and the private means of appropriation in semi-feudal and feudal societies, where the dominant ideology is animistic or Islamic, in which marriage practices are monogamous and/or polygamous, and the positioning of women within them is profoundly problematical.

The whole analysis covers practically the entire ethnically differentiated social geography of Guinea. He combines the historical differentiations that ensue from such a structure into a complex whole. Cabral calibrates the class position of the following social groups: nobles, religious figures, artisans, peasants, workers and chiefs. This enumeration makes clear the historical differentials between the concept of 'class' in an African 'feudal mode of production' and in a capitalist mode of production. Cabral attempts to trace the transitional passageways from the one to the other. Within the embryonic structure of the capitalist mode of production, he situates the concept of the déclassé, which naturally is a problematical category in the feudal order. Cabral unveils the complex social structure of a colonial capitalist order: the formation of the petty bourgeoisie, the metamorphosis of officials (higher officials, middle officials, petty officials), the nature of déclassé people (beggars, prostitutes, lumpen-protetarians). It is within such a complex order that imperialism intervenes to bring about other complications: the evolution and emergence of a national bourgeoisie. This patterning of relationships proves beyond doubt the existence of African history, an existence that imperial history sought to contest and destroy.

323

In making this detailed analysis of Guinea's ethnic geography, Cabral's aim was to locate the patterns of contradictions within which the national liberation struggle could unfold. After all, the historical logic behind the great theoretical project of Amilcar Cabral was to bring about the defeat of imperial hegemony within African history and the expulsion of imperialism and neocolonialism from the African political landscape. Consequently, within the structure of Classical African Marxism, behind theory stands praxis, and before theory stands praxis. It is in this context that a detailed morphological structure of class forms was necessary. And it was on the basis of a combination of theoretical formulation and empirical evidence that Cabral was able to correct Fanon's postulate that in the colonial context only the peasantry is a revolutionary class, and that the proletariat is privileged and reactionary. Cabral makes clear that the role of the peasantry in a national liberation struggle is that of a physical force, which must be distinguished from that of a historical force. According to him, it is only as a physical force against colonialism that the peasant class is revolutionary and not as a historical force. The working class is the revolutionary historical force that can bring about a transition from capitalism to socialism.

Since I have so far emphasized the historical role of Classical African Marxism in restructuring the social geography and conceptual form of African history in dialectical relation with the revolutionary praxis seeking to vanquish imperial domination, it may be thought that this African materialist philosophy was concerned only with these matters. In fact, it was deeply concerned with a range of other projects, from theorizing the nature of revolutionary democracy (socialist democracy) within an African context to the role of a revolutionary party in relation to the masses. I will shortly look at these issues as they concern the future of socialism in Africa. But for the moment let me emphasize that Classical African Marxism theorized the dialectical problematics of culture: here I will focus on Cabral's contributions, since I have elsewhere examined Fanon's ideas about politics and culture.

In a series of remarkable texts given as lectures at American universities, Cabral presented his thoughts on culture and tradition. In one of them, 'National Culture and Liberation', given at Syracuse University in 1970 as a memorial lecture in honor of the father of the Mozambican Revolution, Eduardo Mondlane, Cabral examines the revolutionary potential of African cultures. The other essay, 'Identity and Dignity in the Context of the National Liberation Struggle', given on the occasion of his receiving in 1972 an honorary doctorate from Lincoln University, articulates the dynamic between culture and tradition. In 'National Culture and Liberation', Cabral argues that as much as imperialist intrusion constituted an act of suppressing the different African national histories, likewise on the cultural plane, this intrusion was a form of negating African national cultures, in the sense that European cultures established hegemony over them. This cultural domination reveals an intimate and dialectical relation between economic exploitation and cultural domination. Culture, according to Cabral, is an expression of people's history, revealing the dialectical unity between humanity and nature. Imperialism sought to obliterate the cultural memory of a people's history. In response forms of cultural resistance emerged. Historically, a national liberation struggle is usually preceded by an increase in the cultural expression of a dominated people. As Cabral writes, 'The value of culture as an element of resistance to foreign domination lies in the fact that culture is the vigorous manifestation on the ideological or idealist plane of the physical and historical reality of the society that is dominated or to be dominated.' Cabral's radical formulation leads him to argue that culture is not only an expression of history, it is actually history itself; it is an expression of the movement of productive forces. In counteracting foreign or imperial cultural domination, a national liberation struggle becomes an act of creating and enlarging the space of culture itself.

For Cabral, though culture has by its very nature a mass character, its distribution on the horizontal and vertical planes of a social formation is very complex and uneven, even among individuals within the same social group. It is in this sense that culture can be seen as not only a historical content, but also as an ideological process. In societies characterized by horizontality, culture is more or less uniformly distributed, whereas in those in which verticality is predominant, culture is complexly and unevenly distributed. These historical differences must be taken into account when national liberation struggles are initiated, and not only when a national cultural history is written. Where there is an imbrication of class, race and ethnicity, the complexity in the distribution of culture is even more profound.

Beyond the invigoration of African national cultures through national liberation struggles, the lineage of African culture shows itself to be a historical storehouse of immense richness. The lineage of cultural achievement from Carthage, Giza, Zimbabwe and Meroe to Benin, Ife, Timbuktu and Kilwa indicates the continuity of African culture. In the spheres of dance, music, oral and written literatures, cosmological and religious systems, as well as philosophy, the universality of African culture should be apparent to all. Given the impact of Africa's expressiveness on the world, ranging from Picasso's adaptations from the African mask to Stravinsky's borrowings from Scott Joplin's music, it is necessary to quote this salutary warning from Amilcar Cabral:

But in the face of the vital need for progress, the following attitudes or behavior will be no less harmful to Africa: indiscriminate compliments; systematic exultation of virtues without condemning faults; blind acceptance of the values of the culture, without considering what presently or potentially regressive elements it contains; confusion between what is the expression of an objective and material historical reality and what appears to be a creation of the mind or the product of a peculiar temperament; absurd linking of artistic creations, whether good or not, with supposed racial characteristics; and finally, the non-scientific or a scientific critical appreciation of the cultural phenomenon.

The task facing Africa today, as Cabral saw, is not so much celebration as much as a series of developments on a cultural front: the development of a popular culture, the development of a national culture, the development of a scientific culture, the development of political and moral awareness and the development of universal culture. It is the combination of these developments that constitutes a new cultural front for the present national liberation struggles.

In the essay 'Identity and Dignity in the Context of the National Liberation Struggle', Cabral sets forth a series of historical arguments concerning the form of African culture. Here Cabral develops the controversial but correct thesis that imperialism was not only negative, but also made its positive contributions to African cultures and societies. The accumulation of capital at the center, appropriated from the periphery through the historical system of imperialism, made possible the development of modern science and technology, and also facilitated the emergence of the Renaissance and the Enlightenment. Cabral's argument here follows the famous classical thesis developed by Marx that capitalism had its positive and negative instances, a dialectic of progression and regression. In forcing the countries that were later to be designated as being in the Third World into modern civilization and in progressively lessening humanity's dependency on nature, capitalism was indeed a great historical achievement. On the other hand, because it destroyed great civilizations like the Aztec and many others, and because it made possible the exploitation of many by the few, capitalism deserves to be destroyed by the forces committed to socialism, forces like Classical African Marxism. It is necessary to recall here Benjamin's maxim, mentioned earlier: that culture is a product of both civilization and barbarism. The logic of this principle reappears in the analysis of the brilliant American Marxist literary scholar Fredric Jameson of the recent emergence of a new bourgeois cultural formation, postmodernism. This new cultural formation is the dialectical embodiment of the negative and the positive. Nevertheless, it should be opposed by the forces of socialism, as Terry Eagleton has made clear. Within the African context, although recognizing the great achievements of capitalism and imperialism, Classical African Marxism has taken up the instruments of warfare in order to defeat them. Only anti-dialecticians can see a contradiction in this.

On the one hand, imperialism has facilitated the expansion of human knowledge in the field of sociology, history, ethnology, ethnography and culture, by studying the dominated countries in order to exploit them better – one has only to think of the great scholarship at the center of Orientalism, however reactionary many of its forms were. The national liberation struggles, for their part, have had to acquire a greater knowledge of their own societies in order to dislodge and defeat imperialism and neo-colonialism. It is this dialectical process that accounts for the extraordinary brilliance of Classical African Marxism. There is nothing in the whole domain of European knowledge and scholarship to compare with the writings of Cabral, Fanon and Nkrumah on matters concerning the Third World, let alone those relevant to Africa. Here it is evident that Classical African Marxism is a direct product of the imperialism that it is historically destined to vanquish: it is similar to the Hegelian relation between master and slave. This is the very essence of materialist dialectics.

While imperialism did have a deleterious effect on the capacity of Africa's national bourgeoisies and elites to forge their own cultural identity, it never did manage to penetrate into the cultural texture of the masses of the people. For Cabral, this cultural resistance on the part of the people has been one of our great victories as Africans. The cultural influence of imperialism and neocolonialism has been confined to a small segment of the population, though tragically enough this elite rules in practically all of the neocolonialist countries with the support of imperialism and its agents. The cultural crisis in Africa today is a crisis of a bourgeois elite and not of the masses of the people, however economically and culturally dominated they are by this bankrupt elite. One of the central tasks of Classical African Marxism is to bring about the hegemony of a peoples' culture, replacing the elite culture of slavery and imitation and servility. The phenomenon of 'return to the source' is only confined to the elites. Cabral writes polemically and controversially:

> It comes as no surprise that the theories of 'movements' such as *Pan-Africanism* or *Négritude* (two pertinent expressions arising mainly from the assumption that all black Africans have a cultural identity) were propounded outside black Africa. More recently, the black Americans' claim to an African identity is another proof, possibly rather a desperate one, of the need for a 'eturn to the source' although clearly it is influenced by a new situation: the fact that the great majority of African people are now independent.

Perhaps what Cabral seeks to convey here is that Classical African Marxism is the first modern philosophical and political system to emerge out of Africa, for it is a product of the contestation over African history. The other great philosophical system, Julius Nyerere's African Socialism, is the other candidate for an intellectual process emerging from within Africa rather than being transported from the diaspora. According to Cabral, the bourgeois concept of 'return to the source' cannot be an *act of struggle,* for it expresses the momentary, secondary contradiction between the national bourgeoisie and imperialism.

Simultaneously with forging a cultural resistance to imperialist cultural penetration, the masses of the people construct an individual and collective identity. During the period of national liberation struggle this individual and collective identity is historically realized through material practice. Cabral makes a salutary distinction between an *original identity*, which is largely determined by a biological element, and an *actual identity*, whose main determinant is sociological. In both forms of identify the dialectic of race and class is important. It is in the former that the element of race predominates, and in the latter it is the concept of class that is the overdetermining factor. The historical mission of the national liberation movements in their struggle is to consolidate the actual identity of the masses of the people. The forging or restoration of a peoples' actual identity, especially in its cultural forms, is in dialectical relation to the restoration of a non-exploitative social structure, for it is on the basis of a dialectically harmonious social structure that this identity can fully emerge. The aim of the actual identity of the majority of the people is to attain supreme dignity.

In order to expel imperialist and colonialist intrusion and penetration into African history, which the spontaneity of masses cannot fully achieve, Classical African Marxism was compelled to invent an instrumentalization process which would be the embodiment of a peoples' will. It was in this circumstance that this materialist philosophy of history theorized the concept of the party within an African context. In addition, the Classical African Marxism of Cabral and Fanon has had to formulate and bring into practice forms of revolutionary democracy. All the different forms of the African Revolution, stretching from Algeria passing through Angola and Guinea-Bissau to Mozambique, have not been led by a party in the Leninist sense, but rather by national fronts, which subsequently transformed themselves into parties, more or less in the Leninist sense. Even the Ethiopian Revolution, probably the only classical revolution of the twentieth century in Africa, in the sense of being compelled largely by internal class contradictions rather than directly by foreign domination, found it necessary to invent a party after the victory of the revolution. The concept of the party emerged while these instruments of history were still national fronts, in the same way that the African National Congress is a national front. In his Havana lecture, 'The Weapon of Theory', Cabral makes clear that the concept of *party* or a *single party* is something unique to Africa's historical conditions, and should not be confused with the European concept of the party.

In a series of nine lectures, widely known as 'Party Principles and Political Practice', which were given to PAIGC (African Party for the Independence of Guinea and Cape Verde) cadres in 1965, Cabral formulated certain Marxist principles of a party within an African context. First, the party should embody unity and struggle. By unity Cabral meant unifying a diversity of positions towards achieving a specific aim or goal. In this sense, unity is a dynamic process of movement. By struggle he meant the practice of opposing imposed hegemony; the process of acquiring knowledge in order to intervene in social reality. In the colonial context, this principle means the unity and struggle of the different classes in opposition to imperial domination; in the neocolonial context, it means a class struggle. In other words, unity and struggle together form a process of overcoming social and historical contradictions. Second, for unity and struggle to be possible, the party must know the fundamental nature of the social reality in which its praxis intervenes. This historical reality is the unity of cultural reality, social reality, economic reality and political reality. Third, the party should be led by people committed to the interests of the masses; a political leadership that is comparable to revolutionary intellectuals. Fourth, that within the party there should be independence of thought and action. Fifth, the party itself should be faithful in the implementation of these principles. This means that the members of the party should reject all forms of opportunism. Last but most crucial, the party must establish revolutionary democracy. Cabral writes:

> As I have said, we must constantly go forward to put power into the hands of our people, to make a profound change in the life of our people, even to put all the means for defense into the hands of our people, so that it is our people who defend our revolution. This is what revolutionary democracy will be in fact tomorrow in our land. Anyone who rules his people but fears the people is in a bad way. We must never fear the people.

In short, it could be said with justice that the one singular historical aim of Classical African Marxism has been to bring about the realization of revolutionary democracy.

In conclusion, then, it can be seen that Classical African Marxism is not only a product of the African Revolution, but is also an expression of the unity of theory and praxis in theorizing that historical moment. Fundamentally also, this materialist philosophy has reconstituted the continent of African history. Unrelentingly, its principal aim has been to defeat the neocolonialism that so dominates Africa today. Classical African Marxism can only claim total victory upon expelling a new form of imperialism, neocolonialism, from Africa, as much as Classical Pan-Africanism claimed total victory upon the expulsion of classical colonialism. Upon achieving this historical aim, Classical Pan-Africanism lost its historical significance, hence its replacement on the stage of history by Classical African Marxism. Today Classical Pan-Africanism, which seeks to unify Black people across different historical moments, cultural patterns and social formations, is a historical impossibility. It succeeded magnificently in its one historic mission, which was in defeating classical colonialism. And after defeating neocolonialism, Classical African Marxism will in turn lose its historical legitimacy. This is equally true of Marxism as well: upon its victory in placing the working class in political and economic power all over the world, it will disappear from history. It may then remain as an ideology, much as Christianity remains today as an ideology, but not as a *living philosophy*.

The historical tasks of Classical African Marxism are still unfinished: it has still to theorize the chain of revolutions that broke out on the African continent in the 1970s. What was the projection of their socialist orientation? What should be the forms of socialist democracy in Africa today? Is the political and economic unification of the continent possible, given the intractable problems of nationalism? Can this philosophy of African history grasp and carry through the upcoming revolutionary storm in South Africa? Because of the nature these issues, Classical African Marxism is still in its infancy and must be extended and deepened by committed African Marxist intellectuals.

Note

This essay was originally presented in German in a forum on contemporary Marxism organized by Peoples' University on 1 May 1988. The Peoples' University is a three-day event held annually in celebration of May Day at the Technical University of Berlin. The force behind this fascinating intellectual forum is the great German Marxist philosopher Wolfgang Fritz Haug and his journal *Das Argument*. I would like to thank Wolfgang Fritz Haug for having invited me to make this presentation. The argument this essay sought to put forth was that Western Marxism had exhausted itself, and in order to replenish itself, it should seek inspiration in African Marxism, whose existence it had never acknowledged. Since 1989 much has changed: for all practical purposes European Marxism has collapsed and socialism has disappeared from the continent of Europe. English Marxism, the latest metamorphosis of European Marxism, has gravitated to Southern California. I have not found it necessary to alter the argument in this essay since then because Classical African Marxism is still the dominant intellectual force in contemporary African cultural history, finding continuation in the incomparable voice of Ngugi wa Thiong'o.

17

The Politics of Cultural Existence:

Pan-Africanism, Historical

Materialism and Afrocentricity

Sidney J. Lemelle

> Knowledge is not a goal in itself, but a path to wisdom;
> it bestows not privilege so much as duty, not power so much as
> responsibility. And it brings with it a desire to learn even as one teaches,
> to teach even as one learns. It is used not to compete with one's fellow
> beings for some unending standard of life, but to achieve for them, as
> for oneself, a higher quality of life.
>
> *A. Sivanandan*

In the wake of Reaganomics, Thatcherism and the rise of neoconservativism in the 1980s, Black people around the world have begun a desperate search for new avenues of counter-hegemonic discourse – often through the creation or resurrection of cultural representations and icons (for example, Malcolm X caps, rap music and African dress). This, in turn, has rekindled an old debate which first surfaced in 1900, again in the 1920s, 1930s and 1960s, and now in the 1990s. The main points of the debate can be divided into several basic questions: Does the African experience contain 'universal' beliefs and institutions which facilitate resistance to oppression by diaspora Blacks (that is, people of African descent in the Americas, Caribbean and Europe)? What, if any, are the relationships between African and Black Atlantic cultures? To what degree have Eurocentric conceptualizations affected/distorted African and Black Atlantic cultures, cultural productions and image representations? To what extent do the affects of Eurocentrism (white chauvinism/racism) keep Africans and Blacks from 'knowing themselves' and resisting that which oppresses them?

This essay is an attempt to come to terms with some of these questions, as well as the key ideas and strategies which have long been part of the debate on the 'politics of Black nationalism' and Pan-Africanism.[1] We must emphasize at the outset that this is not simply an internal 'Black debate' on strategies and tactics; nor is it a part of the irrelevant right-wing 'nondebate' on political correctness (PC) now raging on American college campuses.[2] Instead, it is an attempt to gauge the importance of Pan-Africanist and Black nationalist thought as forces for change through a historical and contemporary examination of their influence on popular consciousness and liberation struggles.

The historiography of Black nationalist and Pan-Africanist thought has undergone many changes since its origins in the nineteenth century. T.T. Fortune, Martin Delany, E.W. Blyden, Alexander Crummell, J.E. Caseley-Hayford, J. Africanus Beale Horton and other early pioneers on the subject wrote extensively about the glories of African peoples and their descendants in the 'new world'. The writings of these authors were by no means all the same, yet their basic intellectual and philosophical underpinnings had a common provenance. As we will demonstrate below, the 'liberal' school of historical interpretation, which dominated Western education in the nineteenth century, has influenced and continues to influence the basic assumptions and conclusions of nationalist writers about Pan-Africanism.

As might be expected, this liberal school brought forth a reaction from more radical theorists. Post–World War II scholar-activists such as C.L.R. James, W.E.B. Du Bois and Eric Williams wrote radical critiques of the earlier literature.[3] Their interpretations were to varying degrees rooted in, or at least influenced by, Marxist-Leninist attacks on European capitalist exploitation. The aim of these radical critiques was not only to rebuke the early liberal historiography of Pan-Africanism – steeped in nineteenth-century European beliefs in uplift and progress within European capitalism – but also to criticize dogmatic, reductionist and non-revolutionary 'cultural nationalist' views.

In the 1970s and 1980s, books and essays on Black nationalism and Pan-Africanism by Cedric Robinson, Walter Rodney, Bernard Magubane and A. Sivanandan, to name just a few, continued the radical tradition.[4] In particular, these radical diasporan authors were influenced by the writings of Antonio Gramsci on cultural hegemony and the capitalist state, and the works of Frantz Fanon on the psychology of racism.[5] Their works grappled with the historical and philosophical contradictions within the diasporan Pan-African movement and specifically the means of achieving African and Black liberation – a debate which continues today.

This essay will begin answering the questions posed above by highlighting some of the philosophical contradictions contained in the current Pan-

African debate. I will then examine the practical implications of this debate by contrasting the works of several important groups of writers and theorists. The first group is represented by Molefi Kete Asante, a well-known scholar and editor who has popularized a modern-day version of liberal cultural nationalism. The second group is represented by several radical diasporan authors including A. Sivanandan, an organic intellectual, writer and editor in Britain, as well as Cedric Robinson, Manning Marable, Bernard Magubane and George Lipsitz. All have provided a historical materialist critique of such notions for many years. While both groups have argued convincingly that an understanding of culture and politics is essential in the struggle for Black liberation in Africa and the diaspora, I maintain that the philosophical and practical implications of their arguments are quite different. Within this context, it should be borne in mind that classifying intellectual perspectives is always arbitrary and fraught with contradictions, yet it can be useful in heuristic terms – particularly when trying to gauge the philosophical 'residue' in more current debates and their potential for liberation.

Finally, I will analyze the implications of the works of both groups vis à vis Pan-Africanism and Afrocentricity – from a historical materialist prospective.[6] I will argue that the potential of Revolutionary Pan-Africanism as a counter-hegemonic discourse and tool for working-class liberation is superior to Afrocentricity, because it allows for a concrete, material analysis of society that breaks with the dominant idealistic discourse in a way that Afrocentricity cannot.

Idealism, Essentialism and Afrocentricity

Molefi Asante, chair of the Department of African-American Studies at Temple University, has become one of the chief spokespersons for a movement that uses scholarship 'to forge a distinct view of the world, one in which Europeans and their white descendants no longer occupy the central and exalted position' – that is, Afrocentrism.[7] In his books and articles, Asante lays out the basic justifications for, and necessity of, his 'unique' Afrocentric philosophy.[8] He begins his book *The Afrocentric Idea* by stating that his work is 'a radical critique of the Eurocentric ideology that masquerades as a universal view.'[9] He is providing a 'different view ... and new perspectives' that he calls 'Afrocentricity'.

Asante defines his new perspective as 'the most complete philosophical totalization of the African being-at-the-center of his or her existence.'[10] The basic argument maintains that to understand the 'African experience' (in either Africa or the Americas) it must be approached from the perspective of Africans themselves – not from a distorted Eurocentric view. This is a valid, yet not necessarily new, concept.[11] Asante claims to be innovative in developing an entire discourse, devoid of Eurocentric philosophy (such as materialism or positivism), for analyzing rhetoric. Yet in the process of explicating his 'new methodology', Asante reverts to the most prevalent Eurocentric strain of philosophy: idealism.[12] Thus, at the base of Asante's Afrocentric conceptualization is the primacy of ideas over material reality. He claims that by using 'ideas' and 'words' to critique a society and its ruling ideology, his words will 'provide a radical assessment of a given reality' and thus 'create, among other things, another reality.'[13] Put another way, Asante's ideas, as reflected in the words he uses in his critique, will alter, indeed create, another material reality.

Similarly, Asante's interpretation of current history locates the basic force of social evolution in the ideas and theories of Afrocentricity. In this sense Asante stands squarely within the tradition of nineteenth-century idealist philosophy associated with such European intellectuals as Georg Friedrich Hegel, Otto Bauer and Thomas Carlyle.[14] Hegel, for example, believed that the 'absolute idea' (akin to Asante's Afrocentricity) governed the lives of people and moved society forward. Similarly, Bauer and Carlyle believed, as does Asante, that each society moves forward because of its individual (invariably male) 'personality'.

In numerous works, Asante explains the social and cultural evolution of African-Americans in terms of individual personality and ideas, attributing to them a uniquely creative role in Black history. By concentrating on Black male intellectuals like Booker T. Washington, W.E.B. Du Bois, Marcus Garvey and Bishop Henry McNeal Turner, Elijah Muhammad, Malcolm X and Maulana Karenga, Asante implies that these individual 'prophets' and 'heroes' made history by themselves – standing above the Black masses. For him these 'exceptional personalities . . . stood against the storm and kept the lights burning to point the way.'[15] Yet from the perspective of a historical materialist, it is not 'heroes' who make history but vice versa. It is people – common, ordinary, everyday women and men – who select their heroes and move history onward. This is not to say that outstanding individuals do not play an important part in the life of society; they do – but only insofar as they are capable of acting upon social conditions and stimulating people to act to improve their lot.[16]

Aside from outright 'hero-worship', such masculinist discourse, E. Francis White has argued, invents a past which is subject to 'sexist pitfalls' and fosters a 'conservative agenda on gender and sexuality'.[17] This feeling is also captured in Anne McClintock's haunting indictment of the type of nationalism represented by Afrocentricity: 'all nationalisms are gendered, all are invented, and all are dangerous'.[18] Most Black feminist scholars agree that the Afrocentric position toward women is filled with contradictory and condescending attitudes. Black feminist scholars such as bell hooks and Patricia Hill Collins have also challenged the androcentric biases of Asante's Afrocentric analysis 'by calling attention to interlocking systems of domination – sex, race, and class.'[19] For Asante, race remains 'the most dominant aspect of intersocial relations', although, mindful of Black feminist criticisms, he adds 'gender also must be seen as a substantial research area'. Yet from his own androcentric/Afrocentric position, Asante can rationalize: 'Since the liberation of women is not an act of charity but a basic premise of the Afrocentric project, the researcher must be cognizant of sexist language, terminology, and perspective.'[20] Not surprisingly, Asante has rejected the work of such Black feminists (or 'Afrofemcentrists' as he chooses to refer to them) who separate 'sex and race' in their work. Instead he praises the 'Africana Womanist project' of scholars like Vivian Gordon, Clenora Hudson Weems, Brenda Verner, Kariamu Welsh Asante and Dona Marimba Richards, who 'have found their models . . . in the ancient models of Auset-Ausar and Mawu-Lisa.'[21]

Asante also finds himself replicating much of current Eurocentric sociology, which maintains that in the evolution of social life the basic factor is not the productive forces in society, but the 'unity of soul and will' among 'Africans'. Hence, the determining force in society is not a struggle of classes against sexism, nor the activity of the masses of Black people, but the strong 'cultural identity' and personalities of Black male leaders.[22] This is another way of saying that ideas make history, obscuring the fact that historical development brings about the rise of new ideas and leaders.

Asante's Afrocentric critique claims to incorporate an 'African perspective' that will somehow transform the 'Eurocentric reality'. In formulating this 'African perspective', he is guilty of essentializing an entire people and constructing an abstract, non-existent 'Africa'. Indeed, he has incorporated many of the European misconceptions which V.Y. Mudimbe critiques in his book *The Invention of Africa*.[23] Asante's Africa is an idealized 'Africa', a 'society [which] is essentially a society of harmonies, inasmuch as the coherence or compatibility of persons, things and modalities is at the root of traditional African philosophy.'[24] Perhaps sensing his essentialism and the imminent critiques of his position, Asante states, 'When we speak of Africans, we are usually talking about a multitude of attitudes, people, and cosmologies; and in this circumstance, to speak of an African mind is to speak cautiously.' He then adds, 'Nevertheless, we speak broadly of traditional African society – perhaps, even African culture.'[25] In another article, Asante explains: 'By "African" I clearly mean a "composite African" not a specific discrete African ethnicity.'[26] These attempts to rationalize his essentialism show that Asante has yet to come to grips with his philosophical utilitarianism.

Anyone who has seriously studied African history and its peoples and cultures realizes that a multitude of attitudes and cosmologies produced many African cultures – none of which were 'universal'. Africa is made up of people from different ethnic, religious and linguistic groupings. Furthermore, 'traditions' in most African societies were created and recreated by people, often to defend against destructive assaults on their economic, political and cultural bases.[27] As Anne McClintock has written: 'Traditions are not the sacrosanct and timeless essences of a people; they are social inventions often of very recent origin – both the outcome and the record of political contests and power. . . .' Thus, 'all too often', she observes, 'the doors of tradition are slammed in women's faces.'[28] Asante's conception of 'tradition' implies a static and unproblematic existence which deprives Africa and its peoples and cultures of their dynamism.

Thus what Asante and other Afrocentrists claim to be 'traditional African ways' are in actuality their own reconstructions of customs and mores taken from many different societies of Africa. For example, Afrocentrists have invented a 'traditional African' holiday (*Kwanza*) celebrated nowhere else in the world except the United States, a 'traditional African ideology' (*Njia*) also unknown outside the Western Hemisphere, and an Afrocentric study of phenomena, events, ideas, and personalities related to Africa (*Africology*).[29] Thus even though Asante claims that 'Afrocentricity is not a black version of Eurocentricity', in developing an 'alternative view' he and other Afrocentric scholars substitute a set of culturally constructed 'African traditions' for ones that are supposedly 'European'.[30] In the final analysis, Asante's Afrocentric vision and its philosophical contradictions have important practical implications – political and economic – for the liberation struggle of African peoples worldwide.

The Liberation of the Black Intellectual

Other scholars and theoreticians have taken different approaches to Black liberation, despite having gone through transformational processes similar to Asante's. Scholars like A. Sivanandan and Cedric Robinson were 'educated' within colonial/neocolonial systems (British and American, respectively). They came of age intellectually during the 1950s and 1960s – the era of African decolonization and liberation movements in Africa and the diaspora, and searched for their cultural identity as a means of fighting oppression. Sivanandan and Robinson thus provide some insights into Asante's idealistic/essentialist philosophy.[31]

For Asante, 'seeing' the need for change 'based on people's needs and experiences' is primarily at the existential and intellectual level. According to him, 'Invariably, rhetoric allies itself with the socio-economic . . . dominant culture. Therefore, the dilemma of the scholar who would break out of these restricting chains is fundamentally *an ideological one*.' Asante also says that 'liberation from the captivity of racist language is the first order of the intellectual.'[32] Unfortunately, the means by which this break is to be accomplished remain unclear.

Sivanandan, in his 'The Liberation of the Black Intellectual', describes the transition of the 'coloured intellectual' into the 'Black intellectual'. The former is a colonial construct, a product of colonial education and imbued with a Eurocentric value system. The challenge of the 'coloured intellectual' is (as Asante would agree) to overcome Eurocentric brainwashing and unite with one's people – to become a Black intellectual.

According to Sivanandan, for 'coloured intellectuals' the search for identity is a complicated process: 'In coming to consciousness of the oppressed, [they] take conscience of [themselves]' and, at that moment of reconciliation 'between the existential and the intellectual, between the subjective and objective realities of [their] oppression . . . [are] delivered from the marginality and stand revealed as neither "coloured" nor "intellectual" – but BLACK.'[33] Yet for Black intellectuals the process does not stop there. By accepting their Blackness, they seek to define it in a world filled with Eurocentric values and must 'come to see the need for radical change in both the values and structure of that society.'[34]

In a similar vein Cedric Robinson discusses in his book *Black Marxism* 'the formation of an intelligensia' – which includes George Padmore, C.L.R. James, Eric Williams, Oliver C. Cox, Aimé Césaire, W.E.B. Du Bois and Richard Wright. As 'Black petty bourgeois intellectuals' they all passed through 'the prepossessing claims of bourgeois ideology for Western cultural superiority with their only modestly disguised radicalism. But eventually they would emerge convinced that a larger and different achievement was required . . . each in his own time, turned his face to the historical tradition of Black liberation and became Black radicals.' But Robinson also points out 'that their brilliance was also derivative. The truer genius was in the midst of the people of whom they wrote. There the struggle was more than words or ideas but life itself.'[35]

Perhaps one of the most insightful analyses of the contradiction of the 'Black intellectual' comes from George Lipsitz's biography of Ivory Perry – a worker and civil rights activist-organizer. In *A Life in the Struggle*, Lipsitz, borrowing freely from Gramsci, portrays Perry as an 'organic intellectual' of the working class.[36] In Gramsci's view, 'organic' intellectuals are the 'thinking and organising element of a particularly fundamental social class'; their function is in 'directing the ideas and aspirations of the class to which they organically belong.'[37] Herein lies the difference between an organic intellectual like Ivory Perry and a 'traditional' professional intellectual like Asante (both of whom have working-class origins). According to Gramsci, 'The mode of being' of the organic intellectual 'can no longer consist in eloquence, which is an exterior and momentary mover of feelings and passions, but in active participation in practical life, as constructor, organiser, "permanent persuader" and not just a simple orator.'[38]

Sivanandan, Robinson and Lipsitz all believe that Black intellectuals (that is, organic intellectuals) must develop a socio-political 'mode' of opposition as a step towards breaking with the dominant discourse. They not only 'analyze and interpret the world, they originate and circulate their ideas through social contestation . . . [they] learn about the world by trying to change it, and they change the world by learning about it from the perspective of the needs and aspirations of their social group.'[39] Thus what distinguishes the transformation of Asante from that of Ivory Perry is not simply ideology, but the fact that Asante – through his reliance on Afrocentric rhetoric – is divorced from oppositional activities connected with social contestation. He has broken his 'organic' ties to the working class and thus remains constrained by the dominant bourgeois ideology. Indeed, the 'break' that Asante insists is so fundamental is not made. We will return to this point later.

Obviously, the decision to break with the dominant ideology is often difficult for the Black intellectual, given the contradictions of a society where, as Sivanandan views it, 'even the revolutionary ideologies that envisage such a change are unable to take into their perspective the nature of his particular oppression and its implications for revolutionary strategies.'[40] Here he is polemicizing against (and unfortunately also caricaturing) white radicals (mostly Marxists) who, in the 1960s and 1970s, were involved in anti-war, anti-racist, labor union and coalition struggles. Sivanandan argues that many (although by no means all) misunderstood the relationship between race and class:

> White radicals continue to maintain that colour oppression is not more than an aspect of class oppression, that color discrimination is only another aspect of working class exploitation, that the capitalist system is the common enemy of the white worker and black alike . . .
>
> But what these radicals fail to realise is that the black man by virtue of his particular oppression, is closer to his bourgeois brothers (by colour) than his white comrade. . . . Indeed his white comrade is a party to his oppression. . . . He too benefits from the exploitation of the black man, however indirectly.[41]

Asante would agree with this indictment of white Marxist radicals, but would go further: 'Because it emerged from the Western consciousness, Marxism is mechanistic in its approach to social understanding and development, and it has often adopted forms of social Darwinism when explaining cultural and social phenomena ... [thus] Marxism is not helpful in developing Afrocentric concepts and methods. ...'[42] Sivanandan confirms that 'Marxism, after all, was formulated in a European context and must, on its own showing, be Eurocentric.'[43] Similarly, Robinson also notes 'in his criticisms of Marxism, ... [Richard] Wright was not entirely rejecting it but was attempting to locate it, to provide a sense of the boundaries of its authority.'[44] Thus rather than discarding the entire methodology because of its Eurocentric provenance, Wright and Sivanandan would instead reconceptualize and 'revolutionize' the Marxist methodological approach to culture as a way of breaking the alliance with dominant culture:

> [I]n their preoccupation with the economic factors of capitalist oppression, they [white Marxists] have ignored the importance of its existential consequences, in effect its consequences to culture. The whole structure of white racism [Eurocentrism] is built no doubt on economic exploitation but it is cemented with white culture. *In other words, the racism inherent in white society is determined economically, but defined culturally.* And any revolutionary ideology that is relevant to the times must envisage not merely a change in the ownership of the means of production, but a definition of that ownership: who shall own, whites only or blacks as well? It must envisage, that is, a fundamental change in the concepts of man and society contained in white culture – it must envisage a revolutionary culture. For, as Gramsci has said, revolutionary theory requires a revolutionary culture.[45]

It should be noted that Sivanandan (and to a lesser extent Robinson and Lipsitz) might be guilty of essentializing 'white' culture in much the same way Asante idealizes 'African' culture – in effect inventing a 'West' devoid of class struggle, cultural dynamism and diversity. Indeed, much of what is understood and claimed as 'white culture' was made possible by the labor-power of African and other peoples from the 'Third World'. Nevertheless, these radical theorists give insight into the necessity for revolutionary theory which leads to societal change, and ultimately to revolutionary culture.

Since Asante rejects the counter-hegemonic cultural vision of historical materialists, especially the idea that any European or Eurocentric notion is capable of promoting change for Blacks, we must ask the question: Can an Afrocentric view break with the dominant culture and bring forth a revolutionary culture? Let us see how Sivanandan, Robinson, Lipsitz and Manning Marable approached this question in the 1960s by analyzing a very similar debate associated with the Black Power movement.

Culture and Identity

Sivanandan's 1971 article 'Black Power: The Politics of Existence' and Manning Marable's chapters in *Race, Reform and Rebellion* give critical insight into the evolution (or devolution) of Asante's Afrocentric philosophy.[46] Each analyzes the two contending force of nationalism in the 1960s and 1970s: cultural nationalists and revolutionary nationalists. As Sivanandan and Marable illustrate, the Black Power movement during that period was viewed by the state as a threat to its dominance and was therefore targeted for elimination.[47] Due in part to real ideological difference, but also to misinformation disseminated through the FBI's Counterintelligence Programs (COINTELPRO), these two camps were involved in a heated, and sometimes deadly, struggle against each other. Similar to Marable, Sivanandan subdivides the nationalist groups into various categories: in the first he places the most recent generation of Asante's philosophical primogenitors, poet-activist Imamu Baraka (a.k.a. LeRoi Jones) and the founder of US (United Slaves Organization), Maulana Ron Karenga. In the second category of revolutionary nationalists Sivanandan uses the Black Panther Party (BPP) as the prime example.[48]

According to Sivanandan, the cultural nationalist 'tacitly acknowledges the conception of a pluralist society and hopes, within it, to find power that will give the Afro-American a choice of opting out of or into white society.'[49] On the other hand, revolutionary nationalists like Newton and Seale (who were influenced by Frantz Fanon's *Wretched of the Earth*) realized to some degree that in an inherently racist class society like the United States or Britain, such 'power' and 'choice' remain purely at the level of idealistic and individualistic rhetoric – still operating within the realm of dominant culture and politics. Thus, borrowing from Frantz Fanon, the revolutionary nationalist 'recognises that racism is a symptom of the malaise in capitalist society and therefore society will itself have to be restructured – and the black man is the obvious historical agent of that process.'[50] Asante, a contemporary and product of both forms of 'nationalism', appears to have conflated the two and incorporated (but not reconciled) both into his concept of Afrocentricity.

In revolutionary nationalist fashion, Asante acknowledges 'non-free people, who are exploited by ruling classes ... are challenged to struggle against structural discourse that denies their right to freedom and, indeed, their right to exist.'[51] Yet borrowing 'important theoretical impetus' from the cultural nationalist Maulana Ron Karenga, Asante maintains that 'freedom is a mental state'. He advocates 'the empowering of the oppressed by listening to their voices' through the use of the 'African' concepts of *nommo* (Akan) 'the generative and productive power of the spoken word', and *Njia*

(Kiswahili) 'the ideology of victorious thought'.[52] He states confidently: 'To the degree that [Afrocentricity] is incorporated into the lives of the millions of Africans on the continent and in the Diaspora, it will become revolutionary.'[53] While it may be true that the pen (or in this case the *nommo*) is more powerful than the sword, it would appear, given the power of the capitalist state, that one must go beyond rhetoric to become 'revolutionary' and effect change in a sexist, classist and racist society.

Yet is it not possible that African identity can be a force for change among African-Americans? Asante claims that it is a false (that is, Eurocentric) assertion that 'Africans in the Americas are not Africans connected to their *spatial origin* . . . African American culture and history represent developments in African culture and history, *inseparably from place and time*. Analysis of African American culture that is not based on Afrocentric premises is bound to lead to incorrect conclusions.'[54] Asante, in groping for some timeless 'essence', sees little or no difference between a poor Zimbabwean peasant woman and a rich male Barbados banker. Likewise, for him there is a spatial and temporal connection between Menelik II struggling against Italian imperialism in the 1890s and US Supreme Court Justice Clarence Thomas struggling against pro-choice forces in the 1990s. It would seem more appropriate, however, to turn Asante's statement around and say that an analysis of Black culture that *is* based solely on Afrocentric premises will lead to incorrect political conclusions. Sivanandan argues:

> A Black American is not just a displaced African. He cannot find himself by relating solely to the African ethos. Africa is no more a clue to his identity than America. But they [African and American] are both his history: one tells him whence he came, and the other where he is at – two strands of the same consciousness. To accept the one to the exclusion of the other is to submit once again to the type of 'double consciousness' that Du Bois spoke of in another context: 'a sense of always looking at one's self through the eyes of others.' For the Black American can no more be at home in an African milieu than the American Jew in the Middle East. And the forced cultivation of a purely African persona can only damage the Black American psyche even further and lead to the type of obsessive, inward-looking nationalism which one has come to identify with the Zionists.[55]

Asante has countered that 'African Americans can never achieve their full psychological potential until they find congruence between who they are and what their environment says ought to be.'[56] To which Sivanandan replies:

> Culture certainly tells us 'who we are, what we must do, and how we can do it.' But creating ourselves in terms of our culture and reshaping our society in terms

of that creation are part and parcel of the same process. *Becoming and doing belong to the same continuum.* To abstract our culture from its social milieu in order to give it coherence is to lose out on its vitality. And once a culture loses its social dynamic, identity becomes an indulgence. *It becomes, that is, an end in itself and not a guide to effective action.*[57] [emphasis added]

But what of this 'effective action'; how does it manifest itself? Many would argue that 'freeing the mind' and 'finding a sense of self', while necessary, should not be 'ends' in and of themselves. The all-important question is not whether revolutionary consciousness should be a one-phase or two-phase process. From the perspective of most historical materialists, the all-important question is *praxis:* the use to which one puts that consciousness and identity.

Although Asante is primarily involved in understanding rhetoric as resistance, he sees Afrocentricity as 'not merely an artistic or literary movement . . . it [is] an individual or collective quest for authenticity, . . . [and] above all the total use of method to effect psychological, political, social, cultural and economic change. The Afrocentric idea is beyond decolonizing the mind.'[58] Thus it is a quest for identity *and* a way of 'empowering . . . the oppressed'. Yet, as Harold Cruse has asked, 'Where is the practice?' 'The answer in African American Studies at Temple', Asante replies, 'is the doctoral program itself, a product of Afrocentric theory and practice.'[59] Indeed, Asante has argued that 'Afrocentric scholarship is itself *praxis*. . . .'[60] But one must question Asante's definition of praxis; surely it is different from Manning Marable's understanding:

> To have any practical relevancy to the actual conditions and problems experienced by African American people, Black Studies must conceive itself as a type of *praxis*, a unity of theory and practical action. It is insufficient for black scholars to scale the pristine walls of the academic tower, looking below with calculated indifference to the ongoing struggles of black people . . . There are Black Studies programs at major universities. . . . Yet, much of this work is abstract and disconnected; . . . it replicates the stilted, obtuse language which characterizes much of the Western intellectual tradition.[61]

Here Marable casts doubt on the unity of 'stilted, obtuse' theories like Afrocentricity and the practical struggles of Black people. Black Studies programs are without value unless they bear a message which 'nourished the hope, dignity and resistance of Black people'. Thus if real liberation and political change are to occur we must understand how identity interacts with culture and consciousness, to inform praxis:

Identity may emanate from the consciousness of our culture, but its operational function can only be meaningful in political terms. Our culture, therefore, needs to be coherent and dynamic at the same time. A culture that takes time off to furbish itself produces a personality without a purpose. There is no point in finding out who I am if I do not know what to do with that knowledge. For knowing who I am does not by itself confer on me the ability to do what is socially necessary. . . . Furthermore, to seek one's identity in seclusion is to become, inbreeding, self-righteous, and, to that extent, inhumane. It keeps one from finding, in Fanon's indomitable phrase, 'the universality inherent in the human condition.[62]

Yet beyond psychological discourse and 'propaedeutic value', does Asante's Afrocentric 'method' or Marable's and Sivanandan's 'utilitarian/functional' analysis have anything concrete to offer to the notions of liberation and 'identity as political change'? One should keep in mind that in the real world of working people, the process of identity, association and cultural liberation are far more dialectical. On the one hand, the struggle for an 'African' identity is always a process of re-invention and is never separated completely from struggle. Today's youth, sporting Malcolm X hats, Kente cloth and reciting raps by Ice T or Public Enemy are recreating the Black militant message of the 1960s to fit their oppressed situation in the 1990s. This history has become part of the collective memory of Black people 'emerging from the vernacular, folk tradition of resistance, survival and struggle in our inner cities.'[63] Unfortunately, the forces of the state, using racism as the key means of maintaining cultural hegemony, often penalize young Black folks for their dress, styles, attitudes – even their music. As Marable reminds us about rap music:

. . . is [it not] accidental that rap has erupted precisely at an historical moment when African American unemployment is massive, when crack has become a crippling epidemic, and as prisons and the criminal justice system have become a means for the institutional regulation of hundreds of thousands of young black people? Rap at its best represents a critique of the system of domination and exploitation, projecting into artistic form the political economy advanced by Malcolm X. By searching the contours of culture, we illuminate the essence of our political, economic and social environment.[64]

Nevertheless, the question remains: Will these youths be motivated to change their objective reality simply because they have freed their minds and recreated a sense of self; or to paraphrase the language of popular culture: 'If they free their mind, will their ass follow?'[65]

What is important to recognize here is that while Afrocentricity may give insight into identity and racism as social practices with their own changing history and symbolic regularities, it cannot explain how both capital and the state – and indeed some members of the working class – use these social practices for their own instrumental purposes. Eurocentric racism was not invented by capitalists simply to confuse the white working class. The Afrocentric approach advocated by Asante does little to explain the specifics of economic and political exploitation. Asante's advocacy of a return to a static and idealist interpretation of an unproblematic 'African past', where oppression and exclusion did not exist, explains little – and accomplishes less. Instead we suggest, along with Gramsci, that consciousness and culture, especially revolutionary consciousness and revolutionary culture, does not proceed in an unmediated fashion – either from the manipulations of state and capital or from the direct experience of discrimination and class struggle.

For the sake of argument, if one rejects Afrocentricity as an answer, the question arises: How can one revolutionize consciousness and culture? Marxists would suggest that Black people must first make a radical assessment of their culture. That assessment, that revolutionary perspective, is provided by the Black man and woman by virtue of their historical situation, that is, they contend with the cultural manifestations of racism in their daily lives. They recognize that racial prejudice and discrimination are not a matter of individual attitudes, but the 'sickness' of a whole society carried in its culture. They also realize that their survival as Black men and women in 'white' society requires that they constantly question and challenge every aspect of 'white' life. In their everyday lives they must fight the particulars of 'white cultural superiority'. In the process they may or may not engender a revolutionary culture, but certainly will engender a revolutionary practice within that culture.[66]

On these points, many Marxists and Afrocentrists would most likely agree; however, where they would part company would be on how to make revolutionary practice 'blossom' into a revolutionary culture. As Sivanandan sees it:

> For that practice to blossom into a revolutionary culture . . . requires the participation of the masses, not just blacks . . . For the black man [and woman], however, the consciousness of class is instinctive to [their] consciousness of colour. Even as they begin to throw away the shackles of [their] particular slavery, [they] see that there are others besides [themselves] who are enslaved too. [They] see that racism is only one dimension of oppression in a whole system of exploitation and racial discrimination, the particular tool of a whole exploitative creed. [They] see also that the culture of competition, individualism and elitism that fostered their intellect and gives it a habitation and a name is an accessory to the exploitation of the masses as a whole, and not merely of the blacks.[67]

Thus revolutionary practice and revolutionary culture are intimately intertwined with class, culture, consciousness, race and sexuality, and anyone who seeks the liberation of all people – that is, not just intellectuals in academe, but all people – must understand these interconnections. As Bernard Magubane has argued:

> Important as it is to establish one's cultural roots, if no revoultion takes place in the productive forces that alienates black labor power, culture will lack substance. Re-establishing Afro-America's cultural roots must not be mere 'folklore' but must be something that validates itself through revolutionary struggles to emancipate human labor from the shackles of capital. Bringing to life the culture of an oppressed people is not just a question of looking back to the past, but in understanding the past in order to transcend it.[68]

Implications for Pan-African Liberation

From a historical materialist perspective, Asante's conception of Afrocentric 'ideas' is both ahistorical and idealistic. Contrary to his Afrocentric notions, ideas are a reflection of material reality in human consciousness, a link by which people relate to their surrounding world. The character of the social structure and the prevailing conditions of life heavily influence the formation of ideas. In a class society, ideas like Afrocentricity have both a social bearing *and* a class character. These ideas, in turn, can have either a positive or negative relationship to the interests of different classes and cultural formations. The characteristic assumption of idealistic philosophy is that an idea has an external existence, immune to change and independent of concrete reality. However, such notions (Afrocentricity included) indirectly lend support to the efforts of exploiting classes to justify the conception of a changeless and hierarchical order of society – an 'order' permeated by class and masculine privileges and racial/cultural oppression.

This understanding of Asante's idealistic discourse holds important implications for Pan-Africanism as a revolutionary practice. For revolutionaries, the 'theoretical' significance of this question has 'practical' implications. As Gramsci has noted, a philosophy must 'cease to be arbitrary and become necessary – rational – real' if its aim is 'to modify the world and to revolutionise praxis'.[69] One could say therefore that a 'philosophy of praxis' must become actual, not simply existing socially and historically in the ideas of individual intellectuals.

Today we must understand that ideas like Afrocentricity and Pan-Africanism are rooted in objective class interests and reflect the contradictions inherent in the current economic, political and social crisis. The political economy of the 1990s is changing so rapidly it is sometimes difficult to comprehend, but it must provide the context within which we view the current crises. We are witnessing the global transformation of capitalism: high technology and robotics are replacing human labor in industry after industry. The use of new methods of computerized controls of workers and materials and downsizing of the work force is eliminating nearly 25 million jobs (or nearly 30 percent of the existing jobs in private enterprises.[70] This will obviously have tremendous consequences for the political and social structure of the country. Industry is abandoning modern US cities (which are increasingly impoverished and offer no political power for their Black and Latino residents) and moving their plants to rural, low-wage areas. Increasingly we see industry moving out of the United States altogether (Mexico, Central America, South Africa, Asia), creating what some call global apartheid. The combination of job-flight and declining social services is widening the base of the 'new poverty', while state and federal governments refuse to allocate their declining resources to the poor. The result is increased unemployment, cuts in social services and homelessness. Working people in America (women, men, Black, brown, white, blue collar, white collar, gay or straight) are becoming 'disposable'. This growing economic crisis is producing political and social crises – complicated by factors of sexism, racism, Eurocentrism and elitism.

If we view Pan-Africanism and Afrocentricity within this overall context, as dialectical ends of a revolutionary spectrum, we can understand the contradictions inherent in the current debate – a debate about how best to resist economic regression and hegemonic social control while achieving Black empowerment. The question to be asked is simply this: Which of these oppositional philosophies – Afrocentricity or Pan-Africanism – both counters racism and sexism and challenges the hierarchical order of society, instead of lending support to that hierarchy? Pan-Africanism has the *potential* to be such a revolutionary 'philosophy of praxis'.

We must also keep in mind that nationalism is not 'transhistorical'; as McClintock reminds us, history reveals a myriad of nationalisms, and all take very different shapes in different contexts.[71] Today Pan-Africanism has developed two variations, similar to the two competing forms of 1960s nationalism, each expressing the interests of one of the two groups of classes which clash in contemporary Africa and the diaspora. Those who can transcend the idealistic limitations of Afrocentricity, and can grasp the necessity of struggle beyond rhetoric, will form a vanguard element and become Revolutionary Pan-Africanists. In this context, Revolutionary Pan-Africanism must be trans-racial and trans-gendered; it must be inclusive (not exclusive) and internationalist (rather than simply nationalist). It must be capable of forging transnational alliances. It must express the interests of male and female members of the Black working class and peasantry; but it must also include all those White, Brown, Red, Yellow and Black working-class 'organic intellectuals' and petty bourgeois elements who are willing to commit class, gender and racial 'suicide' and join the struggle. There are many (including Afrocentrists) who would label such notions 'utopian'. Yet today, as just noted above, revolution in the productive forces and in the economy in general, is creating revolutionaries in the global society. The Black and Brown youth of Los Angeles, the West Bank and Johannesburg, rebelling against racist oppression and economic exploitation, represent encouraging examples of Revolutionary Pan-African consciousness in action.

Counterposed to Revolutionary Pan-Africanists are those Afrocentric elements who cannot (or will not) make the transition to political action and who become 'demogogic' Pan-Africanists.[72] They are products of the type of existential, traditional (inorganic) 'intellectualized' practice advocated by Asante. Consciously or unconsciously, they express the interests of the imperialist ruling class and their African and African-American allies. Included in this group are 'coloured intellectuals' and 'government officials' who often use race/racism as a blind for their class interest. We have ample examples among the Colin Powells, Clarence Thomases and Gatsha Buthelezis of the world – that is, apologists for local and global apartheid.

While this may appear to some as an unusually harsh criticism and total dismissal of all Afrocentric thinking, it should rather be seen as a warning sign. We would stop short of drawing a parallel between Asante and other Afrocentrists in the 1990s, and those that Addison Gayle labelled 'nihilistic cultural nationalists' and 'black fascists' in the 1970s. It must be understood that Afrocentricity could potentially 'serve as a liaison between the black community uptown and the [white] Man downtown. . . . '[73]

Our critique also points to the absolute necessity of making a complete break with idealistic and hegemonic rhetoric and practices. It is critical that Revolutionary Pan-Africanists do not conflate or essentialize the issues of class, culture, gender and identity – an extremely difficult task when bombarded by racism and sexism in postmodern society – but instead put them into context of working-class struggles. This is best illustrated by Manning Marable's discussion of 1960s Black nationalism and Frantz Fanon:

> Militant nationalists praised Fanon's advocacy of revolutionary violence, and his polemical thrusts aimed at the Negro petty bourgeoisie in colonial Africa. But what did Fanon think about the Afro-American struggle? . . . For Fanon, the struggle to destroy white oppression was not in essence a racial dialectic, but an anti-racist movement that welcomed the participation of committed whites. In *Black Skin, White Masks* (1952), Fanon's most 'nationalist-oriented' work, he explained that his ultimate vision for the US was the liberation of all exploited

people: 'I can already see a white man and a black man hand in hand.' The question here is not so much that of intellectual dishonesty, but a failure of many Black Powerites [and Afrocentrists] to relate their eclectic versions of nationalism to the actual material needs and aspirations of the black working class and the poor.[74]

Obviously the validity of Revolutionary Pan-Africanism as a liberating 'idea' can only be born out in 'praxis'. Yet it should be fairly obvious that an idea like Afrocentricity, which is not based on reality but on some metaphysical ideation of 'Africa', has limited practical use in a liberation struggle beyond providing 'origin stories'. Asante has accused the critics of Afrocentricity of 'not reading or quoting [his] works but of responding to a popular cachet.'[75] On the contrary, using Asante's own words, we might say of Afrocentricity, that 'the invalidity of an idea arises, not from its exponents, but from its own fundamental flaws.'[76]

Notes

I would like to thank all those who have read drafts of this work, including Craig Gilmore, Ruth Wilson Gilmore, Robin D.G. Kelley, Bill Watkins, Ken Wolf, Patritia K. Telaghani, Trevor A. Campbell and Salima Lemelle. The quote by A.Sivanandan that begins this article is from *A Different Hunger*, London, 1987, p. 89.

1. See Kinfe Abraham, *Politics of Black Nationalism*, Trenton, N.J. 1991. and Cedric J. Robinson, *Black Marxism*, 2nd edn, London 1991.

2. For example, see 'Taking Offense: Is This the New Enlightenment on Campus or the New McCarthyism?' *Newsweek*, 24 December 1990, pp. 48–55; John Taylor, 'Are You Politically Correct?' *New York Magazine*, 21 January 1991, pp. 33–40; Dinesh D'Souza, 'The Visigoths in Tweed', *Forbes*, 1 April 1991, pp. 81–6; Michael Bérubé, 'Public Image Limited: Political Correctness and the Media's Big Lie', *Village Voice*, 18 June 1991, pp. 31–6; 'African Dreams', *Newsweek*, 23 September 1991, pp. 42–50.

3. C.L.R. James, *A History of Pan-African Revolt*, Washington D.C. 1969 [1938]; W.E.B. Du Bois, *The World and Africa*, New York 1946; Eric Williams, *Capitalism and Slavery*, Chapel Hill, N.C. 1944.

4. Robinson, *Black Marxism*; Walter Rodney 'Towards the Sixth Pan-African Congress', in *Pan Africanism*, Horace Campbell, ed., Toronto 1976; Bernard M. Magubane, *The Ties That Bind: African-American Consciousness of Africa*, Trenton, N.J. 1987. See also V.P. Thompson, *Africa and Unity: The Evolution of Pan-Africanism*, New York 1969; Wilson J. Moses, *The Golden Age of Black Nationalism, 1850–1925*, New York 1978.

5. Antonio Gramsci, *Selections from the Prison Notebooks*, New York 1987, and Frantz Fanon, *The Wretched of the Earth*, New York 1963; *Black Skin, White Masks*, New York 1952; and *Towards the African Revolution*, New York 1967.

6. While I hesitate to label this analysis 'Marxist', it is a work heavily influenced by the theory of historical materialism as developed by Marx and Engels and utilized by Marxist intellectuals. Also note that people from Diane Ravitch, William Raspberry, Henry Louis Gates, Jr, Manning Marable, Michele Wallace, Orlando Patterson, Arthur Schlesinger, Jr, and Glenn Loury to George Will have also critiqued Afrocentricity. Molefe K. Asante, 'African American Studies: The Future of the Discipline', *The Black Scholar*, vol. 22, no. 3 (1992), p. 21.

7. 'African Dreams', p. 42.

8. Asante is by no means the only academic proponent of Afrocentricity; equally well-known are Professor Leonard Jeffries, former chair of Black Studies at the City University of New York and Professor Asa Hilliard of Georgia State University. See 'African Dreams', pp. 42–3, and 'Politically Correct?', pp. 39–40.

9. Molefi Kete Asante, *The Afrocentric Idea*, Philadelphia 1987, p. 3; while we will concentrate on this work, also see *Afrocentricity: The Theory of Social Change*, Buffalo 1980, and the enlarged third edition, *Afrocentricity*, Trenton, N.J. 1989; Molefi K. Asante and K.W. Asante, *African Culture: The Rhythms of Unity*, Trenton, N.J. 1988; Molefi K. Asante, *Kemet, Afrocentricity, and Knowledge*, Trenton, 1990; 'Putting Africa at the Center', *Newsweek*, 23 September 1991, p. 46. For Sivanandan's work, see *A Different Hunger* and *Communities of Resistance*, both London 1990.

10. Ibid., p. 25.

11. Many scholars made much the same point years ago. Among others see W.E.B. Du Bois, *The World and Africa*, New York 1946, and A. Temu and B. Swai, *Historians and Africanist History: A Critique*, London 1981.

12. Tom Bottomore, *A Dictionary of Marxist Thought*, Cambridge, Mass. 1991. Also see Robinson, *Black Marxism*, Part I.

13. Asante, *Afrocentric Idea*, p. 5.

14. See Robinson, *Black Marxism*, Chs 3–4.

15 Asante, *Afrocentricity*, p. 1, and *Afrocentric Idea*, pp. 149–56.

16. The best authority on this topic remains G.K.Plekhanov, *The Role of the Individual in History*, New York 1940. For an 'idealist' interpretation, see Sidney Hook, *The Hero in History*, Boston 1943.

17. E. Francis White, 'Africa on My Mind: Gender, Counter-Discourse and African-American Nationalism', *Journal of Women's History*, vol. 2, no. 1 (Spring 1990), pp. 73–4.

18. Anne McClintock, '"No Longer in a Future Heaven": Women and Nationalism in South Africa', *Transition*, no. 51 (1991), p 104.

19. Darlene Clark Hine, 'The Black Studies Movement: Afrocentric-Traditionalist-Feminist Paradigms for the Next Stage', *The Black Scholar*, vol. 22, no. 3 (1992), p. 15. See bell hooks, 'Feminism: A Transformational Politic', in Debroah L. Rhodes, ed., *Theoretical Perspectives on Sexual Difference*, New Haven, Conn. 1990, and Patricia Hills Collins, *Black Feminist Thought: Knowledge, Consciousness and the Politics of Empowerment*, Boston 1990.

20. Asante, 'African American Studies', p. 24.

21. Ibid. p. 27

22. See Asante, *Afrocentricity* (1989 edn), Ch. 1 and 'Putting Africa at the Center', *Newsweek*, 23 September 1991, p. 46.

23. V.Y. Mudimbe, *The Invention of Africa*, Bloomington, Ind. 1988, especially Chs 1 and 4.

24. Asante, *Afrocentric Idea*, p. 65.

25. Ibid.

26. Asante, 'African American Studies', p. 27

27. See Sidney J. Lemelle, 'Ritual, Resistance and Social Reproduction', *Journal of Historical Sociology*, vol. 5, no. 2 (June 1992).

28. McClintock, 'Future Heaven', p. 122.

29. Asante, 'African American Studies', p. 27.

30. E. Francis White has made a similar point in her critique of Afrocentricity. See White, 'Africa on My Mind', pp 84–5: see also Asante, 'African American Studies', p. 22.

31. A. Sivanandan, 'The Liberation of the Black Intellectual', in *A Different Hunger*, pp. 82–98.

32. Asante, *Afrocentric Idea*, p. 167, and *Afrocentricity*, p. 31.

33. Ibid., pp. 85–6.

34. Ibid., pp. 89–93.

35. Robinson, *Black Marxism*, p. 260.

36. George Lipsitz, *A Life in the Struggle: Ivory Perry and the Culture of Opposition*, Philadelphia 1988, p. 9.

37. Antonio Gramsci, *Selections from the Prison Notebooks*, New York 1987, p. 3.

38. Ibid., p. 10

39. Ibid., p. 4

40. Sivanandan, 'Black Intellectual', p. 93.
41. Ibid.
42. Asante, *Afrocentric Idea*, p. 8. See also *Afrocentricity* (1989 edn), p. 17. It is interesting that Asante must resort to philosophical gymnastics to maintain the coherence of his argument by saying, 'Du Bois became more and more African in his outlook . . . he rejected the inherent racism in capitalism and pursued socialist thought. He moved toward the rejection of material-ism which was deeply imbedded in Marxist thought. Because Du Bois was beyond the limita-tions of a Eurocentric analysis, he could never be restricted by Marxist thought.'
43. Sivanandan, 'Black Intellectual', p. 94.
44. Robinson, *Black Marxism*, p. 434.
45. Sivanandan, 'Black Intellectual', p. 94.
46. A. Sivanandan, 'Black Power: The Politics of Existence', in *A Different Hunger*, pp. 57–66.
47. Manning Marable, *Race, Reform and Rebellion*, Jackson, Miss. 1992, p. 125.
48. Sivanandan, 'Black Power', p. 59. It should be noted that Sivanandan lumped Baraka and Karenga together as cultural nationalists before either claimed their current 'socialist' ori-entation. For an interesting treatment of this period, see Ward Churchill and Jim Vander Wall, *Agents of Repression*, Boston 1990, ch. 3. Also see Marable, *Race, Reform and Rebellion*, Ch. 5. For related struggles in the U.K., see Paul Gilroy, *There Ain't No Black in the Union Jack,* Chicago 1991, Chs 3 and 5; Center for Contemporary Cultural Studies, *The Empire Strikes Back: Race and Racism in 70's Britain*, London 1988.
49. Sivanandan, 'Black Power', p. 59.
50. Ibid., p. 60.
51. Asante, *Afrocentric Idea*, p. 22.
52. Ibid., p. 17, and *Afrocentricity*, p. 1.
53. Ibid.
54. *Afrocentric Idea*, p. 10. See also Asante, 'African American Studies', p. 27.
55. A. Sivanandan, 'Culture and Identity', *Liberator,* vol. 10, no.6 (June 1970), p. 11.
56. Asante, *Afrocentric Idea*, p. 98.
57. Sivanandan, 'Culture and Identity', p. 11.
58. Asante, *Afrocentric Idea*, p. 125.
59. Asante, 'African American Studies', p. 21.
60. Asante, *Afrocentric Idea*, p. 175; Asante, *Afrocentricity* (1989 edn), p. 31.
61. Manning Marable, 'Blueprint for Black Studies and Multiculturalism', *The Black Scholar,* vol. 22, no. 3 (1992), p. 32.
62. Sivanandan, 'Culture and Identity', p. 11.
63. Marable, 'Blueprint', p. 32.
64. Ibid.
65. Originally a lyric by George Clinton Parliament/Funkadelic. The term has been used by many, among them Digital Underground, 'Free Your Mind', on the album *Sons of the P,* 1991.
66. Sivanandan, 'Black Intellectual', p. 95.
67. Ibid.
68. Robinson, *Black Marxism*, p. 234.
69. Gramsci, *Notebook*, p. 368.
70. *Wall Street Journal,* 16 March 1993; *New York Times,* 15 March 1993. See also Trevor A. Campbell, 'The Political Economy of Restructuring and the Process of Global Capitalist Inte-gration', *California Sociologist* (1992), pp. 179–213.
71. McClintock, 'Future Heaven', p. 120.
72. See Elenga M'buyinga, *Pan Africanism or Neo-Colonialism*, London 1982.
73. Marable, *Race, Reform and Rebellion*, p. 120–21.
74. Ibid., p. 120.
75. Asante, 'African American Studies', p. 21.
76. Asante, *Afrocentric Idea*, p. 9.

Appendix A

The Seventh Pan-African

Congress: Notes from

North American Delegates

William H. Watkins, Abdul Alkalimat
and Marian Kramer

As we attempt to summarize our experiences at the Seventh Pan-African Congress (PAC), we wish our readers to know that our thoughts are as personal and emotional as they are political and intellectual. Having experienced the 'roots' phenomenon and visited Africa, we believe it impossible for Black Americans to travel to the motherland without being filled with a certain sense of longing, curiosity and fulfillment. It is much the feeling of a lost people returning home.

Departing from Chicago, we quickly became acquainted with other North American delegates. We were a collection of representatives from mass movements, unions, community organizations and the academy, but all were activists committed to fundamental social change, and with extensive credentials in the movement. In our midst was a most remarkable woman, Kay Struthers, a lifelong veteran of the revolutionary movement, who was making her first trip to the motherland. Kay would prove to be a most energetic and valuable asset to the North American delegation.

Although one of us had spent an extended time in Nigeria in 1983, this would be our first visit to the eastern part of the continent. Anyone listening to the American news media immediately associates East Africa with the curses of starvation, rampant AIDS and political instability. In spite of this conditioning, we were on our way to Africa, and we could hardly contain our eagerness to deplane. But first there would be an eternity of travel. The flights seemed endless. A seven-hour layover at London's Heathrow Airport prompted the inevitable bid whist game, along with the requisite signifying. Another ten to twelve hours to Nairobi followed, during which we seized the opportunity to review and reflect on the background of the Pan-African Congress. We knew the history of the six preceding congresses, of course, but we wanted to refresh our memories, and took this opportunity to review our 'Handbook of Struggle', prepared by the Seventh PAC North American coordinator, Abdul Alkalimat.

The handbook reminded delegates that the First Pan-African Congress convened in London in 1900. Among its leaders were W.E.B. Du Bois, H. Sylvester Williams, Henry P. Brown and Bishop Alexander Walters, all of whom wanted an assemblage of 'men and women of African blood, to deliberate solemnly upon the present situation and the outlook for the darker races of mankind.'[1] The historic resolution of the first congress called for racial progress, 'raising nine millions of human beings from slavery to manhood',[2] international respect for Africa and an end to the 'unrighteous oppression toward the American Negro.'[3]

The Second Pan-African Congress, held in Paris in 1919, called upon the League of Nations and the Western powers to deal with Africa and her people fairly. Resolutions asked that natural resources be 'held in trust for the natives,'[4] that forced labor be abolished, that education be expanded, and that fundamental principles of citizenship and consent be honored.

In 1921, the Third Pan-African Congress's London Manifesto reiterated the themes of self-government, political freedom and restrained European expropriation of African wealth. In addition, this manifesto called for the 'absolute equality of races',[5] the advancement of all civilization, world peace, an end to economic and cultural oppression and to the 'worst abuses' of colonialism. Most important, this document pointed to the problems of capital enslaving labor, thus creating an egregious maldistribution of wealth caused by the tyranny of monopoly.

The Pan-African movement increased in importance as World War II ushered in a shift in the world balance of power. The Fifth Pan-African Congress convened in Manchester, England in 1945. Reflecting the increasingly assertive voice of oppressed peoples, this gathering was characterized by intensified demands and more radical resolutions, and it is generally agreed that the Fifth Pan-African Congress was a watershed event, playing a significant role in stimulating the anti-colonial struggles and wars of liberation of the 1950s and early 1960s. Its 'Declaration to the Colonial Peoples' still resonates:

> We affirm the right of all colonial peoples to control their own destiny. All colonies must be free from foreign imperialist control, whether political or economic.
>
> The peoples of the colonies must have the right to elect their own Governments, without restrictions from foreign Powers. We say to the peoples of the colonies that they must fight for these ends by all means at their disposal.

The object of imperialist Powers is to exploit. By granting the right to colonial peoples to govern themselves that object is defeated. Therefore, the struggle for political power by colonial and subject peoples is the first step towards, and the necessary prerequisite to, complete social, economic and political emancipation. The Fifth Pan-African Congress therefore calls on the workers and farmers of the Colonies to organise effectively. Colonial workers must be in front of the battle against imperialism. Your weapons – the strike and the boycott – are invincible.

We also call upon the intellectuals and professional classes of the colonies to awaken to their responsibilities. By fighting for trade union rights, the right to form co-operatives, freedom of the Press, assembly, demonstration and strike, freedom to print and read the literature which is necessary for the education of the masses, you will be using the only means by which your liberties will be won and maintained. Today there is only one road to effective action – the organisation of the masses. And in that organisation the educated colonials must join. Colonial and subject peoples of the world, unite![6]

The Sixth Pan-African Congress, held in 1974 in Dar es Salaam, Tanzania, offered an examination of the historical development of Pan-Africanism and the current situation. It noted that the Pan-African movement was inextricably linked to the worldwide struggles of oppressed peoples. It called upon workers, peasants and intellectuals of the world's oppressed territories to unite for independence and self-determination.

Of great importance, the Sixth PAC recognized the revolutionary potential of Pan-Africanism: Pan-Africanism must be a dynamic force for liberation 'within the context of the class struggle',[7] and must help bring solidarity to the oppressed of the world.[8] The charge of revolutionary Pan-Africanism would be to help end foreign domination.

The Women's Conference

At last we reached the motherland--only to wait another eight hours in the Nairobi airport. With videocams rolling and flashbulbs popping, we were in the land of our ancestors. Transferring from British Airways to Uganda's national airline emphasized that we were in a different place. The ninety-minute flight from Nairobi to Kampala, Uganda found our collective anxiety escalating. For weary travelers, the bus ride from Entebbe Airport to Kampala was like a jolt of caffeine. Most of the delegates were on African soil for the first time. We were transfixed as we rode through villages and saw African people in an African context. The sight of lush land, children playing, and people going about their everyday lives hypnotized us all.

When we arrived at Mackerere, the prestigious university built by the British, our busy schedule had just begun. With time only to drop our bags, we were immediately escorted uphill to the women's pre-conference meeting that we had so eagerly anticipated. Long before departing, North American delegates had been informed that for the first time a Pan-African Congress would be accompanied by a women's pre-conference gathering. One could sense the enthusiasm generated by the prospect of such a meeting. Not only were the North American women excited, but the politically conscious men understood how divisive the 'woman question' had been, not only in Africa, but throughout the Third World – or, indeed, in the US. History and justice demanded that the complex problems facing women in the motherland be addressed.

During our long layover at Nairobi, the North American women had convened a spirited caucus at breakfast. Those who had been assigned responsibilities to conduct workshops or present papers reviewed their tasks. All resolved to be aggressive, assertive and vocal in support of African women and the struggles of women everywhere. It had been falsely rumored that men might not be able to attend the women's meeting, but in any case, all workshops would be conducted by women. The male delegates understood, and similarly resolved to be assertive in supporting women's struggles.

Arriving at Mackerere's assembly hall, we were thrust immediately into sessions in progress. The two-day gathering would convene six workshops: The Effects of Structural Adjustment on African Women; The African Woman and Her Environment; The Position and Status of the African Woman, African Women and the Law; Towards Increasing Survival of the African Woman and Child; and The Role of Women in Cultural Development.[9] Having previously selected our workshops, we moved quickly to our places – and the arrival of the boisterous North American delegates was noted by all.

To satisfy our curiosity about the rest of the pre-conference, some of us left our workshops to visit the other five. The women's meeting was truly in full force: some of the sessions were hot to the touch. Millennia of grievances and oppression were bubbling to the surface. The Bible says, sow the wind, reap the whirlwind. In every workshop we saw African women holding forth. Reluctantly, the controversial issue of female genital mutilation was brought to the attention of the delegates. As predicted, this was a time for the women of Africa to speak their pièce, not peace.

The plenary sessions of the women's conference marked the high point, however. Because most of us were reared in the Black church, we had experienced hundreds of emotionally charged services and meetings – and this one ranked up there with the best. As we entered the large, church-like room, filled mostly with women, we knew we were in for a special experience. Taking our seats, we noted that we were sitting directly behind Dr Betty Shabazz, widow of our 'prince', Malcolm X.

As the meeting unfolded, one dynamic woman after another seized the floor and began to speak her mind. Among the many women, and men, who spoke of their struggles, the high point came when sister Brenda Matthews of Chicago, a member of our little delegation, rose to speak. Though we had flown to Africa with her, we couldn't possibly have been prepared for what we were about to hear. Brenda, a working-class woman from Chicago's West Side, set forth a dissertation on struggle the likes of which we had seldom heard. She effectively challenged every bastion of patriarchy, capitalism and reaction. Arms flailing and invectives flying, this was a woman to be reckoned with. Brenda, and the other women, made their point. The old days were gone forever! Women will never be the same, Africa will never be the same – and we had better know it.

Sessions, Ceremonies and More Sessions

In preparation for the congress, all conference delegates were to caucus with other delegates from their own region. Our group from Chicago met many other delegates from across the US, electing Leona Smith, president of the National Union of the Homeless, to the Congress Presidium representing North America, and Prof. William Watkins as political representative for the delegation. Repeated disagreements during the caucus discussion made it clear that many North American delegates had come to engage in the kind of 'ideological struggle' that had hampered the Sixth PAC. Our approach, by contrast, was to advance the 'political struggle' on the concrete issues facing the victims of poverty and the police state. We had thought that by now everyone understood that the only ideological struggle of nineties is how to get some biscuits on the table, get a job, find some healthcare, and pay the rent. But clearly the word hadn't trickled down to everyone.

Delegates from North America were representing organizations, and therefore conference voting procedures did not require a consensus. By the third day, several factions had formed and were pursuing their different interests. People found their counterparts and the activists from the Chicago delegation began to connect with grassroots practical leaders of the African revolution.

Like many large gatherings, this congress was organized into workshops and plenums.[10] Having concluded our regional meeting, the second half of the first day was occupied with the opening plenary session, where we got a feel for the congress as a whole. Panning across the conference center was a stimulating and heartwarming experience. With cameras clicking, people were settling in as we marveled at the diverse African people from both sides of the Atlantic. Delegates wearing indigenous dress and speaking many languages had come together in a grand gathering. Although we were aware of the differing political and organizational positions represented in the room, we all had a sense of unity and purpose.

The first and second days' plenums were taken up with an array of introductions, opening statements from dignitaries, solidarity statements from the world over, and an ill-fated attempt to receive a closed-circuit satellite message from Libya's Colonel Kaddafi. Among the highlights were addresses by Colonel Kahinda Otahire, the chair and convener of the conference; the keynote address by H.E. Yoweri Kaguta Museveni, president of Uganda; and North American professor Abdul Alkalimat of the International Preparatory Committee. Together, these presentations set the tone and framed many issues for the delegates to consider.

After Tuesday morning's plenary, delegates went on to their various workshops: Pan-African Strategies to Consolidate African Trading Blocks; From Debt Crises to Recolonization; Economic Cooperation; Liberating Education and Culture; and Regaining Control of Our Environment. All were chaired by notables in their field.

Wednesday's eight workshops included Pan-Africanism and Liberation; How Can We Interpret the Unfolding Gender, Class and Mass Struggle?; The Crusade for Reparations; Democracy, Human and People's Rights; The Military, Civil Wars and Conflict Resolution; Information and Communication Strategy for Development: Pan-African Agenda; Youth and the Future of Pan-Africanism; African Perspectives on Gender; and The Boundaries of Africa, the OAU and the Future. A proposal from two US delegates, Ashaki Binta of the Black Workers for Justice and General Baker of the National Organizing Committee, led to a special workshop on trade union activism.

Each workshop developed its own character, depending on the subject, chair, presentations, and composition. Although it's always difficult to iron out complex positions in short sessions with disparate groups of people, the workshops we observed were characterized by enthusiastic participation and a desire to find solutions, although political and ideological differences periodically emerged. However, in one or two workshops where the prospect of factional dispute was real, the voice of consensus and 'conflict resolution' prevailed.

After hearing presentations and engaging in discussion, each workshop composed a summary report, and this task naturally elicited the most spirited dialogue. Inevitably, these reports represented the political spectrum of those present, and perhaps of the Pan-African movement generally, from liberals and reformers to radicals. The hope is that all engage in a broadly based unity of action supporting the just struggles of African peoples against colonialism, barbarism and international exploitation.

Receptions and cultural activities accompanied the workshops and plenaries. The highlights for us included a marvelous musical play entitled 'The African Guest of Honour', written by Alex Mukulu and performed by an international cast at Uganda's national theater. In addition, there were a reception hosted by His Royal Highness, Ronald Muwenda Mutebe II of Buganda at the Bulange Gardens and several other receptions at the Nile Hotel Gardens. These events allowed the delegates an opportunity to interact with a wide range of people from different corners of the globe.

The General Declaration

The crowning achievement of any conference is its final statement. In this case, the General Declaration of each Pan-African Congress summarizes not only intent, but a collective political analysis of the world and world events, particularly with respect to the African continent and African people. The draft declaration was submitted by Abdul Alkalimat to the entire body: as amended and approved by the delegates, the final declaration articulates the collective sentiments of the Seventh Pan-African Congress.

The declaration begins with an overview, noting that changes in the world political and economic structure pose threats to Africa and to African people scattered across the planet. Africa and her peoples are as a result confronted with new levels of violence, fascism and recolonization. Pan-Africanism has evolved and must continue to evolve as a movement for liberation and unity in these perilous times.

The statement moves on to describe the political and historical development of colonialism throughout the twentieth century. Dramatic advances in science and technology have forever altered industrial production and the social and political system built upon such production. Massive displacements and changes in the processes of commodity production have accompanied by international realignments, the end of the Cold War, and increased state repression.

Long plagued by foreign debt, Africa suffers from these new arrangements. World Bank and International Monetary Fund policies assure that cash-starved African countries remain dependent. Thus 'structural adjustment' policies guarantee the continuation of high unemployment, food and housing shortages, poor healthcare, and social decay. Africa is left open to unchecked diseases, chemical genocide, and mass poverty. Estimates of Africa's outflow of value as a result of loans and resource looting come to

$150 million per day.[11] The 'new world order' offers little to Africa in terms of development and progress.

The declaration concludes with a revolutionary program for the twenty-first century. The program for the emancipation of Africa and the diaspora calls for increased resistance and mass action. The strategy for liberation includes concrete programs of action. Among them is extrication from the stranglehold of imperialist debt. Africa's debt, now exceeding $500 billion, can be reversed by a combination of renegotiations, reparations, and democratic self-determination or refusal to pay. Africa must develop its own energy and communications systems and other infrastructure. Another theme is that of popular democracy. Popular fronts must oppose foreign domination, industrial exploitation and gender bias, and support the struggles of youth and trade unions and foster political democracy.

Finally, the declaration firmly upholds the revolutionary character of Pan-Africanism in a time of international crises. Pan-Africanism stands for the unity of African people, both on the continent and in the diaspora. Pan-Africanism and the Pan-African Congress pledge to continue the struggle against the oppression and exploitation of African people.

Some Final Reflections

After the ideological struggles and divisions of the Sixth Pan-Africanist Congress, that the Seventh PAC actually convened was a minor miracle. Beyond the Pan-Africanist movement itself, the differences between 'liberation' movements, as well as long-standing tribal and ethnic differences make holding such a gathering difficult. The coming together of the Seventh Pan-Africanist Congress despite such problems is perhaps most indicative of the rapidly changing world political economy.

The electronic-technological revolution in the industrial countries has contributed to massive unemployment, dramatic human displacement and an even narrower concentration of wealth. African people on the continent and in the diaspora, along with other oppressed and exploited people, face not only relative poverty, but *absolute* poverty.

In these rapidly changing times, policies change and new forces emerge: new conditions for struggle are inevitably created. A wave of militant protest can be observed among the world's dispossessed, homeless, hungry, unemployed, underemployed, ill-clothed, and forgotten. Even in the wealthy United States, a new study reveals that one in five full-time employees earns wages below the poverty level.[12] Established corporations are filing bankruptcy, 'retrenching', 'regrouping', and 'downsizing'. Jobs are vanishing, never to return. Something profound is happening! We must situate the Seventh Pan-Africanist Congress in this historical context.

The congress called our attention to several issues likely to grow in importance and shape the coming period. The politics of recolonization, South African liberation, state violence, the transformative role of the women's movement, and the call for a new unity of struggle were among those themes. The political economy of colonialism is well known to all. Western industrial nations built their empires on Africa, Africa's resources, and on the backs of Africa's people and their labor. Recolonization represents a continuation of the politics of colonialism and neocolonialism practiced over the past several centuries. Modern-day recolonization is marked by deepening client-state indebtedness, economic embargoes, the continued extraction of raw materials, labor expropriation, dumping of hazardous wastes, and chemical warfare. Africa's ultimate hope is to free itself from the grip of foreign domination, subordination and the abyss of debt.

All must understand that the 'new world order' and the so-called 'end of communism' signal a new ferociousness and aggressiveness in imperialist foreign policy. The imperialists brazenly interfere in the internal politics of Somalia, Haiti, Panama, Mexico, North Korea and a host of other countries throughout Africa, the Caribbean and the Americas. The international front against imperialist aggression must be supported.

People the world over celebrated the victory of the African National Congress and its leader Nelson Mandela in the April 1994 elections. As we cheer the end of the brutal apartheid regime, we also recognize that this was a negotiated settlement. As such, the struggle to redistribute land and wealth is only beginning. Thirteen percent of the population still controls more than 85 percent of the land.[13] Unemployment for Blacks is intolerably high, and most of the profits from industrial commodity production are repatriated to Western countries. This electoral victory signals a new stage of struggle, not final victory. The Pan-African Congress must be a reminder that the unity of African peoples everywhere must continue. We must not waver in our commitment to the people of South Africa in the difficult period ahead.

Regarding violence, one need not look very far to find an escalation of police violence against peoples of color and especially those of African descent, who continue to be scapegoated for the economic and political crises paralyzing many nations. Repressive regimes are desperately trying to beat back the growing upsurge of suffering people. From Zaire to Mexico City to South Central Los Angeles to London to New York City, the story is the same. Police, the military, and often paramilitary organizations have become hit squads. Pan-Africanists are reminded that fascism means that the rule of force replaces the rule of law. Fascism and imperialism have been and continue to be companions in the scheme of reaction and domination.

An old adage suggests that the progress of a society can be measured by the progress of its women. Likewise, revolutionary movements have long understood that the struggle for women's full equality and liberation is at the heart of political and social change. As mentioned, the women's pre-conference meeting at the Seventh Pan-African Congress was a milestone. Far from being imposed from the outside, it was an outgrowth of the inevitable historical and political movement for democracy, equality and socialism in Africa. Africa's women are among the most socially abused. Their struggles are our struggles. Comrade Winnie Mandela and the sisters of the struggles for African liberation will continue to stand as beacons.

Finally, if Pan-Africanism means anything, it means unity. As African people in every country are now irreparably divided by economic and social class, ideology and privilege, the Pan-African movement becomes even more important. Pan-Africanism and the Pan-African Congresses must support the broad front of struggle necessary to challenge the international forces of national oppression, exploitation, and reaction. If Africa and Latin America represent the barometers of international capitalism's exploitation, then the Pan-African movement must articulate the vision for freedom and liberation in the twenty-first century.

Notes

1. *Address to the Nations of the World by the Pan-African Congress,* London, 1900, printed in J. Ayodele Langley, ed., *Ideologies of Liberation in Black Africa,* London 1979, p. 738.

2. Ibid., p. 739.

3. Ibid.

4. Ibid., p. 740.

5. Ibid., p. 749.

6. Ibid., p. 760.

7. Ibid., p. 760–61.

8. *Resolutions and Selected Speeches from the 6th Pan-African Congress,* Dar es Salaam 1976, p. 89.

9. An interesting and analytical discussion of the Sixth Pan-African Congress is Walter Rodney's 'Towards the Sixth Pan-African Congress: Aspects of the International Class Struggle in Africa, the Caribbean and America', in *Resolutions and Selected Speeches from the Sixth Pan-African Congress,* pp. 18–41.

10. All workshop information is published in *Pan-African Congress: Programme,* p. 9.

11. A complete transcription of all plenums can be found in *Pan-African Congress: Programme.*

12. The entire declaration is entitled *Kampala Declaration: Resist Recolonisation.*

13. Abdul Alkalimat, 'Declaration of the Seventh Pan-African Congress, Draft of the Final Statement'issued by the Congress, 3–8 April 1994.

14. The study, entitled *The Earnings Ladder,* was issued by the Bureau of the Census, US Department of Commerce.

15. Abdul Alkalimat, 'South African Election: Prelude to Revolutionary Upsurge', *People's Tribune,* 16 May 1994, vol. 21, no. 20, p. 6.

16. Further information and documents of the Seventh Pan-African Congress can be obtained from Black Liberation Committee, c/o National Organizing Committee, P.O. Box 47711, Chicago, IL 60647, USA.

Appendix B

Resist Recolonisation!:

General Declaration by the Delegates

and Participants at the 7th

Pan-African Congress

We convened the 7th Pan-African Congress to organise politics of mass resistance to the new conditions that are threatening Africa and African peoples in more dangerous ways than ever before. The African continent is facing a real threat of recolonization while our people in the diaspora are confronting the rise of fascism and fascist violence in Europe and America. Pan-Africanism has always been a global calling to advance the cause of liberation, freedom and unity of African peoples at home and abroad. A viable Pan-Africanist movement for the 1990s entails new and creative methods of fostering solidarity among Africans and people of African descent worldwide. In the age of information and communication explosion, Pan-Africanism must move with the times and be in a proactive position to propel the pace of African unity.

The 20th-century Pan-African movement found its organised expression and was institutionalised in 1900 with the 1st Pan-African Conference and has since held six Congresses (1919, 1921, 1923, 1927, 1945, 1974). The main focus began as a collective effort to fight slavery, racism, colonialism and assert the right to self-determination. The efforts culiminated in the 1945, 5th Pan-African Congress (Manchester, England) calling for the end of colonial rule.

On the continent of Africa, the mass character of Pan-Africanism was bolstered when Ghana became independent and President Kwame Nkrumah declared that 'the independence of Ghana is meaningless unless linked with the total liberation of the entire continent'. This became the theme for mass mobilisation and liberation of the African peoples. The All African Peoples Conference of 1958 brought together liberation movements mainly from across the continent. The liberation movements called for African independence by any means necessary including armed struggle.

Pan-Africanism and Liberation

The emergence of newly independent countries in Africa led to the creation of the Organisation of African Unity in 1963, motivated by the need for a unified continental government. During this period, further impetus was given to the liberation struggle by the creation of a Coordinating Committee for the Liberation of Africa to accelerate the liberation of the rest of the continent. Sacrifices by governments and peoples committed to the ideas of Pan-Africanism particularly in Ghana, Nigeria, Tanzania, Guinea, Algeria, Cuba, Libya, Egypt and Zambia as well as liberation support groups in the diaspora, advanced the struggle to liberate the last bastion of settler colonialism on the African continent, namely South Africa.

While remnants of the colonial system remain, as in Puerto Rico, Guadeloupe and Martinique in the Caribbean, Western Sahara and La Union in Africa, many of the newly independent states fell victims to neo-colonialism. Neo-colonialism chained the continent and hampered it from taking part in the global and technological transformation. Africa has been deliberately marginalised from acquiring and utilising modern technology for the development of our people to the extent that it has remained a producer of primary products and a dumping ground for foreign industrial goods.

The New Imperialism

The end of the cold war ushered in a new period of domination. The cold war has now been replaced by the unleashing of an intensified economic war against Africa spearheaded by the IMF and the World Bank. This war will lead to a new scramble for the recolonization of Africa.

The 7th Pan-African Congress maintains that the IMF and the World Bank are supervising an economic order which does not provide the means for African development and growth, but instead structurally adjusts Africa into increasing poverty, the debt burden and underdevelopment. This equally applies to African peoples and governments in the diaspora.

We face a breakdown of our families, communities and societies. Our people cry out for food, housing, health care, education, jobs, justice, and freedom from police terror, drugs, and AIDS (HIV). African women and children has been especially hard hit. However, they have demonstrated an indomitable spirit of resistance by waging a tireless struggle around these issues while being in the forefront of all facets of political mobilisation. It is undeniable that African women will continue to make significant contributions to the struggle for African liberation.

The control of Africa remains in foreign hands. In most African countries, imperialism has the cooperation and compliance of the ruling elites. The overall result is that Africa is being forced into dangerous levels of economic impoverishment, social decay, and chemical genocide. In Africa and the diaspora mass uprisings manifesting themselves from Cairo to Chicago, from Somalia to Los Angeles, and from Detroit to Durban.

South Africa

We look forward to the emergence of a new and free South Africa evolving out of the combination of peaceful and armed struggle of the people of South Africa. However, the 7th Pan-African Congress expresses grave concern over the escalating state-sponsored political violence through the use of mercenaries. These mercenaries, who were trained by South Africa to destabilise neighbouring countries, are now being deployed internally to destablise the democratisation process. The 7th Pan-African Congress condemns the use of mercenaries to kill African people and hopes that the new political dispensation will finally put an end of all destabilisation policies in the region.

The 7th Pan-African Congress is looking forward to an emerging new South Africa as an equal partner rather than as a dominant political and economic power (in the region). We further call on the liberation movements in South Africa to advocate for new foreign and defence policies that will be Africa oriented.

In addition, we condemn the 'New World Order' created and maintained by United States imperialism with particular reference to Somalia, Libya and Cuba. The Congress condemns United States foreign policy in Africa and Latin America, and calls upon the United Nations to demand the lifting of the economic embargo against the people of Libya and Cuba, countries which we express complete solidarity with. We further demand that the USA and its allied European powers ensure the return of Palestinian land and statehood and guarantee, in freedom, the safety of the people of Palestine.

Towards a 21st-Century Programme

We declare the following political programme for the Pan-African movement as we enter into the 21st century. In order to effectively implement the programme, it must be disseminated, discussed and debated at the grassroots level in all African languages and be applied to the concrete conditions.

The 7th Pan-African Congress has been convened to formulate a general programme of action for an overall political and economic strategy for the final liberation of Africa under one union Government with full citizenship rights to Africans in the diaspora. Economic integration must be guided by creating the material basis for objective economic complementarity.

Cognisant of the fact that science and technology are fundamental to human development and liberation; and that imperialism uses the power of science and technology to exploit, dominate and terrorise African peoples, the 7th Pan-African Congress calls upon people in Africa and the diaspora to make science and technology a principal link in our struggle for economic and social liberation.

Our strategy must include the removal of the stranglehold of imperialist debt by collectively fighting to cancel the debt (presently over 500 billion dollars in Africa and the diaspora) on the basis of the 'odious debt' principle as accepted in international law. African people are legally justified to resort to this principle for protection, because the debts were incurred without their approval. For every programme and project we see in Africa funded by imperialist loans and 'aid' there is correspondingly, a massive outflow of value in the form of debt servicing and looting, siphoning needed resources to the tune of 150 million dollars a day.

The 7th Pan-African Congress endorses the fight for European/US reparations for the African Holocaust. This must be effected through large-scale Africa-wide infrastructure projects, e.g., solar energy development, a trans-Africa road system, railways and river/canal transportation, linking our massive rivers and lakes for better utilization of Africa's water resources, above and below ground for the benefit of the entire continent. Similar projects must also apply to Africans in the diaspora.

The realisation of our political unity must be through organised mass action at the grassroots level comprised of African women, students, youth, workers, trade unions and revolutionary organisations. We call upon African peoples to form a popular front for the liberation of Africa from foreign exploitation, dispossession and domination. Our goal is to liberate African peoples based on collective mobilisation through popular democracy. A central component of this struggle is to oppose all forms of oppression and exploitation of women both in the public and private domain. The democratisation process includes the transformation of gender relations includes on the continent and in the diaspora.

Tasks

One of the major tasks is to expose how the enemies of Pan-Africanism are exploiting and promoting religious and ethnic divisions to divide and weaken us in order to continue our subjugation and domination as being experienced in Angola, Liberia, Zaire, Kenya, Somalia, Rwanda, Burundi and the Sudan. Our goal is to promote tolerance, peace and understanding among all African peoples and seek to convert religious and ethnic diversities into a source of strength rather than weakness.

We recognize that the youth and children of African are part of a labour force that plays a crucial role in the reproduction of our societies. We believe that failure to recognize this contribution and their resilience would be a weakness which we cannot afford. The future of Africa is their future.

Further, we will work for the immediate removal of all foreign military bases, the cessation of all foreign military activity, including the establishment of military bases and the deployment of troops, whether under the auspices of the UN or as unilateral action. We declare Africa a nuclear free zone.

To realise the above, we must build a movement based on local self-reliance guided by international strategic planning and the forging of tactics on regional and local levels.

Our Vision

We dare to dream the same dream that has always filled the villages, ghettos, townships and slave quarters with hope, that has always animated the spirit of resistance, that has united the oppressed, the dispossessed, and the exploited masses of our people for genuine liberation. However, we held the 7th Pan-African Congress to do more than dream, for we have come together to make concrete plans for action action that will rid the world of a curse that has plagued humanity for over five centuries.

We the African people are our own liberators and thinkers whose task is to make a mighty stride towards genuine freedom by any means necessary. The great Pan-Africanist W.E.B. Du Bois wrote of his vision and we take this to be our own:

> Awake, awake, put on thy
> strength, O Africa! Reject

the weakness of missionaries
of false good and evil states
who teach neither love nor
brotherhood, but chiefly
the virtues of private profit
from capital, stolen from
your land and labour.

Africa, awake! Put on your beautiful
robes of Pan-Africanism, and fight!
Our salvation lies in our own hands.
We are our own liberators.

RESIST RECOLONISATION!
DON'T AGONISE, ORGANISE!

Contributors

Adul Alkalimat is associate professor of Black Studies at Northeastern University in Boston. He has authored books on Macolm X and Harold Washington, and is senior author of *An Introduction to Afro-American Studies*. Professor Alkalimat was an organizer and regional director of the 7th Pan-African Congress and is a member of the International Planning Committee for the 50th Anniversary Symposium for the 5th Pan-African Congress, to be held in Manchester, England in 1995.

Barbara Bair served as associate editor of volumes five and six of the *Marcus Garvey and UNIA Papers* (University of California Press, 1986–89), and associate editor of *Marcus Garvey: Life and Lessons,* coedited with Robert A. Hill (University of California Press, 1987). She is currently working on a history of women in the UNIA.

Patrick Bellegarde-Smith was born in Haiti. He is chair of the Department of Africological Studies at the University of Wisconsin-Milwaukee. He has written articles on social and political development and philosophical throught, as well as two books, *In the Shadow of Powers* (Humanities Press, 1985) and *Haiti: The Breached Citadel* (Westview Press, 1988).

Paul Buhle is director of the Oral History Project of the American Left at Tamiment Library, New York University. He is also a founding editor of *Radical America* and contributes regularly to the *Village Voice* and *minnesota review*. His many books include *Marxism in the USA* (Verso, 1986) and *C.L.R. James: The Artist as Revolutionary* (Verso, 1989).

Horace Campbell, a native of Jamaica, has taught in the U.K., Africa and the United States. He is a regular contributor to *The Black Scholar* and other Pan-Africanist journals, and is the author of *Rasta and Resistance: From Marcus Garvey to Walter Rodney* (Africa World Press, 1987).

Maryse Conde is from Guadeloupe. She is a novelist, journalist, literary critic, university professor, political activist and a 1987–88 Guggenheim Fellow. She has published fifteen novels, including *Heremakhonon,* and a widely acclaimed trilogy on the African Kingdom of Segu. Her most recent novel is *La Colonie du nouveau monde* (1993).

Paul Gilroy is a senior lecturer in sociology at Goldsmiths' College, University of London, and teaches at Yale University. He is the author of *There Ain't No Black in the Union Jack* (University of Chicago, 1987) and *The Black Atlantic* (1993).

Barbara Harlow is professor of English at the University of Texas, Austin, and is the author of *Banned: Women, Writing and Political Detention* (1992) and *Resistance Literature* (1987.

Robin D.G. Kelley is a professor of History and Africana Studies at New York University. He is the author of the prize-winning book *Hammer and Hoe: Alabama Communists During the Great Depression* (University of North Carolina Press, 1990); *Race Rebels: Culture, Politics and the Black Working Class* (1994); and *Into the Fire: African Americans Since 1970* (forthcoming), volume 10 of the 'Young Oxford History of African Americans' (Oxford University Press). His articles have appeared in the *Journal of American History, American History Review, Nation, Labor History* and *Radical History Review.*

Marian Kramer is president of the National Welfare Rights Union and co-president of the National Up and Out of Poverty Now Campaign. In the front lines of the welfare rights movement from its origins in the 1960s, Ms. Kramer speaks all over the US on behalf of people who have been replaced by technology.

Sidney J. Lemelle is associate professor of history at Pomona College and a member and former chair of the Intercollegiate Department of Black Studies at the Claremont Colleges. He has also been a lecturer at the University of Dar es Salaam, Tanzania and a teaching fellow at the University of California, Los Angeles. Dr Lemelle is the author of *Pan-Africanism for Beginners,* as well as articles on African and African-American history and culture. He is currently working on a book about the relationships between mining labor and the state in colonial Tanzania.

Ntongela Masilela is assistant professor of English and world literature at Pitzer College. Dr Masilela, a South African by birth, was educated at the

University of California, Los Angeles, and has done research in Poland. He is currently working on Black American cinema, particularly the UCLA school of African and African-American filmmakers.

Gersham A. Nelson is a Jamaican who teaches Latin American and African history at Frostburg State University (Maryland). He is currently working on a book about the peasantry and the working class in Jamaican politics.

Kathy J. Ogren is associate professor of history at the University of Redlands and author of *The Jazz Revolution* (Oxford University Press, 1989). She is currently working on a second book dealing with New Orleans jazz.

Cedric J. Robinson is professor and chair of the Department of Political Science at the University of California, Santa Barbara. He has written several articles on Black radicalism and Marxist theory, served on the editorial board of *Race and Class,* and published *Black Marxism: The Making of the Black Radical Tradition* (Zed Press, 1983).

Ann Seidman is professor of economics at Clark University and served in 1989–89 as president of the African Studies Association. She has published many articles and books of Africa and African economics, including *Unity or Poverty?: The Economics of Panafricanism* (Penguin, 1969) with Reg Green, *U.S. Multinationals in Southern Africa* (Tanzania Publishing House, 1977), coauthored with Neva Seidman, *The Roots of Crisis in Southern Africa* (Africa World Press, 1986), and *Apartheid, Militarism and the U.S. Southeast* (Africa World Press, 1990).

Lako Tongun was born in Sudan and educated in Kenya and the United States. He is associate professor of political studies and head of the Third World Studies Program at Pitzer College. He is currently working on U.S. relations with the Third World and African political systems.

William H. Watkins is associate professor of education at the University of Utah. He has written numerous articles on educational policy and curriculum development; he has also written extensively on issues related to Africa and African-American communities.

Index

Index